The Human Resource Management Handbook

The Human Resource Management Handbook

Part III

Edited by **DAVID LEWIN**
Anderson Graduate School of Management
University of California, Los Angeles

DANIEL J.B. MITCHELL
Anderson Graduate School of Management
and School of Public Policy and Social Research
University of California, Los Angeles

MAHMOOD A. ZAIDI
Carlson School of Management
University of Minnesota

 **JAI PRESS INC.**

Greenwich, Connecticut   *London, England*

Library of Congress Cataloging-in-Publication Data

The human resource management book / edited by David Lewin, Daniel
J.B. Mitchell, and Mahmood A. Zaidi.
   p. cm.
   Includes bibliographical references and indexes.
   ISBN 0-7623-0246-1 (set). — ISBN 0-7623-0247-X (pt. 1). — ISBN
0-7623-0248-8 (pt. 2). — ISBN 0-7623-0249-6 (pt. 3)
   1. Management. 2. Personnel management. 3. Human capital.
   I. Lewin, David, 1943-   II. Mitchell, Daniel J. B.   III. Zaidi,
Mahmood A.
HD31.H8124   1997
658.3—DC21

                                 96-38022
                                   CIP

Copyright © 1997 JAI PRESS INC.
55 Old Post Road, No. 2
Greenwich, Connecticut 06836

JAI PRESS LTD.
38 Tavistock Street
Covent Garden
London WC2E 7PB
England

ISBN: 0-7623-0247-X (Part I)
0-7623-0248-8 (Part II)
0-7623-0249-6 (Part III)
0-7623-0246-1 (Set)

Library of Congress Catalog Card Number: 96-38022

Manufactured in the United States of America

CONTENTS

CONCLUSION

PART I

SECTION I.   EMPLOYEE PARTICIPATION: NONFINANCIAL

SECTION II.   EMPLOYEE PARTICIPATION: FINANCIAL

PART II

SECTION I.   EMPLOYER FLEXIBILITY

SECTION II.   UNIONS AND COLLECTIVE BARGAINING

SECTION III.   WORKPLACE DISPUTE RESOLUTION

Contents

SECTION 1

STAFFING AND REWARD

SELECTION AND JOB MATCHING

Cheri Ostroff and Teresa J. Rothausen

Organizations rarely, if ever, hire people randomly. In the selection process the desired characteristics of employees are identified based on some aspect of success or job performance to be predicted, individuals are recruited and assessed in terms of these desired characteristics, hiring decisions are made, and the success of the process is evaluated (Guion, 1991). Through this process it is possible to identify those individuals who possess characteristics that will best *match* or *fit* the requirements of the job and/or organization. A good match will lead to positive outcomes, such as high performance, satisfaction, attendance, and retention (Brousseau, 1984; Caldwell & O'Reilly, 1990; Rounds, Dawis, & Lofquist, 1987; Ostroff, 1993; Schneider, 1983)

The selection systems in organizations involve a large number of decisions and interrelated activities (Begin, 1991; Schuler, 1987). Selection affects and is affected by other human resource (HR) activities such as the amount and type of training employees receive after hire and the type of rewards used to motivate employees. Decisions about the selection system also reflect the company's goals, values, and strategies, the role of the HR function in the company, and external influences such as government regulations, labor markets, economic considerations, and so forth. Depending on a wide range of organization and external factors, the hiring and matching practices will vary widely for different organizations and different jobs (Jackson, Schuler, & Rivero, 1989). For example, in one company a goal may be to increase diversity in the workforce. In another company a goal may be to select individuals with very specific skills, while in a third company a satisfied, committed workforce is the goal. These goals and objectives dictate the specific kind of selection process that develops.

3

While the employer is attempting to identify and choose those individuals who will best match or fit the organization's requirements, individuals are simultaneously identifying and choosing jobs and organizations which match or fit their own requirements (Rynes, 1991; Wanous, 1992). Individuals proceed through a conscious or unconscious process of defining the desired characteristics of the job and organization for which they would like to work, searching for career and job opportunities, choosing an organization, and then evaluating the success of this process in terms of their own satisfaction, personal development, and progress toward career goals. Depending on a number of factors, the specific process may vary widely from one individual to the next. The individual's background, aptitudes, family concerns, and desires as well as the larger economy and labor market conditions influence the job search and organizational choice process of individuals (Rynes & Gerhart, 1990; Schneider & Schmitt, 1986; Super, 1953).

The organization's recruiting process and individuals' search processes first come together when individuals become applicants for the job, resulting in an applicant pool for the organization. From here, when the organization's and any one individual's search and choice processes match or come together, an employment relationship will result. That is, an organization may identify and offer jobs to a number of people whose characteristics fit or match the organization's requirements and goals; whether or not these offers will ultimately be accepted or result in a "hire" depends on how well the job and organization's characteristics match the requirements of the individuals (Wanous, 1992). Thus, selection is a mutual process with both the organization and individual actively participating. The underlying assumption is that identifying and choosing the kinds of people who will be effective and satisfied with the job and organization will promote the accomplishment of both individual and organizational goals (Schneider & Schmitt, 1986).

A well-designed selection process will allow both the individual and the organization to meet their respective requirements, not only in terms of initial employment, but also in terms of continued employment in the organization. Appropriate selection in conjunction with training and development, rewards, performance management, and monitoring systems helps to ensure that those selected will contribute to the organization over time. When these systems provide individuals with desired rewards and allow individuals to achieve their own career and development goals, the individual will seek to remain in the organization (Dawis & Lofquist, 1984). Organizations continue to employ those who fulfill their requirements and individuals remain in an organization when their needs are met (Mitchell, 1989).

The selection system is complex and integrally tied to other systems. Figure 1 represents these processes and systems and the role that selection plays in the overall organization and system.

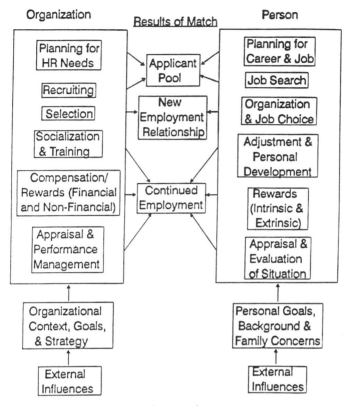

Figure 1. The Matching Process

In this chapter our primary emphasis is on the selection process from the organization's perspective. First, selection is briefly considered in the context of other human resource activities, organizational features, and environmental influences. Next, the general selection model is described, various methods of selection are reviewed, and means for evaluating their usefulness are discussed. A set of selection policy decisions are offered as broad choices that must be made about selection systems. Maintaining the focus on the selection model, the individual's perspective and role in the process is briefly considered. Finally, we address how simultaneous consideration of both the organizational system and individual system results in a "match" to accomplish both the organization's and individual's objectives.

SELECTION AND ORGANIZATIONAL SYSTEMS

Effective selection requires a consideration of the entire HR function (see Figure 1). It is generally cheaper for most companies to retain workers over long periods of time than to constantly hire new ones since recruiting, selection, and training can be very costly. Thus, an important goal is to develop procedures that will allow for continued employment of the "right" people with the "right" skills and attributes for the organization (Mitchell, 1989). This goal is not likely to be reached unless selection is appropriately integrated with other HR functions.

Most researchers (e.g., Butler, Ferris, & Napier, 1991; Mahoney & Deckop, 1986; Schuler & Jackson, 1987) and textbook authors indicate that the HR function includes a set of six interrelated activities: planning, recruitment, selection, development (socialization, training), rewards and compensation, and performance management (appraisal, productivity programs). The selection process impacts and is impacted by these other HR activities. To illustrate, during the HR planning process HR needs are specified in terms of the number and types of employees that are needed in various parts of the company. This information is used to make decisions about the manner in which employees should be recruited and selected. Recruiting activities are designed to obtain an applicant pool from which employees who meet the organization's needs can be selected. In selecting employees, training issues must be considered since selection provides the "raw materials" for training. Decisions about the relative emphasis to place on selection versus training must be made. One approach is to devote resources to recruiting and selecting individuals with the needed attributes so that little training is needed. Alternatively, minimal standards in selection can be set and employees trained extensively after hire. Selection is also related to reward systems. Selecting people who will not be motivated by the particular type of reward and incentive program used in the company can result in lower performance, poor attitudes, and high turnover. Similarly, compensation plans and selection must be appropriately integrated. For example, a selection process designed to hire "the best in the nation" coupled with a compensation plan designed to provide average or below average wages for the industry will not be successful. Finally, since selection systems are not perfect, some poor quality workers will be hired. Evaluations and monitoring of performance can be used to weed out these poor workers or to transfer them to jobs for which they are better suited. Workers with the appropriate attributes can be kept productive with performance management programs, including supervisory practices, redesigning jobs, motivation programs, and incentives. Clearly, the development of an effective selection system requires that selection be viewed as but one sub-function of the entire HR function.

Selection and HR must also be viewed in the broader context of the organization (Zedeck & Cascio, 1984). One important issue is the interface between HR and the organization's strategy (Butler, Ferris, & Napier, 1991). Organizations determine a general strategy or strategic direction (e.g., growth, innovation, cost reduction) to pursue. This strategic direction is used to develop specific strategic plans (e.g., acquire another company, develop a new product) and ways to implement this plan so that the overall mission of the firm can be achieved. Selection and staffing choices can be used to implement the organization's strategy in order to gain a strategic advantage and enhance strategic objectives (Barney, 1991; Butler, Ferris, & Napier, 1991). To illustrate, an organization may decide to adopt a more advanced technological process in an effort to achieve its strategic goal of cost-efficient production. This choice forces decisions about whether to replace current workers with workers already trained for the new technology or equipment, or whether to provide existing employees with opportunities to learn new skills (Butler, Ferris, & Napier, 1991). Another organization may adopt a growth strategy and plan to expand rapidly into a new and relatively unstable product market. The success of this strategy will depend on whether or not employees with the right skills and abilities can be made available (recruited, selected, and trained) at the right time. New employees with the established skills may need to be hired. However, if skilled employees are not available at the wages the firm can offer, the strategic plan will fail. Thus, HR plans and strategic plans should be integrated. At the very least, selection and HR managers should be made aware, early on, of the strategic choices made by top management so that selection and HR systems to support this objective can be developed. Ideally, selection and HR managers would participate in the strategic planning process, providing input about the feasibility of the plans since HR issues can affect the eventual success of the chosen strategy (Butler, Ferris, & Napier, 1991).

Clearly, strategic plans and implementation of these plans involves HR issues. Further, strategy is closely related to other contextual features, including organizational goals, structure, design of tasks, technological processes, size, resources, and culture, all of which impact selection (Begin, 1991; Quinn, 1980). The majority of research and theory on selection has given little consideration to the impact that these contextual features have on selection and HR practices. There is, however, a strong and growing sentiment that these contextual features explain some of the differences in the types of selection and HR practices that develop across organizations (Begin, 1991; Butler, Ferris, & Napier, 1991; Jackson, Schuler, & Rivero, 1989; Olian & Rynes, 1984). Throughout this chapter we will highlight the role that various features of the organizational context have on the development of selection processes.

Finally, the HR function, and selection in particular, are impacted by the larger environment including legal and economic considerations such as government regulation, labor markets, and unions. Legal regulations represent one of the strongest external influences on selection and will be discussed separately. External labor markets influence selection activities in terms of the availability of people the organization can choose from. For example, when more employees are seeking employment than there are job openings, a firm can be more selective and raise its selection standards. In the opposite situation, firms may compete with one another to obtain the limited number of employees who meet their requirements by increasing recruiting and the compensation offered, or by lowering selection standards and providing more training (Mitchell, 1989). Finally, firms in which workers are represented by a union may have additional constraints imposed on their selection and HR systems. Through the collective bargaining process the union becomes a partner in determining selection and HR activities, including the types of procedures used to select employees, production standards, retraining of individuals for other jobs, and promotion practices (Kochan, 1980).

SELECTION AND THE LAW

Companies must comply with an increasing number of laws, executive orders, and legislative policies that have been enacted in an attempt to ensure that all individuals have an equal chance for employment. Any method used to hire employees (e.g., application forms, resumes, interviews, written tests, psychological evaluations) is subject to Equal Employment Opportunity (EEO) laws, regardless of how formally the process is carried out. If legal policies are not respected, the organization will be vulnerable to a charge of discrimination. Thus, employers must simultaneously consider how to maximize the probability of making accurate selection decisions about applicants while also ensuring that these decisions are carried out in such a way as to minimize the chance of a judgment of discrimination being brought against the organization. A brief overview of the role that equal employment opportunity (EEO) regulations play in selection is provided below. For more details, we recommend texts (e.g., Arvey & Faley, 1988; Ledvinka & Scarpello, 1991) as well as subscription sources (e.g., Fair Employment Practices Series, Fair Practices Guide) which periodically send updated material on statutes, regulations, court opinions, and interpretations of the law.

Major Laws

Title VII of the 1964 Civil Rights Act and the 1991 Civil Rights Act makes it illegal for an employer to discriminate against any individual with respect to employment opportunities, including hiring, compensation, terms, conditions, or privileges of employment because of an individual's race, color, religion, sex, or national origin. Other relevant laws include the Age Discrimination in Employment Act which prohibits discrimination on the basis of age, the Equal Pay Act which prohibits discrimination on the basis of sex in the payment of wages, and the Pregnancy Discrimination Act which protects pregnant women and women who have had an abortion from discrimination.

The Americans with Disabilities Act (ADA) of 1990 prohibits discrimination in all employment practices against qualified individuals with disabilities. If a disabled person can perform the essential job duties (with or without a "reasonable accommodation"), the individual cannot be denied employment even if he or she is unable to perform marginal or less essential job duties. An employer must make "reasonable accommodations," both on the job and during pre-employment screening and testing, unless such an accommodation would pose undue hardship on the organization (based on cost of the accommodation and the financial resources of the employer). The ADA also prohibits medical testing prior to an offer of employment. At present, there is much confusion about which disabilities are covered, what constitutes a medical test, and how an essential task is defined (Landy, Shanster, & Kohler, 1994).

These federal laws apply to employers with 15 or more employees. The Equal Employment Opportunity Commission (EEOC) is the enforcement agency for these laws and has offered a set of Uniform Guidelines on Employee Selection Procedures (1978) to help employers comply with federal employment laws. Similar laws and executive orders have been enacted which apply to contractors or employers who do business with the federal government (e.g., the Vocational Rehabilitation Act, Vietnam Era Veteran's Readjustment Act, and Executive Orders 11246, 11375, 11478, 11141). In addition to prohibiting discrimination, they require contractors to engage in affirmative action plans to encourage employers to actively recruit individuals of protected classes and increase minority representation in the workplace.

Issues in Discrimination

Discrimination can be an overt act (e.g., an employment notice stating males-only need apply) or the intentional application of different standards to individuals based on their membership in a protected group (e.g., a practice of hiring individuals of one race for cleaning jobs while similarly qualified individuals of another race are hired for more skilled jobs). However, discrimination can also occur unintentionally, resulting in adverse impact or disparate impact. Adverse impact refers to situations in which the same standards are applied uniformly to all applicants (e.g., a high school diploma is required), but the result of the process is that members of one group have a reduced likelihood of being hired. The most common measure of adverse impact is the EEOC's four-fifth's rule—if the proportion of applicants hired for any racial, sex, or protected subgroup is less than 80 percent of the proportion of applicants hired for the non-protected group, evidence of adverse impact exists.

If evidence of discrimination or adverse impact exists, the organization can cease using the procedure, modify the procedure to eliminate discrimination, or continue using the procedure and be willing to provide evidence to defend the practice if challenged with a charge of discrimination. According to the

Civil Rights Act of 1991, once a prima facie case of discrimination has been made, the burden of proof shifts to the employer who defends the selection practices by showing that the employment practice is a "business necessity." The employer provides a legitimate nondiscriminatory goal that it hoped to achieve with the employment practice. Further, the organization must produce evidence indicating that the selection procedure is relevant to the job. Job-relatedness refers to the extent to which characteristics assessed with the test or selection procedure are important for performance on the job.

Further, the 1991 Civil Rights Act included a prohibition against adjustment of test scores or using different cutoff scores for different groups. Adjusting scores on selection tests and procedures was a fairly common practice when the average score for a protected group was lower than the average score for the "majority" group. This prohibition has resulted in many employers abandoning a number of commonly used selection tests, because without score adjustments, fewer members of a protected group would be hired.

It is important to note that employers are not obligated by law to use job-relevant procedures. With the exception of banned procedures (e.g., polygraphs except in limited cases), an employer can use any hiring practice, regardless of how well it captures attributes important for the job, so long as the employer does not discriminate against employees as defined by the various laws.

THE SELECTION MODEL

In selection, the goal is to choose individuals who are likely to work well at their jobs (Guion, 1991). Traditionally, selection researchers and experts have viewed this system as a process of matching people to jobs. Worker characteristics are matched to the requirements of the job, under the assumption that a better fit or match will result in better performance on the job (Burke & Pearlman, 1988). Conventional selection systems have focused on facilitating or optimizing the match between the skills and abilities of individuals, and the skills and abilities required by the tasks and duties of the job.

In recent years, there has been growing recognition that this ability-task match is too narrow and that other work context issues may be important. In the traditional system of skill-job match, little explicit attention has been devoted to matching people to the work or organizational context. More recently, a number of authors (e.g., Bowen, Ledford, & Nathan, 1991; Jackson, Schuler, & Rivero, 1989; Schneider, 1987; Schuler & Jackson, 1987) have advocated moving to a broader focus of person-organization match which focuses on matching the person to the job and organizational context. Organizations differ in their goals, values, reward systems, culture and so forth. People who are likely to work well in an organization may need more than specific skills that fit the job requirements; they may need personal attributes and personalities that fit the broader context of the organization (e.g., Chatman, 1991). The implication is that different selection practices will be needed in different organizations, because different kinds of people with different competencies and personal attributes are needed in organizations of different types (e.g., Guthrie & Olian, 1991; Jackson, Schuler, & Rivero, 1989; Olian & Rynes, 1984; Schneider, 1983). Nevertheless, a widely accepted "generic model" can be offered for designing a selection system.

Developing a selection system entails five basic steps. Guion (1991) advocates that this process be viewed from a predictive hypothesis testing framework. That is, selection professionals and researchers develop formal or informal hypotheses about the characteristics that will best predict performance or success. This hypothesis requires an understanding of the job and organization (step 1), specifying the criterion of job performance or success to be predicted (step 2), and determining the predictors or applicant characteristics that are believed to predict that criterion (step 3). Evaluation of the tenability of the hypothesis requires collection of evidence regarding the relationship between the predictor and criterion (step 4), and evaluating the utility or success of the process (step 5). It is important to note that the development and refinement of this basic model over the years has been driven by the job-skill match perspective, with job specific performance as the criterion. In our discussion of this model, we explain how the broader approach of person-job organization and broader views of performance and success can be incorporated in the model.

Job and Organizational Analysis (Step 1)

It is impossible to design a selection system without gathering information about and gaining an understanding of the job and organization. This information is used in all subsequent steps. Traditionally, selection experts have concentrated on defining the content of jobs through job analysis procedures (Landy, Shankster, & Kohler, 1994). Job analysis involves collecting information on the important task-related aspects of the job. This information is used to define the array of employee skills and characteristics which will fit the job's requirements, and to determine the types of selection procedures that should be used. In theory, these systems should also encompass characteristics of the context in which work is performed; yet, little attempt has been made to do so (Burke & Pearlman, 1988). Given the recent emphasis on broader types of fit between people and organizations, we also include organizational analysis procedures which elucidate the system-wide components of the organization. Such procedures are not traditionally included as part of the selection model, hence their direct impact on the various components of the selection model are just developing.

Job Analysis

Job analysis involves the description of the content of the job. The end result of a job analysis can range from a simple descriptive paragraph to a long report detailing highly specific tasks and attributes. A wide variety of techniques for collecting job analysis information are available, each of which provides different information. Several excellent sources are available that provide reviews of the process and details about specific job analysis techniques (e.g., Gael, 1988; Guion, 1991; Harvey, 1991; Levine, 1983; Schneider & Schmitt, 1986; Wright & Wexley, 1985). Based on a review of this literature, the dimensions along which different job analysis methods can be differentiated are provided below.

1. Nature of information. The most important distinguishing feature of different job analysis procedures pertains to the nature of the information obtained. Information can be obtained about the specific tasks, duties, responsibilities (TDR), and activities performed on the job; or information can be obtained about the worker characteristics, the knowledge, skills, and abilities, (KSA) needed to perform the job TDR. Work-oriented procedures focus on describing the job in terms of the specific tasks and activities performed, the process of performing the tasks, and/or the products resulting from job performance (e.g., makes boxes, maintains an inventory of parts). Worker-oriented approaches focus on the characteristics workers need to perform the tasks, in particular, KSA required. The interest is not in specific job activities, but rather in the general characteristics of workers which are needed to perform specific job activities (e.g., knowledge of first aid procedures, typing skills, ability to think clearly).

2. Standardization of information. Position-specific approaches provide information that is detailed and specific to a single, given job, whereas standardized methods provide a standard form which can be applied to all jobs, such as a list of common tasks that are performed across many jobs or a taxonomy of abilities that represent enduring attributes of individuals in performance. Standard formats allow for comparisons of jobs to one another, but provide less specific information about the particular job content.

3. Specificity of information. The degree of behavioral and technological detail provided by job analysis items ranges from low (e.g., a narrative description of the job) to high (e.g., a detailed list of the exact duties, tasks, skills, abilities, or worker attributes needed for job performance).

4. Method of Obtaining Information. There are three primary methods for obtaining job analysis information: (1) observation of workers, (2) interviews with groups of workers and/or supervisors, and (3) questionnaires completed by a job analyst, workers, and/or supervisors. A given job analysis may include one or all of these methods.

5. Scale metric. Some methods are based on obtaining qualitative data, such as a narrative report or a general descriptive summary. Quantitatively based procedures utilize numerical ratings (e.g., asking workers to rate the importance of a task on a 1-10 point scale).

6. Source of information. Information can be obtained from supervisors, job incumbents, experienced workers, or trained job analysts who observe performance and interview workers. Differences in job analysis information have been found as a function of incumbents' sex, tenure, and performance level, and between supervisors and incumbents. At present, there are no definitive conclusions regarding the importance and implications of these findings. The safest strategy is to collect information from as many informed sources as possible.

The distinguishing features presented here are not mutually exclusive. For example, a common job analysis procedure, the Position Analysis Questionnaire, (or PAQ; McCormick, Jeanerette, & Mecham, 1972), is a standardized questionnaire that provides fairly specific, worker-oriented information, and quantitative ratings. Further, more than one job analysis procedure can be used to gather more complete information, (e.g., to gather both TDR and KSA information) and each has its advantages and disadvantages.

Organizational Analysis

Organizational analysis refers to the examination of the system-wide components of the organization beyond individual job tasks and duties. This information is important because organizational features, such as leadership, reward systems, organizational style, values, culture, climate, technology, and structure impact employees attitudes and behaviors in organizations as well as aggregate levels of performance and productivity (cf. Chatman, 1991; Ostroff, 1993; Ostroff & Schmitt, 1993; Sutton & Rousseau, 1979). Analysis of the organizational context can be used to infer the desired personal characteristics of people who will fit the broad features of the organization and allow for effective organizational functioning.

Organizational analysis techniques are not nearly as well developed as job analysis techniques. Nevertheless, a review of the literature indicates that several important categories of the organizational context should be analyzed. For more specific techniques and details, see Perrow (1961) for organizational goals; Porter (1985) for strategy, Nadler (1977) for perceptions of organizational members; Harrison (1994) for a diagnosis of organizational components and informal processes; Chatman (1989) and Siehl and Martin (1988) for values and culture; Hackman and Oldham (1975) and Lawler (1981) for rewards; Rousseau (1979) for technology; and the training needs assessment literature, such as Camp, Blanchard, and Huszczo (1986) and Goldstein (1986) for a general overview of organizational analysis. These contextual features of jobs are briefly described below.

1. Organizational environment. The analysis of the organizational environment includes examination of the external technological sector, commercial sector, and market environment as well as the stability of these environments. Organizations operating in different types of larger environments will develop different types of jobs, styles, structures, and ways of making decisions (Katz & Kahn, 1978). Additionally, many U.S. businesses have been expanding into foreign markets, and must prepare employees for international assignments. In such companies, analysis of the cultural and business norms of the host countries is important (Schuler, 1987).

2. Goals/Objectives. Virtually all organizations have formal mechanisms for setting and amending goals. The goals provide direction and indicate the future state of affairs the organization wishes to attain. Goals guide decisions made about all aspects of organizational functioning (Gross & Etzioni, 1985), including the number and types of employees needed to help achieve these goals.

3. Strategy. Strategic emphasis has a critical impact on the types of people who are needed to promote organizational effectiveness, and the types of selection procedures that are appropriate (Begin, 1991). A widely accepted typology is Porter's (1985) three generic strategic types—cost leadership, differentiation, and focus. The cost strategy emphasizes improving efficiency, cost reduction, and being the lowest cost producer, as opposed to seeking out new opportunities. The differentiation strategy emphasizes innovation, product development, aggressive pursuit of market opportunities, and providing unique products and services. The focus strategy emphasizes a concentration on a specific market, product line, or customer group; within this particular market niche, the organization may compete on the basis of either cost or differentiation.

Further, the firm's strategic orientation is related to the company's goals, external opportunities, and its internal forces including structure, culture, values, and resources (Miles & Snow, 1984; Quinn, 1980), all of which influence selection systems. For example, organizations with a cost-efficiency strategy tend to develop centralized structures for decision making which in turn influences the characteristics of people (e.g., desire for hierarchical authority) who will best serve the organization.

4. Structure. Organizations develop internal structures that enable them to manage and coordinate their internal and external environments. For example, employees can be organized into functional divisions (e.g., accounting, marketing) or into product or service divisions (e.g., all employees needed to produce the product are grouped together). Further, structural choices include mechanisms for integrating and coordinating processes in both vertical and horizontal directions, such as different supervisory practices and degree of standardization of work processes (Lawrence & Lorsch, 1967; Mintzberg,

1983). Based on the structural considerations, different degrees of formalization of behavior, specialization of jobs, and decision-making authority of workers results, thus workers with different types of skills are needed.

5. Technology. Various taxonomies of technology exist (cf. Perrow, 1967; Thompson, 1967; Emery & Trist, 1960). At the most basic level, technological processes can be defined as ranging from simple (e.g., routine processes, predictable work, requiring little coordination and interdependence) to complex (e.g., diverse technical processes, requiring a high degree of coordination and interdependence). The technological or work-flow transformation process has a large impact on the types of jobs and the job content. Further, different technologies may require people of different types (e.g., cooperative people in complex technologies).

6. Climate/Culture/Style. Organizations differ in the cultures and value systems that develop, the climates or shared perceptions of how an organization deals with its members and environments, and the general management styles and philosophies that represent the kinds of assumptions management makes about the nature of workers. These characteristics influence the types of people who will best fit in the organization as a whole (Schneider, 1983, 1987).

7. Reward systems. Organizations design and use different reward styles, patterns, and mechanisms that reflect beliefs about the treatment of workers and the motivation of employees. Important issues concern the equity and fairness of reward distributions, linking rewards to performance, and whether rewards are based on the individual's, units' or groups', and/or organization's performance (Schneider & Schmitt, 1986). Nonfinancial, informal rewards, such as praise and recognition, may also be used to varying extents. At a more micro level, the reward attributes of jobs, such as the amount of autonomy, feedback, and variety provided, are important considerations. At all levels, workers whose needs correspond with the rewards provided will be more effective (Hackman & Oldham, 1980).

Organizational analysis of these features provides information about the content and activities of the organization, much like task or work-oriented job analysis procedures define the content and activities of the job. Unfortunately, there has been little research that systematically associates characteristics of organizations and individual behavior patterns (Bowen, Ledford, & Nathan, 1991) or that defines the characteristics of people needed to support different organization activities. Schuler and Jackson (1987) provide a taxonomy of some of the broad employee behaviors that are needed for various strategic types and their associated organizational conditions. A potentially useful procedure for gaining an understanding about the attributes of people needed to work in the organizational context is to apply job analysis techniques to glean organization-wide information. This procedure was advanced as part of large selection and classification study (Project A) in the armed forces (Campbell, Ford, Rumsey, Pulakos, Borman, Felker, De Vera, & Riegelhaupt,

1990). Supervisors and incumbents delineated army-wide or organizational-wide behaviors and factors to define the components that are the same for every job in the army (e.g., maintaining proper physical fitness, displaying honesty and integrity, adhering to regulations and procedures).

Issues

There is no single "best" job analysis or organizational analysis procedure. Each produces different types of information, which may be more or less relevant in different situations. From the selection perspective, enough information and detail is needed to enable the selection expert or researcher to identify the important behaviors and attributes necessary for success on the job and in the organization, develop hypotheses about potential predictors of the behavior, and determine the most promising method of assessing the predictors and criteria (Guion, 1991).

Some employers conduct job analyses primarily to defend against potential employment discrimination charges (Harvey, 1991). In employment discrimination cases, courts have generally interpreted Title VII to mean that a comprehensive and highly specific job analysis must be conducted, describing the full spectrum of TDR performed and KSA needed, and identifying the most important behaviors for the job (Thompson & Thompson, 1982). This legal emphasis helps explain why far more attention has been devoted to job analysis procedures which define specific job content than procedures which focus on the organizational context. The procedure used by Campbell and his colleagues (1990) may be promising in this respect since job analysis techniques were used to define the content and components of specific jobs (as traditionally done in job analysis) as well as organizational-wide behaviors that are the same for every job.

Determining the Criteria (Step 2)

Once important attributes of the job and organization are analyzed, criteria are identified. Criteria represent the ultimate goals of selection (Thorndike, 1949), the behaviors and outcomes at work that constitute standards of excellence or performance standards to be achieved (Schneider & Schmitt, 1986), or the outcomes and job behaviors we try to predict with selection devices (Guion, 1991). It is important to begin with a conceptual criterion, that is, a definition of the behaviors, outcomes, or attributes that are desired and relevant for the organization. Once this is accomplished, attention is devoted to operationalizing the criteria or choosing the actual measures of criteria (e.g., production indexes, performance ratings).

In selection, criteria essentially represent what constitutes "doing well" at the job. "Doing well" can take different forms. Campbell and Campbell (1988) make a distinction between behavior, performance, and effectiveness. At work, individuals "do" a variety of things or exhibit different observable behaviors. For example, in a hospital, nurses might discuss patient care procedures with their colleagues, listen to patients' problems, or gossip about their co-workers. They might administer medication to patients, help their co-workers, or read a novel. Clearly some of these behaviors are more desirable from an organization's point of view than others. Performance is defined as "the aggregate of those behaviors that are relevant for the organization's goals and that can be scaled (measured) in terms of the individual's contribution to the goal(s) of interest" (Campbell & Campbell, 1988, p. 85). That is, an individual's performance represents the level of expertise an individual exhibits in episodes of behavior that are judged to be relevant or critical for one or more of the organization's goals. Effectiveness refers to an aggregate of the outcomes of performance across individuals in the unit or organization, that is, a measure of the organization's performance or success.

Ideally, criteria represent the organization's goals and values (e.g., Guion, 1991; Schneider & Schmitt, 1986). The culture, climate, and philosophy of the organization results in the development of objectives and certain standards of performance against which people are evaluated. These goals and standards should be translated into actual measures of employee performance (Schneider & Schmitt, 1986). Unfortunately, this notion has not been given direct attention in selection, partially because job analysis information is usually used to define criteria. That is, "doing well" has been traditionally defined as job-based performance (Borman, 1991; Landy, Shankster, & Kohler, 1994; Werner, 1994). Selection experts assume that the behaviors that are relevant to the organization's goals are those based on performance of specific job tasks and duties (Olian & Rynes, 1984). This is an important but limited view.

Both strategy experts and organizational behavior researchers (e.g., Bowen, Ledford, & Nathan, 1991; Miles & Snow, 1984; Jackson et al., 1989; Tichy, Frombrun, & Devanna, 1982) have recognized that selection criteria should reflect more than immediate job requirements. Organizations differ in their goals and contextual features (e.g., culture, strategy, structure). These contextual features of the organization determine broader patterns of behaviors that employees need to exhibit to make the organization function effectively. That is, among employees in jobs of many different types, there are overarching common patterns of employee behaviors needed within the organization in order for the organization to be effective. For example, risk-taking behaviors and experimenting with new ideas are needed in an organization attempting to compete in the marketplace by being more innovative (Jackson et al., 1989). Thus, "performance" as the aggregate of behaviors that are relevant for the organization's goals may be based on characteristics that are important in terms of their compatibility with the organization's values, policies, goals, and strategies, not just the performance of specific tasks (Rynes & Gerhart, 1990).

Further, depending on the organization's goals and context, criteria that are not directly based on performance may be important. In the person-organization fit model, selection focuses on identifying the kinds of people whose skills, personalities, values, and needs match the values, goals, climate, and systems of the organization. The assumption is that individuals and organizations will be more effective when the attributes of the person and the organization match or are congruent (Schneider, 1987). Here, criteria which reflect the extent to which fit has been achieved (e.g., adjustment, satisfaction) may be relevant. The extent to which criteria will reflect the organization's overall goals and values depends on whether organizational analysis information is also considered and used to define and choose criteria.

The most traditionally used measures of criteria will be listed (see Austin & Villanova, 1991; Borman, 1991; Cascio, 1991a, Guion, 1991 for a more thorough review). Given the view that fit to the organization, not just the job, should be more explicitly addressed in selection, we also describe some nontraditional criteria.

Traditional Criteria

The most frequently used criteria are judgments or *ratings* of job performance, particularly supervisory ratings. An enormous amount of research has been devoted to devising, improving, and refining such measures in order to improve their accuracy and understand the sources of biases and other influences on raters' decisions (see Bernardin & Beatty, 1984; Murphy & Cleveland, 1991 for reviews of rating types and issues). A wide variety of different rating formats have been developed, but there are no conclusive findings regarding the superiority of one type of format over another.

Production measures include assessments of work output, such as, units produced, dollar volume of sales, number of letters typed, or commission earnings, as well as quality measures such as number of errors detected, or number of customer complaints. Further, criteria can include *personnel data*, such as attendance or absenteeism, tenure, and promotion rates. These criteria can be useful. Organizations with problems in these areas may try to select individuals who will attend and remain in the organization, since both absenteeism and turnover are costly. *Training success* criteria typically reflect the level of proficiency after an individual completes a training program. Since training can be costly, the ability to predict who will succeed in training can be of interest in selection.

In some cases, specially devised *work sample tests* are used as criteria. These tests require individuals to perform the major tasks of the job under controlled conditions. Employees perform the same set of tasks, under the same conditions, with standardized instruction, and then performance on this test is scored.

Nontraditional Criteria

The traditional criteria all focus on ability to perform aspects of the job or job duties either directly (e.g., production measures, rating of performance) or indirectly (e.g., absenteeism). Nontraditional criteria focus on more general aspects of success in the organization, and go beyond an employee's performance in his or her stated duties. In fact, some researchers have indicated that supervisory ratings of job performance are implicitly or unconsciously influenced by these more general factors (Organ, 1987; Werner, 1994). Suggestions have been made that we include "contextual performance" or general aspects that most employers desire, but are not directly involved in task performance (Borman & Motowidlo, 1993). For example, prosocial behaviors, altruism, volunteering for tasks, helping others, and extra effort go beyond the boundaries of specific job-related performance (Borman, 1991; Smither, Reilly, Millsap, Pearlman, & Stoffey, 1993). These behaviors are likely to be reflected in criteria such as organizational citizenship, commitment, and socialization behaviors. Further, nontraditional criteria such as job satisfaction can be important for selection because they may contribute to organizational effectiveness. Some evidence suggests that organizations with more satisfied, committed, and adjusted employees are more effective and better performing organizations (Ostroff, 1992). Other work has demonstrated that employees' satisfaction and commitment plays an important role in absenteeism and turnover (Mowday, Porter, & Steers, 1982; Tett & Meyer, 1993), both of which are costly to the organization.

Issues

Regardless of the measure(s) chosen, it is most important that criteria are relevant (Borman, 1991; Schneider & Schmitt, 1986). Relevance refers to the extent to which the criterion measure corresponds to the relevant aspects of performance or job success. A relevant criterion taps the entire range of job performance or behaviors important to the job or organization. Relevance is limited to the extent that the criterion is deficient, or fails to capture one or more of the important performance areas. Relevance is also limited when the criterion includes contaminants, or aspects irrelevant for successful performance on the job (e.g., dollar volume of sales for different auto salespersons may be influenced by region of the country in which they operate).

According to the Uniform Guidelines, job analysis is a key factor in demonstrating that criteria are relevant and represent important work behaviors or work outcomes. Criteria that can be used without a full job analysis include production rates, error rates, tardiness, absenteeism, and tenure. Criteria that will be closely reviewed for job relevance and should be developed based on a thorough job analysis include ratings of performance and measures consisting of paper and pencil tests. When training success is used as a criterion, the relevance of training must be shown, either by comparing the content of the training program to the important behaviors and tasks on the job, or by demonstrating that measures of training success are related to measures of job performance. While not currently addressed, it is likely that the job relevance of nontraditional criteria would need to be demonstrated in cases of a discrimination charge against the employer. Arguments have been made (Borman, 1991; Borman & Motowidlo, 1993) that as long as such behaviors and attributes can be shown to contribute to an organization's effectiveness, then such measures can be considered relevant performance criteria. However, demonstrating relevance for such criteria is likely to be more difficult than for traditional criteria which are more directly based on job content.

Further, an important issue is whether performance or success should be viewed unidimensionally, using or creating an overall measure, or whether it should be viewed multidimensionally, using multiple criteria to capture various components or aspects of performance or success (Borman, 1991). Recently, based on work in the Project A Army Selection and Classification Project, Campbell and his colleagues (Campbell, 1990; Campbell, McHenry, & Wise, 1990; Campbell, McCloy, & Oppler, 1993) have suggested a theory of job performance that includes eight parameters or components which make up overall performance. This body of work is particularly useful in defining the broad categories that comprise work performance (e.g., specific technical proficiency, general proficiency, personal discipline). Further, results of Project A indicated that these distinct performance categories were predicted by different things (McHenry, Hough, Toquam, Hanson, & Ashworth, 1990; Wise, McHenry, & Campbell, 1990).

In selection, the choice of whether to use an overall criterion or multiple criteria depends on one's goals. If the goal is to select persons with the highest predicted overall performance or success, then a single criterion is most useful. If the goal is to understand more precisely which predictors are best able to predict which aspects of performance and success, then multiple criteria are needed (Borman, 1991). Viewing performance multidimensionally and using multiple criteria does not preclude using a single overall index as the criteria. That is, an organization can weight the importance of each major performance or success factor and then combine the weighted scores into an overall composite index that best reflects what the organization desires and is trying to accomplish (Campbell, McHenry, & Wise, 1990).

Choosing Predictors (Step 3)

Criteria define what represents effective performance and success in the organization. Once this is determined, the attributes or characteristics of individuals that are needed to achieve success on the job and in the organization are delineated. Information from the job analysis is used to develop hypotheses about the worker characteristics that will best predict performance and success. Then, measures of these characteristics (predictors) are developed or chosen. The choice of predictors is based on these hypotheses and on previous research evidence about different predictors (cf. Lubinski & Dawis, 1990). Many types of predictors are used, including application blanks, interviews, written tests, and work samples, each of which assesses a different set of individual characteristics. Although predictors take many forms, we use the term *test* to refer to any type of predictor. Understanding the usefulness of predictors requires an understanding of the concepts of validity and utility; thus, the review of different predictors follows the discussion of validity and utility below.

Analyzing Predictor-Criterion Relationships (Step 4)

In selection, the accuracy with which criteria can be predicted from the traits or characteristics measured by the selection devices is of primary concern. Validation of tests and measures refers to the degree to which the inferences that are drawn from scores on the measure are accurate (Guion, 1991). Different procedures provide different types of validity evidence. The essentials of validation are presented here based on several sources (Ghiselli, Campbell, & Zedeck, 1981; Guion, 1991; Schneider & Schmitt, 1986). More comprehensive coverage can be found in these sources.

Criterion-Related Validation

In the selection context, criterion-related validity evidence is most common. Evidence of criterion-related validation is based on the degree to which predictor and criterion scores are correlated. The degree of correlation indicates how well we will be able to predict the performance of applicants based on information about their test scores.

There are two basic designs to this approach. In a concurrent design predictor and criterion data are collected at the same time from a sample of job incumbents, and the two sets of scores are correlated. This approach is relatively quick and easy. In a predictive design predictor test data is collected from applicants and then at some later point in time (e.g., after new hires have served six months on the job), performance measures are collected, and the two sets of scores are correlated. Evidence suggests that correlations obtained from concurrent and predictive designs are similar. The quality of the validation study depends on the size of the sample, the reliability of the predictor and criterion measures, and the degree to which the sample is representative of the applicant pool for which the test will ultimately be used.

The EEOC's Uniform Guidelines address the requirements for a criterion-related validity study and provide some additional direction for designing a good validation study. A job analysis for each of the jobs for which the validation study is being conducted is important to justify the tests and criteria. Further, the sample of employees should be based to as great extent as feasible on a sample which is representative of the people and jobs to which the results are to be generalized. In particular, the proportion of women and minorities in the sample used for the validation study must be adequate. If technically feasible, the employer should demonstrate the test's fairness by showing that it predicts performance in the same way for all groups involved (see Arvey & Faley, 1988 for assessment of fairness). Further, a test is not considered valid if it assesses KSA that are learned after a short time on the job. It is also not acceptable to use tests validated on a higher-level job to select applicants for lower-level jobs, except when there is a reasonable likelihood that the individual in the lower-level job will be promoted to the higher-level job.

Content Validation

In content validation evidence is collected regarding the degree to which responses required by items in the selection measure are representative of the sample of the behaviors exhibited on the job. Essentially, content validation is concerned with the construction of the measure. Content validity evidence focuses on a description of the degree to which the content of the measure represents the tasks performed on the job, rather than the ability to make predictions about performance.

In a content validity study, experts (e.g., job incumbents, supervisors) evaluate the job relevance of the items in the test or measure. Experts judge or rate which knowledge, skill, or ability the item measures, and the extent to which the K, S, or A measured by the item is essential or necessary for successful job performance. These ratings can be summarized into a content validity ratio (see Lawshe, 1975).

Content validity is applicable to both predictors and criteria measures. Further, content validity evidence is appropriate primarily for measures of observable work behavior or products rather than for abstract traits (e.g., intelligence). This is because the inferential leap that must be made to determine if the measure assesses the content of the job is likely to be smaller for assessments of work behavior than for general traits.

The Uniform Guidelines point out some requirements for a content validation study. A job analysis must fully enumerate the tasks, KSA, and their importance since it is used to identify the content domain of the job. Also, since most content-valid measures require a demonstration of task-specific knowledge or skills that are actually performed on the job, content validity is inappropriate if individuals are to receive training on these job tasks or require job experience to perform the tasks.

Construct Validation

Construct validation evidence is used to estimate the degree to which the characteristic assessed by the test or measure corresponds to the characteristic as defined. For example, if we purport that a test measures intelligence, construct validity indicates the extent to which the test actually measures intelligence. In a sense, construct validation focuses on an internal assessment of the quality of the measure.

Estimation of construct validation is complex and requires an accumulation of evidence from different sources and different studies. A frequently used approach is the multi-trait multi-method matrix. This procedure requires the inclusion of measures of the same or similar traits (e.g., conscientiousness, honesty), assessed with different types of methods (e.g., interview, written test). Further, different traits (e.g., honesty, intelligence) are assessed with different methods. The scores from the different measures are correlated. The basic assumptions underlying this approach are that a measure should correlate highly with other measures purported to assess the same construct, and a test should not correlate strongly with a measures of different constructs or traits. The highest correlations should be observed for measures of the same trait, assessed with the same method.

Recently, more sophisticated statistical and analytical procedures have been offered for assessing construct validity, such as the use of factor analysis and path analysis (see Arvey, 1992; Arvey, Landon, Nutting, & Maxwell, 1992 for more details).

Broader Perspectives

In the past, it was generally assumed that the results of a criterion-related validation study were specific to the situation or job for which the study was conducted. This assumption was based on the findings that different validities for the same test were found from one study to another, even when the jobs were practically identical. The implication of this was that a validity study had to be conducted each time the test was used in a new situation (e.g, a different organization, different plant, or different job). More recently, it has been shown that much of the differences in observed validities across situations are simply due to statistical artifacts (e.g., low sample size, unreliability of measures). Work by Schmidt, Hunter, and their colleagues (e.g., Hunter & Schmidt, 1990; Schmidt & Hunter, 1977; Schmidt, Hunter, & Pearlman, 1981) provided evidence that validity results are generalizable from one situation to the next. Validity generalization techniques essentially combine the results of many validity studies to provide the best estimate of the true validity of the test. By combining studies, the validity estimate is based on a much larger sample size, and corrections for statistical artifacts are made. A large number of research publications provide evidence that validity is generalizable across similar jobs and across organizations. This evidence is available for a large number of predictor measures.

When validity generalization evidence is available, it is possible that the evidence can be used to support the validity of the test, without conducting an independent study. To use validity generalization evidence, it is important to conduct a job analysis to show the similarity between the job in question and the jobs for which the validity evidence is reported. Further, it is important to show the similarity between the samples and tests used in the studies comprising the validity generalization project and the sample and test currently in question. It should be noted that validity generalization has been well received in recent years, both by selection experts and courts, although debate continues about specific validity generalization procedures.

Issues

Ideally, validation includes criterion, content, and construct validity evidence. From a practical point of view, evidence of a test's job relatedness and evidence of strong correlation between the criterion and predictor is useful even without a precise understanding of what exactly the predictor measures. For example, we may be able to predict job performance well with a structured interview, even though we do not have a clear understanding of the exact constructs that are measured with the interview.

Earlier, we focused on validation between a single predictor and a criterion. In many cases, using more than one predictor simultaneously (a test battery) can improve prediction since different tests may assess different attributes needed for job success (Schneider & Schmitt, 1986). To increase criterion-related validity by using multiple predictors, predictors should be chosen such that each predictor is correlated with the criterion and the predictors have relatively low correlations with each other. Multiple regression, and more recently, path analysis techniques, are typically used to assess the effectiveness and overall validity of test batteries. This approach is termed a compensatory model since a low score on one test can be compensated for by a high score on another test.

Alternatively, a cutoff approach can be used whereby job candidates must "pass" each test. This procedure is useful when some minimal amount of the ability or attribute is critical in order to succeed on the job. No one is selected who does not meet the minimum cutoff level, but among those who meet the cutoff other considerations can be used to select people. Research devoted to determining cutoff scores provides no clear direction about choosing one cutoff score over another or about the best methods for choosing cutoffs (cf. Angoff, 1971; Cascio, Alexander, & Barrett, 1988; Martin & Raju, 1992; Maurer, Alexander, Callahan, Bailey, & Dambrot, 1991). From a legal standpoint, courts tend to look for an articulated rationale for the cutoff score, based on the level of job performance needed on the job and the test score needed to achieve this performance level. The Uniform Guidelines state that cutoff scores should be set so as to be reasonable and consistent with normal expectations of acceptable proficiency within the workforce. Further, the guidelines call for cutoff scores, as opposed to rank ordering candidates based on their test scores, when the tests are validated solely on the basis of content validity.

Usefulness and Utility (Step 5)

Researchers have often used validity coefficients as proof of the test's usefulness, that is, the greater the relationship between selection test scores and performance, the more useful the procedure for acquiring people who will perform well and be productive. However, validity coefficients do not provide information about the "bottom line" practical utility of selection procedures. Thus, utility procedures have been developed to translate validity into dollar values. Since utility analysis can be quite complex; only a brief mention of the concepts involved are provided here. Two excellent sources covering utility analysis are Cascio (1991b) and Boudreau (1991).

Utility concerns the overall value of the selection system and can be viewed as analogous to a cost-benefit ratio. Application of utility formulations provides an estimate of the increase in productivity in dollars to be expected from the use of the selection procedure. The basic premise is that a more valid selection procedure will result in an average increase in the performance of those hired. The more selective the organization (e.g., the ratio of those hired to applicants is small), the higher the average performance will be when people are selected with the test. The dollar value or worth to the company of this increase in job performance is estimated. Greater benefits are achieved as the number of people hired increases and as the average tenure of those hired increases. Of course, there are costs associated with a selection procedure (e.g., the cost of recruiting, cost testing). Thus, costs are subtracted from the overall dollar value estimate of the selection procedure.

The results of utility analyses are particularly useful for comparing two selection devices. For example, one selection device may be very valid such that our chances of hiring successful performers is increased, but at the same time, it may be very costly to use. Another procedure may be less valid, but low cost and easy to administer. Utility analysis can help determine which will result in the best overall benefit to the organization in terms of the increased productivity associated with the use of the test.

Further, we believe it is important to consider broader issues aside from specific job performance and to consider evaluation at a more global level, as opposed to basing evaluation primarily on the relationship between an individual's predictor score and an individual's criterion score. For example, many organizations have begun using work teams. Since we select new people to move into existing teams or work groups, we might evaluate the extent to which the newcomer influences the group's performance (Guion, 1991). Other analyses might include an examination of the extent to which the organization's HR needs, in terms of the number of people with the required skills, are being met. Examination of the aggregate satisfaction levels of hired employees, turnover rates or absenteeism rates could also provide useful information about the success of the selection program. Some recent work (Terpstra & Rozell, 1993) has focused on the success of selection at the organizational level, showing a positive relationship between the extent to which organization's use staffing practices recommended in the academic literature (e.g., recruiting studies, validation studies, structured interviewing) and organizational level measures of performance.

Another relevant factor in examining the usefulness of selection practices concerns applicants' reactions to the procedure. The most valid and effective selection systems are of little value if qualified job seekers do not apply (Barber & Roehling, 1993). The way applicants view job posting, the way they are treated during the hiring process, and the types of selection tests utilized suggest to applicants how much the organization cares for its human resources and how fairly employees are treated. Applicants' perceptions that a test is unfair can result in negative consequences for the organization, such as reduced acceptance of job offers, decreased likelihood of purchasing the organization's products or services, increased likelihood of discrimination charges, and if hired, increased likelihood of having negative attitudes and lower commitment (e.g., Gilliland, 1993; Rynes, Bretz, & Gerhart, 1991). Further, applicant reactions may indirectly influence the validity and utility of the procedures. Perceived unfairness may lower motivation to perform resulting in biased or inaccurate scores for validation purposes, and decreased organizational attractiveness may result in significant utility losses when qualified applicants refuse jobs (Smither, Reilly, Millsap, Pearlman, & Stoffey, 1993). Thus, an important evaluative mechanism would focus on examining applicants' reactions to selection processes.

PREDICTOR MEASURES

Selection is complex. A wide variety of different types of predictors that measure a wide variety of individual characteristics are available. Given limited time and resources, it is necessary to collect as much relevant information about an applicant as possible in an efficient and timely manner (Schmitt & Klimoski, 1991). In the following section, techniques that have been developed for this purpose are briefly reviewed (for overviews and more details, see Cascio, 1991a; Guion 1991; Reilly & Chao 1982; Schmitt, Gooding, Noe, & Kirsch, 1984;

Schmitt & Klimoski 1991). Unless otherwise noted, all references to validity refer to criterion-related validity, the correlation coefficient between predictor scores and performance-based criterion scores.

Interviews

Interviews are a common and enduring predictor used by organizations. Many interviews take the form of unstructured discussions between an organizational representative and a job applicant. Due to the subjective nature embodied in this process, decisions about applicants are often influenced by interviewer biases and irrelevant factors (Anderson, 1992). Research indicates that the validity of unstructured interviews is extremely low, around 0.1 to 0.2 (Hunter & Hunter, 1984; Schmitt et al., 1984), and their use may result in some adverse impact against women and minorities (Arvey & Faley, 1988; Reilly & Chao, 1982).

In an effort to improve the validity of the interview, several types of structured interviews have been developed (Janz, 1982; Latham, Saari, Pursell, & Campion, 1980; Motowildo et al., 1992). Structured interviews include a standard format, deliberate application of systematic and predetermined rules for observation and evaluation, and uniform application of rules for every applicant (Motowidlo et al., 1992). Structuring the interview process and focusing the content of the interview on gathering job-relevant information helps control subjectivity and the influence of irrelevant factors. Recent reviews (Huffcutt & Arthur, 1994; Marchese & Muchinsky, 1993; Wiesner & Cronshaw, 1988; Wright, Lichtenfels, & Pursell, 1989) suggest that the validity of structured interviews is good, around 0.4. Further, the validity of interviews can be increased by using a panel of interviewers and by training interviewers (Anderson, 1992).

Background Information and Biographical Data

Employers have long collected information about individuals' background from application forms and in resumes, including education, previous training and work experience, and special skills. The assumption behind using this information in selection is that behavior tends to be consistent; hence, a good predictor of future behavior is past behavior (Guion, 1991; Mael, 1991). Background data should be useful for screening applicants, but it is often used subjectively. One procedure that combats this subjectivity is the weighted application blank (WAB), whereby items that are related to job success are identified and weighted before using them to make decisions (England, 1971).

Biographical information forms (biodata) also assess personal history, but include a much broader spectrum of items, such as hobbies, social relations, and other life experiences. Similar to WAB, those items that are statistically related to job success are combined and used for making decisions about applicants. Research evidence suggests that biodata is among the most valid predictors, with validities in the 0.3 to 0.5 range (Hunter & Hunter, 1984; Reilly & Chao, 1982). However, validity may diminish over time due to the sole reliance on empirical relationships to identify useful items (Wernimont, 1976). Because many personal and background experiences may be related to age, gender, and race, adverse impact is a potential concern, but it depends on the biodata items used and the criteria that is predicted (Reilly & Chao, 1982).

Reference Checks

Reference checks involve gathering information about an applicant's background and character from people who have worked with or had contact with the individual (Ash & Levine, 1985) through reference letters, telephone interviews, or in-person contacts. Information from reference checks can be used to verify other information (e.g., previous jobs) received from the candidate. Or, the information can be used to predict job success. For prediction, the validity of reference checks is poor, around 0.2 (Hunter & Hunter, 1984). The low validity is likely due to the subjective nature of the process and the fact that most evaluations of candidates are very positive. Also, recent court rulings for slander make reference-givers reluctant to say negative things about a candidate. There is little available evidence on the adverse impact of reference checks (Arvey & Faley, 1988; Reilly & Chao, 1982).

Cognitive Ability Tests

There are many different types of human abilities (Fleishman & Mumford, 1991; Lubinski & Dawis, 1990). Cognitive ability tests are usually paper-and-pencil measures designed to assess mental abilities or mental functioning. Most cognitive ability tests include assessments of multiple abilities or aptitudes, such as verbal, quantitative, and reasoning abilities, spatial orientation, form perception, and finger dexterity. Scores can be derived for each of the different facets of ability; or, an average score across the verbal, quantitative, and reasoning ability facets can be computed to represent "g" or general cognitive ability. General cognitive ability is interpreted as general intelligence or ability to learn (Gottfredson, 1986; Hunter & Hunter, 1984; Lubinski & Dawis, 1990).

Results of validity generalization studies show that g has some validity for nearly all jobs, with validities in the range of 0.2 to 0.4. (Hunter & Hunter, 1984; Schmitt et al., 1984). Thus, cognitive ability tests are highly generalizable and can be used in different organizations for different jobs, with the expectation that the test will have some degree of validity. However, some jobs require only a limited number of the facets of ability. As the complexity of the job increases, the validity of general cognitive ability increases, whereas for less complex jobs, other specific abilities (e.g., perceptual, psychomotor) may be more valid (Hunter & Hunter, 1984). Tests of more specific abilities generally show criterion-related validities in the range of 0.3 (Schmitt et al., 1984), but they are less generalizable across different jobs. Unfortunately, cognitive ability tests exhibit sizeable differences in test scores between blacks and whites, hence they almost always result in adverse impact against blacks when used in hiring (Arvey & Faley, 1988; Hartigan & Wigdor, 1989; Hunter, Schmidt, & Hunter, 1979; Reilly & Chao, 1982).

Physical Ability Tests

Due to recent laws (ADA, EEO) and the concern with health care costs, assessment of physical ability (e.g., strength, endurance, coordination) has been receiving more attention during selection. Recent work (Arvey, Landon, Nutting, & Maxwell, 1992; Hogan, 1991a, 1991b) has shown that physical ability tests are highly valid for physically demanding jobs or jobs in which physical abilities are critical in crisis times (e.g., police officers, fire fighters). However, physical ability tests generally have adverse impact against women and are likely to have adverse impact against some minority groups, disabled individuals, and older workers (Hogan, 1991a). Thus, in using physical ability tests as predictors, it is important to demonstrate job-relatedness, showing that the physical abilities assessed are necessary for safe and effective job performance.

Work Samples

Work samples, or simulations, are essentially small replications of the actual job. These tests provide direct evidence of an applicant's ability to perform particular tasks, by having applicants complete some activity (either motor or verbal) that closely resembles the actual job situation (Asher & Sciarrino, 1974). Occasionally, written work sample tests are used to assess specific job knowledge. Content-oriented procedures (e.g., basing items on tasks defined in a job analysis) are used to construct work samples to ensure that they closely resemble the content of the job (e.g., Schmitt & Ostroff, 1986), hence they typically demonstrate high content validity. The criterion-related validity of these procedures also tends to be high, in the range of 0.4 to 0.5 (Hunter & Hunter, 1984; Schmitt, Gooding, Noe, & Kirsch, 1984). There is little evidence available regarding the adverse impact of work samples, but it appears to be considerably less than that of paper-and-pencil cognitive ability tests (Arvey & Faley, 1988).

Assessment Centers

An assessment center is a collection of work sample and other tests which job candidates proceed through over a period of a day to one week. In the selection context, assessment centers have been primarily used to predict managerial performance (Gaugler, Rosenthal, Thornton, & Bentson, 1987) by assessing attributes such as decision-making ability, administrative skills, interpersonal skills, and delegation. These attributes are assessed with different simulations, such as role-playing exercises, group discussions, and an "in-basket" which contains memos and documentation of hypothetical issues requiring action. In addition, participants may be interviewed and may complete written tests of intelligence and interests. Candidates are observed and evaluated by multiple, trained raters who then meet to reach a consensus rating for each candidate. Content validity should be high since assessment centers represent a form of work sampling, although dissenting opinions exist (e.g., Sackett, 1987). Assessment centers typically demonstrate strong criterion-related validity, around .4 to .5 (Schmitt et al., 1984). Adverse impact for race, age, and sex have been reported, however much less so than in other selection procedures (Arvey & Faley, 1998).

Personality Tests

Personality tests are designed to assess human nature and character traits of individuals with paper-and-pencil tests or with evaluations made by clinical psychologists or psychiatrists (Hogan, 1991). Initial interest in personality assessment during selection declined as discouraging validity evidence was compiled in the 1960s (e.g., Guion & Gottier, 1965). However, the majority of personality tests used during that period were designed to explain the origins of psychopathology; hence, they may have been largely irrelevant for the work context (Hogan, 1991; Weiss & Adler, 1984). With the development of paper-and-pencil personality tests designed to assess the dynamics of everyday social behavior (Hogan, 1991) and the tailoring of personality inventories to the job (e.g., Mills & Bohanon, 1980; Ostroff, 1993), interest of in these measures in selection has been growing and validity evidence has been mounting (cf. Barrick & Mount, 1991; Hough, Eaton, Dunnette, Camp, & McCloy, 1990).

In both personality and organizational research, a great deal of research attention has been devoted to the construct validity of personality measures, resulting in the notion that there are five basic personality dimensions (e.g., conscientiousness, extroversion) of individuals (Hogan, 1991). Although some argue that it is insufficient to assess only five broad personality categories (e.g., Hogan, 1991), the criterion-related validity of some of the "Big Five" personality traits for predicting performance-based criteria has been established and is in 0.2 to 0.3 range (Barrick & Mount, 1991; Hough et al., 1990; Tett, Jackson, & Rothstein, 1991). Finally, while some personality tests are race- and gender-blind (Hogan, 1991), others require that different scoring keys be used for males and females, which is problematic since the Civil Rights Act of 1991 prohibits differential scoring for different groups.

Integrity Testing

The use of paper-and-pencil integrity tests to assess the honesty and integrity of applicants has been growing since the Polygraph Act of 1988 severely limited the use of lie-detector tests for selection. There are two basic types of integrity tests—overt and personality-based (Sackett, Burris, & Callahan, 1989). Overt tests are designed to assess and predict theft by asking candidates about their attitudes toward theft and dishonesty and to admit to past theft and other illegal behaviors. Personality-based tests are designed to assess broader constructs such as "employee deviance," attitudes toward authority, trustworthiness, and conscientiousness (Sackett, Burris, & Callahan, 1989). They are used to predict theft, as well as counterproductive behaviors, such as disciplinary problems and absenteeism.

Ones, Viswesvaran, and Schmidt (1993) found that integrity tests are reasonably valid (0.2 to 0.4) for job performance, counterproductive behaviors, self-reported theft, and actual theft, with the strongest validities for predicting counterproductive behaviors, as opposed to actual theft. Little evidence of adverse impact exists; however, there are legal and ethical issues involved since some states have made them illegal and they are considered by some to be an invasion of privacy.

Issues

Most work on developing and validating predictors has been based on the concept of matching skills to job requirements in order to predict job performance. Several researchers (e.g., DuBois, Sackett, Zedeck, & Fogli, 1993; Sackett, Zedeck, & Fogli, 1988) have argued that the prediction of job performance requires an understanding of maximum and typical performance. Maximum performance reflects what a worker is capable of doing when performance is monitored and the greatest effort is put forth over a short period of time. Maximum performance is primarily a function of individuals' knowledge, skills, and abilities, so the best predictors of it should be those measures designed to assess capabilities (i.e., ability tests, work samples, and assessment centers). Also, supervisory ratings of job performance have been shown to largely reflect maximum performance (Sackett, Zedeck, & Fogli, 1988). Since the majority of measures of job performance used as criteria in validation studies are supervisory ratings, it is not surprising that the highest validities are often reported for these skill- and ability-based predictors.

However, an exclusive focus on maximum performance may be a deficient strategy. Predictors of maximum performance may allow us to predict the level of performance individuals are capable of, but not whether individuals will actually achieve this performance level on a regular basis. Typical performance is a function of both ability and motivation (DuBois, Sackett, Zedeck, & Fogli,

1993). Motivation is affected by the fit between the worker's needs and values and the values, opportunities, and rewards available from the job and organization (Dawis, 1991; Schmitt & Klimoski, 1991). Thus, typical performance should be best predicted by measures that assess both capabilities and motivational components. Biodata, interviews, reference checks, and personality tests may be used to assess both components to varying degrees, while personality-based tests reflect only the nonability component of typical job performance. Validities of these measures for predicting typical performance are not well known; however, they are likely to be higher than those most often reported in the literature for these predictors.

The implication of this distinction is that typical performance is a function of both capabilities and fit between personal attributes and organizational attributes. A selection strategy that includes only assessment of capabilities is likely to result in choosing people who could do the job, but may not. A selection strategy that emphasizes person-organization fit only is likely to result in employees who want to do the job, but may not be able to. Hence, to predict typical performance, it may be necessary to include both ability-based and personality-based tests. Alternatively, predictors that allow for assessing both (e.g., biodata, interview) can be designed in such a way as to ensure that both components are included in the assessment.

Finally, far less research has been conducted on developing and validating predictors for nontraditional criteria such as satisfaction, commitment, adjustment, and citizenship. These criteria may be important in their own right as goals for the organization (Schneider & Schmitt, 1986). They may also be important because they are indicators of fit, and fit is a component of typical performance. Personality-based tests or value inventories are useful for predicting nontraditional criteria and fit (Chatman, 1991; Caldwell & O'Reilly, 1990) and may be more useful for predicting satisfaction and fit than for predicting job performance (Ostroff, 1993; Schneider & Schmitt, 1986).

SELECTION POLICY CHOICES

As detailed in the preceding sections, a variety of options exist and a complex array of considerations must be taken into account when designing a selection system. Thus, to organize these issues, we focus on a broader framework that reflects a set of general choices which must be made about the selection system as a whole. Expanding on the framework of Schuler and Jackson (1987) and based on our own review of the selection literature, eight major selection policy choices are presented.

Each policy choice is presented as a continuum between two extreme points (e.g., skill fit to organization fit). Any point along the continuum can be chosen. The best point on each continuum for an organization should be logically tied to contextual features, and the goals and strategy of the organization (Jackson, Schuler, & Rivero, 1989; Schuler & Jackson, 1987; Schuler, 1987). However, selection policy choices and priorities may also be based on the demands of the powerful or politically active constituencies in the organization (Tsui, 1987; Tsui & Milkovich, 1987).

Job Specific—Organization Fit

There is no universally accepted definition of fit in the selection context (Rynes & Gerhart, 1990). At one end of the continuum is the traditional, job task specific view of selection in which fit is defined as correspondence between an individual's KSA and the KSA required to do the job. Job specific fit enhances job performance and productivity (Burke & Pearlman, 1988). At the other end of the continuum is person-organization fit defined in terms of the correspondence between individuals' personal attributes and the organization's norms, culture, climate, and values. People who fit the organization are more likely to be satisfied, committed, adjusted, and remain for longer periods of time (e.g., Chatman, 1991; O'Reilly, Chatman, & Caldwell, 1991; Ostroff, 1993).

An emphasis on job-specific fit requires a job analysis detailing the tasks and KSA, identification of job performance criteria, and development of selection procedures that are skill-based, such as ability tests or work samples. An emphasis on organization fit requires a different view of the selection model. The system-wide components of the organization must be delineated and desired attributes of employees inferred from this analysis. Selection procedures, such as personality tests, integrity tests, or interviews, are more likely to capture different types of personal attributes compared to skill-based methods, and may be useful for predicting the nontraditional criteria (e.g., citizenship, satisfaction) which reflect organizational fit.

The choice need not be exclusively on one type of fit or the other; both can be used simultaneously to select the "whole" person. For example, a multi-stage process could be used to identify individuals with the requisite skills needed for the job; then, from this pool of candidates, selection procedures would focus on identifying those that fit the organization (Bowen, Ledford, & Nathan, 1991). It has been argued that people will perform at levels that match their ability or perform up to their potential to the extent that the work environment fits their expectations and preferences (Schneider, 1972; Schneider & Bartlett, 1970). Thus, consideration of both types of fit during selection is important.

Nevertheless, in some organizations, or in some circumstances, it may be necessary to place more emphasis on one type of fit in selection than another. For example, many personality traits and personal characteristics are relatively enduring and stable, and are not likely to be changed with training (Pervin, 1994). If a particular trait (e.g., sociability, service-orientation, or desire to learn) is deemed critical for the job and organization, then either people must be hired who have this attribute, or the organization must function, perhaps less effectively, without it. Here, selection might focus on ensuring that people with the right personal attributes are hired, and then trained in the technical skills required. In other circumstances, skills may be more important. For example, when training times are long or during periods of rapid growth when the organization needs to upgrade skills, it may be necessary to hire employees who better fit the job's requirements than the organizational context (Bowen, Ledford, & Nathan, 1991).

It is important to point out that a high degree of fit may not always be a desirable state for organizations. For example, when the external environment changes, an organization may have trouble adapting to the change because it has not selected and retained people with the appropriate job skills and personal characteristics to deal with the new external environment. Schneider (1987) argues that for long-term effectiveness and survival, organizations should actively seek and select some individuals who do not completely fit the current organizational context. New "right types" should be selected who share some attributes of current employees but differ in other attributes (Schneider, 1983). Selection practices should be designed to move beyond matching individuals to the current state and consider the skill and general behavioral styles and attributes that will match the organization's future objectives and directions (Schneider, 1983).

Continuity—Change

Selection policies can promote continuity by hiring people who fit the current job or organization, or they can foster change in an organization by identifying employees with job skills or personal characteristics that differ from those of job incumbents (Butler, Ferris, & Napier, 1991). The traditional selection model fosters continuity because the basic premise is that selection criteria should be aligned with the behaviors and activities performed by job incumbents. Information obtained from the job analysis procedures is typically gathered from incumbents, and then this information is used for selection test development. Further, continuity of personal characteristics (and to some degree job skills) occurs through processes of attraction-selection-attrition. Schneider (1983, 1987) argues that individuals are attracted to organizations with characteristics similar to their own, and organizations select people who have the particular competencies needed for organizational effectiveness. Individuals who do not fit the organization tend to leave. Over time, this process results in organizations comprised of employees with very similar types of personal attributes.

Some deviations from the traditional model are needed when selection is to be used as a tool to foster desired changes in the organization. For example, if an organization implements a new technological process, job requirements change and different job skills are needed. Here, job analysis information cannot be gathered from incumbents; instead information from workers in other companies that have similar jobs might be useful. Further, procedures are being developed to use information about tasks from current jobs to forecast the demands of future jobs (Arvey, Salas, & Giallucca, 1992). Alternatively, organizations desiring to change their culture or climate may need to focus on selecting new "right types" to reinforce the desired cultural change. Here, input from top management about the desired changes in people may help in developing appropriate selection procedures.

Specific—Broad Skills

Choices about the level of skills needed by employees must be made in designing selection systems. Organizations may need or desire "specialists" who have a narrow range of highly specific skills relevant for a specific job or set of related jobs, or "generalists" might be required, who have a broad range of skills applicable to a wider variety of jobs. For example, in firms that are organized by functions (e.g., marketing, sales, production), no single function is responsible for producing the entire product or service. Here, specialists with skills relevant to one particular function are more likely to be needed. Alternatively, in firms that are organized by distinct products, each product division is self-contained and must manage processes across different functional areas. Here, generalists, who are competent in all aspects of the business, are more likely to be needed (Jackson, Schuler, & Rivero, 1989). In selection, specific skills could be assessed with multi-attribute ability tests (not general ability) and work sample tests, while general skills could be assessed with cognitive ability tests, interviews, or application forms.

Immediate—Potential Performance

Selection can focus on choosing individuals capable of performing the job immediately, with little or no training, or the focus can be on selecting individuals with a general ability or aptitude level who have the potential to learn, and then training them for the job or various jobs. Using the selection model, selection for immediate performance would require a detailed task and KSA analysis. Relevant selection measures would be work sample tests or simulations. For potential to perform, a focus on general skills and abilities is needed and selection devices which assess general aptitudes such as a cognitive ability test would be appropriate.

Single Job—Job Family

The selection model can be followed and procedures developed for each individual job in the organization. Alternatively, similar jobs can be classified into broad families of related jobs and a single selection procedure can be developed for the entire job family. Some have argued that selection for a broad family of jobs may be a more effective and efficient policy than trying to distinguish clearly the prediction of performance in jobs that do not differ much (Pearlman, 1980), especially since some validity generalization evidence suggests that differences between jobs are not as large as originally believed in terms of our ability to predict job performance (Guion, 1991). Job analysis information is used to group jobs requiring the same skills into families. Then, selection measures are chosen, validated, and evaluated based on the entire job family, not each individual job comprising the family. A job-family focus assumes a more general skill focus since there will be differences in the specific tasks that are performed in the jobs that comprise the job family. A single-job focus makes it possible to use and validate selection methods (e.g., work sample) that are more directly related to specific job tasks and skills.

Internal—External Candidates

Selection occurs after a pool of job applicants has been recruited. The pool of job candidates can be drawn from current employees who will be promoted or transferred, or it can be drawn from external applicants. The extent to which each is used depends on the extent of the organization's training and development of current employees, the extent to which current employees possess the needed skills, and the organization's general philosophy regarding worker retention. The use of an internal labor pool should enable selection to focus more on job fit relative to organization fit. Incumbents should already fit in the organization since they have previously been selected by the organization, and have chosen to join and remain in the organization (Schneider, 1983). Thus, assessment of incumbent employees skills for the particular job opening would form the basis of the selection procedure. With external applicants, issues of both job and organizational fit described earlier are relevant.

Permanent—Contingent Employees

The use of contingent workers (contract, vendor, or temporary employees), has been growing in organizations (Pfeffer & Baron, 1988). One reason for this trend is that companies have been adopting a "right-sizing" approach in which a core of permanent workers is supplemented by contract workers who come and go as product or service demand fluctuates or as different expertise is needed (Pfeffer & Baron, 1988). Thus, contractors allow for more flexibility, help prevent the need for layoffs and mass hirings, and lower costs.

The extent to which contractors can be used effectively depends, in part, on the general strategy and culture of the organization (Ouchi, 1980; Pearce, 1993). For example, if the goal is to develop a committed, trusting, cooperative, and sharing organization, then contractors should be used less, since the presence of contract workers among permanent employees may undermine the trust permanent employees have in the organization (Pearce, 1993). With an efficiency focus, it may be desirable to increase the use of contractors since labor costs can often be reduced by limiting the number of permanent employees and hiring contractors (Pfeffer & Baron, 1988). The extent to which contractors can realistically be used depends on the degree to which firm-specific job skills for completing tasks are needed (Pearce, 1993). Job analysis information can be used to determine the extent to which firm-specific skills are needed and the extent to which managers could re-assign job tasks so that contractors would perform independent tasks and permanent employees would perform tasks that require firm-specific knowledge and interdependence among employees.

Diversity—Validity

Tests vary in their degree of validity and in the extent to which they are likely to produce adverse impact. The validity and adverse impact of the most commonly used selection procedures was reported earlier. The EEOC guideline's state that when available selection procedures are substantially equal in validity and serve the user's legitimate interests in an efficient way, then the procedure which has less adverse impact should be used.

Unfortunately, the choice is not always so simple. Decision makers may be faced with a tradeoff between using the test with the highest validity thereby maximizing the chances of selecting high performers, or using the test that better allows for increasing diversity in the workplace, but has less validity (Maxwell & Arvey, 1993). For example, cognitive ability tests tend to be more valid than unstructured interviews, but nearly always result in adverse impact. The decision can be further complicated by the utility of the selection procedures. For example, work sample tests, which have little demonstrated adverse impact, tend to have higher validity than cognitive ability tests; yet work samples are more costly to develop and administer. Thus, the overall utility of a work sample could be less than that for cognitive ability test even though the work sample is more valid and is less likely to produce adverse impact. The choice between selection measures depends on which better serves the organization's goals. In making such decisions, organizations need to consider factors such as the benefit to the minority group, benefits of a diversified workforce, potential performance losses, and the costs associated with litigation if a charge of discrimination is brought against the organization.

Considerations of factors beyond the impact on performance may ultimately outweigh the importance of using the procedure with the highest validity for predicting specific job performance (Silva & Jacobs, 1993). Obviously, the ideal choice is to identify those procedures that promote both goals. For example, biodata forms are valid predictors and performance and can have little adverse impact. Personality tests may be valid for predicting fit in the organization and tend to have little adverse impact against ethnic minorities.

All eight selection policy decisions must be coordinated, and tradeoffs among them may be necessary. The goal is to develop a configuration of selection policy choices that contributes to the organization's goals and strategies. For example, firms with a cost reduction strategy have a general goal of efficient production. Thus, they tend to define a narrow range of specific skills that are required of employees and employees are trained extensively in these skills. Personal employee characteristics for organizational fit may be of lesser concern, but include a low tolerance for ambiguity, low flexibility to change, and a desire for predictable repetitive behavior. Contract workers may be used more extensively in such firms in an effort to control labor costs. Further, since such firms typically operate in a relatively stable environment, more emphasis may be placed on continuity as opposed to procedures that will promote large changes in the organization. On the other hand, a differentiation or innovation strategy places an emphasis on creativity and cooperation. Employees in these firms are expected to exhibit behaviors such as taking risks, cooperating with others, tolerating ambiguity, and developing new ideas. Since specific jobs may change often, broadly defined skills and general job descriptions are provided, thereby placing greater emphasis on organizationally relevant personal characteristics as opposed to job-specific skills (Begin, 1991; Schuler & Jackson, 1987; Sonnenfeld & Peiperl, 1988).

THE INDIVIDUALS' PERSPECTIVE

We began this chapter by emphasizing that the overall goal of selection is to match individuals and jobs or organizations in order to enhance the job performance and success of those individuals and thereby the success of the organization. We discussed at length the organization selection system model and issues that affect it. While organizations' selection systems are affected by internal and external contextual considerations (e.g. legal, economic, strategic, and structural constraints, as discussed in previous sections), selection systems are also affected by another consideration, and that is the individuals themselves. In a process analogous to selection of individuals by organizations, individuals also select organizations in which they want to work. The two processes, individual and organizational, occur simultaneously.

From the individual's perspective, the process of selecting a job and organization is related to other career activities (see Figure 1). Individuals begin with a conscious or unconscious career planning process. They develop preferences for types of jobs that would meet their needs and for which they would be qualified (Dawis & Lofquist, 1984; Super, 1953), and develop a plan to obtain such a job. Once this initial planning is done, individuals engage in search processes in which they identify possible job openings and opportunities. Individuals then gather initial information, screen their possible opportunities, and make decisions about which jobs to apply for. At this point individuals becomes applicants to a number of different organizations, and encounter these organizations' recruiting and selection processes. During this process, individuals gather further information about the organization (Rynes, 1991) and compare this information to their original preferences to arrive at an organization choice. Once individuals accept a job offer and become new employees, they begin work, but they also continue to develop job and personal skills. Often, as the employment relationship progresses, individuals appraise their careers and organizational situations to determine if they are successful by evaluating their career success and job satisfaction (Cytrynbaum & Crites, 1989). If successful and satisfied, they will want to remain in the job and organization. The individuals' job and organization search and choice process and its implications for the organization are described briefly below.

The Selection of the Organization by the Individual

Individuals develop a set of preferences with respect to jobs and organizations (Taylor & Giannantonio, 1993). Individuals' vocational preferences are sets of desired job characteristics, and job context and organizational attributes which they prefer over alternative sets of characteristics and attributes. These preferences are often based on individuals' interests and values (Dawis, 1991). Numerous theories describe how these preferences are developed throughout the lifetime of individuals, becoming more refined as individuals approach adulthood (Dawis & Lofquist, 1984, Holland, 1985; Super, 1953). Experience working also affects the individuals' set of preferred job characteristics (Dawis & Lofquist, 1984; Rynes, Bretz, & Gerhart, 1991; Super, 1953). Preferences for different types of characteristics of jobs, contexts, and organizations have been noted in the literature, including preferences for: reward and pay levels, structures and systems of the organization (Dawis & Lofquist, 1984; Cable & Judge, 1994), geographic location (Barber & Roehling, 1993), types of skills required and the work itself (Dawis & Lofquist, 1984; Taylor & Giannantonio, 1993), the environment of the job (Holland, 1985), values of the organization (Judge & Bretz, 1992), prestige of the job (Gottfredson, 1981), and the climate of the organization (Schneider, 1987). These preferences will be weighted differently by different individuals, and each individual's unique set of preferences define the type of job and organization that will meet the individual's needs. Further, demographic characteristics of individuals, such as sex, work experience, and educational success, as well as lifestyle and general life issues, such as religion and family concerns, can impact the kind of job that individuals will seek and find acceptable (Levinson, 1978; Rothausen, 1994; Rynes, Bretz, & Gerhart, 1991; Sharf, 1992).

Just as organizations go through a formal or informal employee selection process, individuals go through a conscious or unconscious job selection process, referred to as job search and choice. The job search and choice process of individuals is influenced by their unique sets of preferences and constraints. Individuals' job choice can be viewed as having two aspects, a "type of work" aspect and a "type of organization" aspect. In other words, some individuals may choose what type of work they want to do first, and then investigate a number organizations in order to identify the best one in which to practice this career. On the other hand, individuals may target an organization or a select group of organizations and then examine the types of jobs within the organization that they are qualified for. Once individuals choose their job search strategy, they will identify opportunities and, based on some preliminary information about the job and organization, decide which jobs to apply for.

In identifying job openings for which they are qualified and which potentially meet their needs, individuals gather information about actual job openings or opportunities. This gathering of information occurs in stages, and is often incomplete. In the initial job search, individuals may gather information from an advertisement or job posting (Barber & Roehling, 1993) or by word of mouth from friends or professional contacts. Individuals then choose to apply to a number of these organizations based on an initial assessment of the job and organization attributes using their set of preferences and constraints and other alternative openings as comparisons. After applying, individuals proceed through the selection systems of the organizations to which they applied; these hiring and selection systems provide additional information to applicants about the jobs and organizations. For individuals, proceeding through the selection processes may culminate in one or more job offers. At this point, individuals may gather more information about the jobs and organizations from which they have offers. Finally, individuals compare their unique sets of preferences and constraints to the job and organizational characteristics of the different companies, and then make a choice about which job and which organization to accept.

Organizational Implications of the Individual Processes

Organizations have little control over the preferences of individuals before the employment relationship begins. However, the organization has considerable influence on whom they focus their recruiting efforts and on the information that the individual will gather about the organization. Thus the organization can affect the individual's job search and choice processes by managing the amount and type of information that the individual gets about the organization and the job. While individuals may apply to a number of different organizations, successful candidates may have to narrow their search because of the costs of the job search process in terms of time (Barber & Roehling, 1993). One factor that may influence which jobs are eliminated from consideration in the initial stages of job search is the amount of information that is in the job posting or initial notification. Candidates appear to be more likely to apply for jobs when the job posting contains more complete and specific information (Barber & Roehling, 1993).

Organizations may engage in impression management in their recruiting processes; in other words, the organization may be selective in the release of information to the applicants. The organization may even exaggerate or distort certain qualities of the job that it views as attractive, while downplaying less attractive features. Research on realistic job previews (Wanous, 1992; Wanous, Premack, & Poland, 1992) indicates that more realistic and balanced information discourages some candidates from pursuing the job, but leads to higher retention rates and more job satisfaction later.

Rynes, Bretz, and Gerhart (1991) found that some applicant characteristics affect applicant reaction to job information. Some types or categories of workers may be more open to particular types of jobs and organizations. While organizations typically cannot change any given individual's preferences in this stage of the employment relationship, the organization may choose to target specific types of candidates in order to enhance applicant attraction, or for other (e.g., EEO) reasons. Rynes and Barber (1990) suggest that targeting nontraditional and less marketable candidates will increase the organization's ability to attract qualified individuals.

Finally, the organization affects applicant attraction by managing recruiter characteristics. Some evidence suggests that the type of person employed by the organization may be an important job attribute for which individuals have a preference. Applicants may view recruiter characteristics such as competence, warmth, and personableness as representative of the organization. Recruiters that seem competent and personable are more likely to attract applicants to pursue the job (Martin & Nagao, 1989; Rynes, Bretz, & Gerhart, 1991). Unfortunately, there is little research in this area, and therefore organizations may have to determine the recruiter characteristics that seem to work best for them. In addition to amount and accuracy of information, target applicant pool and recruiter characteristics, Rynes and Barber (1990) hypothesize that recruitment sources and recruitment timing may affect applicant attraction to jobs.

Smither, Reilly, Millsap, Pearlman, and Stoffey (1993) argue that applicant reactions to selection procedures are important because they can influence the candidate's pursuit of the job or acceptance of job offers and what that applicant will say about the company to other applicants and consumers. In addition, applicant reactions may be related to the likelihood of litigation regarding unfair selection procedures. Thus, the applicant job search and choice process can affect a company's reputation and the utility of its selection procedures. In addition, we are moving from a standard model of employment which included hierarchical career progression, loyalty to the company, and lifetime employment to a newer model in which employees are valued for skills, move from company to company, and make lateral moves within a company. At the same time, families are changing from the traditional model of working father, stay-at-home mother to dual-career and dual-job families. As management is faced with attracting quality employees at a time when the pool of this type of worker may be shrinking, considerations of individual job search and choice behaviors may become more important.

Employers must recognize that selection is not a one-sided process. Although the research in this area is in its infancy, a tentative conclusion can be drawn: the individual's job search and choice process is important to the success of the organization's selection process, specifically its success in getting a large enough applicant pool from which to select employees, its success in having applicants accept offers, and the subsequent success of these individuals in the organization. Although not typically discussed in research on selection, the simultaneous selection of the firm by the individual may have a big impact on the organization's ability to attract, retain, and motivate employees.

SUMMARY AND CONCLUSIONS

At the same time that individuals are searching for jobs and organizations that meet their needs and their requirements, organizations are seeking to find individuals who possess the characteristics that best meet their requirements. Multiple individuals and multiple organizations come together in the recruiting and job search processes, resulting in an applicant pool. Organizations then gather additional information about these applicants during the selection process in order to narrow the applicant pool to those who will receive job offers. Individuals gather further information about organizations during the job choice process to decide which organizations they would accept offers from, if given that choice. New employment relationships are established when both the individual and the organization select or choose each other (see Figure 1). These selection processes, when well designed, allow the individual and the organization to meet their own unique goals not only at this point, but throughout the ensuing employment relationship. When both the individual's and the organization's goals for the relationship are met, the relationship will continue (Dawis & Lofquist, 1984).

These processes are extremely important to both the individual and the organization. For the organization, selecting employees who match the requirements of the job and organization will result in better performance and longer tenure of employees, thereby increasing the organization's productivity and success. Similarly, for most individuals a good match at work has broad implications. A good match will lead to job satisfaction (Dawis & Lofquist, 1984), and job satisfaction is related to overall life satisfaction (Tait, Padgett, & Baldwin, 1989). Those who are happier at work are happier in general. Thus, both individuals' and organizations' success can be maximized with carefully planned choice and selection processes that are designed to produce a greater degree of match.

Even without formal choice and selection process, matches are made; however, the quality of these matches may suffer. In this chapter we outlined the procedures recommended by human resource experts for designing and planning a good selection system. Of critical importance is the use of valid predictors. However, many organizations continue to use unvalidated selection procedures. In a 1983 survey of 437 companies, only 16 percent indicated that they validated one or more of their selection tests (Bureau of National Affairs, 1983). Ten years later, in a study of 201 organizations, only 24 percent reported that they validated tests (Terpstra & Rozell, 1993). In addition, many companies do not use the predictors that have generally proven to be more valid. For example, Terpstra and Rozell (1993) report that only 29 percent of companies use structured interviews, 20 percent use cognitive ability tests, and 17 percent use biodata-type predictors, even though these procedures are among those with the highest documented validity. On the other hand, the majority of companies reported using devices that have little documented validity, for example, 97 percent of companies reported using reference checks and 81 percent reported using unstructured interviews (Bureau of National Affairs, 1983). We believe this is unfortunate as it suggests that many companies are not tapping a valuable resource, namely human resources, to the extent that they could. Based on utility analysis estimates, the use of a valid test can result in millions of dollars in productivity increases per year for some organizations (Boudreau, 1991). Further, recent evidence suggests that using solid HR practices, including good selection procedures, impacts a company's bottom line financial performance (Gomez-Mejia, 1985; Ichniowski, 1990; Katz, Kochan, & Weber, 1985; Terpstra & Rozell, 1993). Thus, from both the organization's and the individual's standpoint, systems designed to increase the match between people, jobs, and organizations will provide the largest benefits.

REFERENCES

Angoff, W.H. (1971). Scales, norms, and equivalent scores. In R.L. Thorndike (Ed.), *Educational measurement* (pp. 508-600). Washington, DC: American Council on Education.

Anderson, N.R. (1992). Eight decades of employment interview research: A retrospective meta-review and a prospective commentary. *European Work and Organizational Psychologist,* 2, 1-32.

Arvey, R.D. (1992). Constructs and construct validation: Definitions and Issues. *Human Performance,* 5, 59-69.

Arvey, R.D., Landon, T.E., Nutting, S.M., & Maxwell, S.E. (1992). Development of physical ability tests for police officers: A construct validation approach. *Journal of Applied Psychology,* 77, 996-1009.

Arvey, R.D., & Faley, R.H. (1988). *Fairness in selecting employees* (2nd ed.). Reading, MA: Addison Wesley.

Arvey, R.D., Salas, E., & Giallucca, K.A. (1992). Using task inventories to forecast skills and abilities. *Human Performance,* 5, 171-190.

Ash, R.A., & Levine, E.L. (1985). Job applicant training and work experience evaluation: An empirical comparison of four methods. *Journal of Applied Psychology,* 70, 572-576.

Asher, J.J., & Sciarrino, J.A. (1974). Realistic work sample tests: A review. *Personnel Psychology,* 27, 519-533.

Austin, J.T., & Villanova, P. (1992). The criterion problem: 1917-1992. *Journal of Applied Psychology,* 77, 836-874.

Barber, A.E., & Roehling, M.V. (1993). Job postings and the decision to interview: A verbal protocol analysis. *Journal of Applied Psychology,* 78, 845-856.

Barney, J.B. (1991). Integrating organizational behavior and strategy formulation research: A resource-based analysis. *Advances in Strategic Management,* 8, 39-61.

Barrick, M.R., & Mount, M.K. (1991). The big five personality dimensions and job performance: A meta-analysis. *Personnel Psychology,* 44, 1-25.

Begin, J.P. (1991). *Strategic Employment Policy.* Englewood Cliffs, NJ: Prentice Hall.

Bernardin, H.J., & Beatty, R.W. (1984). *Performance appraisal: Assessing human behavior at work.* Boston: PWS-Kent.

Borman, W.C. (1991). Job behavior, performance, and effectiveness. In M.D. Dunnette & L.M. Hough (Eds.), *Handbook of industrial organizational psychology* (2nd ed., pp. 271-326). Palo Alto, CA: Consulting Psychologists Press, Inc.

Borman, W.C., & Motowidlo, S.J. (1993). Expanding the criterion domain to include elements of contextual performance. In N. Schmitt, W.C. Borman, & Assoc. (Eds.), *Personnel Selection in Organizations* (pp. 71-98). San Francisco: Jossey Bass.

Boudreau, J.W. (1991). Utility analysis for decisions in human resource management. In M.D. Dunnette & L.M. Hough (Eds.), *Handbook of industrial organizational psychology* (2nd ed., pp. 621-652). Palo Alto, CA: Consulting Psychologists Press, Inc.

Bowen, D.E., Ledford, G.E., & Nathan, B.R. (1991). Hiring for the organization, not the job. *Academy of Management Executive,* 5, 35-51.

Brousseau, K.R. (1984). Job-person dynamics and career development. In K.M. Roland & G.R. Ferris (Eds.), *Research in personnel and human resources management* (volume 2, pp. 125-154), Greenwich, CT: JAI Press.

Burke, M.J., & Pearlman, K. (1988). Recruiting, selecting and matching people with jobs. In J.P. Campbell & R.J. Campbell, & Associates (Eds.), *Productivity in organizations.* San Francisco: Jossey Bass.

Butler, J.E., Ferris, G.R., & Napier, N.K. (1991). *Strategy and human resources management.* Cincinnati, OH: South-Western Publishing Co.

Cable, D.M., & Judge, T.A. (1994). Pay preferences and job search decisions: a person-organization fit perspective. *Personnel Psychology,* 47, 317-348.

Caldwell, D.F. & O'Reilly, C.A., III (1990). Measuring person-job fit with a profile comparison process. *Journal of Applied Psychology,* 75, 648-657.

Camp, R.R., Blanchard, P.N., & Huszczo, G.E. (1986). *Toward a more organizationally effective training strategy and practice.* Englewood Cliffs, NJ: Prentice Hall.

Campbell, C.H., Ford, P., Rumsey, M.G., Pulakos, E.D., Borman, W.C., Felker, D.B., De Vera, M.V., & Riegelhaupt, B.J. (1990). Development of multiple job performance measures in a representative sample of jobs. *Personnel Psychology, 43,* 277-300.

Campbell, J.P. (1990). Modeling the performance prediction problem. In M.D. Dunnette & L.M. Hough (Eds.), *Handbook of industrial organizational psychology* (2nd ed., pp. 687-732). Palo Alto, CA: Consulting Psychologists Press, Inc.

Campbell, J.P., McCloy, R.A., & Oppler, S.H. (1993). A theory of performance. In N. Schmitt, W.C. Borman, & Associates (Eds.), *Personnel selection in organizations* (pp. 35-70). San Francisco: Jossey Bass.

Campbell, J.P., McHenry, J.J., & Wise, L.L. (1990). Modeling job performance in a population of jobs. *Personnel Psychology, 43,* 313-333.

Campbell, J.P. & Campbell, R.J. (1988). Industrial-organizational psychology and productivity: The goodness of fit. In J.P. Campbell, R.J. Campbell & Associates (Eds), *Productivity in organizations.* San Francisco: Jossey Bass.

Cascio, W.F. (1991a). *Applied psychology in personnel management.* Englewood Cliffs, NJ: Prentice Hall.

————. (1991b). *Costing human resources: The financial impact of behavior in organizations.* Boston: PWS-Kent.

Cascio, W.F., Alexander, R.A., & Barrett, G.V. (1988). Setting cutoff scores: Legal, psychometric, and professional issues and guidelines. *Personnel Psychology, 41,* 1-24.

Chatman, J.A. (1989). Improving interactional organizational research: A model of person-organization fit. *Academy of Management Review, 14,* 333-349.

————. (1991). Matching people and organizations: selection and socialization in public accounting firms. *Administrative Science Quarterly, 36,* 459-484.

Cytrynbaum, S., & Crites, J.O. (1989). The utility of adult development theory in understanding career adjustment process. In M.B. Arthur, D.T. Hall, & B.S. Lawrence (Eds.), *Handbook of career theory.* New York: Cambridge University Press.

Dawis, R.V. (1991). Interests, preferences, and values. In M.D. Dunnette & L.M. Hough (Eds.), *Handbook of industrial organizational psychology* (2nd ed., pp. 833-871). Palo Alto, CA: Consulting Psychologists Press, Inc.

Dawis, R.V., & Lofquist, L.H. (1984). *A psychological theory of work adjustment: An individual-differences model and its applications.* Minneapolis, MN: University of Minnesota Press.

Dubois, C.L.Z., Sackett, P.R., Zedeck, S., & Fogli, L. (1993). Further exploration of typical and maximum performance criteria: Definitional issues, prediction, and black-white differences. *Journal of Applied Psychology, 78,* 205-211.

Emery, F.E., & Trist, E.L. (1960). Socio-technical systems. In *Management science models and techniques* (vol. 2). London: Pergamon.

England, G.W. (1971). *Development and use of weighted application blanks.* Minneapolis, MN: University of Minnesota, Industrial Relations Center.

Equal Employment Opportunity Commission (1978). Uniform guidelines on employee selection procedures. *Federal Register, 43,* 38290-38315.

Fair Employment Practices Series (subscription). Washington, DC: Bureau of National Affairs.

Fair Practices Guide. (subscription) Chicago, IL: Commerce Clearing House Inc.

Fleishman, E.A., & Mumford, M.D. (1991). Evaluating classifications of job behavior: A construct validation of the ability requirements scales. *Personnel Psychology, 44,* 523-575.

Gael, S. (Ed.) (1988). *The job analysis handbook for business, industry and government.* New York: Wiley.

Gaugler, B.B., Rosenthal, D.B., Thornton, G.C., III, & Bentson, C. (1987). Meta-analysis of assessment center validity. *Journal of Applied Psychology, 74,* 611-618.

Ghiselli, E.E., Campbell, J.P., & Zedeck, S. (1981). *Measurement theory for the behavioral sciences.* San Francisco: Freeman and Co.

Gilliland, S.W. (1993). The perceived fairness of selection systems: An organizational justice perspective. *Academy of Management Review, 18,* 694-734.

Gomez-Mejia, L.R. (1985). Dimensions and correlates of the personnel audit as an organizational assessment tool. *Personnel Psychology, 38,* 293-308.

Gottfredson, L.S. (1981). Circumscription and compromise: A developmental theory of occupational aspirations. *Journal of Counseling Psychology, 28,* 545-579.

————. (1986). The g factor in employment. *Journal of Vocational Behavior, 29,* 293-296.

Goldstein, I.L. (1986). *Training in organizations* (2nd ed.). Monterey, CA: Brooks/Cole.

Gross, E., & Etzioni, A. (1985). *Organizations in society.* Englewood Cliffs, NJ: Prentice Hall.

Guion, R.M. (1991). Personnel Assessment, Selection, and Placement. In M.D. Dunnette & L.M. Hough (Eds.), *Handbook of industrial organizational psychology* (2nd ed., pp. 327-398). Palo Alto, CA: Consulting Psychologists Press, Inc.

Guion, R.M., & Gottier, R.F. (1965). Validity of personality measures in personnel selection. *Personnel Psychology, 18,* 49-65.

Guthrie, J.P., & Olian, J.D. (1991). Does context affect staffing decisions? the case of general managers. *Personnel Psychology, 44,* 263-292.

Hackman, J.R., & Oldham, G.R. (1975). Development of the job diagnostic survey. *Journal of Applied Psychology, 60,* 159-170.

Harrison, M.I. (1994). *Diagnosing organizations: Methods, models, and processes.* Thousand Oaks, CA: Sage.

Hartigan, J.A., & Wigdor, A.K. (Eds.) (1989). *Fairness in employment testing: validity generalization, minority issues, and the general aptitude test battery.* Washington, DC: National Academy Press.

Harvey, R.J. (1991). Job analysis. In M.D. Dunnette & L.M. Hough (Eds.), *Handbook of industrial organizational psychology* (2nd ed., pp. 71-164). Palo Alto, CA: Consulting Psychologists Press, Inc.

Hogan, J. (1991a). Physical abilities. In M.D. Dunnette & L.M. Hough (Eds.), *Handbook of industrial and organizational psychology* (volume II, pp. 753-831). Palo Alto, CA: Consulting Psychologists Press, Inc.

————. (1991b). Structure of physical performance in occupational tasks. *Journal of Applied Psychology, 76,* 495-507.

Hogan, R.T. (1991). Personality and personality measurement. In M.D. Dunnette & L.M. Hough (Eds.), *Handbook of industrial and organizational psychology* (volume II, pp. 873-919). Palo Alto, CA: Consulting Psychologists Press, Inc.

Holland, J.L. (1985). *Making vocational choices: A theory of vocational personalities and work environments* (2nd ed.). Englewood Cliffs, NJ: Prentice-Hall.

Hough, L.M., Eaton, N.K., Dunnette, M.D., Camp, J.D., & McCloy, R.A. (1990). Criterion-related validities of personality constructs and the effect of response distortion on those validities. *Journal of Applied Psychology, 75,* 467-476.

Huffcutt, A.I., & Arthur, W. (1994). Hunter & Hunter (1984) revisited: Interview validity for entry-level jobs. *Journal of Applied Psychology, 79,* 184-190.

Hunter, J.E., & Hunter, R.F. (1984). Validity and utility of alternative predictors of job performance. *Psychological Bulletin, 96,* 72-98.

Hunter, J.E. & Schmidt, F.L. (1990). *Methods of meta-analysis.* Beverly Hills, CA: Sage.

Hunter, J.E., Schmidt, F.L., & Hunter, R.F. (1979). Differential validity of employment tests by race: A comprehensive review and analysis. *Psychological Bulletin, 85,* 721-735.

Ichniowski, C. (1990). Human resource management systems and the performance of U.S. manufacturing businesses. Working paper #3449. National Bureau of Economic Research.

Jackson, S.E., Schuler, R.S., & Rivero, J.C. (1989). Organizational characteristics as predictors of personnel practices. *Personnel Psychology, 42*, 727-786.

Janz, T. (1982). Initial comparisons of patterned behavior description interviews versus unstructured interviews. *Journal of Applied Psychology, 67*, 577-580.

Judge, T.A., & Bretz, R.D. (1992). Effects of work values on job choice decisions. *Journal of Applied Psychology, 77*, 261-271.

Katz, D., & Kahn, R.L. (1978). *The social psychology of organizations.* New York: Wiley & Sons.

Katz, H.C., Kochan, T.A. & Huber, M.R. (1985). Assessing the effects of industrial relations systems and efforts to improve the quality of working life on organizational effectiveness. *Academy of Management Journal, 28*, 509-526.

Kochan, T.A. (1980). Collective bargaining and organizational behavior research. In B.M. Staw & L.L. Cummings (Eds.), *Research in organizational behavior* (pp. 129-176). Greenwich, CT: JAI Press.

Landy, F.J., Shankster, L.J., & Kohler, S.S. (1994). Personnel selection and placement. *Annual Review of Psychology, 45*, 261-296

Latham, G.P., Saari, L.M., Pursell, E.D. & Campion, M.A. (1980) The situational interview. *Journal of Applied Psychology, 65*, 422-427.

Lawler, E.E., III (1981). *Pay and organizational development.* Reading, MA: Addison Wesley.

Lawrence, P.R., & Lorsch, J.W. (1967). *Organization and environment.* Boston: Harvard Business School.

Lawshe, C.H. (1975). A quantitative approach to content validity. *Personnel Psychology, 28*, 563-575.

Ledvinka, J., & Scarpello, V.G. (1989). *Federal regulation of personnel and human resource management* (2nd ed.). Boston, MA: PWS-Kent.

Levine, E.L. (1983). *Everything you always wanted to know about job analysis.* Tampa, FL: Mariner Publishing, Co.

Levinson, D.J. (1978). *Seasons in a man's life.* New York: Knopf.

Lubinski, D., & Dawis, R.V. (1990). Aptitudes, skills, and proficiencies. In M.D. Dunnette & L.M. Hough (Eds.), *Handbook of industrial and organizational psychology* (volume I, pp. 1-59). Palo Alto, CA: Consulting Psychologists Press, Inc.

Mael, F.A. (1991). A conceptual rationale for the domain and attributes of biodata items. *Personnel Psychology, 44*, 763-792.

Mahoney, T.A., & Deckop, J.R. (1986). Evolution of concept and practice in personnel administration/human resource management (PA/HRM). *Journal of Management, 12*, 223-241.

Marchese, M.C., & Muchinsky, P.M. (1993). The validity of the employment interview: A meta-analysis. *International Journal of Selection and Assessment, 1*, 18-26.

Martin, C.L., & Nagao, D.H. (1989). Some effects of computerized interviewing on job applicant responses. *Journal of Applied Psychology, 74*, 72-80.

Martin, S.L., & Raju, N.S. (1992). Determining cut of scores that optimize utility: A recognition of recruiting costs. *Journal of Applied Psychology, 77*, 15-23.

Maurer, T.J., Alexander, R.A., Callahan, C.M., Bailey, J.J., & Dambrot, F.H. (1991). Methodological and psychometric issues in setting cutoff scores using the Angoff method. *Personnel Psychology, 44*, 235-261.

Maxwell, S.E., & Arvey, R.D. (1993). The search for predictors with high validity and low adverse impact? Compatible or incompatible goals? *Journal of Applied Psychology, 78*, 433-437.

McCormick, E.J., Jeanerette, P.R., & Mecham, R.C. (1972). A study of job dimensions as based on the Position Analysis Questionnaire. *Journal of Applied Psychology, 56*, 347-368.

McHenry, J.J., Hough, L.M., Toquam, J.L., Hanson, M.A., & Ashworth, S. (1990). Project A validity results: The relationship between predictor and criterion domains. *Personnel Psychology, 43*, 335-354.

Miles, R., & Snow, C. (1978). *Organizational strategy, structure, and process.* New York: McGraw-Hill.

————. (1984). Designing strategic human resource management systems. *Organizational Dynamics, 13*, 36-52.

Mills, C.J., & Bohannon, W.E. (1980). Personality characteristics of effective state police officers. *Journal of Applied Psychology, 66*, 680-684.

Mintzberg, H. (1983). *Structure in fives: Designing effective organizations.* Englewood Cliffs, NJ: Prentice Hall.

Mitchell, D.J.B. (1989). *Human resource management: An economic approach.* Boston: PWS-Kent.

Motowidlo, S.J., Carter, G.W., Dunnette, M.D., Tippins, N., Werner, S., Burnett, J.R., & Vaughan, M.J. (1992). Studies of the structured behavioral interview. *Journal of Applied Psychology, 77*, 571-587.

Mowday, R.T., Porter L.W., & Steers, R.M. (1982). *Employee-organization linkages: The psychology of commitment, absenteeism, and turnover.* New York: Academic Press.

Murphy, K.R., & Cleveland, J.N. (1991). *Performance appraisal: An organizational perspective.* Boston: Allyn & Bacon.

Nadler, D.A. (1977). *Feedback and organizational development: Using data-based methods.* Reading, MA: Addison-Wesley.

Olian, J.D., & Rynes, S.L. (1984). Organizational staffing: Integrating practice with strategy. *Industrial Relations, 23*, 170-183.

Ones, D.S., Viswesvaran, C., & Schmidt, F.L. (1993). Comprehensive meta-analysis of integrity test validities: Findings and implications for personnel selection and theories of job performance. *Journal of Applied Psychology, 78*, 679-703.

O'Reilly, C.A., III, Chatman, J., & Caldwell, D.F. (1991). People and organizational culture: A profile comparison approach to assessing person-organization fit. *Academy of Management Journal, 34*, 487-516.

Organ, D.W. (1987). A reappraisal and reinterpretation of the satisfaction-performance hypothesis. *Academy of Management Review, 12*, 46-53.

Ostroff, C. (1992). The relationship between satisfaction, attitudes and performance: An organizational level analysis. *Journal of Applied Psychology, 77*, 963-974.

————. (1993). The effects of climate and personal influences on individual behavior and attitudes in organizations. *Organizational Behavior and Human Decision Processes, 56*, 56-90.

Ostroff, C., & Schmitt, N. (1993). Configurations of organizational effectiveness and efficiency. *Academy of Management Journal, 36*, 1345-1361.

Ouchi, W.G. (1980). Markets, bureaucracies, and clans. *Administrative Science Quarterly, 25*, 129-141.

Pearlman, K. (1980). Job families: A review and discussion of their implications for personnel selection. *Psychological Bulletin, 87*, 1-28.

Perrow, C. (1961). The analysis of goals in complex organizations. *American Sociological Review, 66*, 335-347.

————. (1967). A framework for a comparative analysis of organizations. *American Sociological Review, 32*, 194-208.

Pearce, J.L. (1993). Toward an organizational behavior of contract laborers: Their psychological involvement and the effects on employee co-workers. *Academy of Management Journal, 5*, 1082-1096.

Pervin, L.A. (1994). Personality stability, personality change, and the question of process. In T.F. Heatherton & J.L. Weinberger (Eds.), *Can personality change?* Washington, DC: American Psychological Association.

Pfeffer, J., & Baron, J.N. (1988). Taking the workers back out: Recent trends in the structuring of employment. In L.L. Cummings & B. Staw (Eds.), *Research in organizational behavior* (pp. 257-303). Greenwich, CT: JAI Press.

Porter, M. (1985). *Competitive advantage*. New York: Free Press.

Quinn, J. (1980). *Strategies for change: Logical incrementalism*. Homewood, IL: Irwin.

Reilly, R.R., & Chao, G.T. (1982). Validity and fairness of some alternative employee selection procedures. *Personnel Psychology, 35*, 1-62.

Rothausen, T.J. (1994). Job satisfaction and the parent worker: The role of flexibility and reward. *Journal of Vocational Behavior, 44*, 317-336.

Rounds, J.B., Dawis, R.V., & Lofquist, L.H. (1987). Measurement of person-environment fit and prediction of satisfaction in the theory of work adjustment. *Journal of Vocational Behavior, 31*, 297-318.

Rousseau, D.M. (1979). Assessment of technology in organizations: closed versus open systems approaches. *Academy of Management Review, 4*, 531-542.

Rynes, S.L. (1991). Recruitment, Job choice, and post-hire consequences: A call for new research directions. In M.D. Dunnette & L.M. Hough (Eds.), *Handbook of industrial organizational psychology* (2nd ed., pp. 399-444). Palo Alto, CA: Consulting Psychologists Press, Inc.

Rynes, S.L., Bretz, R.D. Jr., & Gerhart, B. (1991). The importance of recruitment in job choice: A different way of looking. *Personnel Psychology, 44*, 487-521.

Rynes, S.L., & Gerhart, B. (1990). Interviewer assessments an applicant "fit": An exploratory investigation. *Personnel Psychology, 43*, 13-35.

Rynes, S.L. & Barber, A.E. (1990). Applicant attraction strategies: An organizational perspective. *Academy of Management Review, 15*, 286-310.

Sackett, P.R. (1987). Assessment centers and content validity: Some neglected issues. *Personnel Psychology, 40*, 13-25.

Sackett, P.R., Zedeck, S., & Fogli, L. (1988). Relations between measures of typical and maximum job performance. *Journal of Applied Psychology, 73*, 482-486.

Sackett, P.R., Burris, L.R., & Callahan, C. (1989). Integrity testing for personnel selection: An update. *Personnel Psychology, 42*, 491-529.

Schmidt, F.L., & Hunter, J.E. (1977). Development of a general solution to the problem of validity generalization. *Journal of Applied Psychology, 62*, 529-540.

Schmidt, F.L., Hunter, J.E., & Pearlman, K. (1981). Task differences as moderators of aptitude test validity in selection: A red herring. *Journal of Applied Psychology, 66*, 166-185.

Schmitt, N., Gooding, R.Z., Noe, R.A., & Kirsch, M. (1984). Metaanalyses of validity studies published between 1964 and 1982 and the investigation of study characteristics. *Personnel Psychology, 37*, 407-422.

Schmitt, N., & Ostroff, C. (1986). Operationalizing the "behavioral consistency" approach: Selection test development based on a content-oriented strategy. *Personnel Psychology, 39*, 91-108.

Schmitt, N.W., & Klimoski, R.J. (1991). *Research methods in human resources management*. Cincinnati, OH: South-Western Publishing.

Schneider, B. (1972). Implications of the conference: A personal view. *Personnel Psychology, 31*, 299-304.

––––––– . (1983). Interactional psychology and organizational behavior. In L.L. Cummings & B. Staw (Eds.), *Research in organizational behavior* (pp. 1-31). Greenwich, CT: JAI Press.

––––––– . (1987). The people make the place. *Personnel Psychology, 40*, 437-454.

Schneider, B., & Bartlett, C.J. (1970). Individual differences and organizational climate II: Measurement of organizational climate by the multi-trait, multi-rater matrix. *Personnel Psychology, 23*, 493-512.

Schneider, B., & Schmitt, N. (1986). *Staffing organizations*. Glenview, IL: Scott, Foresman & Co.

Schuler, R.S. (1987). Personnel and human resource management choices and organizational strategy. *Human Resource Planning, 10*, 1-17.

Schuler, R.S., & Jackson, S.E. (1987). Linking competitive strategies with human resource management practices. *Academy of Management Executive, 1*, 207-219.

Sharf, Richard S. (1992). *Applying career development theory to counseling.* Pacific Grove, CA: Brooks/Cole Publishing Company.

Siehl, C., & Martin, J. (1988). Measuring organizational culture: mixing qualitative and quantitative methods. In M.O. Jones, M. Moore, & R. Schneider (Eds.), *Organizational ethnography: Field studies of culture and symbolism.* Newbury Park, CA: Sage.

Silva, J.M., & Jacobs, R.R. (1993). Performance as a function of increased minority hiring. *Journal of Applied Psychology, 78*, 591-601.

Smither, J.W., Reilly, R.R., Millsap, R.E., Pearlman, K., & Stoffey, R.W. (1993). Applicant reactions to selection procedures. *Personnel Psychology, 46*, 49-76.

Sonnenfeld, J.A., & Peiperl, M.A. (1988). Staffing policy as a strategic response: A typology of career systems. *Academy of Management Review, 13*, 588-600.

Super, D.E. (1953). A theory of vocational development. *American Psychologist, 8*, 185-190.

Sutton, R.I., & Rousseau, D.M. (1979). Structure, technology, and dependence on a parent organization: Organizational and environmental correlates of individual responses. *Journal of Applied Psychology, 64*, 675-687.

Tait, M., Padgett, M.Y., & Baldwin, T.T. (1989). Job and life satisfaction: A reevaluation of the strength of the relationship and gender effects as a function of the date of study. *Journal of Applied Psychology, 74*, 502-507.

Taylor, M.S., & Giannantonio, C.M. (1993). Forming, adapting, and terminations the employment relationship: A review of the literature from individual, organizational, & interactionist perspectives. *Journal of Management, 19*, 461-515.

Terpstra, D.E., & Rozell, E.J. (1993). The relationship of staffing practices to organizational level measures of performance. *Personnel Psychology, 46*, 27-48.

Tett, R.P., & Meyer, J.P. (1993). Job satisfaction, organizational commitment, turnover intention, and turnover: Path analyses basad on meta-analytic findings. *Personnel Psychology, 46*, 259-293.

Tett, R.P., Jackson, D.N., & Rothstein, M. (1991). Personality measures as predictors of job performance: A meta-analytic review. *Personnel Psychology, 44*, 703-742

Thompson, D.E., & Thompson, T.A. (1982). Court standards for job analysis in test validation. *Personnel Psychology, 35*, 865-874.

Thompson, J.D. (1967). *Organizations in action.* New York: McGraw-Hill.

Thorndike, R.L. (1949). *Personnel selection.* New York: Wiley.

Tichy, N.M., Fombrun, C.J., & Devanna, M.A. (1982). Strategic human resource management. *Sloan Management Review, 23*, 47-60.

Tsui, A.S. (1987). Defining the activities and effectiveness of the human resource department: A multiple constituency approach. *Human Resource Management, 26*, 35-69.

Tsui, A.S., & Milkovich, G.T. (1987). Personnel department activities: Constituency perspectives and preferences. *Personnel Psychology, 46*, 519-537.

Wanous, J.P. (1992). *Organizational entry* (2nd ed.). Reading, MA: Addison Wesley.

Wanous, J.P., Poland, T.D., Premack, S.L., & Davis, K.S. (1992). The effects of met expectations on newcomer attitudes and behaviors: A review and meta-analysis. *Journal of Applied Psychology, 77*, 288-297.

Werner, J.M. (1994). Dimensions that make a difference: Examining the impact of in-role and extrarole behaviors in supervisory ratings. *Journal of Applied Psychology, 79*, 98-107.

Wernimont, P. (1962). Re-evaluation of a weighted application blank for office personnel, *Journal of Applied Psychology, 46*, 417-419.

Weiss, H.M., & Adler, S. (1984). Personality and organizational behavior. In L.L. Cummings & B. Staw (Eds.), *Research in organizational behavior* (volume 6, pp. 1-50). Greenwich, CT: JAI Press.

Wiesner, W., & Cronshaw, S. (1988). A meta-analytic investigation of the impact of interview format and degree of structure on the validity of the employment interview. *Journal of Occupational Psychology, 61*, 275-290.

Wise, L.L., McHenry, J., & Campbell, J.P. (1990). Identifying optimal predictor composites and testing for generalizability across jobs and performance factors. *Personnel Psychology, 43*, 355-366.

Wright, P., & Wexley, K. (1985, May). How to choose the job analysis method your really need. *Personnel*, 51-55.

Wright, P.M., Lichtenfels, P.A., & Pursell, E.D. (1989). The structured interview: Additional studies and a meta-analysis. *Journal of Occupational Psychology, 62*, 191-199.

Zedeck, S., & Cascio, W.F. (1984). Psychological issues in personnel decisions. In M.R. Rosenzweig & L.W. Porter (Eds), *Annual review of psychology* (volume 35, pp. 461-519). Palo Alto, CA: Annual Reviews, Inc.

THE ECONOMICS OF TRAINING

Orley Ashenfelter and Robert LaLonde

INTRODUCTION

When an expensive machine is erected, the extraordinary work to be performed by it before it is worn out, it must be expected, will replace the capital laid out upon it, with at least ordinary profits. A man educated at the expense of much labor and time to any of those employments which require extraordinary dexterity and skill, may be compared to one of those expensive machines. The work which he learns to perform, it must be expected, over and above the usual wages of common labor, will replace to him the whole expense of his education, with at least ordinary profits of an equally valuable capital.
–Adam Smith, 1776

More than 200 years ago Adam Smith articulated the idea that the incentives to augment workers' skills are analogous to the incentives to invest in physical capital. Workers or their employers will invest in "human capital" if the discounted future "returns" from this investment exceed the cost of acquiring new skills. These returns manifests themselves in increased wages or salaries and fringe benefits for workers, and in increased profits for employers.

In recent years interest in the incentives to invest in human capital and how such investments are allocated among workers has intensified. Several economic developments have motivated this increased interest in training. Among these has been the slowdown in the rate of U.S. productivity growth beginning in the mid-1970s. Concern about this slowdown has been heightened by comparisons to Germany and Japan, where productivity growth has been faster, and where vocational training appears to be a more common experience in the workplace (Lynch, 1994).

Another development that has increased interest in the incentives to provide training is the increase in earnings inequality during the last 30 years. Some of this widening earnings inequality has resulted from the substantial structural changes experienced first in the goods-producing sector and more recently by the services sector (Farber, 1993). Workers displaced from their jobs as a result of these changes have experienced substantial and long-term declines in their living standards (Jacobson, LaLonde, & Sullivan, 1993). One explanation for these declines is that displacement meant that some of these workers' skills had become obsolete.

An even more important contributor to the rise in earnings inequality has been the decline in employers' demand for the services of relatively unskilled workers (Katz & Murphy, 1992). At the same time, there have been reports citing evidence that U.S. students appear to end their formal schooling less skilled than both their predecessors and their counterparts in other industrialized and emerging nations. Some studies suggest that because U.S. workers are more poorly educated when they enter the workplace, that a larger share of employers' training expenditures are on remedial skills than is the case for employers abroad.

Commentators argue that one reason for these developments is that employers and their employees lack adequate incentives to invest in vocational training. They point to the relatively high turnover rates in U.S. firms and how these rates discourage employer financed investments in training. Some argue that either direct or indirect involvement of the public sector in firms' training decision would mitigate these disincentives and may help offset some of the losses associated with worker displacement and the apparent shortcomings of formal schooling. This paper will not attempt to resolve these contentions. Instead, we summarize the theoretical issues concerning the incentives to invest in training and survey some of the existing evidence on the incidence and intensity of vocational training in the private sector.

The plan for the remainder of this chapter is as follows. In the second section we review the theory on investments in human capital. Included in this discussion we distinguish among incentives to invest in general as opposed to firm-specific skills. In the third section we survey the evidence on the incidence and intensity of vocational training. The fourth section demonstrates different approaches for estimating the costs of training and the fifth section summarizes the empirical evidence on the returns to training. Finally some concluding remarks follow in the last section.

INVESTING IN ON-THE-JOB TRAINING

Employers train their employees if the future discounted profits generated by a more skilled workforce exceed the costs of training. These training costs include not only the physical resources expended on training, but the forgone output associated with the trainee's and other co-workers' time (Becker, 1980). These forgone costs include having a new employee "shadow" a co-worker, having co-workers leave their own work to show a new employee how to operate an unfamiliar machine, or having supervisors spend less time on their customary tasks in order to observe new employees performing their jobs.

To make these ideas more concrete, consider a case in which an employee is unskilled when he begins his career, and his career lasts just two periods. A firm will train this employee during the first period only if the costs associated with this training are less than the discounted gains in profits realized during the second period. The cost of training to the employer during the first period is the actual cost of the training program (denoted by K), and the difference between the employee's productivity (marginal product) and wage (denoted by W) while in training. Presumably, while an employee's productivity suffers during the time that he acquires new skills. The employer realizes increased profits from training during the second period when the trained worker's productivity (or marginal product denoted by VMP) exceeds the wage paid by the firm.

The employer's decision to train an employee may be expressed more formally in terms of the following inequality:

$$[VMP_1^U - W_1] + K < [VMP_2^S - W_2]/(1+r). \tag{1}$$

In (1), the terms VMP_t^U and VMP_t^S denote the value of untrained and trained workers' productivity (marginal product) during each period. The expression to the left of the inequality is the cost associated with training an unskilled employee. When the employee is being trained, the firm pays K dollars in training costs and $VMP_1^U - W_1$ dollars in forgone profits. The expression to the right of the inequality is the net gain in profits associated with employing a trained worker. In a competitive labor market, the cost of training equals its benefits for the last worker trained, because firms expand their workforces to the point where the wage of the last worker trained equals his contribution to the firm's output.

In this example, worker's wages need not change between the first and second periods. Indeed, increased wages for the employee as a result of such an investment by the firm would imply that some of these returns are being realized by the worker. But, if the firm is to have sufficient incentive to invest in training it must realize the returns from training. Therefore, if the firm paid the full cost of training, we should expect their workers' wages to remain the same in both periods.

A problem with this characterization of the firm's decision to train is that recently trained employees have an incentive to seek new higher paying jobs commensurate with their increased productivity. At the same time, other employers have an incentive to hire the newly trained workers because of the gap between these workers' productivity and their wages. This prospect reduces employers' incentives to train. Once the trained employee separates from the firm, the employer cannot recoup its investment. Therefore, in order for employers to have sufficient incentives to incur the costs of training, they must anticipate that the employment relationship will continue once training is completed.

Whether the potential for employee turnover imposes a barrier to firm-financed training depends on how easy it is for employees to apply their new skills in other firms. Hence, when considering the incentives that firms have to train their employees, it is important to distinguish between investments in skills that are useful to other employers and in skills that are useful only to the employer providing the training. Economists refer to these different types of skills as "general" and "specific" human capital. Examples of general human capital include the skills of military pilots whose training raises the demand for their services at commercial airlines, or the skills of doctors who intern at one hospital but find that their training raises the demand for their services at other hospitals.

By contrast, "[c]ompletely specific training can be defined as training that has no effect on the productivity of trainees that would be useful in other firms. Much on-the-job training is neither completely specific nor completely general but increases productivity more in firms providing it and falls within the definition of specific training" (Becker, 1980, p. 26). In the military examples of specific human capital are the skills of operators of guided missiles and of tank gunners. In the private sector examples of specific human capital are the skills created by expenditures on employee orientation or on developing "teams." In addition, employers make investments in specific skills when they spend time learning about their firms' bureaucracy or clients. Such skills are likely to raise employee productivity in the firm, but not elsewhere.

General Human Capital

We observed earlier that firms pay the cost of the training only if it expects a return from its investment. To obtain a return on its investment, the employer must pay its trained employees less than their marginal products. However, if firms pay employees with general skills less than their marginal products, other firms have an incentive to hire these generally trained workers by offering higher wages. Other employers can afford to "poach" the firm's employees, because they did not pay the costs of training.

This "externality" associated with general training is potentially important because it suggests that firms will "underinvest" in general skills. A solution to this problem is for workers to pay for their training by accepting lower wages when they are being trained and for their wages to rise once training is complete. Because the firm did not pay the cost of training, it need not capture the subsequent returns. Further, it is not important to the firm that the employment relationship continue once training is complete. The trained worker can receive the return from his investment by applying his new skills either in the firm in which he received the training or in another firm.

In practice there are several ways that the employer could put this policy into effect. First, the employer might require a new employee to post a "bond" as a condition of employment. The employer would then pay for training and would keep the bond if the employee left the firm prior to the employer receiving its return on its investment. The same principal underlies incomplete vesting of a pension plan. Under current law, employers that provide pensions to their employees generally must vest them after their fifth year of service at the company. However, should the employee leave before that time, the employer in effect keeps the money previously allocated to the pension plan. By doing so the employer has been compensated for some of the costs of training. Finally, the firm might have a policy of increasing pay with years of seniority. Employees are willing to accept low wages during their early years at the firm, if they believe that their pay will increase substantially with years of service.

This arrangement solves the "poaching" problem, because the employees, and not the employers, pay for the general training by accepting a training wage equal to the difference between the wage that they would have received without training and the pecuniary cost of training plus any forgone output. Subsequently, trained employees' wages must increase so that they are paid their marginal products, otherwise they will quit their jobs and seek employment elsewhere. This wage increase is the return the employee receives from the investment made in his skills. Therefore, workers who have made investments in general skills receive higher wages and their earnings grow more rapidly with time in the workforce than do the earnings of workers who do not make the same investments in training. Competition in the labor market ensures that the wages of unskilled and skilled workers adjust so that the costs of acquiring training are exactly offset by the subsequent discounted wage gains from training.

Learning by Doing as Training

An alternative way of viewing this process of acquiring general skills is in the context of a "tied-sale" or "package deal." The untrained worker sells the employer his time and at the same time purchases from the employer a job that offers opportunities to learn (Rosen, 1972). In a competitive market there are "implicit" prices associated with each of these two transactions. As a result, workers' wages or salaries equal the difference between the "implicit" price of workers' time and the "implicit" price of the opportunities to learn on the job. All other things equal, jobs that offer workers greater opportunities to acquire new skills will pay less.

A concrete example of this arrangement is an apprenticeship. An apprentice earns considerably less than a "journeyman's" wage, until the training period or the apprenticeship is completed. Although apprenticeships are no longer common in the United States,[1] they are common among young persons in Germany and Great Britain (Blanchflower & Lynch, 1994). During the 1970s and early 1980s approximately 60 percent of German 16-19 year olds and 35 percent of British 16-19 year olds worked in apprenticeships (Soskice, 1994; Blanchflower & Lynch, 1994). In Germany apprentices were paid approximately one-third the wages received by workers who had completed their apprenticeships compared to the approximately two-thirds ratio earned by apprentices in Great Britain (Oulton & Steedman, 1994). As the theory would suggest, this difference in the relative pay received by apprentices in the two countries is consistent with the perception that German apprenticeships teach more general skills than do British apprenticeships.[2]

It is no surprise to find that apprenticeships are held by younger workers. We expect that workers would seek jobs with greater opportunities to learn when they are young, because they have a longer remaining career over which they can realize the returns to this new knowledge. As workers become older, they will increasingly seek jobs that pay higher wages, but offer fewer opportunities to learn new skills. Such behavior on the part of workers would tend to make earnings rise relatively rapidly when workers were young and "flatten" out latter in their careers.

This view of training also explains why more educated workers are likely to seek jobs that offer more opportunities for learning. If education and ability to learn on the job complement each other, skill enhancing job opportunities at any given market "price" are more attractive to better educated as opposed to less educated workers. Similarly, even among workers with the same schooling, those with more ability or motivation are more likely to seek jobs that provide opportunities to learn. By doing so they drive up the "price" of these jobs and discourage less able workers from seeking them. Because more able workers are more likely to be concentrated in jobs offering the greatest opportunity for learning, the earnings of workers even with the same level of schooling will "fan out" or increase in variance as their experience in the labor force increases.

The observation that workers are heterogeneous, even among those with the same schooling, suggests that it will be difficult in practice to detect an inverse relationship between the amount of training that workers acquire in their jobs and their wages during the early years of their careers. In the absence of training, more able workers will be paid more than their less able counterparts. However, because more able persons are more productive learners, they seek jobs that provide more opportunities for training. This behavior causes their wages to decline. However, whether they usually decline below the level of their less able counterparts who are in jobs that provide less training is unknown. Indeed empirical studies suggest that workers' starting wages do not depend on the amount of training that they receive during their first few months on the job (Barron, Black, & Lowenstein, 1989).[3]

Specific Human Capital

Some researchers contend that workers lack sufficient incentive to invest in general skills because they cannot easily demonstrate to other potential employers that they posses these skills. Workers invest in general skills because they expect that if their current employer will not compensate them for their increased productivity, they can find other employers who will. But, if the skills that they acquire are difficult to verify, they may be unable to find an employer who will compensate them accordingly. As a result, once employees have invested in these skills, this cost is "sunk," and their current employer can pay them less then their marginal products without fear that they might quit their jobs. This prospect discourages workers from investing in general skills in the first place (Katz & Ziderman, 1990).

One solution to this problem might be to have a third party certify different types of general skills. For example, state governments could expand their already pervasive practice of granting occupational licenses. Such a certification process would make it easier for prospective employers to identify skilled job seekers and thereby increase incentive for workers to invest in general skills.

In practice, there is too much variation in the skills demanded by employers for a expanded system of certification to overcome the problem that seemingly general skills may not be easily portable. This problem suggests that a portion of the general skills acquired by workers were specific rather than general. As we observed earlier, specific skills differ from general skills in that they raise an employee's productivity by more in his current firm than in other firms. But when employees possess specific skills, their employers have little incentive to pay them their marginal products. As a result, workers will not pay for such training on their own.

Such an outcome might mean that workers will underinvest in specific skills. To avoid this problem the firm could pay for the portion of their employees' training that provides specific skills and receive a return for this investment by subsequently paying them less than their marginal products. This gap between their employees' productivity and wages compensates the firm for its investment. However, this solution is not satisfactory, because it leaves the trained worker indifferent between staying at the firm and working elsewhere. The firm paid the full cost of specific training and therefore reaped its full benefit. But, their employees' wages reflect only their investments in general skills for which they can just as easily be compensated in another firm. In order for firms' training investments to pay off it is essential that their trained employees not quit their jobs. Once a trained worker severs the employment relationship, the employer cannot receive the returns from its investment in specific skills.

One way to provide employees with incentives to acquire specific skills is to alter their wages in such a way that both workers and employers have an incentive to maintain the employment relationship once training is complete. A solution to this problem is to have both parties share the costs and the returns to specific training (Becker, 1980; Hashimoto, 1981). In the context of our two-period example introduced previously, the employee pays some of the cost of specific training by accepting a wage below his alternative (or untrained) wage during the first period, $W_1^U - W_1^S > 0$. The employer also makes an investment during the first period, because the employee's wage is not low enough to cover the cost of training plus any forgone output.

In order for both parties to have incentive to make this investment in specific skills, they each must receive a return in the second period. Therefore, the wage that the employee receives in the second period must be above the wage he could earn at another firm. But, to ensure a return for the employer, this wage must be less than the employee's marginal product. An attractive feature of this arrangement is that both parties have an incentive to maintain the employment relationship. The employee is unlikely to quit his job, because his wages are higher than he could receive elsewhere. Similarly, the employer is unlikely to permanently lay off the employee, because the employee's marginal product exceeds his wage.

This solution of shared training costs does not completely solve the problems associated with investing in specific skills, because it depends on the parties' "goodwill" to share the subsequent returns to training. A firm wishing to increase its share of the returns subsequently may attempt to cut its employees wages somewhat, while still leaving them above their alternative wages. Likewise, an employee organization, such as a labor union, may try to use the threat of a strike to increase the employees' share of this return.[4] The prospect that such behavior may occur once training has ended, reduces both parties incentives to invest in specific skills.

LIMITATIONS OF DATA ON TRAINING

The forgoing discussion indicates that competitive markets provide workers and employers with incentives to invest in training. But how much training is actually acquired? There are several reasons why we do not know enough from existing data sources about the incidence and intensity of training received by the workforce. First, most data sources contain only unrefined measures of the incidence, the source, and duration of training as reported by the employee.[5] Further, these data sources do not include measures of the costs of training other than the employee's wage. If more effort were made to survey employers about their training expenditures, there would still be the problem that the firms themselves often do not keep a separate account of the resources spent on employee training. For example, among the 140 large firms that were members of the Bureau of National Affairs' Personnel Policy Forum in 1985, only one-half reported that they had a separate training budget (Brown, 1990).

A second barrier to obtaining reliable measures of investments in training, is that training is conceptually difficult to measure. When training occurs in the context of a formal program administered by the firm, it is relatively straightforward to measure the number of hours spent in training and the dollars spent on the program. However, in the United States much private sector training is informal. Employees can acquire new skills by trial and error, or by watching co-workers and supervisors perform their jobs. Such training represents an investment because the employer incurs the costs associated with a new employee's lower productivity, with the wages they pay them to observe other workers, and with the lost output associated with the time that other workers spend away from their jobs.

The significance of informal training in the workplace is demonstrated in the findings from one of the few large surveys of employers. This 1982 survey of 1,901 U.S. firms asked employers about the number of hours they spent training their most recent hires during their first three months on the job. As shown by Table 1, company personnel spent 17.8 hours providing their new employee with job orientation and job-specific skills in a formal setting.

Table 1. On-the-Job Training of New Employees
(average hours per employee during first 3 months on the job)

Type of Training	Hours
Formal Training:	
Hours spent by company personnel providing job orientation.	5.9
Hours spent by specifically trained personnel providing formal training.	10.9
Total Formal Training	17.8
Informal Training:	
Hours spent by line supervisors and management providing individualized training and extra supervision.	54.3
Hours spent by co-workers away from other tasks providing individualized training and extra supervision.	26.9
Hours spent by new employee watching other workers do the job rather than doing it himself	53.1
Total Informal Training	134.3

Source: Barron, Black, and Loewenstein 1989, p. 5, Table 1. Sample of 1,901 employers from the Employment and Opportunity Pilot Projects Surveys.

However, as also shown by the table, the majority of time in training occurred while the employee was on the job. This informal training involved not only substantial amounts of the new employee's time, but also the time of co-workers and supervisors (Barron, Black, & Lowenstein, 1989).

The potential importance of informal training in the labor market also is indicated by surveys of representative samples of the U.S. labor force. Two special supplements to the U.S. Bureau of the Census January 1983 and January 1991 Current Population Surveys (CPS) asked respondents (1) whether they needed specific skills or training to be qualified for their current (or last) job; (2) whether they had taken any training to improve their skills in their current job; and (3) the sources of any training that they had received. As shown by Table 2, among those responding that they needed specific skills in order to qualify for their current (or last) job, 47 percent reported that they acquired this training informally either on another job with the same employer or from a previous employer. Further, among those reporting that they had acquired training while on their current jobs, 37 percent said that those skills had been acquired informally while on the job.

A third barrier to obtaining reliable measures of training investments is that workers receive much of their job-related training in different types of schools, and not in the workplace. As shown by Table 2, schools appear to be as important a setting for vocational training as are firms. Nearly 60 percent of the workers who reported that they needed special training to qualify for their current (or last) jobs, and approximately one-third who reported having received training while in their current jobs received this training in school.

Table 2.   Sources of Training for U.S. Workers Receiving Training
(percent reporting receiving training from source)

	Qualifying for Present or Last Job	Skill Improvement in Current Job
Sources of Training:		
School	58%	32%
...High School Vocational Program	7	0
...Post H.S. Vocational Program	5	2
...Junior College or Tech. Institute	14	10
...4 Year Colleges	35	12
On-the-Job:		
...Formal Training Program	21	39
...Informal Training	47	37
Armed Forces	4	0
Other	14	17

Source: January 1991 CPS, Bulletin 2407, Tables 6, 14, 42, 49, pp. 8, 13, 34, 37. Respondents could report more than one training source. Schooling subcategories do not have to sum to the total for schooling.

The primary sources of this school-based training were junior and four-year colleges. Not only do employees acquire training from these schools on their own, but firms often subcontract with these institutions to provide their employees with specialized training (Krueger & Rouse, 1995).

THE INCIDENCE OF TRAINING

Graduation from some level of schooling does not signify the completion of a training process. It is usually the end of a more general and preparatory stage and the beginning of a more specialized and often prolonged process of acquisition of occupational skill, after entry into the labor force (Mincer, 1962).

There are several sources of information on the incidence of training in the United States. Besides the two supplements to the CPS discussed earlier, there also exist several smaller databases that report to varying degrees the incidence, sources, and durations of vocational training. Although the CPS's measures of training are relatively unrefined, they provide some evidence about the incidence of training for a large representative sample of U.S. workers. As shown by Table 3, the survey indicates that a majority of (but by no means all) workers were employed in jobs that required specialized training. In addition, 41 percent of U.S. workers reported that they had received additional training while in their current job.

Table 3.   Incidence of Vocational-related Training in the United States
(percent reporting having received training)

Demographic group	Needed Special Training to Qualify For Current Job		Received Training While in In Current Job	
	1983	*1991*	*1983*	*1991*
All Workers	55%	57%	35%	41%
Education:				
High School or Less	42	41	26	29
Some College	62	63	41	46
College Graduate	84	84	54	61
Occupation:				
Managerial	71	72	47	53
Professional	93	92	61	67
Technical	85	86	52	59
Sales	43	43	32	40
Clerical	57	55	32	40
Craft and Repair	57	55	35	38
Operatives	37	38	22	25
Service Workers	36	37	25	29
Laborers	16	20	14	15

Source: U.S. DOL Bulletin 2407, Tables 1, 38, pp. 5, 30.

Complementarity Between Formal Schooling and Training

Statistics from the CPS indicate that vocational training is relatively common, especially for well-educated workers. As shown by Table 3, these workers as well as those employed in higher paying occupations were more likely to report that they needed training to qualify for their current jobs and that they had received additional training in those jobs. Studies using other data sets confirm that one of the strongest predictors of whether a person reports receiving training is their years of schooling. Workers with high school degrees receive more of all forms of training than their counterparts who are high school dropouts (Lillard & Tan, 1992; Lynch, 1992). Likewise, workers with college degrees report receiving significantly more training than high school graduates (Altonji & Spletzer, 1991; Lillard & Tan, 1992). This finding holds especially for formal company programs and training received off the job. However, the relationship between schooling and training appears to be less strong when the training is informal.[6] These findings suggest that vocational training is not a substitute for less formal schooling. When making decisions on who to train, employers usually do not compensate for the lower skills of their less educated employees by providing them with more training.

The positive relationship between schooling and the receipt of training suggests that training is more productively provided to more skilled workers. Evidence supporting this contention is found in studies showing that even among persons who have attained similar levels of schooling, the better educated among them receive more training. Among those with the same level of formal schooling, those with higher scores on standardized tests, with higher class ranks, or who took more rigorous classes while in school are more likely to participate in off-the-job training programs and to enroll in regular schooling programs in which the tuition has been subsidized by the employer (Altonji & Spletzer, 1991). Indeed, because more able persons tend to acquire more schooling, these other indicators of skills also explain a modest amount of the correlation between schooling and training.

One reason that better educated workers received more training is that they are more likely employed in jobs that require vocational training. These jobs are usually in the managerial, professional, and technical occupations. As shown by Table 4, workers in these occupations are more likely to report (1) that they are receiving training in their current jobs, and (2) that it takes more than two years for a new worker in their position to become fully trained. By contrast, workers employed in semiskilled and unskilled occupations report that it took on average less than one year to become fully trained (Duncan & Hoffman, 1979). The amount of training that employees receive differs among jobs in part because firms provide more training for jobs that demand greater quantitative skills. Employees holding such jobs, such as those in the managerial, professional, and technical occupations, are significantly more

Table 4. Average Years of Training Required For Current Job
(persons 18-64 years old in 1975)

	Number of Years Needed To Become Fully Qualified In Current Job	Percent in Training In Their Current Job
Occupation:		
Managers, not self employed	2.76	33%
Accountants	2.40	45
Engineers, architects, chemits	2.89	30
Technicians	1.96	28
Sales workers	1.40	23
Skilled craftsmen	2.54	31
Secretaries	0.80	14
Non-transportation operatives	0.71	9
Unskilled laborers	0.63	8
Non-household service workers	0.60	10
Demographic Group:		
White men	2.3	26%
Black men	1.0	9
White women	0.9	14
Black women	0.8	9

Source: Duncan and Hoffman, 1979, Table 2 , p. 597. Based on samples of approximately 3,000 males and 2,000 females from the 1976 wave of the Panel Study of Income Dynamics who worked at least 500 hours in 1975.

likely to report receiving formal and informal on-the-job training, and to report spending more hours receiving training than workers employed in jobs that require greater clerical or manual skills (Altonji & Spletzer, 1991).

The strong complementarity between workers' prior skills and on-the-job training has several important implications for public policy.[7] First, that people with limited or poor quality schooling also are likely to receive limited additional training once they enter the labor force. Evidence supporting this contention is found in a survey of economically disadvantaged persons.[8] In that survey only 11 percent of the male respondents and 12 percent of female respondents reported receiving vocational training from any source during the previous 18 months. By comparison, the percentage of young adults in the population at large that would report receiving training during a similar period would be approximately 25 percent (Lillard & Tan, 1992).

A second implication of the complementarity between workers' skills and training is that the incidence and intensity of private sector training should increase if the quality of formal schooling and the average educational attainment of the workforce were raised. The tendency for employers to train better educated employees and for better educated employees to seek more vocational-related training on their own suggests that training these people is more productive because it is less costly. By increasing the supply of better educated persons in the workforce, incentives to train workers also increase.

Incidence Among Demographic Groups

Information on vocational training also provides some insight into the differences in wages and salaries received by people from different demographic groups. Many studies show that nonwhite males and women earn less than white males and also experience slower earnings growth during their working lives. Several surveys indicate that these groups also receive less post-secondary training than white males (Freeman, 1974; Lillard & Tan, 1992; Lynch, 1992). This difference results because nonwhite males and women are less likely to participate in formal company training programs or to enroll in vocational training programs off the job.[9] In particular, people in these groups report receiving less formal company training, because they are less likely to receive training for higher paying managerial, professional, and technical positions. In light of these findings, it is not surprising, as shown by Table 4, that these groups are more likely to occupy jobs that require fewer years of training. These differences in the receipt of vocational training can explain up to 20 percent of the differences in earnings among these demographic groups (Duncan & Hoffman, 1979).

Although, nonwhite men and women receive less training than their white male counterparts, these groups experience similar benefits or "returns" from the training that they receive (Freeman, 1974; Duncan & Hoffman, 1979). For example, participation in a three-month company training program has approximately the same impact on nonwhite males' subsequent earnings as it does on the earnings of white males. Therefore, differences in the way the private sector rewards vocational training does not explain any of the differences among demographic groups' earnings or earnings growth. Nonwhites' and women's earnings grow more slowly once they enter the labor force, because they are less likely to hold jobs that provide vocational training which would raise their productivity and cause their earnings to grow as rapidly as those of white males.

ESTIMATING AMOUNT INVESTED IN TRAINING

Although the available measures of training intensity are unrefined, it is still possible to estimate the amount invested in training each year in the United States. Mincer has proposed using two different approaches. The "direct" approach estimates the annual costs of training by simply adding together the value of the time that workers spent being trained or training others plus the resource costs of providing the training. The "indirect" approach does not use statistics on training, but instead infers the amount of training from differences among workers' earnings growth during their careers. Those with greater earnings growth are assumed to have received more vocational training. Remarkably, both approaches suggest that the annual cost of vocational training amounts to between $150 and $200 billion per year. By comparison, the annual costs of formal schooling, including the forgone earnings while students are in school, have been estimated at around $500 billion dollars.

Mincer applied the "direct" approach to information collected from a 1976 survey that asked respondents about the amount of time that they had spent in training during the previous week. We reproduce the results from this survey as well as Mincer's calculations in Table 5. As shown by the table, young adults reported that during the previous week they received an average of 4.9 hours of training. Because the survey questioned a representative sample of the population, it is reasonable to multiply the time spent in training per worker by the number of workers under 25 years of age to arrive at an estimate of the time spent in training by all young adults. To estimate the opportunity costs of their weekly training, Mincer then multiplied the resulting figure of 97 million hours by young adults' average wage. He concluded that the annual costs of young adults' training was approximately $19 billion. He computed the annual costs for other workers similarly. Adding together these estimates for each age group, he concluded that in 1976 the opportunity cost of vocational training amounted to $57 billion. Converting this figure to 1993 dollars, this estimate of annual training costs amounts to $145 billion.

This approach is likely to understate the magnitude of the annual investment in vocational training for several reasons. First, to the extent that respondents understate their time in informal on-the-job training this estimate will be too low. Second, the survey did not ask respondents about the time that they spent training others while on the job, or about the material costs associated with

Table 5. Direct Opportunity Costs of Training
(from responses to 1976 wave of panel study of income dynamics)

Age Group	Hours in Training Previous Week (per resondent)	Number Employed (millions)	Total Hours (weekly in millions)	Average Wage (weekly)	Weekly Costs (millions)	Annual Costs (billions)
Under 25	4.86	20.0	97.3	$3.70	$360	$19.7
25-34	3.10	22.5	69.7	5.60	390	20.3
35-44	2.20	16.5	36.4	6.20	225	11.7
45-54	1.06	16.1	17.0	6.70	114	5.9
55-64	0.32	10.9	3.5	6.3	22	1.1

Source: Mincer, 1994, Table 8.

their training. As shown by Table 1, the costs associated with co-workers and supervisors lost output when they are training new employees may be substantial.

A third reason that the "direct" approach probably underestimates the annual investment in training is that since 1976 the amount of vocational training probably has increased. Although evidence supporting this contention is sparse, there are both theoretical and empirical reasons for believing that it is true. On theoretical grounds, the well-documented rise in the returns to education and skills since the 1970s suggests that both employers and their employees should be investing more in vocational training. On empirical grounds, the two CPS surveys suggest that between 1983 and 1991 there was a rise in the number of people reporting that they received training in their current jobs. In keeping with the trend toward greater earnings inequality, this increase was particularly pronounced among college graduates and among workers with more than 20 years of experience in the labor market (Constantine & Neumark, 1994). CPS questions about training during the 1970s suggest that the amount of workplace training did not fall and may have risen during that decade (Brown, 1989). Although it is impossible to know from the CPS whether the intensity of training increased by as much as the reported incidence, a crude calculation based on the figures in Table 3 suggest that the amount of vocational training has risen by 15 percent since the mid-1980s.

Mincer also applied the "indirect" approach to arrive at an alternative estimate of the annual cost of vocational training. The idea underlying this calculation is that college graduates' earnings grow more rapidly during their careers than do high school graduates' earnings, because college graduates receive more on-the-job training. College graduates' higher educational attainment explains why their earnings exceed those of high school graduates, but their educational attainment cannot explain why their earnings also continue to grow more rapidly, even after they are settled in the labor force. This faster earnings growth likely results, at least in part, from having received more on-the-job training.

Mincer observes that if we attribute a normal rate of return to the investment made in schooling, we can arrive at an estimate of the amount invested in training by subtracting this return from workers' actual earnings. To make this point more concrete, consider the example illustrated in Table 6. To generate the figures in the table, we assume that high school graduates begin work after graduation and receive no on-the-job training for the rest of their careers. By contrast, college graduates delay their entry into the labor force for four years while acquiring more formal schooling. During thcsc years, college graduates make a substantial investment in their human capital. As shown by column 4 of the table, the magnitude of this investment equals the difference between the earnings of high school graduates and college students plus the tuition costs of college. Further, by going to college one additional year, college students

Table 6. Estimating the Investments in
Training Using Mincer's Indirect Approach

	Earnings if Works After High School (1)	Earnings if Goes to College (2)	Tuition Costs of College (3)	Net Difference in Earnings + Tuition (4)	Return on Cost Last Year Column (7) times 0.08 (5)	Total Returns on all Previous Costs (6)	Foregone Earnings Cost at Age j of all Training (7)	Total Foregone Earnings Cost of all On-the-job Training (8)
Age								
18	16,000	0	-10,000	26,000	0	0	26000	0
19	16,000	0	-10,000	26,000	2080	2080	28080	0
20	16,000	0	-10,000	26,000	2246	4326	30326	0
21	16,000	0	-10,000	26,000	2426	6752	32752	0
22	16,000	18,000	0	-2000	2620	9372	7372	7,372
23	16,000	20,000	0	-4000	590	9962	5962	13,334
24	16,000	22,000	0	-6000	477	10439	4439	17,773
25	16,000	24,000	0	-8000	355	10794	2794	20,567
26	16,000	26,000	0	-1000	224	11018	1018	21,585
27	16,000	27,099	0	-11099	81	11099	0	21,585
28	16,000	27,107	0	-11107	0	11107	0	21,585

Notes: The table presents a hypothetical example of a high school graduate's earnings and a college graduate's earnings starting at age 18. The high school graduate is assumed to begin work after high school and not to receive any subsequent vocational training.

also lose the returns they would have earned from investments made during previous years. The returns associated with all previous investments are presented in column 6. The cumulative forgone annual earnings are presented in column 7.

After students graduate from college and enter the workforce, their earnings should reflect their previous investment in formal schooling. In this example, the earnings of 22-year-old college graduates are only $2,000 above those of high school graduates. But, according to column 6 of the table, college graduates should be earning a return of $9,372 from their previous investments in schooling. Because their earnings are $7,372 lower, Mincer would attribute the gap to investments made in on-the-job training by college graduates during their first year in the labor market. In the following year, when the college graduates are 23, their earnings should reflect both the returns to schooling and the returns to the previous year's investment in training. However, despite their earnings having grown by an additional $2,000, they remain below the level expected based on previous investments in human capital. This process continues until the college graduates' earnings "level off" at a point where they are collecting a normal return both from their investments in formal schooling and in training. The earnings profile depicted in column 2 of the table suggests that these college graduates "invested" in $21,585 worth of new skills after they left school.

Applying this "indirect" approach to actual U.S. earnings data, Mincer concluded that in 1976 (the same year he had used for the "direct" approach) approximately $88 billion were invested in training. However, he conceded that this estimate was probably too large because some of the growth in earnings resulted not from the returns to training, but from the returns to job search. Studies indicate that wage growth associated with workers' switching jobs is a significant source of lifetime earnings growth (Topel & Ward, 1992). This source of wage growth may have nothing to do with the returns to skills. But, instead it results from the returns associated with the "quality of the match" between workers' skills and the job requirements of employers. Mincer estimated that this source of wage growth accounted for approximately 15 percent of career earnings gains. Applying this percentage to his original estimate based on the "indirect" approach leaves an adjusted figure of $75 billion or $190 billion in 1993 dollars. As expected, the estimate based on the "indirect" approach is larger than the corresponding estimate based on the "direct" approach, because it implicitly includes the costs of materials and co-workers' and supervisors' time.

DOES TRAINING WORK?

Many studies find that there is a strong positive relationship between both employee and employer reported measures of training and workers' subsequent productivity or wages. Whether this relationship reflects the returns to training depends on whether those workers with high wages and productivity would have received high wages or had high levels of productivity even in the absence of training. Answering this question is difficult, because employers do not provide training randomly to their employees nor do workers randomly acquire training on their own. As we observed earlier, better educated persons are more likely to acquire vocational training both on and off the job. Because of their higher levels of schooling, better educated workers are likely to receive higher wages and be more productive whether or not they receive training.

By itself, this positive correlation between educational attainment and training does not pose an insurmountable barrier to measuring the returns to training. These returns could be measured by comparing the relationship between measures of vocational training and wages for those with the same schooling. The ambiguity associated with such a measure of the returns to training is that other measures of ability also are correlated with the propensity to receive training (Altonji & Spletzer, 1991). More importantly, if employees' observed attributes are correlated with having received training, it may be reasonable to assume that there exists other unobserved attributes, such as employee motivation, that also are correlated with both their receipt of training and their productivity. As a result, the returns that we infer from any positive relationship between measures of training and wages (or productivity), even for those with the same observable attributes, would be too large. Some or all of this correlation may result because reported measures of training serve as a "proxy" for workers' motivation.

If employees were randomly assigned to receive different levels of training, we could measure the impact of training simply by comparing the wages (or productivity) of workers receiving larger amounts of training to the wages (or productivity) of workers receiving less training. In this instance, randomization ensures that the propensity to receive training is not correlated any unobserved attribute of the employee. To be sure, it would rarely make sense for an employer to allocate training opportunities randomly among its employees. Indeed, our discussion indicates that it makes more sense to provide training to those who are the easiest to train. There are, however, several instances in government-sponsored training programs where training opportunities have been randomly provided to eligible low-income persons and displaced workers. The outcome of these "experiments" are instructive because they demonstrate that training can significantly raise recipients' earnings and presumably their productivity (LaLonde, 1995).

Because training opportunities in the private sector are not randomly allocated among workers, analysts have used a statistical technique known as multiple regression to attempt to account for the correlation between workers' characteristics and their receipt of training. This technique generates estimates of the return to training that holds constant other attributes of employees that determine their wage levels or productivity. The results of these studies indicate that even after accounting for observed differences between workers' attributes, there remains a significant positive relationship between wages and reported measures of the incidence and duration of training. The "gross" returns to workers' wages from a years worth of vocational training is approximately 10 percent per year or more (Mincer, 1994). Further, these returns can explain a substantial portion of the tendency for employees' earnings to rise with seniority in their firm. Employees wage growth is largest when they report that they are receiving training in their current positions. As they begin to report that they are receiving less training in their current jobs, their wage growth also slows (Brown, 1989).[10]

As we observed, if workers receive training that raise their general skills, the foregoing wage gains should correspond to their productivity gains. But, if some of the skills that workers acquire are specific, the estimated wage gains will be smaller than the productivity gains from training. Among the few studies that examine the relationship between training and productivity, two of them indicate that the effect of training received during the first few months on the job may be as much as twice as large as its effect on wages (Barron, Black, & Lowenstein, 1989; Bishop, 1994). This finding suggests that a significant component of vocational training involves specific skills.

The evidence suggests that the impact of vocational training is comparable if not larger than the returns to formal schooling. One explanation for this finding is that despite analysts' best efforts, they still have not satisfactorily accounted for unobserved attributes that simultaneously influence wages (or productivity) and the propensity to receive training.[11] There are several reasons, however, to expect that the "gross" returns to training would be larger than the returns to formal schooling. First, the returns from formal schooling may be lower than the returns from training because some schooling costs probably are better characterized as consumption instead of as an investment. Second, because workers acquire some specific skills and at the same time may leave the firm, the returns to training need to be larger than the returns to schooling in order to compensate both the worker and the employer for the risk associated with turnover. Third, as new technologies are introduced some skills may become obsolete. One study suggests that the value of workers' skills may depreciate by as much as 10 percent per year (Lillard & Tan, 1992). As a result, if workers' skills are likely to depreciate, the returns to training must be larger in order for there to be sufficient incentive to invest in training in the first place.

CONCLUSIONS

This chapter has examined the incentives for workers to acquire and their employers to provide vocational training. A competitive labor market provides these incentives by compensating workers with higher wages and salaries and firms with increased profits. To be sure, there are instances where these "market" incentives may be insufficient. These cases depend on the likelihood of employee turnover and the "portability" of vocational skills from one employer to another. The possibility that employers can "poach" other firms' employees diminishes incentives to provide training. Likewise, if employees cannot easily sell their new skills to another employer, their incentives to invest in training on their own also is diminished.

Concern about these incentives, and crude evidence that U.S. workers receive less vocational training than their counterparts abroad, have led some analysts to argue that U.S. workers underinvest in training. One proposal to remedy this perceived shortfall is to adopt France's and Australia's practice of mandating that employers spend a certain percentage of their payroll on training.[12] Those firms that did not comply with this requirement would be taxed this amount and the proceeds would be distributed to firms that provide more than the required amount of training.

An alternative practice that governments can use to induce increased training in the private sector is to provide direct subsidies to firms. During the 1980s, 46 U.S. states experimented with this concept by providing modest-sized training grants to a limited number of small and medium-sized companies. States stipulated that these grants be used to cover the costs of instruction and supplies (but not forgone output) in on-the-job training programs. When awarding these grants, states often gave preference to firms that were adopting new technologies. Few studies examine whether this policy led to increased training or its costs. But a study of Michigan's program found that companies receiving grants provided their employees significantly more training than did employers who applied for but did not receive a subsidy from the state (Holzer, Block, Cheatham, & Knott, 1993). The study's authors concluded that each hour of additional training cost the state government $6 to $7 dollars per employee.

The merits of these policies that involve the public sector taking an active role in private sector training depend on whether companies and their employees underinvest in training. Such a contention remains open for debate. This chapter suggests that there are several reasons why this debate will be difficult to resolve. First, measures of vocational training tend to be unrefined and often not comparable among studies of the same country, much less studies of different countries. Second, some components of training, especially informal on-the-job training are conceptually difficult to measure. Evidence presented here indicates that this informal training is an important source of training in the United States. Indeed, comparative studies suggest that this source of training may play a bigger role in the United States than in other industrialized economies (Lynch, 1994). Finally, even if a consensus were reached that the United States underinvests in vocational training, the conceptual difficulties associated with measuring different types of training suggest that it will be difficult to enforce employer mandates to provide more training.

Whether or not one believes that firm's "underinvest" in training, the evidence surveyed in this chapter does suggest that public policy can increase the amount of vocational training by improving formal schooling. The strong positive correlation between educational attainment and the receipt of training indicates that training investments will increase as the workforce becomes better educated. Current concerns about the effectiveness of the public school system also carry over to the institutions that provide vocational training. These institutions' effectiveness should improve as the formal schooling of new labor force entrants improves.

APPENDIX

Survey Questions on the Incidence and Duration of Training

Panel Study of Income Dynamics, 1976-1980

"On a job like yours, how long would it take the average person to become fully qualified?"

"Are you learning skills on the current job which could lead to a better job or promotion?"

National Longitudinal Survey, Young Men and Young Women, Mature Men Cohorts

"Did you receive of use additional training (other than schooling) on your job?"

"What was the longest type of training you have had since the last interview?"

Current Population Survey, January 1983 and 1991

"Did you need specific skills or training to obtain your current (last) job?" (If respondents answered yes then they were asked to identify the source(s) of training.)

"Since you obtained your present job, did you take any training to improve your skills?" (If respondents answered yes then they were asked to identify the source(s) of training.)

Employment Opportunity Pilot Survey, Individual Survey, May-September 1980

"Describe up to four training events occurring between January 1979 and the interview date."

Employment Opportunity Pilot Survey, Employer Survey, February-June 1982

Directed employer to select "the last new employee your company hired prior to August 1981 regardless of whether that person is still employed by your company."

"Number of hours typically spent by a new employee in the position last filled watching other people doing the job rather than doing it himself during the first three months of employment."

"Number of hours a new employee in the position spends in formal training."

National Federation of Independent Business Survey, January-June 1987

Directed employer to select the job that it had "hired the most people over the last two or three years." It then asked the employer to select the "last person hired for this job (job X) by your firm prior to August 1986 regardless of whether that person is still employed by your firm. Call this individual person A. The individual hired for job X immediately before person A is called person B. Do not include rehires of former employees."

"How many hours did you or an employee spend training or closely supervising A or B?"

"How many additional hours (beyond training and close supervision) did A/B spend learning the job by watching others rather than doing it?"

"How many hours did A/B spend reading manuals and such, in order to learn the job?"

National Longitudinal Survey, Youth Cohort

"In addition to your schooling, military, and government-sponsored training programs, during the previous year did you receive any other type of training for more than one month?" (Those responding yes also are asked about up to three training spells.)

Which category best describes where you received this training?" (Those responding yes to the previous question are asked about the category of up to three training spells.)

National Child Development Survey—Great Britain, persons born in 1958.

"Have you ever been on any training courses which involved at least 14 days or 100 hours of attendance a college, training centre, or skill centre?"

Respondents asked about up to three training courses.

German Socioeconomic Panel (GSOEP)—West Germany, panel of 6,000 households.

"There are various possibilities for work related training. Thinking about the past three years, for your own job related education have you read books and journals, participated in conferences and congresses, or participated in work related courses?"

Respondents asked about the costs, duration, and content of training

Sources: Lynch (1992, Table 1, p. 301); U.S. DOL, Bulletin 2407, p. 1; Bishop (1994, pp. 169-70, 195); Blanchflower and Lynch (1994); Pishchke (1996).

ACKNOWLEDGMENT

We thank Canice Prendergast and the editors for comments on an earlier draft.

NOTES

1. Statistics from the National Longitudinal Survey of Youths indicate that approximately 1 percent of U.S. 19-year-old males report holding an apprenticeship. Percentages for males of other ages and females are smaller (Blanchflower & Lynch, 1994). For a description of the apprenticeships system in the U.S. automobile industry see Berg (1994).

2. To be sure, depending on the value of training and the supply of people seeking it, there is no reason that an apprentice's wage has to be greater than zero. During the nineteenth century workers sometimes paid skilled craftsmen for the right to work free of charge in their shops. Indeed, it was sometimes considered a criminal offence for a apprentice to leave his employer before his apprenticeship had been completed.

3. Lillard and Tan (1992) find in the National Longitudinal Survey of Young Men that those who report that they currently receiving training also have regression-adjusted wages that are 2 percent lower than those of other workers. However this gap is not statistically significant at conventional levels.

4. Long-term collective bargaining agreements can mitigate these disincentives if they (1) stipulate wages and employment levels and (2) the union agrees formally not to strike while the contract is in effect.

5. See the Appendix for a list of questions asked employees about their training activities on different surveys.

6. This weaker relationship might be an artifact of the greater difficulty associated with measuring informal training.

7. This relationship between worker skills and the propensity to receive training is not unique to the United States. Studies of worker training in Great Britain and Germany during the 1970s and 1980s both reveal significant positive correlations between employees' formal schooling, other prior qualifications, their occupation, and the likelihood that they report receiving formal on-the-job training (Nickell, 1982; Greenlaugh & Stewart, 1987; Booth, 1991; Pischke, 1996).

8. Employment Opportunity Pilot Projects Survey, May through September 1980.

9. A study of the NLS High School Class of 1972 indicates that blacks are more likely to receive formal company training than whites (Altonji & Spletzer, 1991). But, when blacks received such training it lasted less time than did the training received by comparable educated whites.

10. Relatively few other studies besides this one examine the relationship between the tendency for workers earnings to rise with years of service with their firm and the incidence of on-the-job training. The studies that do report different results. Mincer and Higuchi's (1988) study of U.S. and Japanese manufacturing industries finds that workers in industries in which firms provide more training also have earnings that rise more rapidly with years of service. Bartel (1992) in an unusual study examines professional employees in a single large U.S. manufacturing firm. She finds that about 18 percent of these employees' earnings growth can be explained by participation in the company's formal on-the-job training programs. Levine (1993) examines a sample of manufacturing firms in metropolitan Indianapolis, Indiana, and Atsugi, Japan and finds little relationship between earnings growth and participation in training.

11. One study of young adults explicitly accounted for the effects of unobserved attributes that do not change (Lynch, 1992).

12. During the 1960s and 1970s the Industrial Training Boards (ITB) in Great Britain had the authority to tax employers in order to raise revenues for the county's apprenticeship programs. During the 1980s the ITBs were abolished by the government (Blanchflower & Lynch, 1994).

REFERENCES

Altonji, J.G., & Spletzer, J.R. (1991). Worker characteristics, job characteristics, and receipt of on-the-job training. *Industrial and Labor Relations Review, 45,* 58-79.

Barron, J.M., Black, D.A., & Lowenstein, M.A. (1989). Job matching and on-the-job training. *Journal of Labor Economics, 7,* 1-19.

Bartel, A.P. (1992). Training, wage growth and job performance: Evidence from a company database. Working Paper No. 4027, National Bureau of Economic Research, March.

Becker, G.S. (1980). Investment in human capital: Effects on earnings. In *Human capital* (2nd ed.) (chap. 2, pp. 15-44). Chicago: University of Chicago Press.

Berg, P. (1994). Strategic adjustments in training: A comparison with Germany. In L. Lynch (Ed.), *Training and the private sector* (pp. 77-107). Chicago: University of Chicago Press.

Bishop, J. (1994). The impact of previous training on productivity and wages. In L. Lynch (Ed.), *Training and the private sector* (pp. 161-199). Chicago: University of Chicago Press.

Blanchflower, D., & Lynch, L. (1994). Training at work: A comparison of U.S. and British youths. In L. Lynch (Ed.), *Training and the private sector* (pp. 233-260). Chicago: University of Chicago Press.

Booth, A. (1991). Job-related formal training: Who receives it and what is it worth? *Oxford Bulletin of Economics and Statistics, 53* (3), 281-294.

Brown, C. (1990). Empirical evidence on private training. In R. Ehrenberg (Ed.), *Research in labor economics* (volume 11, pp. 97-113). Greenwich, CT: JAI Press Inc.

Brown, J.N. (1989). Why do wages increase with tenure? On-the-job training and life cycle wage growth observed within firms. *American Economic Review, 79,* 971-991.

Constantine, J.M., & Neumark, D. (1994). Training and the growth of wage inequality. Working Paper, No. 4729, National Bureau of Economic Research, May.

Duncan, G.J., & Hoffman, S. (1979). On-the-job training and earnings differences by race and sex. *Review of Economics and Statistics* (last issue of year), 594-602.

Farber, H.S. (1993). The incidence and costs of job loss: 1982-91. *Brookings Papers on Economic Activity: Microeconomics, 1,* 73-119.

Freeman, R. (1974). Occupational training in proprietary schools and technical institutes. *Review of Economics and Statistics, 63,* 310-318.

Greenhalgh, C., & Stewart, M. (1987, May). The effects and determinants of training. *Oxford Bulletin of Economics and Statistics, 49,* 171-190.

Hashimoto, M. (1981, December). Firm-specific human capital as a shared investment. *American Economic Review, 72,* 1070-87.

Holzer, H., Block, R., Cheatham, M., & Knott, J. (1993, July). Are training subsidies for firms effective? The Michigan experience. *Industrial and Labor Relations Review, 46* (4), 625-636.

Jacobson, L., LaLonde, R., & Sullivan, D. (1993, September). Earnings losses of displaced workers. *American Economic Review, 83* (4), 685-709.

Katz, E., & Ziderman, A. (1990, December). Investment in general training: The role of information and labour mobility. *The Economic Journal, 100,* 1147-1158.

Katz, L., & Murphy, K. (1992, February). Changes in relative wages, 1963-1987: Supply and demand factor. *Quarterly Journal of Economics, 57* (1), 35-78.

Krueger, A., & Rouse, C. (1995). New evidence on workplace education. Unpublished mimeograph, Princeton University.

Levine, D.I. (1993, October). Worth waiting for? Delayed compensation, training, and turnover in the United States and Japan. *Journal of Labor Economics, 11* (4), 724-52.

Lillard, L.A., & Tan, H.W. (1992). Private sector training: Who gets it and what are its effects? In R. Ehrenberg (Ed.), *Research in labor economics* (volume 13, pp. 1- 62). Greenwich, CT: JAI Press.

Lynch, L. (1992). Private sector training and the earnings of young workers. *American Economic Review, 82*, 299-312.

_____ . (1994). Payoff to alternative training strategies at work. In R. Freeman (Ed.), *Working under different rules.* New York: Russell Sage Foundation.

LaLonde, R. (1995, Spring). The promise of public sector-sponsored training programs. *Journal of Economic Perspectives, 9* (1).

Mincer, J. (1962). On-the-job training: Costs, returns, and some implications. *Journal of Political Economy, 70* (Supplement), 50-79.

_____ . (1994). Investment in U.S. education and training. Working Paper No. 4844, National Bureau of Economic Research, August.

Mincer, J., & Higuchi, Y. (1993). Wage structures and labor turnover in the United States and Japan. *Journal of Japanese and International Economics, 2*, 97-133.

Nickell, S. (1982). The determinants of occupational success in Britain. *Review of Economic Studies, XLIX*, 43-53.

Oulton, N., & Steedman, H. (1994). The British system of youth training: A comparison with Germany. In L. Lynch (Ed.), *Training and the private sector* (pp. 61-76). Chicago, University of Chicago Press.

Pishchke, J. (1996). Continuous training in Germany. National Bureau of Economic Research Inc, Working Paper 5829, Cambridge, MA, November.

Rosen, S. (1972, Summer). Learning and experience in the labor market. *Journal of Human Resources, 7*, 326 -342.

Soskice, D. (1994). Reconciling markets and institutions: The German apprenticeship system. In L. Lynch (Ed.), *Training and the private sector* (pp. 25-60). Chicago: University of Chicago Press.

Topel, R., & Ward, M. (1992). Job mobility and the careers of young men. *Quarterly Journal of Economics, 57* (2), 439-479.

THE ASSESSMENT OF JOB PERFORMANCE:
FOCUSING ATTENTION ON CONTEXT, PROCESS, AND GROUP ISSUES

Robert L. Heneman and Courtney von Hippel

Since the early 1980s there have been two profound shifts in the manner in which job performance is assessed in organizations and is studied by organizational researchers. Specifically, there is now less emphasis on the performance assessment instrument and greater emphasis has been placed on the measurement of group rather than individual performance. Prior to the early 1980s organizations were primarily concerned with trying to develop the best possible instrument with which to make performance assessments (Patten, 1982). In a complementary fashion, researchers focused on making instruments reliable and free from bias (Landy & Farr, 1980). The focus today is no longer on the performance assessment instrument, but has instead shifted to understanding the processes used in making assessments of performance (Ilgen, Barnes-Farrel, & McKellin, 1993) and the context in which these processes take place (Murphy & Cleveland, 1991).

The current focus indicates that in order for assessments of employee performance to be effective, it is not sufficient to have only a well-developed assessment instrument. Rather, the instrument itself is only one part of the total system needed for effective performance assessment (Lawler, 1994). While a well-developed assessment instrument is a necessary condition for effective performance assessment, an understanding of how the assessment instrument is used under various circumstances is also required. By having this understanding, a complete system can be developed for effective performance assessment.

Additionally, prior to the early 1980s emphasis was placed by organizations on measuring the performance of the individual rather than of a team, business unit, or organization to which the individual belongs. Today many organizations continue to assess individual performance, but increasingly also assess the performance of the team, business unit, or organization. The reason for this shift in measurement from the individual to the group has to do with the design of work in organizations. In the past, work was designed primarily to be centered around the individual. Increasingly, today's organizations are shifting toward work designed around the group. For example, in automobile assembly plants, employees used to be responsible for placing certain parts on an engine. Today, in some auto plants, employees are responsible as a team for assembling the entire engine together.

In order for assessments of employee performance to be effective, it is critical that performance of the group be measured along with performance of the individual. By making assessments of the group, organizations can make strategic decisions regarding the direction of the organization and resource allocations. That is, financial, technological, and human resources can be allocated in such a manner that the groups operate in accordance with the desired direction of the organization. Unfortunately, there is very little research on the assessment of performance at the group level, and thus, there is a crying need for performance assessment researchers to turn their attention to this important topic. As will be shown in this chapter, most of the research on performance of the group thus far has simply been descriptive. This state of affairs leaves us with many questions regarding which practices are effective and why they are effective at the group level.

The objective of this chapter is to show how an understanding of the assessment process and the context of the assessment can be used to make more effective assessments of performance. In order to meet this objective, current research illustrative of this new focus will be reviewed. Specifically, we will address issues dealing with context followed by issues addressing process. The literature will be introduced with a discussion of the purposes of performance assessments in organizations and the criteria used to gauge the effectiveness of performance assessments. Because of the limited amount of research conducted on the assessment of group performance, most of the information presented will center around performance assessment at the individual level.

PURPOSES OF PERFORMANCE ASSESSMENT

Performance assessment refers to a formal evaluation of an employee's contribution to the organization, usually conducted on a yearly basis. These assessments, often referred to as performance appraisals, performance reviews, or performance evaluations, are used in a variety of different ways in organizations. Some of the more important purposes of these assessments include management decisions, developmental feedback, and staffing and training support.

Management Decisions

Evaluations of employee performance are used to make management decisions. These decisions include rewards, promotion, demotions and terminations, and job assignments. In order to motivate continued good performance, rewards are allocated on the basis of performance on both an informal and formal basis. On an informal basis, praise is provided on the basis of good performance during day to day coaching. On a formal basis, rewards are allocated for good individual and group performance. Individual performance is most often formally recognized in organizations with a merit pay increase whereby pay allocations are made on the basis of one's performance assessment and position in the pay range (Heneman, 1992). Group performance is often rewarded through gainsharing plans which make pay increase allocations to individuals on the basis of the productivity of the work group or the entire organization (Mitchell, Lewin, & Lawler, 1990; McAdams & Hawk, 1994). In order to retain the best performers, promotion, demotions, and terminations should also be made on the basis of performance assessments. Job assignments are made on the basis of performance to ensure that assignments are successfully completed. The quality of these decisions regarding rewards and the movement of employees in the organization is highly dependent on the effectiveness of the performance assessments made.

Developmental Feedback

Performance assessments are an important source of developmental feedback to employees. In order for employees to maintain and improve upon present performance, it is important that specific and challenging goals be set. The research clearly shows that when specific and challenging goals are set and accepted by employees, performance is improved (Locke & Latham, 1990). Performance assessments are the vehicles used by managers to set specific and challenging goals for and with employees (Latham & Wexley, 1994); the more effective the assessment, the more likely that employee development will occur.

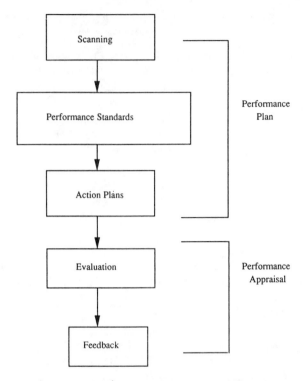

Figure 1.   Performance Management Process

Performance assessment is one component of the developmental process in organizations known as *performance management*. Managers use the performance management process to help employees develop in ways which are consistent with the goals of the organization. Stages and steps involved in the performance management process are shown in Figure 1.

The first stage in the process is the development of a performance plan which consists of setting goals for the employee. Goals define standards for good performance and typically are jointly set by the manager and employee. Along with goals, performance plans also contain action plans which are developed to specify the activities that must be undertaken to accomplish the goals. Both goals and action plans are linked to organizational goals by the first step in the performance planning stage, which is to scan the organization for business planning documents that can be used to develop goals for the positions which are consistent with the goals of the organization. The second stage of the process is actually to appraise employee performance once a plan has been developed. The initial step here is the assessment of performance where the employee's actual performance is compared to the organization's standards. The next step is to provide the employee with feedback on how well he has done relative to the standards and what must be done to improve on or maintain job performance. Also, a discussion of additional resources needed by the employee to facilitate goal accomplishment, such as training, is provided as a part of such feedback.

Staffing and Training Support

Performance assessments help to facilitate the recruitment, selection, and training of employees. In terms of recruitment, performance assessments can be used as a "realistic job preview" to inform job applicants of the type of work and the levels of performance they would be expected to perform at as an employee. When realistic job information is presented to current employees, it gives them the opportunity to decide whether the organization's expectations are consistent with their own. To the extent these expectations are consistent, job applicants who become employees are more likely to be satisfied with their jobs and remain with the organization (Wanous, 1992).

In terms of selection, tools such as interviews and tests are validated against employee performance. A valid selection device is one which allows managers to predict actual performance by the job candidate should the person be hired. In order for actual performance to be predicted, it is important that an effective performance assessment system be in place.

In terms of training, performance assessments are used by managers to assess the need for training and evaluate the effectiveness of training. One reason to provide training is to correct performance deficiencies; performance assessments can be used to show who is in need of training due to deficiencies in performance. It is also important to determine if the training actually affects job performance. Performance assessments should be made before and after training and compared to employees who do receive training to determine if the training actually affects job performance.

As can be seen from these three sets of purposes, performance assessment plays a critical role in helping organizations manage human resources. The old stereotype, namely, that performance appraisals are "...just another stupid form to be filled out for the personnel department," is clearly incorrect. Performance assessments are an important part of the total management process; in order to be useful, however, they must be effective. The criteria used to gauge the effectiveness of performance assessments will now be reviewed.

EFFECTIVENESS CRITERIA

The quality of decisions made by managers regarding human resources using job performance as the criterion are only as good as the quality of their assessments of employee performance. In order to make high quality or effective performance assessments, it is important to know how effectiveness is gauged, which is typically measured via multiple indicators (Austin, Villanova, Kane, & Bernardin, 1991). These indicators serve as the goals of effective performance assessment and will be used to judge the effectiveness of recommended performance assessment practices in subsequent sections of this chapter. A brief summary of these indicators from a variety of sources (Heneman, 1992; Latham & Wexley, 1994; Thorndike, 1949; Smith, 1976) follows, and are arranged from the micro to the macro level of analysis.

Reliability

Reliability refers to the consistency of assessments across raters, measures, and time. If multiple evaluators are assessing the same person or group, using the same form, after observing the person or group perform the same work, their evaluations should be similar; this is known as interrater reliability. If two measures of the same concept are used by the same evaluator, the evaluations should be correlated; this is known as internal consistency reliability. For example, if customer ratings of "courtesy" and "friendliness" are designed to measure an aspect of customer service, then these ratings should be correlated with one another. If an assessment is completed twice at different points in time (when actual performance is not expected to change), then the evaluations should be similar; this is known as test-retest reliability. For example, output should be correlated at two different points in time if the same person is using the same machine set at the same pace. Consistency is essential to the performance assessment process. If performance assessments are not consistent, then the wrong employees may be targeted for rewards, promotions, and dismissals.

Validity

Validity refers to the degree to which the assessment measures what it actually purports to measure. In order to be valid, a performance assessment should be accurate and free from bias. Accuracy refers to the extent to which the assessment captures all dimensions of actual job performance. That is, the assessment instrument should contain all of the relevant components of the job, as spelled out in a job analysis. For example, simply measuring an individual employee's productivity in a team setting would be a deficient measure. It would ignore another important element of the job, which is the need for the team to work together to accomplish team goals. Freedom from bias refers to the extent to which the assessment measures actual performance rather than nonperformance related factors.

Examples of nonperformance factors that bias performance assessments are known as rating errors. Halo error takes place when an evaluator generalizes from one aspect of an employee's performance to other aspects of an employee's performance without regard to the employee's actual performance. An example of halo error is when it is automatically assumed that just because a professor is a good researcher he or she is also a good teacher. Some professors are good at both, but some are better at one dimension of performance than another; hence, it is an error when they are automatically assumed to be good at both. A similar example arises when examining a supervisor's performance on the technical versus managerial aspects of performance. Halo error can also occur in group settings; if one division of a large organization is profitable, and a customer automatically assumes that other divisions are profitable too, then halo error has occurred.

Leniency, a specific type of halo error, occurs when employees are always rated very high or very low on all aspects of their performance. While it is true that some employees are particularly good or bad in all aspects of their performance, most employees, like professors, are good in some aspects and not so good in other aspects. In contrast, central tendency error takes place when employees are rated average in all aspects of their performance. Again, as with leniency, there is little variance in the ratings of different aspects of performance. This tendency is an error given that this lack of variance is at odds with the greater variance in the several aspects of performance usually exhibited by many employees.

The rating process is not only contaminated by the "cold," computer-like rating errors that may occur with the cognitive processing of performance information, it is also influenced by the "hot" affect or "states of feeling" held by the evaluator (Cardy & Dobbins, 1994). Conventional wisdom in organizations suggests that in order to make valid performance assessments, raters should be in a "good" mood. The reality seems to be that when raters are slightly depressed, rather than elated, they tend to be more thorough in their processing of performance information, resulting in more valid appraisals (Harris, 1994; Sinclair, 1988). This finding is a robust one and holds up in certain areas of social judgments (e.g., self-assessments) other than performance assessments (Isen, 1987).

Bias in performance assessments is not simply a function of the mood of the assessor, is also a function of "perverse incentives" built into the assessment system (Lewin & Mitchell, 1995). In many organizations, for example, performance ratings are skewed toward the positive end of the rating scale. That is, almost everyone is rated above average or better. A skewed distribution of this nature may not reflect actual performance levels and, hence, reduce the validity of the assessments. The reason for this bias is that the performance assessment system may have incentives built into it that reward the supervisor for skewed ratings which are perverse to the organization. Incentives for the supervisor/manager to give high ratings include not having to feel the discomfort associated with confronting a poor performing subordinate and being able to garner a larger raise due to the good performance of the manager's subordinates.

Fairness

In order for managers to be willing to make performance assessments and for employees to be willing to act on the results of the assessment, they must believe that the system is fair (Dickinson, 1993). Perceptions of fairness regarding performance assessments can be conceptualized in terms of *distributive* and *procedural justice* (Greenberg, 1987). Distributive justice refers to whether the outcome of the assessment (e.g., positive, negative) is viewed as fair. Procedural justice refers to whether the procedures used to make this determination are seen as fair. Both distributive and procedural justice perceptions are essential for effective performance assessment.

Distributive justice is established on the basis of equity considerations (Adams, 1965). Individuals performing the same job at the same level of performance should receive the same evaluation. Procedural justice is established on the basis of several rules (Leventhal, Karuza, & Fry, 1980). According to these rules, assessments should be consistent across evaluators and over time, be made using accurate information, be correctable, and reflect the concerns of the participants. In addition, bias should be suppressed and evaluations should comply with ethical standards.

Legality

Many laws and regulations govern what can and cannot be done in the context of performance assessments. Two of the major laws, the Civil Rights Act of 1964, 1991, and the Age Discrimination in Employment Act of 1967, make it illegal to assess performance on the basis of age, race, sex, color, religion, and national origin. An effective performance assessment procedure in an organization will not show any statistical pattern of discrimination or discriminatory treatment of an individual in performance assessments for members of these protected groups relative to nonprotected group members.

Practicality

An effective performance assessment system must also be practical to be effective. A practical performance assessment is one that is understandable to the person conducting the evaluation and the person being evaluated. It also has "face validity," which means that the results of the assessment seem plausible to both parties. Additionally, an effective performance assessment will be "user friendly." That is, the assessment procedure will provide clear instruction and the process will not be overly cumbersome to either party.

This list of criteria used to evaluate the effectiveness of performance assessments is an imposing one and reflects the attention that must be devoted to performance assessments by organizations if sound decisions are to be made on the basis of performance. Although it is not possible to develop a system of performance assessment that perfectly meets all of these criteria, these criteria can nevertheless be used to guide system development. Moreover, as will be shown in the next section of this chapter, it is becoming more possible than ever before to meet these criteria with the new emphasis in performance assessment on context and process, rather than focusing solely on the rating instrument.

CONTEXT

A considerable amount of performance assessment research has been conducted in laboratory studies. While this type of research has added to our knowledge of the assessment process, concerns have been expressed over the generalizability of laboratory study results to the "real world" (Ilgen & Favero, 1985). In recognition of this limitation, designers and users of performance assessment must go beyond laboratory research to develop effective performance assessments. In order to do so, fortunately, it is possible to learn from business strategists, legal experts, labor relations specialists, and organizational behavior theorists about real-world variables that must be dealt with in assessing employee performance. Four of these sets of variables— business strategy, organizational culture, unions, and laws and regulations— will now be addressed.

Business Planning

In order for performance assessments to be effective, they must be consistent with the business plans of the organization. By aligning business plans with performance assessments, the goals of the individual and organization are brought into alignment with one another. Operationally, alignment is accomplished by having the performance standards used to assess employee performance developed after business plans of the organization and business units within the organization are established. Not only should performance standards be formed after the formation of the business plan, rather than before, they should also be carefully shaped to be consistent with the core competencies or critical success factors contained in the business plan. These competencies or factors spell out the actions that must be taken by the organization to be effective in their product or service markets. To develop performance standards consistent with core competencies, inferences must be made about job behaviors and results that will contribute to each core competency.

An example of this process comes from Ameritech. At Ameritech one of the critical success factors is customer service. In order to be more successful than competitors in their markets, it is the company's belief that they must offer more effective customer service than their competitors. In order to do so, they have developed customer-based performance standards for their service representatives. These standards spell out a number of dimensions of good customer service, and each dimension is defined by specific behavioral indicators. For example, one dimension is "Personalizes Customer Contacts" and behavioral indicators include "Treats each customer as an individual with individual needs," "Incorporates customer information in conversations," and "Recognizes different personality types and responds appropriately."

One methodology available to strengthen the link between individual and organizational goals is to develop "competency platforms" (Tucker & Cofsky, 1994). A competency platform establishes the underlying competencies needed by employees to accomplish the goals of the business plan. Competencies refer to those characteristics of the employee that predict superior performance consistent with the business plan of the organization. Hence, it links individual employee capabilities to organizational strategies. As such, competency platforms not only spell out desired performance, they go one step further and show the underlying characteristics of employees that are needed to meet these standards. Underlying characteristics of competency plans include knowledge, skills, and abilities. These competencies can then be used to select and train employees as well to monitor their performance. An example of a competency model is shown in Table 1.

Table 1.   Example of a Competency Model for Plant Supervisors and Managers

The following is an example of the competencies that predicted success for the plant supervisors and managers of a large food-processing company:

Leveraging Technical and Business Systems
Using expertise to solve operational problems,
optimize systems and plan for future requirements

Leading For Results
Using initiative and influence to drive
results and promote continuos improvement

Building Work-Force Effectiveness
Coaching individual development and building capability of operational
project or cross-functional teams to achieve business results

Understanding and Meeting Customer Needs
Working with customers to meet overall business objectives

Source: Reprinted from Tucker, and Cofsky, 1994, with permission from the American Compensation Association (ACA).

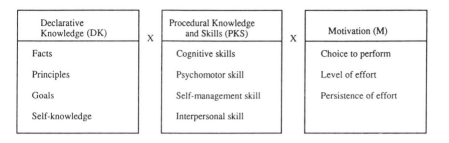

Adapted from Campbell et al. (1993).

Figure 2. Determinants of Job Performance Components

More and better performance assessment theory and research is needed to guide the development of competency platforms. A theory of competency that shows considerable promise is presented in Figure 2. This model holds promise as it incorporates current developments in organizational psychology, but has not yet been empirically tested. Other competency models that have been tested were done in military settings, and thus may not be generalizable (e.g., Borman, White, Pulakos, & Oppler, 1991). The modeling of human performance obviously needs to be further developed and tested in nonmilitary settings.

Organizational Culture

In order for performance assessments to be effective they must not only be consistent with business plans, but must also be consistent with the culture of the organization. The culture represents the shared set of beliefs and values held by members of the organization (Ott, 1989). Different types of cultures support different types of performance assessment systems. Hence, the performance assessment system must be carefully matched to the culture. Two different cultures can be used to illustrate this point (Walton, 1985).

A "control" culture is one that characterizes many large bureaucracies such as the military where jobs are strictly defined and highly specialized, many layers of management prevail, there is little lateral communication, and authority is top down. A "commitment" culture is typically found in smaller organizations that must respond to a rapidly changing business environment. In this type of culture, jobs are broadly defined with few specific duties, there are few layers of management, much lateral communication occurs, and authority resides at all levels of the organization. Table 2 shows the type of performance assessment system appropriate in each of these two cultures.

Table 2.　Culture and Performance Assessment System

Performance Assessment System Characteristics	Culture	
	Control	Commitment
Purpose of Evaluation	Evaluation	Development
Unit of Analysis	Individual	Team and Individual
Source of Evaluation	Superior	Superior Self Peers Subordinates Customers
Performance Standards	Quantity	Quantity Quality Teamwork Customer Service
Appraisal Period	Yearly	Ongoing

The importance of organizational culture can be highlighted with the case of self-directed work teams whereby such teams are formed to be more responsive to the needs of the customer. These teams are directed by the employees so that decisions traditionally made by management are made by employees. Such an approach enables issues raised by the customer to be dealt with immediately rather than having the customer wait for an extended period for the issue to be resolved by management. Self-directed work teams are also formed to take advantage of ideas for better business performance held by employees. Because employees are closer to day-to-day operations than managers, employees have many good ideas not thought of by management which can be immediately used in self-directed teams. The culture with self-directed work teams is one of commitment. If a control-oriented performance assessment system were used here, it could lead to disastrous results. It would suggest to employees that they cannot be trusted to be a part of the appraisal process by rating their own performance and that of their peers. A mistake made by many companies is to tell employees that they are empowered to make decisions as a self-directed team, but then are not given the authority to be part of the performance assessment process. Similarly, customer evaluations should be used to reinforce the customer service focus of service-based teams, and team assessments should be conducted to reinforce this concept of a work team.

Unionized Settings

Many organizations with workforces represented by labor unions do not have performance assessment systems. Instead of making human resource decisions on the basis of performance, managers are sometimes required to make decisions on the basis of seniority as specified in a labor contract negotiated and agreed on by labor and management.

Some unions do allow performance assessments to take place. They may be in favor of performance assessments because it helps members become developed and promoted. It also may help the union to decide which grievances are meritorious and should be processed by the union. Acceptance of a performance assessment system by the union is more likely to take place when it is developed jointly by labor and management. Performance assessments are also more likely to be acceptable to a union when they are used solely for developmental reasons and not used to make pay or promotion decisions.

On the whole, union resistance to performance assessment is strong as evidenced by the fact that only about 15 percent of unionized organizations have incentive pay plans, where pay is made contingent on performance (U.S. Department of Labor, 1981). Even in those organizations that do have performance assessment systems, research suggests that unionized employees are less satisfied than nonunionized employees with the performance assessment process (Gaertner & Gaertner, 1987).

Unions are resistant to performance assessments for several reasons (Balkin, 1989; Freeman, 1982; Barkin, 1948). First, there is an overriding concern that assessments are not conducted fairly because of the subjectivity involved in the assessment process. Concern is often expressed, for example, about how the evaluations are biased by personality conflicts. Second, performance assessment is very costly in terms of the time required by the union to monitor the results of performance assessments to be sure that they are not biased. Third, concern is expressed that when performance is assessed, union members will be in competition with one another, which defeats the goal of solidarity among union members.

Laws and Regulations

As previously noted in this chapter, various laws and regulations govern permissible practices with regard to performance assessments. The laws and court cases ruling on these laws have been subject to narrative (Latham & Wexley, 1994; Martin, Bartol, & Levine, 1987; Nathan & Cascio, 1986) and empirical reviews (Feild & Holley, 1982). Based on these reviews, the following steps should be taken to ensure that performance assessments are legally defensible:

- Performance standards should always be based on a sound job analysis.
- Personality traits should not be evaluated as it is difficult to show their relationship to the job.
- Instructions and training on how to make effective performance assessments should be given to all assessors.
- An appeals procedure should be in place for employees who feel that they have not been fairly treated in the assessment process.
- The completed assessment must be reviewed with the employee being assessed and a signature indicating that a review was conducted with the employee should be given by the employee.

It should be noted that these guidelines do not impose an undue hardship on employers. To the contrary, they are very consistent with sound business practice and research, as will be shown in the next section of this chapter on process issues.

PROCESS

Along with a consideration of contextual issues, another issue that must be considered if effective performance assessments are to be formed is the process used to formulate performance assessments. In the past, this has meant considerable attention being given to the cognitive processes used by evaluators to make performance assessments. While cognitive processes are important, they should not be considered at the expense of organizational processes, which are as important, or perhaps more important, than cognitive processes in determining performance assessments (Ilgen, Barnes-Farrel, & McKellin, 1993; Murphy & Cleveland, 1991).

One way to view process issues that incorporates both individual and organizational processes is shown in Figure 3. According to this perspective, performance assessment is a three-step process that is required as a part of the evaluator's or rater's role. The rater must formulate standards, gather data on how the employee performs, and compare the employee's performance to the standards in order to make final ratings of performance. In executing these steps, the rater draws on two sets of resources: individual and organizational. Individual resources include the ability and motivation to make performance assessments. In order to make an assessment of performance, the rater must be able (Feldman, 1981) and motivated (Dickinson, 1993) to observe performance, store the observations, recall the observations, and integrate them into a summary judgment (Wexley & Klimoski, 1984; DeNisi, Cafferty, & Meglino, 1984). Organizational resources can also be drawn on to perform the rater's role. Organizational resources include the time needed to complete

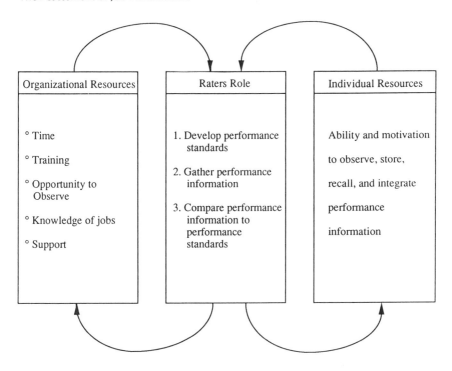

Figure 3. The Performance Assessment Process

the tasks, training on how to conduct the tasks, being placed in a situation where performance can be observed, being provided with information about the nature of the job, and having the support of subordinates, peers, and superiors necessary to complete the three-step rating process. A variety of forces have been identified in the literature as impacting raters as they undertake this process. These factors will now be described as it is these factors that must be managed if effective performance assessments are to be made.

Most of the research that will be reviewed has focused on the ability of the rater to acquire resources needed to make effective assessments. Whenever possible, the motivation to acquire needed resources will also be examined. Motivation is a very important part of the rating process, as it affects even the most basic issues underlying the rating process. For example, one such factor is willingness to complete a performance assessment. In an organization studied by Fried, Tiegs, and Bellamy (1992), about 30 percent of the ratees did not even receive scheduled performance assessments, let alone valid ones. Most of the research conducted regarding motivation has examined the motivation to provide valid ratings. Researchers need to take a step back and consider the willingness of and incentives for managers to even use performance assessments.

Measurement

As indicated throughout this chapter, the assessment instrument or measure is not a panacea for effective performance assessment. The measurement process or steps used to develop the instrument do, however, play a critical role in the effectiveness of performance assessment. Important issues related to the measurement process will now be reviewed.

In order to ensure that performance assessments are accurate and reflect critical elements of the job, a process-flow analysis should be conducted to develop the standards used to assess performance (Zigon, 1994). A process-flow analysis involves identifying the inputs, transformations, and outcomes required to complete major work assignments (Noe, Hollenbeck, Gerhart, & Wright, 1994). Performance standards should be developed at each stage of the work process whereby inputs are transformed into outcomes (e.g., materials are manufactured into products). To make work consistent with the goals of the organization, emphasis should first be placed on the desired outcomes followed by an assessment of activities and inputs required to achieve these outcomes. Desired outcomes should be based on the business plan of the organization. When outcomes are measured in relation to the activities and inputs needed to produce these outcomes, organizational productivity, an important source of competitive advantage, is being assessed (Pritchard, 1992).

Outcomes are often measured in organizations with standards known as objectives. These objectives measure specific products or services provided by employees and are usually calibrated in terms of quality (e.g., scrap rate) or quantity (e.g., sales). Systems used to measure outcomes at the individual or group-based level are usually labeled "Management by Objectives." Although they are frequently used by organizations, little is known about the reliability and validity of these systems. These objectives are quite important, however, as they are related to the "bottom line" of the organization. On the other hand, the bottom-line results may not be under the control of employees because such results are influenced by other factors such as capital, technology, and the economy. Consequently, behaviors that are under the control of employees also need to be considered.

Transformations to inputs are often measured in terms of employee behaviors. These behaviors refer to the manner in which employees carry out their work activities or duties. Behavioral standards that should be emphasized are those which are highly effective for goal accomplishment (Latham & Wexley, 1994). Performance appraisal systems that capture these critical behaviors include behavioral observation scales (BOS) and behaviorally anchored rating scales (BARS), both of which have acceptable levels of reliability and validity. An assessment of these behaviors is important because they help employees learn about the relationship between their activities at work and the goals of the organization.

Behaviors are also important because they allow organizations to measure and manage very important, but more subjective, aspects of employee performance not captured by outcome measures (Heneman, 1986). Increasingly, it is these more subjective and subtle aspects of employee behavior which help organizations to gain competitive advantage in their product and service markets. Examples of these subjective behaviors include customer service, teamwork, corporate social performance, and organizational citizenship behavior. The latter two concepts refer to going above and beyond normal expectations of a business to serve other people outside (Wood, 1991) and inside the organization (Organ, 1988; Borman & Motowidlo, 1993).

Inputs are often measured in terms of personality trait standards. Often these traits are known as graphic rating scales. Using traits to measure inputs is unfortunate because, as previously discussed, there are legal problems with using trait labels such as "aggressiveness" or "temperament" even though they can sometimes be measured in a reliable manner. Also, because personalities are very stable over time and difficult to change (Hogan, 1991), employees do not react positively to feedback about their personality versus feedback about their behavior or results (Wexley, 1984). Moreover, managers are uncomfortable making trait assessments compared to behavioral assessments (Wiersma & Latham, 1986). Most important of all, it is very difficult to tie traits to the business plan of the firm and, as a result, traits fail to take the essential step of integrating context into the performance assessment system.

Given the problems with trait ratings and the need to assess work input under the control of the employee, what else can be used to measure input? In terms of the quantity of input, an objective measure such as labor hours can be used. Unfortunately, however, simply being at work does not necessarily measure the effectiveness of work. A more promising measure is job knowledge, which has been shown to be correlated with overall performance (Hunter, 1986). Unlike traits, it is a standard that is job related and, as a result, is less likely to be subject to legal problems and more likely to be acceptable to employees and managers. Job knowledge has two components—declarative knowledge and procedural knowledge (Campbell, McCloy, Oppler, & Sager, 1993). Declarative knowledge is knowledge about facts and things regarding task requirements; procedural knowledge refers to knowing when and how to accomplish tasks. Declarative knowledge is a necessary, but not sufficient, condition for procedural knowledge.

Most of our knowledge concerning the measurement of performance is at the level of the individual. This is an unfortunate state of affairs because, as previously noted, work is now often being designed at the group level. Little is known, however, about the effectiveness of alternative measures of team, business unit, and organizational performance. One reason for this lack of knowledge regarding effectiveness is the lack of consensus regarding what constitutes performance at the team, business unit, or organizational level (Whetten & Cameron, 1994).

Conflicting opinions abound as to how, when, and where to measure group-level performance. As a result of this confusion, it is very difficult to specify appropriate group-level measures.

Fortunately, there is now the beginning of some theory to end this confusion and provide organizations with guidance to measure performance at the group level. One stream of thought that provides some assistance in formulating group measures of job performance comes from the business planning literature. As reviewed in the section of this chapter on context, group-level measures should be consistent with the strategic objectives of the organization.

A second stream of thought concerning organizational effectiveness is helpful in designing organizational level measures of effectiveness. This perspective suggests that there is no one best conceptualization or measure of organizational effectiveness. Rather, the appropriate measure depends on the purpose of the measure and the situation. Furthermore, it should not be assumed that the goal-directed strategy of the organization solely defines performance at the organization level (Whetten & Cameron, 1994). An example of this perspective comes from Scott (1992), who argues that different stakeholders in the organization look to different measures of organizational performance: stockholders tend to emphasize the accomplishment of strategic objectives; clients and customers focus on outcomes such as quality and quantity; employees look at the accomplishment of activities needed to accomplish outcomes; and staff administrators are most concerned with the structural capabilities of the organization to be effective. This perspective indicates that multiple measures, not a single measure, of group performance are needed. This perspective recognizes that organizations have multiple goals, based on multiple constituencies, resulting in multiple outcomes (Whetten & Cameron, 1994).

A third stream of thought comes from consultants involved in work design. For example, Zigon (1994) takes a multilevel view of the organization which leads to a method of developing performance measures at the team and individual level. His system of developing performance measures is shown in Table 3, and examples of team and individual performance measures are shown in Tables 4 and 5, respectively.

Sources

The rating process is also influenced by those individuals who conduct the assessments. Traditionally, the usual source for assessments was the employee's immediate supervisor. Clearly, supervisors should play a role in assessment as they have knowledge of organizational goals and are ultimately accountable for their subordinate's performance. Increasingly, however, they do not have the resources to be effective by themselves in this role. Recently, organizations have reduced layers of management to cut costs as a source of competitive

Table 3. How To Develop Team Measures

1. **Review and revise organizational and business-unit measures.**
   Do business-unit measures flow from and support corporate strategy? If only financial measures are being used, ask why. Identify measures to evaluate both strategic success and market results.

2. **Review and revise business operating system measures.**
   Are there measures for customer satisfaction? Flexibility or innovation? Productivity?

3. **Map the business process.**
   Identify the teams customers and the products/services the customers need. Identify all major process steps and handoffs that lead to the final product. Change the process to simplify it and increase value to the customer.

4. **Identify team measurement points.**
   Always measure the final product. Decide which process steps and handoffs are worth measuring. Measure processes by waste and cycle time. Measure handoffs by delivery and quality.

5. **Identify individual accomplishments that support the team's process.**
   Build a role-result matrix with team members down the left column, key process steps across the top row and accomplishments needed to support each process step inside each cell.

6. **Develop team and individual performance measures.**
   For each accomplishment, select the general measures that are important (quantity, quality, cost and/or timeliness). For each general measure, answer the question, "How can (quantity, quality, cost and/or timeliness) be measured?" If an accomplishment can be measured with numbers, record the units to be counted (or tracked by percentage). If performance only can be described, list who will judge the work and what factors they will consider.

7. **Develop team and individual performance objectives.**
   The goal is verifiability. If the measure is numeric, ask, "For this measure, what number would represent 'meeting expectations'?" Establish a range of performance above which special recognition is warranted and below which a performance problem exists. If the measure is descriptive, ask, "For each factor the judge will look at, what would this person see that means a good job has been done?" List the judge, factors, and what constitutes a good job for each factor. Ask, "If this description equals 'meeting expectations', what would 'exceeding' look like?" Write what the judge would see happening if these expectations were exceeded.

Source: Reprinted from Zigon, 1994, with permission from the American Compensation Association (ACA).

advantage for the organization (Shaw & Schneier, 1994). In doing so, supervisors have many more people reporting to them along with more job responsibilities themselves. Also, technology has made it possible for employees to work at locations separate from their supervisor. When there is more to do, more subordinates to appraise, and more subordinates in remote locations, opportunities for the supervisor to observe performance are decreased. This decreased opportunity to observe performance reduces the accuracy of performance ratings (Heneman & Wexley, 1983). Consequently, organizations with effective performance assessments will need to move toward multisource or 360-degree performance assessment. With this approach, performance assessments are not made only by the supervisor, but made also by peers, subordinates, the job incumbent (self), and customers who may have more or different opportunities to observe the employee in action than does the supervisor. Each of these sources of performance assessment will be addressed next.

Table 4.   Examples Of Team-Performance Objectives

Category	Team-Performance Objectives
Customer	• 90 to 95 percent of customers say they are "likely" or "very likely" to purchase the product. • 50 to 75 percent of customers say they are "likely" or "very likely" to repurchase. • There is a 10- to 15- percent sales increase that occurs during the first 90 days.
Operations	• There is no negative impact on customer satisfaction scores. • Restaurant managers are satisfied that: —The labor standards are accurate. —They have enough storage capacity and the product is easy to store. —The complexity of the procedure does not prevent them from selling within required service and hold times. —They are able to handle all customer questions about the product. —All needed supplies are received on time and to specification. —The procedure is simple enough to allow the food to be prepared consistently.
Financial	• There is a 45- to 70-percent return on investment.
Project Management	• There is a $5,000 to $10,000 national average capital per store. • The test is completed by September, 1994. • There is no more than a $26.7-million capital project investment.

Source: Reprinted from Zigon, 1994, with permission from the American Compensation Association (ACA).

An excellent, but often overlooked, source of performance information in traditional organizations is peer assessment. Under this approach, members of the organization at the same level provide ratings of peers. Reviews of the literature show that the reliability and validity of peer ratings are as good or better than supervisory ratings (Latham & Wexley, 1994). The correlations between supervisory and peer ratings are fairly strong (Harris & Schaubroeck, 1988), so they can be used as a check on supervisory ratings. On the negative side, employees tend to dislike peer ratings (Love, 1981). One way to minimize this dislike may be to have peers provide anonymous ratings or to use peer ratings for developmental rather than for other human resource decision making. Peer ratings appear to have high potential in modern-day work organizations in which work is designed for work teams with a minimum of supervision. Importantly, peer assessments are consistent with the self-directed and managed philosophy underlying these teams. It should be noted, however, that there are opportunity costs associated with peer ratings in the form of downtime from work. This is especially true if the person works in a large work group requiring many ratings. In order to minimize this cost and to increase the validity of peer ratings, peers should only rate other peer's work with which they are very familiar.

Table 5.

Team Member	Individual-Performance Objectives
Operations Person in Charge of Restaurant Modifications	• 90 to 95 percent of customers say they are satisfied with the following: —Utility hookups are in the right location. —Utility service levels meet the equipment's needs. —There is no negative effect on restaurant operation. —Modification scheduling is coordinated with the restaurant's schedule. —The vice president of operations is satisfied that the modifications support the project's goals. —Modifications are completed by agreed-upon deadlines. —Installation is no more than 10 percent above the estimate.
Marketing Person in Charge of Product Design	• Customers want to buy the product based on multiple-market research test data. • Store managers say the product is doable in the restaurant environment during the single-store test and multiple-store market test. • The design meets or falls below product-cost targets.
Procurement Person in Charge of Equipment	• Restaurant services and research-and-development function sign off on equipment specifications. • Specifications and prototypes are created by agreed-upon deadlines. • Equipment costs are 10 percent or less above budget for capital cost per store. • Installation is completed by agreed-upon deadlines. • Equipment has 99.5 to 99.8 percent up-time. • No retrofits are required. • 90 to 95 percent of service calls are responded to within 24 hours or within the time specified by the service contract. • 88 to 92 percent of repairs are completed correctly during the first visit.
Information Systems Person	• Restaurant managers are satisfied that cash-register changes have resulted in the following: —Key strokes are minimized. —Keyboard overlay matches data. —Download to cash registers occurs in time for training or the night before product rollout.
Training Representative	• Procedure produces a consistent product • Restaurant managers are satisfied that the training package: —communicates the procedures clearly —is complete (e.g., includes job aids, procedures) —fits the restaurant environment —arrives two weeks prior to product rollout date.

Source: Reprinted from Zigon, 1994, with permission from the American Compensation Association (ACA).

A small, but increasing number of organizations are using subordinate ratings of managerial performance. These ratings have been primarily used for the purposes of team-building in organizations (Latham & Wexley, 1994) and as a way to diagnose training deficiencies of managers. That is, they are used for gathering data on how well managers perform the duties most closely observed by employees (e.g., delegation). Little is known about the reliability, validity, or acceptability of these ratings, however. As with peer ratings, they may be best introduced into organizations by being conducted in an anonymous fashion and for developmental purposes only, in order to gather support for this process. Subordinate ratings seem to lend themselves well to innovative organizational arrangements that have empowered self-directed teams to complete the work. Subordinate ratings could be used in this type of context to assess whether managers are providing subordinate teams with the necessary resources (e.g., time, direction, equipment) to get the tasks accomplished properly. As with peer ratings, subordinate ratings are likely to be used more frequently by organizations in the future (Cardy & Dobbins, 1994).

On the face of things, self-ratings seem to be an excellent source of performance information. After all, who knows the job better than the employee herself? While many managers have tried self-appraisals, many have abruptly stopped using them. The reason managers are no longer using them is that they are often inflated as a result of positive leniency, and are not as closely correlated with supervisory ratings as are peer ratings (Borman, 1991; Latham & Wexley, 1994). These problems are correctable, however. One method to decrease leniency is to provide job incumbents who are expected to make self-ratings with instructions on the rating process. Often job incumbents are expected to conduct self-ratings with no preparation. Another way to decrease leniency with self-ratings is to use the ratings for developmental purposes only. Employees should also be encouraged to provide self-ratings because it gives them the opportunity to be part of the performance assessment process. By being a part of the process, they are more likely to be committed to the outcomes of the process (Mohrman, Resnick-West, & Lawler, 1989).

Customer assessments have been used frequently for many years in some sectors of the economy (e.g., hotels and restaurants). Unfortunately, virtually no empirical data have been reported as to their effectiveness (Cardy & Dobbins, 1994). There is a great need for research in this area of performance assessment. Given the focus of most organizations on the customer in the business planning process, these ratings would seem to be a very important source of information for performance assessments. Using customers to help assess the performance of employees is evidence of a strengthened link between performance assessment systems and business plan objectives. Caution should be exercised in using customer ratings, however, as there are both direct and indirect costs to the organization of their use. Customers expect a response from the organization when they take the time to rate employees and, hence, not only must the ratings be processed, but acknowledgments in the form of letters to the customer must be sent which add indirect costs. Direct costs include any actions that must be taken as a result of a letter from a customer to remedy the situation if poor service was provided (e.g., a free meal).

A critical question faced by organizations in the performance assessment process is "Which rating sources should be used?" The answer is threefold. First, in most cases multiple raters should be used as multiple ratings are likely to be more reliable than single ratings (Latham & Wexley, 1994). Second, multiple raters should be very carefully selected. In particular, only those raters who have the opportunity to observe and are knowledgeable about the job of the person being evaluated should be selected (Borman, 1991). Third, raters should be asked only to rate those aspects of the job which they are knowledgeable about (Cardy & Dobbins, 1994). For example, subordinates may be knowledgeable about their manager's performance in delegating assessments, but have little knowledge about their budgeting performance.

Administration

The effectiveness of performance assessments is also dependent on administrative practices, such as how and when ratings are conducted. Often what is required by the organization in terms of making assessments is in conflict with the capabilities of the rater cognitively to process performance information (Heneman, 1992); as a result, the validity of ratings is diminished. Therefore, to increase the validity of ratings, attention must be devoted to making administrative practice more consistent with cognitive processes. Fortunately, recent research in the area of cognition as it applies to performance appraisal provides some guidance about how to make administrative practice congruent with cognitive processes.

The most promising avenue for organizations to pursue in increasing the effectiveness of performance assessments is to provide raters with training. Smith (1986) reviewed 24 studies of performance assessment training and found it effective in increasing the validity of performance assessments under two important conditions. First, the more active the raters are in the training process, the better the outcomes. Raters should be given the opportunity to discuss issues of concern and participate in practice and feedback sessions. Second, raters should be put in practice sessions with the actual performance standards they are expected to use. These standards help structure the observation and judgment of performance which, in turn, leads to more valid ratings. Not only do these two steps help to increase the abilities of evaluators, they motivate raters to make valid assessments as well (Bernardin, Cardy, & Abbott, 1982). Unfortunately, most training programs do not build these steps into the program and instead simply focus on how to fill out and route forms associated with the appraisal process (Bretz, Milkovich, & Read, 1992). Organizations need to devote more resources to these proven training techniques for increasing the validity of performance assessments. These approaches are costly, however, and they may not be possible in smaller organizations.

Another way to increase the validity of ratings, which has received less empirical study thus far but appears to hold great promise, is to hold raters accountable for the results of their ratings. If rewards are provided for valid ratings and announced in advance, then raters do a better job of cognitively processing performance information, which results in more valid ratings (Salvemini, Reilly, & Smither, 1993). Unfortunately, most organizations currently do not generally follow this practice. A study of employer practices in the banking and newspaper industries by Napier and Latham (1986) found that not only do raters not receive tangible rewards for valid ratings, they do not even receive a word of appreciation from the boss!

A notable exception here is Pratt & Whitney which ties rewards for managers directly to how well they conduct performance assessments of their subordinates (Schneier, 1989). This practice can also be followed in the public sector and with smaller organizations as well. For example, in the municipal government of Columbus, Ohio, managers' appraisals include a measure of how well they conduct performance assessments of their subordinates. Criteria evaluated to make this determination include whether they turn the ratings in on time, the level of documentation provided to substantiate their ratings, and whether they provided feedback to the employees. In turn, their performance on these criteria serve as one of several measures used to determine the size of their merit pay increase.

An additional body of literature indicates that raters should keep diaries of critical performance ratings. One reason for this recommendation is that a delay between the observation and recording of performance information reduces the validity of assessments due to memory decay over time (Heneman & Wexley, 1983). Furthermore, demands on memory are lessened with a diary. A second reason for the use of diaries is that the validity of ratings is lower when raters do not have comparative data on how other employees are performing (Heneman, 1986); this is especially true with self-appraisals (Farh & Dobbins, 1989). Diaries can be used so that comparative performance data are available on demand. The effectiveness of diaries was reported in a study by DeNisi, Robbins, and Cafferty (1989). They found that raters who keep a diary were more valid than raters who did not keep a diary. Also, they found that raters who organized their diaries by the ratee, rather than by the task performed by the ratee, were more accurate. This finding indicates that a separate file should be kept on each employee to record critical performance incidents.

The keeping of diaries requires extra time by the evaluator in the rating process. Hence, it may be seen as a cost by the evaluator. In order to minimize the cost, only critical incidents of highly effective or ineffective performance should be recorded, rather than recording everything the employee does. From the organization's perspective, the time cost may be offset by the increased validity of the assessments. Hence, organizations may be willing to provide incentives for diary-keeping by managers. To do so, diary-keeping may be one standard that evaluators are held accountable for in the assessment of the evaluator's performance.

A final administrative issue that needs to be addressed in order to produce effective performance assessments concerns the parties to be involved in the development of performance standards. Traditionally, performance standards were developed by the human resource department for everyone or by managers for their direct reports. Neither practice is recommended, given current theory and research. Managers and employees, not human resource departments or managers alone, should develop performance standards. Friedman and Cornelius (1976) found that when managers participated in the development of performance standards, the ratings were more valid than ratings made when managers were not involved in the process of setting standards. Employees should also be involved in the development of standards being used by their managers to rate their performance. By participating in the process employees are likely to feel that there is greater fairness (procedural justice) than when they do not participate (Greenberg, 1986); another result is likely to be improved motivation on the part of the employee. Silverman and Wexley (1984) reported that employees involved in the setting of performance standards for their positions were more satisfied with the appraisals and more willing to improve their performance than were employees not involved in the setting of standards for their positions.

Incentives may need to be provided by the organization to get managers to undertake participation in standard-setting. Involving employees in the setting of standards takes a considerable amount of time by the manager to teach employees how to do this and to review the standards being set by the employee. Hence, there is a disincentive (the time required) for managers to use participation. From the organization's perspective, however, this cost in the form of time may be offset by the increased validity and acceptability of the assessments. Consequently, the organization may formally require managers to use participation by making it a part of the manager's performance assessment. In turn, the incentive of a pay increase can be tied to this part of the manager's performance assessment.

Social Influence

Although much research has been conducted on characteristics of the rater and ratee which influence the effectiveness of performance ratings, little attention has been directed to the influence of social interactions between raters and ratees (Wexley & Klimoski, 1984). This lack of research has been a problematic oversight in that social interactions have a potentially important influence on the motivation of the rater (Harris, 1994) and affective states of the rater (Wayne & Kacmar, 1991). One promising area of research is the influence of impression management techniques on the effectiveness of performance assessment.

Employees engage in behaviors intended to manage the impressions of the rater (i.e., impression management). The hope, of course, is to create positive impressions of one's self which in turn result in a favorable performance assessment. The available research indicates that there is general support for this intention. Impression management tactics by employees lead to a positive affect ("liking") by the manager, which in turn results in favorable performance ratings (Ferris, Judge, Rowland, & Fitzgibbons, 1994). Not all impression management tactics by employees are successful, however. While being politically connected produces more favorable ratings, (Bartol & Martin, 1990), as does the threat to use such connections, using ingratiation or flattery is not effective (Gould & Penley, 1984; Martin, 1987). Clearly, politics play a very important, but often overlooked, part of the performance appraisal process (Longnecker, Sims, & Gioia, 1987).

Impression management techniques are not only undertaken by the person being evaluated, they are undertaken by the evaluator as well (Harris, 1994). These tactics are used by the evaluators to influence both the people that report to them and the people they report to. Evaluators may give out high ratings with positive leniency to impress their boss—a "perverse incentive" (Lewin & Mitchell, 1995). By having a staff of high performing subordinates, evaluators can boast to their bosses about what a good job they have done at developing their subordinates. In contrast, evaluators may give low ratings with negative leniency to protect themselves from the wrath of their bosses. By having a staff of subordinates with low ratings, the evaluators can attribute their own failures to the staff rather than to themselves. Finally, evaluators may give average ratings with central tendency (error) in order to maintain work group cohesion. By evaluating everyone as average, evaluator's may believe that they have not created any friends (because no high ratings were given), but also have not created any enemies (because no low ratings were given). As can be seen from these examples, impression management techniques can be self-serving for the evaluator as well as the employee.

CONCLUSION

Managers and human resource specialists often become disenchanted with performance assessments. One response to this disenchantment is to eliminate performance assessments. The elimination of performance assessments is not an acceptable practice, however, as it ignores the much needed role that performance assessment plays in making management decisions, providing developmental feedback, and supporting staffing and training practices. Another response to this disenchantment with performance assessments is to attempt to develop an "ideal form" that will lead to performance assessments which are reliable, valid, legal, fair, and practical. Research and practice has clearly demonstrated that it is virtually impossible to create such a form, however.

A better approach to developing effective performance assessments is to come to an understanding of the *context* in which performance assessments are made and the *processes* used by evaluators to make performance assessments. An understanding of the *context* leads to the development of performance assessment systems that are linked to the goals of the organization, rather than merely a form based on the whims and fancies of managers and human resource specialists. Consideration of the context also promotes the development of performance assessment systems that are consistent with the law, the culture of the organization, and labor organizations, rather than a form that can be used in all situations.

An understanding of the *process* leads to measurement issues, sources of assessments, management practices, and social influences that must be accommodated by a performance assessment system. Attention should be devoted to using multiple measures of performance at both the individual and group levels, gathering performance data from multiple sources, recording performance incidents immediately in a diary, providing training to raters, holding raters accountable for their ratings, and involving employees in the development of standards. By taking these steps, we are confident that more effective performance assessments can be made, and that the disappointment associated with the creation of new performance assessment methods will be held in check.

We are still very concerned, however, about the lack of research being conducted on measuring performance at the level of the group. As shown in this chapter, there are some very important reasons to measure performance of the team, as well as the business unit and organization. At the same time, there are also problems with measurement at this level, especially the degree to which the performance of the group can be influenced by individual members of the group. More research is certainly needed here, and we hope that it will be directed at context and process issues concerning group performance rather than being directed at attempting to develop the "best" format to capture group performance.

REFERENCES

Adams, J.S. (1965). Inequity in social exchange. In L.R. Berkowitz (Ed.), *Advances in experimental social psychology* (volume 2, pp. 267-299). New York: Academic Press.

Austin, J.T., Villanova, P., Kane, J.S., & Bernadin, H.J. (1991). Construct validation of performance measures: Definitional issues, development, and evaluation of indicators. In G.R. Ferris & K.M. Rowland (Eds.), *Research in personnel and human resources management* (volume 9, pp. 159-233). Greenwich, CT: JAI Press.

Balkin, D.B. (1989). Union influences on pay policy: A survey. *Journal of Labor Research, 10,* 299-310.

Barkin, S. (1948). Labor's attitude toward wage incentive plans. *Industrial and Labor Relations Review, 1,* 553-572.

Bartol, K.M., & Martin, D.L. (1990). When politics pays: Factors influencing managerial cooperation decisions. *Personnel Psychology, 43,* 599-610.

Bernardin, H.J. Cardy, R.L., & Abbot, J.G. (1982). The effects of individual performance schemata, familiarization with the rating scales and rater motivation on rating effectiveness. Paper presented at the annual Academy of Management meetings.

Borman, W.C. (1991). Job behavior, performance, and effectiveness. In M.D. Dunnette & L.M. Hough (Eds.), *Handbook of industrial/organizational psychology* (2nd ed.) (volume 2). Palo Alto, CA: Consulting Psychologists.

Borman, W.C., & Motowildo, S.J. (1993). Expanding the criterion domain to include elements of contextual performance. In N. Schmitt & W.C. Borman (Eds.), *Personnel selection in organizations* (pp. 71-98). San Francisco: Jossey-Bass.

Borman, W.C., White, L.A., Pulakos, E.D., & Oppler, S.H. (1991). Models of supervisory job performance ratings. *Journal of Applied Psychology, 76,* 863-872.

Bretz, R.D., Jr., Milkovich, G.T., & Read, W. (1992). The current state of performance appraisal research and practice: Concerns, directions, and implications. *Journal of Management, 18,* 321-352.

Campbell, J.P., McCloy, R.A., Oppler, S.H., & Sager, C.E. (1993). A theory of performance. In N. Schmitt & W.C. Borman (Eds.), *Personnel selection in organizations* (pp. 35-70). San Francisco: Jossey-Bass.

Cardy, R.L., & Dobbins, G.H. (1994). *Performance appraisal: Alternative perspectives.* Cincinnati, OH: South-Western.

DeNisi, A.S., Cafferty, T.P., & Meglino, B.M. (1984). A cognitive view of performance appraisal: A model and research propositions. *Organizational Behavior and Human Performance, 33,* 360-396.

DeNisi, A.S., Robbins, T., & Cafferty, T.P. (1989). Organization of information used for performance appraisals: Role of diary keeping. *Journal of Applied Psychology, 74,* 124-129.

Dickinson, T.L. (1993). Attitudes about performance appraisal. In H. Schules, J.L. Farr, & M. Smith (Eds.), *Personnel selection and assessment* (pp. 141-161). Hillsdale, NJ: Lawrence Elsbaum.

Farh, J.L., & Dobbins, G.H. (1989). Effects of comparative performance information on the accuracy of self-ratings and agreement between self and supervisory ratings. *Journal of Applied Psychology, 74,* 606-610.

Feild, H.S., & Holley, W.H. (1982). The relationship of performance appraisal system characteristics to verdicts in selected employment discrimination cases. *Academy of Management Journal, 25,* 392-406.

Feldman, J.M. (1981). Beyond attribution theory: Cognitive processes in performance appraisal. *Journal of Applied Psychology, 66,* 127-148.

Ferris, G.R., Judge, T.A., Rowland, K.M., & Fitzgibbons, D.E. (1994). Subordinate influence on the performance evaluation process: Test of a model. *Organizational Behavior and Human Decision Processes, 58,* 101-135.

Freeman, R.B. (1982). Union wage practices and wage dispersion within establishments. *Industrial and Labor Relations Review, 36,* 3-21.

Fried, Y., Tiegs, R.B., & Bellamy, A. (1992). Personal and interpersonal predictors of supervisors' avoidance of evaluating subordinates. *Journal of Applied Psychology, 77,* 462-468.

Friedman, B.A., & Cornelius, E.T., III. (1976). Effects of rater participation in scale construction on the psychometric characteristics of two rating scale formats. *Journal of Applied Psychology, 61,* 210-216.

Gaertner, K.S., & Gaertner, G.H. (1987). Union membership and attitudes toward participation in determining conditions of work in the federal government. *Human Relations, 40,* 431-444.

Gould, S., & Penley, L.E. (1984). Career strategies and salary progression: A study of their relationships in a municipal bureaucracy. *Organizational Behavior and Human Performance, 34,* 244-265.

Greenberg, J. (1986). Determinants of perceived fairness of performance evaluations. *Journal of Applied Psychology, 71,* 340-342.

─────── . (1987). A taxonomy of organizational justice theories. *Academy of Management Review, 12,* 9-22.

Harris, M.M. (1994). Rater motivation in the performance appraisal context: A theoretical perspective. *Journal of Management, 20,* 737-756.

Harris, M.M., & Schaubroeck, J. (1988). A meta-analysis of self-supervisor, self-peer, and peer-supervisor ratings. *Personnel Psychology, 41,* 43-62.

Heneman, R.L. (1986). The relationship between supervisory ratings and results-oriented measures of performance: A meta-analysis. *Personnel Psychology, 39,* 811-826.

─────── . (1992). *Merit pay: Linking pay increases to performance ratings.* Reading, MA: Addison-Wesley.

Heneman, R.L., & Wexley, K.N. (1983). The effects of time delay in rating and amount of information observed on performance rating accuracy. *Academy of Management Journal, 26,* 677-686.

Hogan, R.T. (1991). Personality and personality measurement. In M.D. Dunnette & L.M. Hough (Eds.), *Handbook of industrial/organizational psychology* (2nd ed.) (volume 2, pp. 873-919). Palo Alto, CA: Consulting Psychologists.

Hunter, J.E. (1986). Cognitive ability, cognitive aptitudes, job knowledge, and job performance. *Journal of Vocational Behavior, 29,* 340-362.

Ilgen, D.R., & Favero, J.L. (1985). Limits in generalizing from psychological research to performance appraisal processes. *Academy of Management Review, 10,* 311-321.

Ilgen, D.R., Barnes-Farrel, J.L., & McKellin, D.B. (1993). Performance appraisal process research in the 1980's: What has contributed to appraisals in use? *Organizational Behavior and Human Decision Processes, 54,* 321-368.

Isen, A.M. (1987). Positive affect, cognitive processes, and social behavior. In L. Berkowitz (Ed.), *Advances in experimental social psychology* (volume 20, pp. 203-253). New York: Academic Press.

Landy, F.J., & Farr, J.L. (1980). Performance ratings. *Psychological Bulletin, 87,* 72-107.

Latham, G.P., & Wexley, K.N. (1994). *Increasing productivity through performance appraisal* (2nd ed.). Reading, MA: Addison-Wesley.

Lawler, E.E., III (1994, May-June). Performance management: The next generation. *Compensation & Benefits Review,* 16-19.

Leventhal, G.S., Karuza, J., & Fry, W.R. (1980). Beyond fairness: A theory of allocation preferences. In J.M. Kula (Ed.), *Justice and social interaction* (pp. 167-218). New York: Springer-Verlag.

Lewin, D., & Mitchell, D.J.P. (1995). *Human resource management: An economic approach* (2nd ed.). Cincinnati, OH: South Western.

Locke, E., & Latham, G.P. (1990). *A theory of goal setting and monetary incentives.* New York: Prentice Hall.

Longnecker, C.O., Sims, H.P., & Gioia, D.A. (1987). Beyond the mask: The politics of employee appraisal. *Academy of Management Executive, 1,* 183-193.

Love, K.G. (1981). Comparisons of peer assessment methods: Reliability, validity, friendship bias, and user reaction. *Journal of Applied Psychology, 66,* 451-457.

Martin, D.C., Bartol, K.M., & Levine, M.J. (1987). The legal ramifications of performance appraisal. *Employee Relations Law Journal, 12,* 370-395.

Martin, D.L. (1987). Factors influencing pay decisions: Balancing managerial vulnerabilities. *Human Relations, 40*, 417-430.

McAdams, J.L., & Hawk, E.J. (1994). *Organizational performance and rewards: 663 experiences in making the link*. Scottsdale, AZ: American Compensation Association.

Mitchell, D.J.B., Lewin, D., & Lawler, E.E., III. (1990). Alternative pay systems, firm performance, and productivity. In A.S. Blinder (Ed.), *Paying for productivity: A look at the evidence* (pp. 15-87). Washington: The Brookings Institution.

Mohrman, A.J., Jr., Resnick-West, S.M., & Lawler, E.E., III. (1989). *Designing performance appraisal systems*. San Francisco: Jossey-Bass.

Murphy, K.R., & Cleveland, J.R. (1991). *Performance appraisal: An organization's perspective*. Boston: Allyn & Bacon.

Napier, N.K., & Latham, G.P. (1986). Outcome expectancies of people who conduct performance appraisals. *Personnel Psychology, 39*, 827-837.

Nathan, B.R., & Cascio, W.F. (1986). Technical and legal standards. In R.A. Berk (Ed.), *Performance assessment* (pp. 1-50). Baltimore: John Hopkins.

Noe, R.A., Hollenbeck, J.R. Geshart, B., & Wright, P.M. (1994). *Human resource management: Gaining a competitive advantage*. Burr Ridge, IL: Irwin.

Organ, D. (1988). *Organizational citizenship behavior: The good soldier syndrome*. Lexington, MA: DC Heath.

Ott, J.S. (1989). *The organizational culture perspective*. Chicago: The Dorsey Press.

Patten, T.H., Jr. (1982). *Performance appraisal: A managers guide*. New York: Free Press.

Pritchard, R.D. (1992). Organizational productivity. In M.D. Dunnette & L.M. Hough (Eds.), *Handbook of Industrial and Organizational Psychology* (2nd ed.) (volume 3, pp. 443-471). Palo Alto, CA: Consulting Psychologists.

Salvemini, N.J., Reilly, R.R., & Smither, J.W. (1993). The influence of rather motivation on assimilation effects and accuracy in performance ratings. *Organizational Behavior and Human Decision Processes, 55*, 41-60.

Schneier, C.E. (1989). Implementing performance management and recognition and reward (PMRR) systems at the strategic level: A line management effort. *Human Resource Planning, 12*, 205-220.

Scott, W.R. (1992). *Organizations: Rational, natural and open systems* (3rd ed.). Englewood Cliffs, NJ: Prentice Hall.

Shaw, D.G., & Scheiner, C.E. (1994). Making organization change happen: The keys to successful delayering. *Human Resource Planning, 16*, 1-18.

Silverman, S.B., & Wexley, K.N. (1984). Reactions of employees to performance appraisal interviews as a function of their participation in scale development. *Personnel Psychology, 37*, 703-710.

Sinclair, R.C. (1988). Mood, categorization breadth, and performance appraisal: The effects of order of information acquisition and affective states on halo, accuracy, information retrieval and evaluations. *Organizational Behavior and Human Decision Processes, 42*, 22-46.

Smith, D.E. (1986). Training programs for performance appraisal: A review. *Academy of Management Review, 11*, 22-40.

Smith, P.L. (1976). Behaviors, results, and organizational effectiveness: The problem of criteria. In M.D. Dunnette (Ed.), *Handbook of industrial and organizational psychology*. Chicago: Rand McNally.

Thorndike, R.L. (1949). *Personnel selection: Tests and measurement*. New York: Wiley.

Tucker, S.A., & Cofsky, K.M. (1994, Spring). Competency-based pay on a banding platform. *ACA Journal*, 30-45.

U.S. Department of Labor (1981). *Characteristics of major collective bargaining agreements*. Washington, DC: G.P.O.

Walton, R.E. (1985, March-April). From control to commitment in the workplace. *Harvard Business Review*, 76-84.

Wanous, J.P. (1992). *Organizational entry: Recruitment, selection, orientation, and socialization of newcomers.* Reading, MA: Addison-Wesley.

Wayne, S.J., & Kacmar, K.M. (1991). The effects of impression management on the performance appraisal process. *Organizational Behavior and Human Decision Processes, 48*, 70-88.

Wexley, K.N. (1984). Appraisal Interview In R.A. Berk (Ed.), *Performance assessment, methods, and applications.* Baltimore: John Hopkins.

Wexley, K.N., & Klimoski, R.J. (1984). Performance appraisal: An update. In G.R. Ferris & K.M. Rowland (Eds.), *Research in personnel and human resources management* (volume 2). Greenwich, CT: JAI Press.

Whetten, D.A., & Cameron, K.S. (1994). Organizational effectiveness: Old models and new constructs. In J. Greenberg (Ed.), *Organizational behavior: State of science* (pp. 135-154). Hillsdale, NJ: Lawrence Erlbaum Associates.

Wiersma, U., & Latham, G.P. (1986). The practicality of behavioral observation scales, and trait scales. *Personnel Psychology, 39*, 619-628.

Wood, D.J. (1991). Corporate social performance revisited. *Academy of Management Journal, 16*, 691-714.

Zigon, J. (1994, Autumn). Measuring the performance of work teams. *ACA Journal*, 18-33, 30.

PAY AND REWARD FOR PERFORMANCE

John A. Fossum and Brian P. McCall

Pay programs have received increased attention from academics and practitioners in both absolute and relative terms since 1980. One might argue that this emphasis roughly parallels the financial markets' unparalleled interest in firms' financial performance. Compensation practice increasingly emphasizes skill-based pay and broadbands, executive bonus and stock option programs, lump sums instead of annual increases in union contracts, elimination of cost-of-living allowances, and placing some portion of employees' pay "at risk" by lowering or freezing base pay rates and using annual individual or organizational performance criteria to determine total earnings. Emphasis on traditional merit pay programs has declined.

This chapter will outline several theoretical propositions on the effects of pay on employee behavior, explore basic theory and research in efficiency wage and tournament models, and relate both to the design and operation of compensation programs. We first examine the measurement of performance and the contribution of individual performance to organizational results. Pay program components are defined next, and the major classes of employee behavior they are intended to influence are identified. Recent research on effects of risk in pay program components on employee behavior and firm performance is examined. This is followed by an examination of theories of pay including expectancy theory, efficiency wage theory, and tournament models. Several comprehensive reviews detail research on many of these topics (Ehrenberg & Milkovich, 1987; Gerhart & Milkovich, 1992; Gerhart, Milkovich, & Murray, 1992; Gomez-Mejia & Balkin, 1992; R. Heneman, 1990; Lazear, 1992; Milkovich & Wigdor, 1991; Mitchell, Lewin, & Lawler, 1990).

111

THE ORIENTATION OF COMPENSATION PROGRAM DESIGN

Compensation program designs are not generally theory driven. Rather, they are designed to facilitate transactions in external and internal labor markets of concern to the employer. However, highly developed models such as expectancy theory (Vroom, 1964) from industrial/organizational psychology, and agency theory from economics (Fama & Jensen, 1983) have been the basis for segments of pay programs in many firms.

Pay structures reflect an implicit understanding of differences between general and specific human capital through the use of job evaluation to slot nonmarket jobs into a pay structure anchored in benchmark market comparisons. But, compensation managers are generally unaware of the concept of risk aversion of employees due to relatively undiversified human capital.

Compensation programs are often designed to imitate those of other employers who are perceived to be "doing well." In the case of pay levels, employers try to approximate the assumptions of "perfect information" in the competitive labor market in order to successfully attract and retain employees. Specific practices, as components of a production process, are assumed to contribute to organizational performance.

PERFORMANCE

Performance must be defined before pay can be linked to it. The contribution of increased individual performance to organizational performance must also be known, and the level at which performance will be measured must be identified. Common units of analysis include the employee, work unit, job, business unit, or organization. The performance measurement method—normative (absolute) or ipsative (relative)—must also be chosen.

Defining Performance

Ultimately, organizational performance is reflected in profit maximization or continually attaining normative goals. CEO performance is almost entirely intangible, but highly measurable. Output of production and service workers is also highly measurable. Quantity of output, in terms of total pieces, quantities during scheduled times, and hours per unit are all measurable. Quality and cost measures can also be closely tracked.

Performance of many clerical and professional jobs is difficult to assess in terms of tangible output or financial measures. Many position-holders in these jobs troubleshoot process problems or work on projects to improve processes. Exempt job position-holders are expected to exercise initiative in improving information flows, improving processes, and engaging in other behaviors whose effect on performance cannot be specified a priori. The relationship between the measurability of individual employee output and job level follows a U-shaped curve with high measurability at the top and bottom levels of the organization, and decreased measurability in the middle. Measures at the top are primarily financial while those at the bottom are primarily tied to physical outputs.

Performance within a position results from endogenous behaviors of the employee and exogenous factors in the employee's environment (both within and outside the organization). For the CEO all exogenous factors can be assumed to occur outside the organization. Following agency theory, CEOs are retained to apply their special expertise to accomplish outcomes of value to principals. Principals hire agent CEOs because the principals do not have the expertise necessary to operate the organization at its current level of complexity. Except for broad prescriptions (such as meeting certain legal requirements), owners seldom specify what the CEO is expected to *do*. On the other hand, they do specify what the CEO is expected to *accomplish* (in financial terms). At the production end of the organization job outputs can be defined clearly, *and* the behaviors required of employees completely described. Thus, the measurability of behavior as a function of job level is negative. At the executive level performance measurability is high and behavioral predictability low.

Relationships Between Individual and Organizational Performance

The relationship between individual and organizational performance depends on the elasticity of demand for the specific type and level of product or service provided by the organization and its job designs. Three basic forms of relationships are suggested (Jacobs, 1981). These are shown in Figure 1. The first describes a situation in which individual performance has only a modest effect on organizational performance. Examples would include machine-paced production processes in which the individual's job has relatively little impact on the attributes, sales, or performance of the company's products or services. These are often jobs involved in production, where product attributes that influence consumer decisions have already been designed in. In the second situation, individual performance has a great impact on organizational performance. For example, product development managers in different firms may create products varying only slightly, but the incremental advantages of product A as compared to product B lead to product A capturing a very large market share. In situation three, beyond a certain level, increments in performance contribute relatively little to organizational performance while low performance is extremely detrimental. Consider airline pilots. Crashes caused by pilot error lead to large costs to the airline. Very high performance

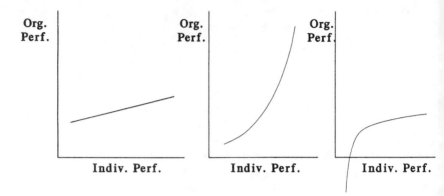

Source: Jacobs (1981, pp. 684-707).

Figure 1.   Possible Individual-Organizational Performance Relationships

might include landings that put the least stress on aircraft consistent with passenger safety. Very high performance probably makes little difference given rules requiring parts replacement at preset service intervals.

Units of Analysis

The organization defines performance. Performance within a job is a combination of organizationally defined behaviors and outputs. As noted earlier, the identifiability and definition of behaviors is an inverse function of job level while output measures have a U-shaped relationship with jobs in the middle most difficult to directly measure.

A study of compensation practices in retail stores (Eisenhart, 1988) indicates that pay is tied to job level and hours of work where behavior can be easily monitored. Where behavior is difficult to monitor, pay is output-based using a commission structure.

Performance requires certain configurations of knowledge, skill, and ability (KSA). Jobs and salary grades explicitly define the breadth and depth of KSAs required in particular positions. Skill-based pay plans (Lawler & Ledford, 1985) explicitly tie pay to proficiency in KSAs and an ability to produce behaviors that require them.

Organizations increasingly measure and reward performance at levels where incremental performance has increasingly large effects on organizational performance (e.g., individual production workers may have relatively little impact on unit costs or quality, but similar measures on work team or plants may substantially influence organizational performance). Relatively small increments in product quality may contribute to a firm's product reputation enabling it to capture a significantly larger market share, thereby boosting profit margins through the more efficient use of capital and a willingness by consumers to pay somewhat higher prices. (Consider, for example, the effects of J.D. Powers's initial quality ratings of motor vehicles.)

Performance measures can be used to increase the unit's ability to influence employee behavior to improve performance. Self-managed work teams and cell manufacturing enable constant monitoring of behavior and quicker feedback on output measures.

Absolute versus Relative Measures

Absolute measures compare an individual, work unit, and so forth to an existing standard. Consider a merit pay program basing increases on performance ratings. An organization implements a five-point summary rating scale (1 = low, 5 = high) within which managers are expected to rate subordinates. Each level of the scale may be associated with some descriptive output or behavior. The employee is assigned to the level most closely reflecting his or her behavior, independent of the ratings of any other employee.

Piece rates, commissions, and stock option plans follow an absolute measurement model. If an output indicator increases for one employee, it does not, in itself, affect measures of other employees. (Obviously, factors exogenous to the individual's position have an effect and can lead to correlated measures across employees within the job. Strong financial performance enhancing share price increases outcomes for all employees with stock options.) Absolute performance measures do not hold exogenous factors constant.

Relative measures lead to rank order outcomes. For example, if the organization indicated, a priori, what proportion of employees in given units must be rated within each of the five levels in the previously defined rating scale, then one's performance depends on how it's perceived in relation to other similar employees. Performance measures capture only endogenous effects (once the set of ratees is defined).

PAY PROGRAM COMPONENTS

Pay programs contain four major components: *pay level, pay structure, pay form*, and *pay system* (H. Heneman & Schwab, 1979). Organizations decide how each will be structured. Pay level relates to the organization's competitive position in the market. Considering benchmark jobs, is the firm paying more, less, or the same as competitors in the organization's relevant labor markets?

Pay structure relates to differentials between jobs and levels within the organization. It consists of job families defined for pay purposes, grade levels and pay differences between them, numbers of grades, proportions of between-grade overlap, and the like. Pay structure includes differences in pay associated with predefined skill blocks in skill-based pay plans.

Pay form defines the manner in which compensation is delivered to the employee: cash, paid time off, insurance, deferred compensation, ownership and options to own, and the like. Pay form includes both legally mandated and voluntary benefits.

Pay system refers to the rules and decision processes used to determine how an individual's pay will change. The pay system includes promotion and merit increases, bonuses, COLAs, individual and group incentives, commissions, stock options, and so on.

EMPLOYEE BEHAVIORS

Pay programs are intended to influence four major classes of employee behavior: joining the firm, staying with or leaving the firm, developing skills for present jobs or future jobs, and performing in present position assignments. Employee satisfaction is influenced by the design and administration of the pay program (H. Heneman, 1985). In turn, satisfaction is related to decisions to stay with or leave the organization.

Pay program components are directed at certain types of employee behavior (e.g., pay level is assumed to influence attraction and retention). Firms paying more than competitors are more successful in attracting applicants. Pay level may also indirectly affect employee quality or effort. People have an established idea about the value of their aptitudes and knowledge, skill, and abilities (KSAs). If they validly judge their abilities, and abilities are related to reservation wages, higher paying companies will attract, on average, more qualified applicants (Holzer, 1990).

Pay structure influences skill development primarily and performance secondarily. The pay structure cues employees about the relative value of various KSA sets, tying worth to the internal opportunity structure. For jobs staffed primarily from within, it provides information about the relative desirability of developing specific human capital (SHC) KSAs rather than general human capital (GHC) KSAs. Pay changes related to movement in the structure are usually larger than pay changes for other reasons. Promotional pay increases are usually permanent as long as the employee remains in the organization.

Pay systems relate primarily to performance in employees' present jobs. Pay changes depend on evaluations or measured output on predefined criteria. Organizations increasingly offer performance-contingent pay at team, group, business unit, or corporate levels.

"AT-RISK" PAY AND EFFECTS ON EMPLOYEE BEHAVIOR

Employers are increasingly implementing so-called "pay-at-risk" components in pay programs. "At-risk" pay involves tying a portion of pay to immediate past performance of the employee, unit, or organization. There is no guarantee employees will receive similar amounts in the future. Amounts are unknown until the performance measures on which the "at-risk" pay is based are known. Contingent rewards are increasingly "at-risk." Base salary increases may occur only when an employee's position within the pay structure changes. Second, increasing attention is being paid to tying contingent pay to organizational financial outcomes. Both of these increase the income risks of employees. They also change employee expectancy perceptions about the degree to which their behavior influences performance and pay outcomes.

Pay System Risk Effects on Employee Behavior and Firm Performance

Employees vary in their response to pay system risk depending on the behaviors the risk is designed to influence: joining, staying, developing skills, or performing. The effect of risk on firm performance can't be directly evaluated for attraction and retention strategies, but is more directly observable for skill development and performance.

Attraction and Retention

Little research addresses how "pay-at-risk" plans affect attraction. One study found college recruits were attracted to decentralized organizations with pay-for-performance policies (although this does not necessarily encompass pay-at-risk). The strength of attraction was greater for those with higher achievement needs. Recruits with low self-esteem favored large, decentralized organizations without pay for performance (Turban & Keon, 1993).

Employers with profit-sharing plans should be more willing to hire additional workers because compensation costs flex with profitability (Weitzman, 1987). Retention is higher in Japan where bonuses make up a relatively large part of pay. In the United States evidence supports a connection between profit-sharing plans and lower turnover for nonexempt employees (Chelius & Smith, 1990). Bonuses and profit-sharing are more often found in cyclical industries. High performer turnover is reduced by individual incentive plans, but increased by group incentive plans (Park, Ofori-Dankwa, & Bishop, 1994), possibly in reaction to "free-rider" problems in group plans.

Managers may try to influence mobility decisions as well as rewarding performance through merit increases. Policy capturing studies indicate salary increases are mostly allocated to performance but significant proportions are also allocated to critical and potentially mobile employees (Bartol & Martin,

1989; Fossum & Fitch, 1985). (However, Schoderbek & Deshpande [1993] did not find a mobility effect.) High performing employees who are mobility-constrained are particularly dissatisfied by these allocations (Rusbult, Campbell, & Price, 1990). Turnover is negatively related to job performance, and this relationship is strengthened by contingent rewards (Williams & Livingstone, 1994). In practice, merit pay programs reward most employees quite similarly. Only very high performers get large increases and very low performers receive nothing. Employers seem interested in retention only at extremes of the performance distribution. Moderately high performers are seen as easily replaceable, and low variation in increases improves overall satisfaction (Zenger, 1992).

Skill Development

"At-risk" pay programs don't directly address skill development. Employees expect investments in KSAs will lead to long-run stable returns. Some evidence exists that skill development (Fossum & Fitch, 1985) or specialized skills (Deshpande & Schoderbek, 1993) is taken into account in allocating merit increases. Cappelli and Cascio (1991) found employers pay a premium for jobs requiring larger proportions of SHC-KSAs.

Performance

Most research on pay examines employee reactions to changes in their pay or the pay system itself. Recently, more of the emphasis has turned toward examining "at-risk" situations. Financial economists and accountants have focused increased attention on executive compensation. This section will examine results of research on employees within major occupational groups, followed by results from experimental studies.

Executives. Overwhelming evidence finds executive financial incentives are linked with increased organizational financial performance. Bonuses contingent on financial performance improved subsequent financial performance and shareholder returns at greater rates than in firms without these plans (Abowd, 1990). Gerhart and Milkovich (1990) found that for managers and executives, pay mix (ratio of bonuses to base salary) was more strongly related to firm performance than pay level. Long-term incentives such as stock options are related to higher return on equity (Leonard, 1990). Executives whose bonuses were most sensitive to performance attainment performed at higher rates in future periods (Kahn & Sherer, 1990).

But, the structure of executive compensation reflects risk aversion among executives. If they were risk neutral, executives would demand bonuses equal to the gains they produced. At the same time, they would be willing to suffer the sum of losses. Since executives cannot afford symmetrical downside losses, they are willing to limit upside gains (Jensen & Murphy, 1990). Evidence suggests the average gain to a CEO for every $1,000 in increased shareholder value is about $3 to $5, far less than a risk neutral agent would demand if solely responsible for success or failure of the firm (Haubrich, 1994).

Incentives based on financial performance are not always appropriate, however. A study found R&D intensity was lower in firms where managers had a large short-run bonus tied to financial performance. Stock options and other long-run mechanisms mitigated this effect somewhat. Linking pay to strategic criteria rather than financial performance improved overall success. Diversified organizations more often used financial performance measures for allocating bonuses (Hoskisson, Hitt, & Hill, 1993).

Nonexecutives. There is great variety in the unit in which contingent compensation is determined for nonexecutives. Some is related to the individual, particularly in sales positions, while other plans relate it to group, business unit, or corporate performance (e.g., gainsharing and profit-sharing plans). There is decreasing interest in implementing or continuing incentive plans at the individual level for production employees as more complex output measures are being implemented and team-based production processes are implemented.

Sales work requiring higher education levels, more experience, and generating more revenue dollars per sale was more likely to be salaried. Salary may be necessary to account for opportunity costs of technical sales work given the relatively high education level required (Coughlan & Narasimhan, 1993). One study of technical sales employees found behavior-based controls increased performance more than output-based measures. In turn, improved sales performance enhanced overall sales organization performance. The study concluded there was only a limited role for incentives in improving technical sales performance (Cravens, Ingram, LaForge, & Young, 1993). A retail sales study found commissions are paid more often when special knowledge is necessary, thus appropriate behavior may not be known to the principal. However, tradition also plays a part in the continuing use of commissions (Eisenhardt, 1988).

DuPont synthetic fibre division employees were placed on a pay-at-risk plan in the late 1980s in which 6 percent of their pay was placed at risk with the expectation of adding 2 percent more annually. If performance equalled 100 percent of the goal, the 6 percent would be returned. One to 12 percent more could be earned for performance between 101 and 150 percent of the goal. Part of the 6 percent would be lost for performance between 80 and 100 percent of target, while the entire 6 percent would be forfeited for results below 80 percent. The plan was dropped later when employees expressed a desire to individually vary the proportion of pay they were willing to risk and organizational performance dropped for exogenous reasons. DuPont would have had to disclose confidential financial data for the division under SEC regulations if it had allowed employees to determine how much of their pay to put at risk (Santora, 1991).

Experimental evidence. An incentive is a preannounced contingent outcome following from a defined and measurable output (e.g., 20 cents per piece; $5 per hundred, less $.10 for each defective piece). Psychological experiments generally vary reward magnitude, task difficulty, demographic makeup of experimental subjects, or assigned performance goals. While situations are somewhat contrived, evidence finds experimental effects generalize to the field, but with lower effect sizes due to variability in organizational environments.

Experiments almost universally find incentives improve performance. They also suggest caution in applying incentives in the field. Studies have found the incentive, rather than its magnitude, influenced performance levels (Dickinson & Gillette, 1993; Frisch & Dickinson, 1990). Men respond to incentives by substantially increasing goals (but not necessarily performance) while women set more realistic goals (Henry, 1994). Larger incentives are perceived to be associated with more difficult tasks, regardless of actual difficulty, possibly reducing willingness to commit to goals with high incentives (Freedman, Cunningham, & Krismer, 1992; Svortdal, 1993). Commitment is higher when incentives are tied to easy goals, but incentives positively influence accomplishment on hard goals only if tied to performance, not goal attainment (Wright, 1992). Incentives improve performance beyond noncontingent conditions. Group performance was higher when incentives required cooperation as compared to either competitive or individual situations. The effect size of the incentive was relatively small, however (Allison, Silverstein, & Gallante, 1992).

Design Considerations

Pay-at-risk and incentive plans often require new or more elaborate performance criteria. They may require additional monitoring to prevent moral hazards. One study finds the choice of a pay plan represents balancing the loss of productivity associated with the lack of incentives against the cost of constructing and operating monitoring systems (Brown, 1990). Pay-at-risk decreases the certainty of pay for employees. Risk-averse individuals may require a premium in a contingent pay environment (Conlon & Parks, 1990).

Expectancy theory suggests performance will be higher if the reward is valued, if a strong link is perceived between performance and reward, and if the person believes he or she can perform. Persons with high pay valence perceptions perform better (Fox, Scott, & Donohue, 1993). The type of behavior to which incentives are tied influences the choice of the most effective incentive. Incentives can be either positive or negative. Both influence behavior, but negative incentives are a more powerful influence where the goal is necessary but the individual is not committed to its accomplishment. Prior attainment of a goal reduces the effectiveness of positive incentives for further performance against a similar goal (Wicker, Brown, Wiehe, & Hagen, 1991).

Bonus programs do not necessarily relate rewards more closely to performance. Schwab and Olson (1990) found with even relatively low reliability performance measures, merit pay more closely tracked long-run performance than bonus based on year-to-year rated performance. Their evidence is robust even when managers rate several dimensions in their pay decisions, such as Deshpande and Joseph's (1994) finding that performance, importance of the employee to accomplishing the manager's goals, and degree of disruption if the employee left, all influenced sizes of recommended merit increases. Deshpande and Joseph (1994) found employees with consistent performance across periods received larger increases.

Employee Satisfaction

Several studies have examined employees' reactions to implementing pay-for-performance and pay-at-risk programs. There are positive effects on satisfaction from pay-for-performance programs and negative effects from pay-at-risk programs.

A cross-section of university professionals felt employees differ in performance, and rewards should be associated with performance. They didn't see merit pay undermining cooperation. More highly educated employees were more in favor of pay-for-performance (Koys, Keaveny, & Allen, 1989). Contingent pay strongly influenced satisfaction in another group, especially among female employees (Huber, Seybolt, & Venemon, 1992).

Among a group of bank employees who had base pay cut and some pay put at risk, satisfaction with both pay level and the method for allocating pay-at-risk declined. Perceived effort-reward relationships and understanding of pay levels decreased (Brown & Huber, 1992). In an insurance company, job satisfaction was higher among employees who perceived they had some control over the performance measures that would determine their incentives and engaged in positive coping mechanisms to deal with change. Those without perceived control engaged in negative coping behavior (George, Brief, & Webster, 1991).

Japanese employees are less resistant to proposed changes in their employment relationship if they believe their employer intends to look out for their welfare and they see their union as having been effective in representing their interests (Morishima, 1992).

Pay Structure Risk Effects on Employee Behavior and Firm Performance

Pay structure is seldom at risk to employees. However, increasing inequality in pay reflects long-run changes in rates of return. Recent increases in pay dispersion are not due primarily to macroeconomic shocks, but rather to increases in capital intensity and the quality of general human capital and knowledge, skill, and abilities (Montgomery & Stockton, 1994). Within organizations, hierarchy has been associated with organizational success, possibly as a sorting mechanism to better enable the evaluation of potential executive talent (Leonard, 1990). Egalitarian structures at the plant level were related to higher quality levels (Cowherd & Levine, 1992).

Garvey and Swan (1992) suggest if managers' responsibility is to avoid bankruptcy before maximizing profits, incentives would vary depending on the degree of leverage in the firm's capital structure and requirements for cooperation among employees. Firms with lower leverage are expected to have flatter pay structures. Where cooperation is essential for output, lower leverage (leading to flatter structures) and smaller teams to facilitate communications would result. When cooperation is important, a manager's role is primarily to structure and manage implicit contracts between employees and the firm and arrange individual incentive plans to encourage cooperation.

Job characteristics are expected to relate to pay. Various theories suggest certain job aspects are desired, require greater effort, or call on increased aptitudes. Job enrichment advocates suggest work offering autonomy is more satisfying. Thus employees should see autonomy as a compensating differential. On the other hand, if autonomy and responsibility are related, traditional job evaluation would increase its pay. A Swedish study (Arai, 1994) finds job autonomy increases pay in the private sector, but decreases it in the public sector.

THEORIES OF PAY

Significant developments in pay theory have paralleled or driven recent changes in compensation practice. These originate primarily in economics and psychology to explain employment behavior. In employment, one can assume employees are interested in maximizing the net present value of their lifetime earnings while employers are interested in minimizing the present value of current and deferred compensation associated with current efforts of employees.

Production Functions

Firms combine capital, materials, and labor to create outputs they sell. Profits and future growth are related to value added by the employer, reflected by the difference between the selling price and the cost of the factor inputs. High profits require either high margins or large markets.

Employers would like to react quickly to changes in the market, particularly when demand shifts occur or competitors reduce prices. Increasingly, the ability to compete requires new production methods, often requiring substantially enhanced skills. Just-in-time (JIT) inventories and subcontracting reduce capital requirements and concentrate effort in areas where the greatest value can be added. Total quality management (TQM) aims to reduce material and capital input while simultaneously improving product marketability. The use of contingent workers, profit sharing, gainsharing, and bonus programs reflect a desire to make labor costs more flexible.

Compensation programs with merit or longevity increases to base pay are attractive to risk averse employees. Promotion structures with increases associated with performance and developing skills indicate paths employees can follow to earn more compensation over time.

Seniority systems are consistent with risk aversion since risk increases as time remaining to earn a payoff from GHC investment shortens. Junior employees are tolerant of more risk, given their greater return periods following retooling. Employees in a given employer probably tolerate moderate risks for new employees in return for reducing the risks of displacement for senior employees. These risks are increased if the employee is heavily invested in SHC.

If employers change the "bargain" by increasing employment and/or pay risk, employees could be expected to be less willing to acquire SHC-KSAs and more likely require employment contracts with higher pay during earlier years of employment. This would also hold true if employers reduce deferred compensation (Lazear, 1989b). Since defined benefit pension plan payouts are usually tied to years of service and terminal earnings, higher net present value of deferred compensation is achieved by behaving in a manner that will enable rapid movement through the compensation structure. If this is based on employer-defined performance, the employee has greater motivation to comply and develop SHC-KSAs.

Increasing the variability of pay leads employees to make the same assessment an investor would for a security with a high "beta" (high price volatility relative to market). Employees would expect a pay premium or would likely quit for positions with lower betas (at the same pay rate). Employees usually require a premium to move reflecting a lack of information about the new employer's job security. If a present employer reduces income or employment security, the premium necessary to induce employees to move to a new employer will decline.

Core Competencies and Resource Dependence

Firm strategy is increasingly focused on identifying core competencies (Hamel & Prahalad, 1990; Milgrom & Roberts, 1992). Core competencies are activities the firm performs particularly well compared to competitors. Competencies usually relate to particular functions (e.g., developing new technologies) and depend on market demand for their outputs. Competencies may involve low-cost production, development of intellectual property (e.g., patents leading to licensing agreements), and/or creation of marketing channels.

Core competencies may result from the application of the firm's employees' KSAs (Pfeffer, 1994). As the firm considers future directions, it's constrained by (or dependent on) its current stock of KSAs (resources) or what can be obtained in time to implement the required strategy.

Resource dependence approaches argue that organizational rewards are disproportionately allocated to employees' whose KSAs are congruent with the organization's ascendant strategy. Where merit programs are the vehicle for conveying pay increases, managers appear to take the criticality and potential loss of a particular employee's skills into account (over and above performance in the current assignment) in making salary decisions (Bartol & Martin, 1989).

Psychological Theories

Expectancy theory (Vroom, 1964; Porter & Lawler, 1968) is a cognitively-based motivation model suggesting individuals make decisions about how to behave based on their beliefs about the attractiveness (valence) of outcomes they expect will result from the behavior. The relative attractiveness of outcomes to individuals more strongly predicts choice than their absolute attractiveness across individuals (Kennedy, Fossum, & White, 1983). Individuals differ in their beliefs about how instrumental work-related activities are in influencing the attainment of outcomes. Pay programs are based on the premise that pay is important to all employees and that employees know the linkage between behavior and/or output and how their pay would change as a result. Figure 2 depicts the relationship between components of the expectancy model.

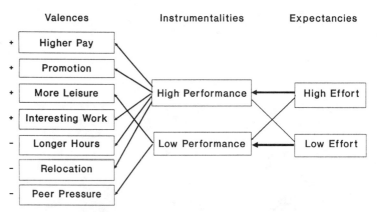

Figure 2. An Expectancy Theory Model

Equity theory (Adams, 1963, 1965) assumes individuals are motivated to maintain a balance in the ratio of the perceived value of their outcomes relative to the cost of their inputs and their ratios with those of others. In employment, comparisons may be other employees in the same job, employees in other jobs requiring different levels of inputs and providing different outcomes, or employees in similar jobs in other firms.

Justice theory (Folger & Konovsky, 1989) includes *distributive* and *procedural* components. Distributive justice is the perception that rewards are divided fairly. Procedural justice is the perception that methods used to divide the rewards are fair. Reactions to procedural injustice are stronger than to distributive injustice. Responses to injustice include quitting or organizing to influence or modify the procedures.

Economic Theories

Economic theories of pay posit (expected) utility maximization on the part of employees, (expected) profit maximization on the part of employers, and, typically, competitive markets. The theories assume the utility or well-being of employees depends not only on the amount of pay they receive but also on the amount of effort they must exert while working. The models typically assume that the amount of effort employees exert in performing their jobs cannot be costlessly observed by the employer, although a "noisy" measure of effort may be freely available.

The firm (principal) is faced with designing the employee's (agent's) pay-for-performance contract (in conjunction with a supervision strategy) to maximize expected profits knowing that not only costs but also revenues may depend on the type of contract (and level of supervision) chosen through its effect on employee performance. In designing the contract the firm is further constrained by market forces in that the employee must be as well off at the firm as in alternative employment opportunities. With such competitive forces firms earn zero economic profits in equilibrium. If employees are risk averse, then the optimal contract will typically balance performance concerns of the employer with risk concerns of the employee (Parsons, 1986). This section will provide an overview of efficiency wage theory and rank-order tournament theory.

Efficiency Wages

Efficiency wage models are based on the notion that the level of wages affect worker productivity (Katz, 1986; Weiss, 1990). Thus, raising wages above the market clearing level may increase profits if the revenues increase due to enhanced productivity outweighs increased wage costs. Several mechanisms through which increased wages increase productivity have been proposed:

nutrition, adverse selection, turnover, "gift exchange," and shirking. The adverse selection and turnover models will be identified and the shirking model discussed in detail.

The turnover model. In this model (Salop, 1979; Schlicht, 1978; Stiglitz, 1974; Weiss, 1990) costly turnover can be reduced by increasing wages. So when determining the wage level, firms will take into account these turnover costs and a wage above the market clearing level may result.

The shirking model. The shirking model assumes employees dislike effort, have some latitude to set their own effort or performance level, and monitoring an employee's effort is costly to the firm. Under these conditions, wages can serve the dual functions of allocating labor and eliciting effort.

A simple efficiency wage model (drawing from Eaton & White, 1983) assumes the utility function of the employee is an increasing function of wages, w, and a decreasing function of effort, e. The employee is assumed to have an alternative employment option available that gives utility $\bar{u}$. Thus, firms are faced with the labor supply constraint

$$u(e,w) \geq \bar{u}. \tag{1}$$

Let $\bar{e}$ denote the firm's desired level of effort. If workers could not vary effort from $\bar{e}$ or if monitoring were costless to the firm, then the labor supply constraint (1) would be the only constraint it faced, and a cost minimizing firm would set the wage w to equal $\bar{w}$ where

$$u(\bar{e},\bar{w}) = \bar{u}. \tag{2}$$

When monitoring employees' performance is costly to the firm and when employees are free to determine their effort level, however, it may be in the firm's interest to set the wage above the "market clearing" level $\bar{w}$. To see this, suppose when an employee shirks, shirking will be detected with probability p by spending m dollars on monitoring (supervision). Let $m = M(p)$ represent this relationship between supervision costs and the probability of detection. Assume M is an increasing function of p that increases at an increasing rate. For simplicity, we assume if the firm detects any shirking, $e < \bar{e}$, then employees forfeit their entire wage ($w = 0$). Under this scenario, if employees shirk at all, they will shirk completely $e = 0$. The firm, under these circumstances, faces the performance constraint

$$u(\bar{e}, w) \geq p\, U(0,0) + (1-p)\, U(0,w) \tag{3}$$

in addition to the labor supply constraint (1).

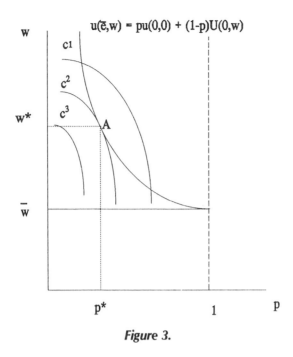

Figure 3.

The firm will then set its wage, w, and monitoring intensity, p, to minimize labor costs

$$C(p,w) = w + M(p) \tag{4}$$

subject to the constraints (1) and (3). This is illustrated in Figure 3. In this figure the labor supply constraint is represented by the horizontal straight line at $\bar{w}$. The isocost curves have negative slopes and are "bowed" away from the origin or concave. Costs decrease as you move in the southwest direction in Figure 3. For illustrative purposes, the performance constraint curve implicitly determined by the equation

$$u(\bar{e}, w) = p \, U(0,0) + (1 - p) \, U(0,w), \tag{5}$$

is negatively sloped and bowed toward the origin or convex. This, however, need not always be the case (see Eaton & White, 1983). The cost minimizing point (p^*, w^*) is achieved where the isocost curve c^2 is tangent to the performance constraint curve at A^*. At this point workers are paid more than is necessary to elicit their labor supply $w^* > \bar{w}$. This is cost efficient for the firm since the cost saving from reduced monitoring $M(\bar{p}) - M(p^*)$ exceeds the increased wage costs $w^* - \bar{w}$.

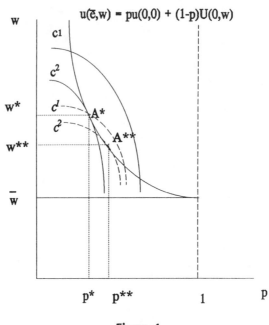

Figure 4.

An increase in the efficiency of monitoring can be represented by a flattening of the isocost curves through point A^* (see Figure 4). In this case, the cost minimizing point, A^{**}, involves more supervision, $p^{**} > p^*$ and lower wages $w^{**} < w^*$. Thus, one empirical prediction of the shirking model is that, all else equal, wages are an increasing function of the marginal cost of supervision.

Krueger (1991) found company-owned fast food restaurants pay higher wages than franchised outlets. In the latter case, since managers are also owners, they have greater incentives to supervise employees closely. So, the necessary wage to elicit appropriate effort is lower. Groshen and Krueger (1990) also found evidence from data on 300 hospitals that wages fall with the extent of supervision for staff nurses.

Using plant-level data, Cappelli and Chauvin (1991) found employee dismissal rates for disciplinary reasons decrease with the wage premium paid at the plant. Although in the simple model outlined earlier no employee shirking occurs, this finding is consistent with efficiency wage models where the amount of shirking decreases with the wage.

Anecdotal evidence for the presence of efficiency wages comes from Henry Ford's raised wages from $2.34 to $5.00 per day while simultaneously lowering the work day from 9 to 8 hours (Raff & Summers, 1987). Both absenteeism and turnover were high prior to the increase, with no visible shortage of labor. After the $5 pay both productivity and profits increased while employee discharges, resignations, and absenteeism fell.

Efficiency wage models may also explain the presence and persistence of interindustry wage differentials (Katz, 1986; Krueger & Summers, 1988). Differences in production technologies across industries may engender different forms of supervision. This, in turn, would lead to differences in the optimal wage and supervision levels across industries (see Figure 4).

Since individuals are better off in jobs paying an efficiency wage than in alternative employment opportunities, they will queue up for these types of jobs. Under usual circumstances, such a queue would drive down the wage. In this situation, firms will not lower their wage since they will then be forced to increase the amount of supervision.

It is necessary that there is some penalty imposed on the employee for shirking (nonperformance). In the Shapiro and Stiglitz (1984) model of shirking, the penalty comes about through workers, in equilibrium, enduring some amount of unemployment after being fired for shirking.

Assume for the moment that the amount of supervision is fixed. At the market clearing wage, an employee fired for shirking can immediately find a new job paying the same wage. Thus, there is no cost to getting caught shirking. By raising its wage above the market clearing level, the firm can induce the employee not to shirk. Here the penalty for getting caught shirking would be having to accept a lower paying job. However, if firms are identical, then they will all simultaneously raise their wage above the market clearing level. As the wage increases, a firm's optimal employment level will fall. Thus, in equilibrium, workers are not penalized by a wage cut, but instead by enduring a spell of unemployment before finding a new job.

While some empirical support for efficiency wage models based on shirking exists, it is unlikely the shirking model explains observed regional variations in unemployment rates. Models based on turnover considerations find empirical support to the extent that many studies find a statistically significant negative relationship between wages and quit rates (Devine & Kiefer, 1991).

Rank-Order Tournaments

Compensation always depends on performance to some extent. Even in models where employees appear to be given a fixed wage, receipt may be contingent on some minimal performance level. For example, in the efficiency wage models discussed earlier employees are paid the efficiency wage only if they are not caught shirking. Another type of compensation contract makes pay contingent on some performance measure. Suppose the measured output of an employee depends on both employee effort and random performance measurement error. Depending on the size and direction of the error component in an employee's performance measure, it's possible for an employee with a higher output measure to actually provide effort with a lower value than another employee whose performance measure includes a negative measurement error. Employers can only observe the measured output of employees (which includes measurement error).

A simple linear incentive plan would use two components to determine pay. First, some base amount would be provided to all employees to balance an employee's aversion to risk (which arises because of the random error component in measured output). Second, an incentive of some predetermined magnitude would be promised to employees based on their measured performance (for a more complete discussion of the optimal linear incentive contract see Parsons, 1986). The incentive will be larger relative to base, the more closely related the performance measure is to interests of the principals (Baker, 1992).

Measured performance may include error from two separate sources, firm-specific and individual-specific components. Firm-specific error is related to common uncertainties faced by all employees within a firm. Individual-specific errors are those related to how individual employee effort and the measurement system interact. Raters who provide performance measures may, for example, inaccurately assess the effects of certain types of effort. If employees are risk averse, then an optimal linear compensation contract would have to account for both the individual-specific *and* firm-specific risks faced by employees, and the optimal amount of employee effort will decrease as the variance of the amount of total error in the performance measure increases.

Using piece rate or quota systems may expose both employers and employees to a great deal of risk (O'Keefe, Viscusi, & Zeckhauser, 1984). Owners may end up paying more than necessary if either the piece rate is set too high or the quota is set too low. Employees may be paid a great deal less if the piece rate is set too low or the quota too high. A benefit of a rank-order tournament is that an employer knows exactly what her costs will be and employees can at least bound their rewards by the top and bottom prizes.

Rank-order tournaments or contests (Lazear & Rosen, 1981) which are instead based on relative performance may dominate linear compensation contracts or, more generally, individualistic reward schemes when either of the above situations hold. In addition, tournaments may be useful when rewards are indivisible in and of themselves (O'Keefe, Viscusi, & Zeckhauser, 1984). For example, for reasons of coordination and control there is only one chief executive officer (CEO) in a company. In this case a tournament may be an efficient method for distributing the CEO prize.

The optimal prize structure for a simple two contestant rank-order tournament model (hereinafter, tournaments) with homogenous contestants is discussed first to illuminate some of the basic features of tournaments. Next, extensions of the basic model including multi-contestant tournaments, multi-period or elimination tournaments, and rank-order tournaments with heterogeneous agents are considered. The section is concluded by discussing some of the empirical research on tournaments as well as discussing some of their limitations.

Two homogenous contestants. Following Lazear and Rosen (1981), assume that an individual's utility is increased by consumption and reduced by effort. The measured output of employees depends linearly on their effort and firm- and individual-specific meaurement error. In a tournament with homogeneous contestants, measured output errors have identical distributions across contestants, but the observed error for any given measure may vary between contestants. The prize structure (consumption possibilities) for a two-contestant tournament provides for a larger prize for the contestant with the higher measured output. The firm's decision problem is to set the prizes in an optimal fashion. This, in turn, depends on how the firm believes the contestants (employees) will react to the prize (compensation) structure. One complication of tournament theory is that a contestant's effort will depend to some extent on the effort of other contestant(s). So, some assumption must be made about how contestants react to each other. Typically, it is assumed that contestants choose their optimal effort level assuming other contestants' effort levels remain fixed (excepting where employees can collude [Parsons, 1986]). Equilibrium effort levels will depend on the size and difference of prizes offered in the tournament. Since contestants are identical, each contestant (employee) is equally likely to win the tournament (be promoted). The employer would like to construct the prize structure to elicit the highest collective effort across contestants given its costs.

Assume firms are risk neutral and face competitive labor market conditions. Then, prizes must be set so as to maximize each contestant's expected utility subject to the constraint that expected profits equal zero. When contestants are risk averse, it is difficult to determine an explicit formula for the optimal spread, however, Lazear and Rosen (1981) and McLaughlin (1988) show the optimal level of effort and the optimal prize spread are both increasing functions of the product price and decreasing functions of the employees' risk aversion. Moreover, the optimal level of effort and the optimal prize spread are decreasing functions of the cost of effort.

It is important to realize that both the optimal effort levels and prize spreads do not depend on the distribution of the firm-specific error. This is not the case for optimal linear incentive contracts. The larger the variance of the firm-specific error (McLaughlin, 1988), the smaller the amount of effort put forth by an employee under the optimal contract. If it is assumed that the individual-specific errors are normally distributed, then a compensation tournament will elicit more employee effort than a optimal linear incentive compensation scheme when the variance of the firm-specific error is large (Green & Stokey, 1983).

Although in a tournament the optimal effort level of an employee does not depend on the firm-specific error term, it does depend on the individual-specific term. Suppose the individual-specific errors are (identically) normally distributed. Increasing the variance of the individual-specific error term leads to a fall in the optimal level of effort. Its effect on the optimal prize spread, however, is ambiguous. Thus tournament compensation schemes will elicit less employee effort when employees' output is subject to large, employee-specific, random fluctuations which are not under their control.

Some problems with the simple model are now examined. Nalebuff and Stiglitz (1984) and O'Keefe, Viscusi, and Zeckhauser (1984) point out that satisfying the "second-order" conditions for a *local* optimum does not insure effort levels are *globally* optimal. For example, contestants may be worse off if they change their effort from the optimal level by a small amount but could become better off if they opt out of the tournament completely. Hence, when faced with a promotion (or other) tournament, some employees may simply "give up."

In some tournaments no Nash equilibrium may exist in pure strategies. This can be seen from the normal form representation of a simple symmetric two-contestant tournament presented in Figure 5 (Fudenberg & Tirole, 1992). In this example there are only two effort levels that an employee may choose: "compete" and "don't compete." As the figure shows both employees have incentives to drop out of the tournament (3 versus 2) when the other employee competes. Both employees opting out of the tournament, however, is also not a Nash equilibrium since each employee has incentives to enter the tournament (10 versus 3) when the other stays out. So, there is no Nash equilibrium in pure strategies. Nevertheless, the normal form game presented in Figure 5 does possess a mixed strategy equilibrium where each employee chooses an effort level with a certain probability (Fudenberg & Tirole, 1992). The mixed strategy equilibrium of the game portrayed in Figure 5 involves each employee opting out of the tournament with probability .56.

O'Keefe, Viscusi, and Zeckhauser (1984) show that for risk neutral contestants, an employer can ensure that employees exert the efficient amount of effort and that the global constraints are satisfied by simultaneously manipulating the precision by which an employer monitors (supervises) employees and the size of the reward spread.

Tournaments with N homogeneous contestants. In the discussion of tournaments with N contestants, first assume that all contestants are risk neutral. Assume also that there is only one winner who receives W and that all the losers receive w. Since increasing the level of effort from the Nash equilibrium level increases the probability of winning the tournament by a smaller amount when there are more contestants, the optimal spread between W and w increases as N increases. This theory then predicts that as the number

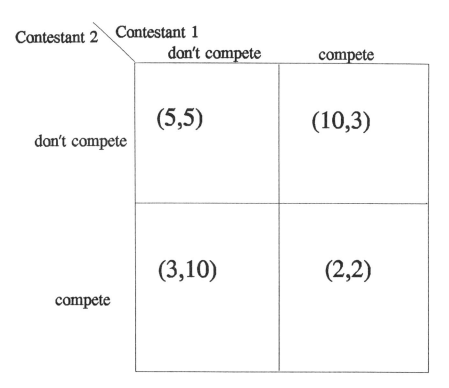

Figure 5.

of vice presidents vying for the chief executive officer (CEO) position increases, the spread of the compensation between the CEO and vice presidents increases. Another interesting feature of the equilibrium is that the optimal effort level is independent of the number of contestants. However, as the number of contestants increases it is more likely that the equilibrium fails to satisfy the global conditions which prevent individuals from opting out of the tournament.

So far we have assumed that there is only one winner. O'Keefe, Viscusi, and Zeckhauser (1984) show that instead of increasing the prize spread, the firm could increase the fraction of winners as the number of contestants increase.

The results that we have described for N contestant tournaments with risk neutral contestants do not generalize to situations with risk averse contestants. If individuals, are risk averse, then the optimal amount of effort is no longer independent of N. Moreover, the optimal spread size will not increase with N. To the contrary, the optimal spread size decreases to 0 as the number of contestants approaches infinity.

Unfair and heterogeneous contestant tournaments. Tournaments may be unfair in the sense that one contestant has a higher probability of winning the contest when both put forth the same amount of effort. This may occur, for example, when there is discrimination, affirmative action, or nepotism (O'Keefe, Viscusi, & Zeckhauser, 1984). If employees are risk neutral, it may still be possible to give them the marginal incentives to achieve the first best level of effort. However, in an unfair tournament disadvantaged employees have greater incentives to opt out of the tournament and collect the bottom prize than in a fair tournament. So, an employer may have to increase the compensation spread between winners and losers and decrease the precision of monitoring to prevent such behavior from occurring. Moreover, unless the disadvantaged employee faces similar disadvantages in alternative employment opportunities, an employer will have to raise the loser's prize w in order to attract disadvantaged contestants to their firm.

In tournaments with unequal or heterogeneous contestants, one employee has an advantage because of her lower marginal costs of effort. If both the employer and employees are, ex ante, ignorant of who possesses the advantage, then tournaments similar to those described earlier for homogenous contestants can be used to elicit the appropriate amount of effort. On the other hand, if both the employer and the employees know, ex ante, who possesses the advantage, then the appropriate incentives can be preserved by handicapping the more able employee. However, in order to attract the more able employee into the tournament, the employer may have to selectively offer them higher prize money for both winning and losing, or pay them a fixed entry fee (O'Keefe, Viscusi, & Zeckhauser, 1984). Alternatively, the employer may segregate employees of different abilities into different tournaments (e.g., "fast track" versus "slow track" careers).

When only the employee knows his own ability it is still possible for a firm to construct tournaments so that employees perform appropriately. This is accomplished by having multiple tournaments with different reward structures (and monitoring precision) that are structured in such a way that employees of different abilities self-select into the different tournaments (O'Keefe, Viscusi, & Zeckhauser, 1984; Bhattacharya & Guasch, 1988). The problem is that in tournaments designed for high ability employees, low ability "climbers" may infiltrate while in tournaments designed for low ability employees, high ability "slummers" may wish to enter. When employees are risk neutral, both climbing and slumming can be prevented and efficient levels of effort maintained by increasing the compensation spread between winners and losers and reducing the precision of supervision in the high ability tournament while simultaneously decreasing the spread between winners and losers and increasing the precision of supervision in the low ability tournament relative to the optimal levels under full information. Reducing the loser's compensation in the high ability tournament makes it unattractive to low ability employees since they are less likely to win and lowering the winner's compensation in the low ability tournament makes it less desirable to high ability employees who are more likely to win.

Elimination tournaments.   Rosen (1986) has shown that in a sequence of elimination tournaments the spread in rewards between winners and losers must increase as the tournament moves to its latter stages. In the early stages of an elimination tournament, part of the reward for winning is the option to continue to the next stage of the tournament. As the tournament progresses, the number of remaining stages and, hence, the value of the option to continue in the tournament, dwindles. Consequently, the spread must increase to maintain performance incentives. This model may help explain why the difference in compensation between the top executive and the second tier of executives in a company may be considerably larger than the difference in compensation between second- and third-tier executives.

Sabotage, collusion, and other issues in tournament theory.   Tournament theory assumes contestants compete by raising their own output. However, as Lazear (1989a) has pointed out, an employee may be able to win a contest by lowering the output of others. Since the incentives for such sabotage increase with the difference in the prize spread between winners and losers, efficiency considerations may lead to some reduction in the prize spread. This theory predicts that greater pay compression and lower productivity will be observed, all else equal, in work environments that are either more conducive to sabotage or whose employees are less averse to sabotage ("sharks").

Large differences between the compensation of winners and losers also give employees incentives to engage in "politicking" (Milgrom, 1988). Thus, employees could spend considerable time and effort ingratiating themselves to their supervisors and/or trying to give the appearance of being highly productive when the spread of prizes is large.

Contestants might also find it mutually beneficial to collude (Dye, 1984). This problem can be especially acute when there are few contestants who work in close proximity to each other. In this situation, all contestants may agree to reduce their effort and share in the prize money. Since total compensation is, ex post, independent of employee performance, all employees can be made better off at the firm's expense.

Dye (1984) has pointed out that tournaments may encounter problems when some companies provide compensation using individual-based contracts. Consider the case with risk-neutral agents. In this case, both individual-based contracts and tournaments produce the efficient level of effort. In a market where some firms offer individual-based contracts, tournament losers may switch to these companies thereby mitigating their losses. This, in turn, would reduce the incentives to win and, hence, lower the effort of all contestants. This argument implicitly assumes a multi-period context. However, with multiple periods a firm can design a multi-period tournament. Moreover, in a multi-period context turnover may occur both in firms with individual based contracts and firms with tournament contracts if measurement errors are correlated across time within a firm. Finally, tournaments contracts can produce more effort than individual based contracts when the variance of the firm-specific error is large and individuals are risk averse.

Empirical and experimental evidence on tournaments.   Rosenbaum (1979) has perhaps the earliest empirical findings relating to tournament theory. Using longitudinal data from a single firm he found evidence of a double-elimination type of tournament. Employees promoted early seem to be put on a "fast track." Employees who are not promoted early, however, can still be promoted. Once promoted, though, their chances for further promotion remain lower than those who were promoted early. Further evidence of individuals being placed on either fast or slow promotion tracks has been found by Baker, Gibbs, and Holmstrom (1994b) who also analyzed personnel data from a single firm.

While these empirical findings are consistent with the economic theory of tournaments presented earlier, they are also consistent with a pure theory of sorting. Employers may not know the abilities of employees when they hire them. As this information is revealed over time employees are sorted into different promotion tracks. Baker, Gibbs, and Holmstrom (1994b) suggest these differential abilities may be the time it takes an employee to become successfully trained for the next job in the corporate hierarchy. Employees need not modify their effort in response to the compensation structure. In addition, employers could base promotions on a fixed standard (e.g., once they have been successfully trained) rather than on relative output.

Tournament theory predicts a convex salary structure with respect to level in the corporate hierarchy and, in particular, predicts high CEO pay. Tournament theory also predicts that the prize spread is an increasing function of the number of contestants. Thus, CEO's should be paid more if they come from a larger pool of vice presidents. Main, O'Reilly, and Wade (1993) found evidence that CEO compensation is an increasing function of the number of their vice presidents, and, holding average compensation constant, returns on a firm's assets are an increasing function of the coefficient of variation of the top executive team's pay. Both Lambert, Larcker, and Weigelt (1993) and Baker, Gibbs, and Holmstrom (1994a) found evidence of convex salary structures with respect to level in the corporate hierarchy. Models with increasing returns to talent in hierarchical production through positive externalities on subordinates, however, lead to similar predictions (Gibbs, 1994).

Using a sample of attorneys practicing in Minnesota, Hoenack and Kleiner (1994) found some evidence that non-partners bill more hours in law firms where the pay differential between non-partners and partners is large. Both tournament theory and (nonlinear) individual contracts based on a fixed promotion standard, however, predict that large compensation increases on promotion lead to greater employee effort.

Some tentative evidence reported in Gibbs (1994) suggests promotion slots are not fixed as postulated by tournament theory. In particular, Gibbs (1994) found that the rate of promotion into a particular job category does not correlate highly with the rate of exit from both turnover and promotions.

Because of the difficulty of empirically distinguishing predictions of tournament theory from competing economic theories using economic data, much of the empirical literature on tournaments has focused on sports tournaments. Using tournament data from both the American and European PGA tours, Ehrenberg and Bognanno (1990a, 1990b) found player performance varies positively with the total prize money awarded in the tournament and with the marginal return to effort in the final round of play. Using auto racing data, Becker and Huselid (1992) found evidence driver performance is positively affected by the prize spread. Further, they found some evidence that driver safety (as measured by the number of caution flags issued during a race) decreases for very large prize spreads.

Finally, in an experimental study of tournaments, Bull, Schotter, and Weigelt (1987) found the mean effort level of the subjects in a symmetric tournament converged toward its theoretical equilibrium level, on average, in an experiment with repeated play. However, even in the last round of play the variance in the effort levels across subject pairs continued to be large and was substantially greater than the variance in effort levels in the last round of a comparable piece rate experiment. This may have to do with the additional complexity of "solving" a tournament problem due to its game structure. In asymmetric tournaments, Bull, Schotter, and Weigelt (1987) found the effort level of the disadvantaged contestant consistently remained above the theoretical equilibrium level. One possible explanation for this finding is that in a tournament, a contestant's utility is not simply a function of the monetary reward and effort but also depends on winning or losing the contest. As noted by Bull, Schotter, and Weigelt (1987), this explanation fails to explain the fact that the advantaged contestants mean effort levels were not significantly different from those predicted by the theoretical equilibrium level. If the disadvantaged contestant increased his effort level, the favored contestant should have also responded by increasing his effort level.

138 JOHN A. FOSSUM and BRIAN P. McCALL

Conclusion

On their face, the topics in this chapter appear disparate, however, they all reflect relatively common themes. They examine how employee efforts are elicited in risky environments where employees are risk averse, and where performance is measured imperfectly and/or unreliably. They also examine the tradeoffs employers confront in eliciting effort and performance from employees.

All of the psychological and economic theories are based on the proposition that individuals pursue their interests. Employment arrangements are structured in ways to link reward attainment with positive employer outcomes. Contractual problems or "action-outcome" difficulties are endemic as recognized by theories of employee justice perceptions and moral hazards, shirking, and sabotage in the various economic theories.

Psychological theories have been particularly helpful in designing pay programs that link rewards with specific behaviors and outputs. They are also helpful in designing work so that stronger action-outcome linkages are established. On the other hand, psychological theories have almost completely ignored the motives of the employer, and have generally operated on the assumption that the employee wants to be productive. Agency, tournament, and efficiency wage theories explicitly deal with the employer's economic interests in productivity, the costs and tradeoffs associated with eliciting performance, and both parties' shifting interests in the form of the employment contract.

The globalization of many segments of the economy has increased risk levels for both employers and employees. Pay programs of the past were designed to reduce risks for employees who have accrued service with their employer and who have acquired specific human capital. There was substantial spillover in practices from collective bargaining agreements. Employees could reduce both pay and employment risks through increasing service and the employer's investment and encouragement in creating SHC-KSAs. Globalization changed the competitive enivronment and helped to reduce the effects of unionization and collective bargaining on compensation. Employers were able to decrease their employment risks by increasing the variability of both pay and employment to employees.

If the variability of employees' pay and employment both increase, one would expect employees would be less willing to invest in and acquire SHC-KSAs in the future. To the extent that the reduction of middle management by many employers requires more coordination and self-supervision to take place at previously nonmanagerial levels, the new production function is not strongly supported by pay-at-risk at the individual level unless other nonsupervisory monitoring mechanisms are feasible. In addition, the absence of an explicit promotion structure makes it more difficult to recognize and reward differences in the rate of skill acquisition and performance. This is probably why skill-based pay and broadbanding have been increasingly used in flatter organization. Without them, the chances of winning a "tournament prize" given the uncertainty in measurement and the dearth of promotional opportunities is too small. It's likely that some restoration of at least an implicit structure will need to take place unless organizational change continues to accelerate. If that occurs, perhaps organizations will require frequent renegotiations of individual employment agreements in the future.

The theory and research reported here emphasizes the variety of employment conditions within which employers must make choices. It also demonstrates, implicitly, the agency problems that exist in designing and implementing these structures, since in most organizations, it is the agents of the agents who are designing the agents compensation program, only loosely supervised by the principals. For both principals and agents, information from theory and research can help to inform whether the reward system is correctly aligned with the outputs necessary given the production process the organization has adopted.

REFERENCES

Abowd, J.M. (1990). Does performance-based managerial compensation affect corporate performance? *Industrial and Labor Relations Review, 43* (3), S52-S73.

Adams, J.S. (1963). Toward an understanding of inequity. *Journal of Abnormal Psychology, 67*, 422-436.

————. (1965). Inequity in social exchange. In L. Berkowitz (Ed.), *Advances in experimental social psychology* (volume 2). New York: Academic Press.

Allison, D.B., Silverstein, J.M., & Gallante, V. (1992). Relative effectiveness and cost-effectiveness of cooperative, competitive, and independent monetary incentive systems. *Journal of Organizational Behavior Management, 13*, 85-112.

Arai, M. (1994). Compensating wage differentials versus efficiency wages: An empirical study of job autonomy and wages. *Industrial Relations, 33*, 249-262.

Baker, G. (1992). Incentives contracts and performance measurement. *Journal of Political Economy, 100*, 598-614.

Baker, G., Gibbs, M., & Holmstrom, B. (1994a). The internal economics of the firm: evidence from personnel data. *Quarterly Journal of Economics, 109*, 881-919.

————. (1994b). The wage policy of a firm. *Quarterly Journal of Economics, 109*, 921-955.

Bartol, K.M., & Martin, D.C. (1989). Effects of dependence, dependency threats, and pay secrecy on management pay allocations. *Journal of Applied Psychology, 74*, 105-113.

Becker, B.E., & Huselid, M.A. (1992). The incentive effects of tournament compensation systems. *Administrative Science Quarterly, 37*, 336-350.

Bhattacharya, S., & Guasch, J.L. (1988). Heterogeneity, tournaments, and hierarchies. *Journal of Political Economy, 96*, 867-881.

Brown, C. (1990). Firms' choice of method of pay. *Industrial and Labor Relations Review, 43* (3), S165-S182.

Brown, K.A., & Huber, V.A. (1992). Lowering floors and raising ceilings: A longitudinal assessment of the effects of an earnings-at-risk plan on pay satisfaction. *Personnel Psychology, 45*, 279-311.

Bull, C., Schotter, A., & Weigelt, K. (1987). Tournaments and piece rates: An experimental study. *Journal of Political Economy, 95*, 1-33.

Cappelli, P., & Cascio, W. (1991). Why some jobs command wage premiums: A test of career tournament and internal labor market. *Academy of Management Journal, 34*, 840-868.

Cappelli, P., & Chauvin. K. (1991). An interplant test of the efficiency wage hypothesis. *Quarterly Journal of Economics, 106*, 769-787.

Chelius, J., & Smith, R. S. (1990). Profit-sharing and employment stability. *Industrial and Labor Relations Review, 43* (3), S256-S273.

Conlon, E.J., & Parks, J.M. (1990). Effects of monitoring and tradition on compensation arrangements: An experiment with principal-agent dyads. *Academy of Management Journal, 33*, 603-622.

Coughlan, A.T., & Narasimhan, C. (1993). An empirical analysis of sales-force compensation plans. *Journal of Business, 65*, 93-121.

Cowherd, D.M., & Levine, D.I. (1992). Product quality and pay equity between lower-level employees and top management. *Administrative Science Quarterly, 37*, 302-320.

Cravens, D.W., Ingram, T.N., LaForge, R.W., & Young, C.E. (1993). Behavior-based and outcome-based salesforce control systems. *Journal of Marketing, 57* (4), 47-59.

Deshpande, S.P., & Joseph, J. (1994). Variation in compensation decisions by managers: An empirical investigation. *Journal of Psychology, 128*, 41-50.

Deshpande, S.P., & Schoderbek, P.P. (1993). Pay allocations by managers: A policy capturing approach. *Human Relations, 46*, 465-479.

Devine, T., & Kiefer, N. (1991). *Empirical labor economics: The search approach.* New York: Oxford University Press.

Dickinson, A.M., & Gillette, K.L. (1993). A comparison of the effect of two individual monetary incentive systems on productivity: Piece rate vs. base pay plus incentive. *Journal of Organizational Behavior Management, 14*, 3-28.

Dye, R. (1984). The trouble with tournaments. *Economic Inquiry, 22*, 147-149.

Eaton, C., & White, W. (1983). The economy of high wages: An agency problem. *Economica, 50*, 175-181.

Ehrenberg, R., & Bognanno, M. (1990a). The incentive effects of tournaments revisited: Evidence from the European PGA tour. *Industrial and Labor Relations Review, 43*, 74S-88S.

———— . (1990b). Do tournaments have incentive effects? *Journal of Political Economy, 98*, 1307-1324.

Ehrenberg, R.G., & Milkovich, G.T. (1987). Compensation and firm performance. In M.M. Kleiner, R.N. Block, M. Roomkin, & S.W. Salsburg (Eds.), *Human resources and the performance of the firm* (pp. 87-122). Madison, WI: Industrial Relations Research Association.

Eisenhardt, K.M. (1988). Agency- and institutional-theory explanations: The case of retail sales compensation. *Academy of Management Journal, 31*, 488-511.

Fama, E.F., & Jensen, M.C. (1983). Separation of ownership and control. *Journal of Law and Economics, 26*, 301-325.

Folger, R., & Konovsky, M.A. (1989). Effects of procedural and distributive justice on reactions to pay raise decisions. *Academy of Management Journal, 32*, 115-130.

Fossum, J.A., & Fitch, M.K. (1985). The effects of individual and contextual attributes on the sizes of recommended salary increases. *Personnel Psychology, 38*, 587-603.

Fox, J.B., Scott, K.D., & Donohue, J.M. (1993). An investigation into pay valence and performance in a pay-for-performance field setting. *Journal of Organizational Behavior, 14*, 687-693.

Freedman, J., Cunningham, J.A., & Krismer, K. (1992). Inferred values and the reverse-incentive effect in induced compliance. *Journal of Personality and Social Psychology, 62*, 357-368.

Frisch, C.J., & Dickinson, A.M. (1990). Work productivity as a function of the percentage of monetary incentives to base pay. *Journal of Organizational Behavior Management, 11*, 13-33.

Fudenberg, D., & Tirole, J. (1992). *Game theory.* Cambridge, MA: MIT Press.

Garvey, G.T., & Swan, P.L. (1992). Managerial objectives, capital structure, and the provision of incentives. *Journal of Labor Economics, 10,* 357-379.

George, J.M., Brief, A.P., & Webster, J. (1991). Organizationally intended and unintended coping: The case of an incentive compensation plan. *Journal of Occupational Psychology, 64,* 193-205.

Gerhart, B., & Milkovich, G.T. (1990). Organizational differences in managerial compensation and financial performance. *Academy of Management Journal, 33,* 663-691.

————. (1992). Employee compensation: Research and practice. In M.D. Dunnette & L.M. Hough (Eds.), *Handbook of industrial and organizational psychology* (2nd ed.) (volume 3, pp. 481-569). Palo Alto, CA: Consulting Psychologists Press.

Gerhart, B., Milkovich, G.T., & Murray, B. (1992). Pay, performance, and participation. In D. Lewin, O.S. Mitchell, & P.D. Sherer (Eds.), *Research frontiers in industrial relations and human resources* (pp. 193-238). Madison, WI: Industrial Relations Research Association.

Gibbs, M. (1994). Testing tournaments? An appraisal of the theory and evidence. *Labor Law Journal, 45,* 493-500.

Gomez-Mejia, L.R., & Balkin, D.B. (1992). *Compensation, organizational strategy, and firm performance.* Cincinnati: South-Western.

Green, J., & Stokey, N. (1983). A comparison of tournaments and contracts. *Journal of Political Economy, 91,* 349-364.

Groshen, E., & Krueger, A. (1990). The structure of supervision and pay in hospitals. *Industrial and Labor Relations Review, 43,* 134S-146S.

Hamel, G., & Prahalad, C.K. (1990). The core competence of the organization. *Harvard Business Review, 68* (3), 79-91.

Haubrich, J.G. (1994). Risk aversion, performance pay, and the principal-agent problem. *Journal of Political Economy, 102,* 258-276.

Heneman, H.G., III, & Schwab, D.P. (1979). Work and rewards theory. In D. Yoder & H.G. Heneman, Jr. (Eds.), *ASPA handbook of personnel and industrial relations.* Washington: Bureau of National Affairs.

Heneman, H.G., III (1985). Pay satisfaction. In K. Rowland & G. Ferris (Eds.), *Research in personnel and human resource management* (volume 3, pp. 115-139). Greenwich, CT: JAI Press.

Heneman, R.L. (1990). Merit pay research. In K. Rowland & G. Ferris (Eds.), *Research in personnel and human resource management* (volume 8, pp. 203-263. Greenwich, CT: JAI Press.

Henry, R.A. (1994). The effect of choice and incentive on the overestimation of future performance. *Organizational Behavior and Human Decision Processes, 57,* 210-225.

Hoenack, S., & Kleiner, M. (1994). Are tournaments really optimal contracts? Mimeo, University of Minnesota.

Holzer, H.J. (1990). Wages, employer costs, and employee performance in the firm. *Industrial and Labor Relations Review, 43* (3), S147-S164.

Hoskisson, R.E., Hitt, M.A., & Hill, C.W.L. (1993). Managerial incentives and investment in R&D in large multiproduct firms. *Organizational Science, 4,* 325-341.

Huber, V.A., Seybolt, P.M., & Venemon, K. (1992). The relationship between individual inputs, perceptions, and multidimensional pay satisfaction. *Journal of Applied Social Psychology, 22,* 1356-1373.

Jacobs, D. (1981). Toward a theory of mobility and behavior in organizations: An inquiry into the consequences of some relationships between individual performance and organizational success, *American Journal of Sociology, 87,* 684-707.

Jensen, M.C., & Murphy, K.J. (1990). Performance pay and top-management incentives. *Journal of Political Economy, 98,* 225-264.

Kahn, L.M., & Sherer, P.D. (1990). Contingent pay and managerial performance. *Industrial and Labor Relations Review, 43* (3), S107-S120.

Katz, L. (1986). Efficiency wage theories: A partial evaluation. In *National bureau of economics macroeconomics annual*. Cambridge, MA: MIT Press.

Kennedy, C.W., Fossum, J.A., & White, B.J. (1983). An empirical comparison of within-subjects and between-subjects expectancy theory models. *Organizational Behavior and Human Performance, 32*, 124-143.

Koys, D.J., Keaveny, T.J., & Allen, R.E. (1989). Employee demographics and attitudes that predict preferences for alternative pay increase policies. *Journal of Business and Psychology, 4*, 27-47.

Krueger, A. (1991). Ownership, agency, and wages: An examination of franchising in the fast food industry. *Quarterly Journal of Economics, 106*, 75-101.

Krueger, A., & Summers, L. (1988). Efficiency wages and inter-industry wage structure. *Econometrica, 56*, 259-294.

Lambert, R., Larcker, D., & Weigelt, K. (1993). The structure of organizational incentives. *Administrative Science Quarterly, 38*, 438-461.

Lawler, E.E., III, & Ledford, G.E. (1985). Skill-based pay: A concept that's catching on. *Personnel, 62* (9), 30-37.

Lazear, E.P. (1989a). Pay equality and industrial politics. *Journal of Political Economy, 97*, 561-580.

_____ . (1989b). Pensions and deferred benefits as strategic compensation. *Industrial Relations, 29*, 263-280.

_____ . (1992). Compensation, productivity, and the new economics of personnel. In D. Lewin, O.S. Mitchell, & P.D. Sherer (Eds.), *Research frontiers in industrial relations and human resources* (pp. 341-380). Madison, WI: Industrial Relations Research Association.

Lazear, E.P., & Rosen, S. (1981). Rank order tournaments as an optimum labor contract. *Journal of Political Economy, 89*, 841-864.

Leonard, J.S. (1990). Executive pay and firm performance. *Industrial and Labor Relations Review, 43* (3), S13-S29.

Main, B., O'Reilly, C., & Wade, J. (1993). Top executive pay: Tournament or teamwork. *Journal of Labor Economics, 11*, 606-628.

McLaughlin, K. (1988). Aspects of tournament models: A survey. In R. Ehreberg (Ed.), *Research in labor economics* (volume 9, pp. 225-256). Greenwich, CT: JAI Press.

Milgrom, P. (1988). Employment contracts, influence activities, and efficient organization design. *Journal of Political Economy, 96*, 42-60.

Milgrom, P.R., & Roberts, J. (1992). *Economics, organization and management*. Englewood Cliffs, NJ: Prentice-Hall.

Milkovich, G.T., & Wigdor, A.K. (1991). *Pay for performance*. Washington, DC: National Academy Press.

Mitchell, D.J.B., Lewin, D., & Lawler, E.E., III (1990). Alternative pay systems, firm performance, and productivity. In A.S. Blinder (Ed.), *Paying for productivity: A look at the evidence* (pp. 15-88). Washington, DC: Brookings Institution.

Montgomery, E., & Stockton, D. (1994). Evidence on the causes of the rising dispersion of relative wages. *Industrial Relations, 33*, 206-228.

Morishima, M. (1992). Japanese employee attitudes toward changes in traditional employment practices. *Industrial Relations, 31*, 433-454.

Nalebuff, B., & Stiglitz, J. (1984). Prizes and incentives: Toward a general theory of compensation and competition. *Bell Journal of Economics, 15*, 21-43.

O'Keefe, M., Viscusi, W.K., & Zeckhauser, R. (1984). Economic contests: Comparative reward structures. *Journal of Labor Economics, 2*, 27-56.

Park, H. Y., Ofori-Dankwa, J., & Bishop, D.R. (1994). Organizational and environmental determinants of functional and dysfunctional turnover: Practice and research implications. *Human Relations, 47*, 353-366.

Parsons, D. (1986). The employment relationship: Job attachment, work effort, and the nature of contracts. In O. Ashenfelter & R. Layard (Eds.), *Handbook of labor economics* (volume 2). Amsterdam: Elsevier Science Publishers.

Pfeffer, J. (1994). *Competitive advantage through people: Unlocking the power of the work force.* Boston: Harvard Business School Press.

Porter, L.W., & Lawler, E.E., III (1968). *Managerial attitudes and performance.* Homewood, IL: Dorsey Press.

Raff, D., & Summers, L. (1987). Did Henry Ford pay efficiency wages? *Journal of Labor Economics, 5,* S57-S85.

Rosen, S. (1986). Prizes and incentives in elimination tournaments. *American Economic Review, 76,* 701-715.

Rosenbaum, J. (1979). Tournament mobility: career patterns in a corporation. *Administrative Science Quarterly, 24,* 220-241.

Rusbult, C., Campbell, S.A., & Price, M.E. (1990). Rational selection exploitation and distress: Employee reactions to performance-based and mobility-based reward allocations. *Journal of Personality and Social Psychology, 59,* 487-500.

Salop, S. (1979). A model of the natural rate of unemployment. *American Economic Review, 69,* 117-125.

Santora, J.E. (1991). DuPont returns to the drawing board. *Personnel Journal, 70* (2), 34-36.

Schlicht, E. (1978). Labor turnover, wage structure, and natural unemployment. *Zetschrift fur die Gesamte Staatswissenschaft, 134,* 337-346.

Schoderbek, P.P., & Deshpande, S.P. (1993). Performance and nonperformance factors in pay allocations made by managers. *Journal of Psychology, 127,* 391-397.

Schwab, D.P., & Olson, C.A. (1990). Merit pay practices: Implications for pay-performance relationships. *Industrial and Labor Relations Review, 43* (3), S237-S255.

Shapiro, C., & Stiglitz, J.E. (1984). Equilibrium unemployment as a worker discipline device. *American Economic Review, 74,* 433-444.

Stiglitz, J. (1974). Alternative theories of wage determination and unemployment in LDC's: The labor turnover model. *Quarterly Journal of Economics, 88,* 194-227.

Svortdal, F. (1993). Working harder for less: Effects of incentive value on force of instrumental response in humans. *Quarterly Journal of Experimental Psychology: Human Experimental Psychology, 46A,* 11-34.

Turban, D.B., & Keon, T.L. (1993). Organizational attractiveness: An interactionist perspective. *Journal of Applied Psychology, 78,* 184-193.

Vroom, V.H. (1964). *Work and motivation.* New York: Wiley.

Weiss, A. (1990). *Efficiency wage: Models of unemployment, layoffs, and wage dispersion.* Princeton, NJ: Princeton University Press.

Weitzman, M.L. (1987). Steady state employment under profit sharing. *Economic Journal, 97,* 86-105.

Wicker, F.W., Brown, G., Wiehe, J.A., & Hagen, A.S. (1991). Differential correlations of positively-based and negatively-based incentives in motivation. *Journal of Psychology, 125,* 567-578.

Williams, C.R., & Livingstone, L.P. (1994). Another look at the relationship between performance and voluntary turnover. *Academy of Management Journal, 37,* 269-298.

Wright, P.M. (1992). An examination of the relationship among monetary incentives, goal level, goal commitment, and performance. *Journal of Management, 18,* 677-693.

Zenger, T.R. (1992). Why do employers only reward extreme performance? Examining the relationships among performance, pay, and turnover. *Administrative Science Quarterly, 37,* 198-219.

NON-WAGE COMPENSATION

Renae Broderick and Barry Gerhart

Non-wage compensation. Fringe benefits. Benefits. Innocuous, even benign words that in the United States of the 1990s provoke visions of out-of-control costs, diminished quality of life, and administrative quagmires for individuals, employers, and policymakers at all levels of organization and government. Recently, the national focus has been on health benefits and ways to control medical costs. However, the cost of all benefits has increased significantly, making cost control a major concern for most employers. Between 1950 and 1993 the United States Chamber of Congress reported that employee benefit costs rose from about 20 to 41 percent of employer payroll costs. Today, not only costs, but all aspects of non-wage compensation are being reexamined as employers rethink the employment relationship (Dyer & Blancero, 1992), as increasing proportions of the labor force are employed in the small business or contract sectors that have not been major benefit providers (Employee Benefit Research Institute, 1994), and as changing demographics force changes in the implicit intergenerational contracts struck to finance Social Security and Medicare (Salisbury & Super Jones, 1994).

Comprehensive examination of all the issues and research on non-wage compensation is beyond the scope of this chapter. Instead, we examine non-wage compensation from the perspective of U.S. employers and human resource (HR) decision makers. This perspective narrows discussion to non-wage compensation that is part of an employer-employee relationship. The term "employee benefits" is hereafter used in place of "non-wage compensation"—compensation of the unemployed and the self-employed is not considered. National-level policy issues, such as benefit related tax incentives

145

for employers or individuals and mandated benefit coverage, are discussed only briefly. Likewise, there will be only minimal discussion of the globalization of business and its implications for employee benefits. The chapter does: (1) define what is meant by the term "employee benefits"; (2) discuss some reasons why employers offer employee benefits; (3) discuss major questions relevant to current employer restructuring of employee benefits; and (4) review major findings about employee benefits from research conducted at the firm level of analysis. The chapter concludes with suggestions about research and policy directions of concern to HR scholars and professionals.

DEFINING EMPLOYEE BENEFITS

A leading compensation text defines employee benefits as that

> part of the total compensation package, other than pay for time worked, provided to employees in whole or in part by employer payments (e.g., life insurance, pension, workers' compensation...(Milkovich & Newman, 1993, p. 396)).

Many standard textbooks on employee benefits (Employee Benefit Research Institute, 1990; Beam & McFadden, 1992; Rosenblum & Hallman, 1991) list six major categories of benefit forms. These range from mandated or legally required social insurance programs, such as social security and workers' compensation, to voluntarily provided benefits such as car pools or health clubs. Table 1 illustrates a typical list of categories and benefit forms. Clearly, the potential scope of benefits goes far beyond the occasional paid holiday.

No Standard Employee Benefit Package

Despite standard textbook lists of benefits, however, U.S. employers offer no standard benefit package. Currently, U.S. employers are not required to provide any benefits to temporary or contract workers.[1] Many employers, especially small business owners, provide full-time workers with only the legally required social insurance benefits along with perhaps a holiday bonus and limited paid time off. For example, the Bureau of Labor Statistics reports that among the 32 million employees working full time in small businesses (fewer than 100 employees) in 1991, only 69 percent had any medical coverage and only 42 percent had pension coverage. This is in contrast to the 92 percent of full-time workers in large or medium-size firms who had medical coverage and the 81 percent who had pension coverage in the same year.

There is also considerable variance in benefit packages among employers who offer a full range of employee benefits. For example, for retirement plans some employers offer defined benefit pension plans, others offer defined

Table 1. Major Employee Benefit Categories and Forms

Legally Required Social Insurance Programs	Extra Cash Payments
Social Security	Educational allowances
Unemployment Compensation	Moving expenses
Workers' Compensation	Savings plans
Non Occupational Disability Insurance	Holiday bonuses
	Meal expenses
Private Insurance and Retirement Plans	**Employee Services**
Life insurance	Subsidized cafeterias
Disability insurance	Recreation facilities
Medical insurance	Clothing allowances
Dental insurance	Car or van pools
Legal insurance	Retirement counseling
Property and liability insurance	Wellness programs
Auto insurance	Day care referral, centers
Defined benefit pension plans	
Defined contribution pension plans	
Payments for Time Not Worked	**Perquisites**
Vacations and holidays	Employment contracts
Sick leave/personal leave	Liberal vacation time
Jury duty	More disability insurance
Rest periods	Personal liability insurance
Sabbatical leaves	Outplacement assistance
Military duty	Company car and driver
	Company airplane, yacht
	Executive home allowance
	Tax and financial counsel

contribution plans, and still others combine the two.[2] Even among employers who offer the same form of pension plan, there can be variations in plan financing, employer contributions to the plan, and plan administration. Benefit packages can also vary in the degree of choice employees have about the benefits they will get and the levels of coverage they will receive. For example, some employers offer the same mix of benefits to all employees, while others use a flexible or "cafeteria" approach that allows employees to structure their own mix of benefits within a framework of options. In addition, though restricted in their offerings by benefit regulations, some employers provide highly paid and critical employees, such as executives, benefits that other employees do not receive.

Thus, it is not only difficult to find standard benefit packages across employers, but even nominally identical packages may vary in terms of their financing, the employer's versus the employee's contributions to them, the levels of coverage they offer employees, and the ways in which they are administered. This situation makes competitive market comparisons and comparative research on employee benefits difficult.

WHY EMPLOYERS OFFER EMPLOYEE BENEFITS

It is clear that the direct and indirect costs of employee benefits are a significant part of total labor costs. It is less clear that benefit costs are offset by the contributions that benefits make to helping employers meet compensation objectives, such as controlling labor costs and attracting and retaining productive employees. Thus it seems reasonable to ask, "why do employers voluntarily offer benefits at all?" This section covers some background rationale, theory, and history on why employers offer employee benefits.[3]

Economic theory suggests that employers should be indifferent about whether they spend $1,000 dollars on wages and salaries or $1,000 on benefits if administrative costs are equal. That is, the composition of total compensation is not an issue, but the level is. Likewise, all else equal, employees should prefer $1,000 in cash to $1,000 in benefits. In comparison to benefits, cash gives employees more discretion in spending. However, employers become less indifferent and employees change their preferences when benefit dollars become worth more or less than cash dollars. For example, in the case of medical insurance, employers with large workforces can buy coverage at rates lower than employees would have to pay as individuals for the same coverage. At the same time, U.S. tax laws make it possible for employers to avoid payroll taxes on the dollars spent on medical insurance, thus making these dollars worth more to employers than dollars spent on wages and salaries. Employees can also avoid adding the dollars spent on medical insurance to their own incomes, thus reducing their income taxes. This is one example among many, but in most cases it is the combination of economies of scale in employers' purchasing power and tax incentives for both employers and employees that might be expected to persuade both groups to trade off some cash for benefits. However, it is important to remember that employers' use of tax incentives is partially offset by the costs of benefit administration and compliance with government benefit regulations.

Theories of internal labor markets in economics and organizational sociology can also provide some insight into why employers offer benefits to employees.[4] Relevant economic theories focus on the development of internal labor markets as efficient means of dealing with market competition in the face of uncertainties posed by workers, jobs, or technology. As applied to employee compensation and benefits, these economic theories suggest that employers with well-developed or "closed" internal labor markets will design compensation so that employees view their pay as part of an implicit long-term contract or career with the organization (Ehrenberg & Smith, 1988; Lewin & Mitchell, 1994). For example, traditional merit increase plans are most valuable if combined with promotions and extended over an employee's career (Milkovich, Wigdor, Broderick, & Mavor, 1991). Pensions also take time to vest, and employer contributions to pensions tend to increase with an employee's tenure (Salisbury

& Super Jones, 1994). Employers who use base pay and benefits that reward career employees provide an incentive for employees to stay with the organization and to perform reasonably well over time. Both employee retention and performance are important to employers who have closed internal labor markets and fill most jobs through internal promotions.

Complementing the market efficiency rationale for the development of internal labor markets, organizational sociologists propose that the ways in which conflicts over power and influence are resolved, both within the organization and in its environment, contribute to the development of specific types of organizational structures, including internal labor market structures (Pfeffer, 1982). In application to employee benefits, these sociological theories suggest that, over time, employer benefit practices have developed as a response to a host of factors: government mandates and regulations, union demands, employee job satisfaction, and labor market competition. However, these theories also suggest that such benefit practices become permanent or institutionalized because, in the absence of compelling information linking benefit practices to organizational outcomes, employers believe that they must maintain benefits in order to be viewed as legitimate by their employees and society at large. A recent empirical study of employer adoption of benefits, such as child care services and flex-time (Goodstein, 1994), suggests that employers do adopt benefits in response to social pressures and to garner a reputation for good work-family practices, especially if benefit adoption is not seen as "overly costly."

The literature in organizational psychology and human resource (HR) management takes a more prescriptive, systems-oriented view of employer decisions about the mix of benefits and cash in a firm. In a systems view of organizations, human resource management programs are ideally designed and implemented to support an organization's overall mission or business strategy (Milkovich & Mahoney, 1976; Lawler, 1981; Fombrun, Tichy, & Devanna, 1984; Dyer & Holder, 1988). In this context, benefit decisions should be consistent with other compensation decisions and with the strategic mission of the organization.

In one application of the systems view to benefit decisions, researchers have proposed that the organization's growth or life cycle stage and its business strategy dictate the organization's ability to pay and thus the level of benefits offered (Broderick, 1987; Carroll, 1987; Lawler, 1990; Gomez-Mejia & Balkin, 1992). For example, in a business that is just getting started, the employer cannot afford a broad benefit package. Moreover, the employer cannot yet offer employees a career and thus has little incentive to provide benefits, such as pensions, to retain employees. Also, if the employer's primary business objective is growth, a compensation strategy that helps attract and retain employees who are risk seekers and innovative problem solvers may be most appropriate. The HR management literature suggests that such a compensation strategy allocates a high proportion of total compensation dollars to incentives that offer large monetary rewards for future performance (Ellig, 1981; Balkin & Gomez-Mejia, 1984; Carroll, 1987). When higher proportions of total compensation are allocated to benefits, the organization tends to attract and retain employees who are more risk averse and interested in predictable job demands and job security.

Also consistent with the systems view, leading compensation texts emphasize that all compensation decisions, including those about benefits, must be viewed as part of a total compensation package that supports organizational objectives (Milkovich & Newman, 1993; Hills, Bergmann, & Scarpello, 1993; Lawler, 1990). Typically, an employer's objectives for total compensation are efficiency, equity, and compliance. The efficiency objective includes controlling labor costs and attracting and retaining the kinds of employees who increase quality, customer service, productivity, and innovation as dictated by organizational strategies. To meet equity objectives it is important for employees to view their total compensation as fair in its recognition of their contributions to the organization and in its design and administration. Employers also want their total compensation plans to comply with federal and state regulations concerning pay.

The history of employer use of employee benefits is consistent with many of the theoretical rationales described earlier. In the early 1900s social reformers and writers awakened the general public to exploitative, dangerous conditions for workers in many U.S. factories and workshops. Employers saw benefits as a way of generating public good will, improving the well-being of their employees, and improving employee productivity and loyalty. The resulting welfare programs included improvements to facilities (better lighting, ventilation, etc.), subsidized food programs, and educational programs to help immigrants learn to read and write English. Following the Great Depression, the period of the New Deal saw legislation mandating social security, unemployment and workers' compensation programs. During World War II national wage and price controls, combined with labor market shortages, resulted in many employers using benefits as a means of attracting and retaining employees. Once wage and price controls were lifted, most employers appeared loathe to remove established benefit packages. In addition, unions, in the past and today, negotiate for benefits as a way of providing value to their memberships despite wage and salary constraints. Many unionized employers offer similar benefits to their nonunionized employees as a means of promoting equity and avoiding further unionization. Employers with no union representation often do likewise for the same reasons.

With regard to applications of the systems view of organizations to benefit decisions, there is little clear evidence. Anecdotes and surveys of benefits show that organizations with fewer employees offer fewer benefits. Although this is consistent with a life cycle view of benefits in organizations, there is little documentation of the growth or life cycle stages these organizations represent.

Prescriptions for making benefit decisions within the framework of total compensation objectives have entered the professional management literature, yet few employers integrate the administration of wages and salaries with benefits. There are practical reasons for this lack of integration. One reason is that in many organizations the responsibility for administering wages and salaries versus benefits has traditionally been held by different staffs. Another reason may be that benefits are much more difficult to survey and compare across organizations than is cash compensation. Many major compensation and benefit consultants are now trying to establish comprehensive, total compensation survey databases, but these efforts are still in their infancy.

Despite its lack of documentation in practice, the systems view of why employers offer benefits does significantly supplement economic and sociological rationales. The systems view assumes that employers make benefit decisions based not primarily on employer indifference to the composition of the wage package, or in response to government regulation or social mores, but on strategic, business, and people management issues within the firm. HR professionals and scholars are recognizing that benefit management will be improved by a better understanding of the impact of benefits on an organization's strategic and total compensation objectives.

MAJOR QUESTIONS IN RESTRUCTURING EMPLOYEE BENEFITS

The controversies surrounding health care reform and especially the employer role in such reform have been prominent in recent media coverage of politics and business in the United States. Most major employers also realize that as discussion of health care reform continues, issues related to retiree medical care and to Social Security, Medicare, and private pension systems will inevitably arise (American Compensation Association, 1994; Salisbury & Super Jones, 1994). The result is considerable uncertainty about the employer's role in the provision of benefits, and thus the need for a more strategic outlook on benefits. At the same time, the more pressing questions for employers over the next few years center on the management of their present employee benefit costs. A 1994 poll of 192 employer members of the American Compensation Association reports that a top priority in benefit management is the control of direct and administrative costs, particularly health care costs (Bennett, 1994).

This section briefly examines some of the more strategic and a few of the operational or tactical questions employers must answer in restructuring their benefit plans.

Strategic Questions in Benefit Planning

The primary question employers need to answer in their strategic benefit planning is, "What role will we play in providing employee benefits?" In order to answer this question, employers and human resource managers are reexamining their benefit mission or philosophy. In the past, if a benefit philosophy was spelled out at all, it looked something like this:

> To provide employee benefits to meet employee needs for leisure time, protection against the risks of old age, loss of health, and loss of life. To provide these benefits on a noncontributory basis, except benefits for dependent coverage for which the employee should pay a portion of the cost. (Beam & McFadden, 1992, pp. 462-463).

This "paternalistic" philosophy has been typical of many *Fortune* 500 companies, perhaps a holdover from the welfare philosophy of the early 1900s. Among organizations considered to have some of the best HR practices, it was not uncommon to talk about a "cradle to grave" perspective on employee benefits (Morrison, 1994). Such a philosophy involves employers in making virtually all choices about benefits for employees. More recently, and in contrast, many employers are developing a "partnership" benefit philosophy. (Barton, 1994; Paul & Grant, 1993). A partnership philosophy might look like this:

> To develop a partnership with employees to share in their protection against catastrophic financial losses due to events such as illness, injury, and death, and to assist them in saving for their retirement years (Barocas, 1992, p. 12).

The logical extreme of this partnership philosophy might involve a complete shift from employer to employee in responsibility for benefit provision, that is, employers getting completely out of the benefit business. Obviously, many smaller employers have historically held this view of benefits. However, some larger employers who have consistently provided generous benefit packages to their employees are now voicing similar views (American Compensation Association, 1994).

Whether with strategic intent or not, many employers have already taken steps consistent with a shift to a partnership benefit philosophy. For example, there has been an increasing use of defined contribution pension plans over defined benefit plans for retirement benefits. Defined contribution plans place more responsibility on the employee to save and invest for retirement; they do not bind the employer to any specific retirement payout. As of 1993, the Internal Revenue Service reported that the number of participants (both workers and retirees) in 401k pension plans (the most common form of defined contribution plan) had doubled in the last decade. The total assets of defined benefit plans still exceed those of 401k plans, but the gap between the two has been narrowing rapidly since 1987.[5] Other concrete evidence of this shift is the increasing number of employers who require higher employee contributions to medical insurance plans. In the ACA 1994 poll of its members, over 80 percent reported that they already had or were planning to increase employees' share of health care insurance premiums.

These examples of shifting responsibility to employees deal with cost. What about the employers' responsibility for educating employees about benefits? One major finding of benefit research is that employees generally have a poor understanding of the value of their benefits and how to choose benefits cost effectively. If employers completely remove themselves from the business of benefits, neither paying for them nor educating employees about them, will this decision come back to haunt them in the form of higher benefit costs and potentially higher government mandated payroll taxes to fund health or pension reform? If employers stay in a benefit partnership, sharing the cost of benefits with employees and shouldering much of the responsibility for benefit education, what liabilities might they incur? There is a fine line between educating employees to make benefit choices that are cost effective for themselves, and educating them to make choices that favor an employer's cost control objectives. In some Western European countries, it is mandatory that employees be involved in decisions about employer-sponsored heath and retirement plans in order to avoid any such loss of individual rights. A middle ground between employees having no responsibility versus complete responsibility for benefit choices might constitute a transition period of employer education.

There are several other major strategic questions about benefits in the employer-employee relationship sketched below.

Benefits Linked to Performance

A 1993 Executive Roundtable sponsored by the American Compensation Association predicted that by the turn of the century most employee pay increases would be based on some combination of individual and company performance. Practice surveys continue to document an accelerating trend in the adoption of performance-based pay increases (Coopers and Lybrand, 1994; The Wyatt Company, 1994). Performance-based pay reflects a compensation philosophy of sharing the risks of organizational ownership between employers and employees. Should the employer contributions to employee benefits (especially medical benefits that are not currently linked to wage and salary levels) be renewable each year, contingent on some measure of employee or organizational performance? Although theories suggest that linking benefits and performance can influence employee or organizational performance there is little empirical research documenting this link. A policy of benefit contingency also runs the risk of violating implicit internal labor market contracts with potentially negative effects on employee retention, motivation, commitment, and employer-employee relations. Yet benefit contingency is consistent with a total compensation philosophy that stresses labor cost control and the sharing of risks and rewards and a benefit philosophy emphasizing a partnership between employer and employee.[6]

Benefits and Employment Stability

Some 94 percent of Americans have health insurance through their employer or a family member's employer. As Daniel Mitchell (1992) points out, there is an irony here. Benefits that are closely linked to specific employers encourage long-term employment relationships. Yet, the rates of employee mobility in the United States are high compared to those of other industrialized countries, suggesting that just the opposite sort of system is needed—one which reduces penalties (loss of medical coverage and reductions in retirement benefits) for changing employers. Or is the tight link between employment and health insurance just what is needed in the United States? Perhaps decoupling health insurance and employment would lead to even higher mobility in the context of the U.S. labor force. In their benefit planning, employers need to consider what employment relationships will be typical of their organization in the future—long-term, short-term, or some combination. Recent research by Pearce (1993) suggests that internal conflicts may occur when long-term, full-time employees work side by side with temporary or contract employees. Despite the fact that long-term employees have a "career" and get benefits from the organization, the actual hourly or monthly take-home pay of contract workers may be higher. Since benefit research shows that employees tend to undervalue their benefits, the result may be that the job and pay satisfaction of full-time, long-term employees will decrease if they can compare their pay to that of contract employees. Will education about the value of benefits be enough to deal with long-term employee dissatisfaction absent more explicit "career" contracts? How much conflict are employers willing to tolerate, especially if future government actions mandate some pro-rated benefit payments to temporary or contract workers? How might benefit portability alleviate potential conflicts among employees with different types of employment contracts?

Benefits and Workforce Diversity

The United States Bureau of Labor Statistics (BLS) reports that the current and projected composition of the labor force reflects increasing diversity (more women and minorities), especially among new entrants (Saunders, 1993). Management literature (Fernandez, 1993; Thomas, 1990) and some research (Fagenson, 1993; Watson, Kumar, & Michaelsen, 1993; Cox & Blake, 1991) suggest that superior problem solving, creativity, and flexibility are characteristic of diverse workforces. Equal employment opportunity laws and regulations also require employer attention to diversity in their labor markets and workforces. Finally, the increasingly global nature of competition for many businesses may require them to rethink benefit packages for globe-trotting employees. At a minimum, employers need to consider these facts in their strategic benefit planning. Certainly flexible benefit plans and more flexible work arrangements appear to be means of accommodating workforce diversity, but, with perhaps the exception of age, there remains little research on major individual or demographic differences in benefit preferences.

Operational and Tactical Questions in Benefit Planning

Operational and tactical questions in benefit planning mainly involve controlling costs. As noted earlier, in 1950 employee benefits represented, on average, less than 20 percent of payroll. Although employers' concerns and efforts at cost containment may have helped dampen the rate of growth in benefit costs, in 1993 they still represented an average 41 percent of payroll (U.S. Chamber of Commerce Research Center, 1994). Moreover, as Table 2 shows, 21 percent of employers' 1993 benefit costs came from legally mandated benefits. Employer control of mandated benefit costs is largely limited to control of headcount and wage and salary growth.[7]

Among the benefit categories under employer control, Table 2 clearly shows that, as of 1993 medical/life insurance category costs, which represent about 28 percent of total benefit costs, remain the most troublesome. Between 1990

Table 2. Average Annual Proportional Costs of 1993 Employee Benefits By Category

	Percentage of Payroll	Percentage of Benefits Cost	Cost in Dollars	Change in Percentage of Payroll since 1990
Legally required	8.7%	21.1%	$ 3,130	- 1.0%
Retirement/savings plans	6.6%	16.0%	$ 2,372	6.5%
Medical/other insurance* ·	11.7%	28.3%	$ 4,193	23.2%
Paid rest periods	2.3%	5.6%	$ 829	-0.4%
Payments for time not worked	10.4%	25.2%	$ 3,725	-1.0%
Miscellaneous**	1.6%	3.8%	$ 559	100.0%
Totals	41.3%	100.0%	$14,708	7.6%

Notes: *Medical insurance represents 11.1% of payroll, 27% of benefit costs, and $3,995 cost in dollars.
**Includes employee services and extra cash payment categories (from Table 1)

Source: Adapted from the U.S. Chamber of Commerce Research Center 1994, Tables 6, 8, 17.

and 1993 employer payments in this category increased from 9.5 to 11.7 percent of payroll, or by 23.2 percent. The only other benefit category that has increased more is miscellaneous (100%), but benefits in this category represent only 1.6 percent of payroll and 3.8 percent of the average employer's total benefit costs. It is significant that neither of these categories are closely linked to changes in wages and salaries. In contrast, payments in the categories of retirement and savings plans and payments for time not worked are linked to wages and salaries. Although these categories represent significant percentages of payroll and total benefit costs, the average growth in each has been declining since at least 1980, mirroring the decline in wage and salary growth as a proportion of total employee compensation.

Employers have struggled with a variety of ways to control the direct cost of benefits as well as with the indirect costs of administering benefits and complying with government regulation.[8] Controlling wage and salary growth, moving from defined benefit to defined contribution retirement plans, and a host of approaches to medical care cost control, which can be grouped broadly under the label of "managed care,"[9] are all representative of efforts to control direct benefit costs. Efforts to control the indirect costs of benefit administration and compliance are reflected in employer investments in information technology, especially automated payroll, record keeping, and reporting systems (Broderick & Boudreau, 1991; Kavanagh, Gueutal, & Tannenbaum, 1990).

There has been more documentation of employer efforts to control costs in the category of medical insurance and health care than in any other benefit category. For example, a survey of 1,021 mid- and large-sized companies by Hay Huggins reported that the number of employers sponsoring managed care plans as the "backbone" of their health care coverage increased from 33 percent in 1991 to 49 percent in 1993 (Hay Huggins, 1994). This same survey found that, in 1993, 76 percent of these employers offered flexible benefit plans, up from 46 percent in 1989. Many questions remain, however, about how effective these cost control efforts have been.

For example, there are questions about how to most efficiently design and implement managed care. The range of financing and delivery options for managed care has multiplied astronomically (Harris, 1993; Billet, 1984), resulting in more employer resources devoted to identifying and negotiating the best options for particular workforces. Regarding medical insurance alone, employers have the option of offering standard indemnity plans, HMO plans, other types of preferred provider plans, point of service plans, or self-insurance. In major metropolitan areas there are many competing providers for each one of these options and each provider may offer a variety of plans. Moreover, as the national debates on health reform have made clear, there is no independent review of the quality/cost tradeoffs offered by most providers' coverage. Employers are learning by trial and error to work their way through the maze of decisions involved in designing and delivering cost-effective, quality managed care, but broad-based, practical guidelines are needed.

Questions about the employer cost advantages of flexible benefit plans also remain. Certainly the plans can offer advantages other than lower costs. By providing choice, flexible plans can motivate employees to learn about the range of benefit choices they face, understand the choices that are best for them, and appreciate the true value of employer provided benefits. Thus flexible plans have the potential to help employers educate employees about benefits and may improve employee benefit satisfaction and retention.

Benefit cost reductions under flexible plans are also possible.[10] For example, in 1990 Xerox's health care costs were growing at an average annual rate of 20 percent. Then the company began limiting its contributions to employee health care costs to the price of the most efficient health maintenance organization (HMO) in each of its geographic areas of operation. Any dollar differences for coverage above this benchmark price had to be paid by the employee, thus providing employees with incentives to choose the most efficient plan coverage. At the same time, Xerox started rating HMO care on a variety of quality standards, including their employees' satisfaction with care. These ratings gave Xerox a basis for selecting among HMOs and negotiating annual coverage costs. The results for Xerox have been an increase in the number of employees using HMOs, and a reduced average annual increase in costs for these employees of only 9 percent in 1993. Xerox now has 75 percent of its employees and dependents enrolled in HMOs, as compared to the 25 to 40 percent that is typical of other companies. Xerox spends nearly $1,000 less per year per employee for those enrolled in HMOs than for those enrolled in traditional indemnity plans (American Management Association, 1994).

Nevertheless, although most anecdotal reports and employee opinion surveys suggest that flexible benefits increase employee understanding of and satisfaction with benefits, and help employers control benefit costs, there is only limited research documenting these or other effects (Rabin, 1994; Barber, Dunham, & Formisano, 1992; Sturman & Boudreau, 1994). Surveys of employers' flexible benefit plans conducted by two major consulting firms reported that only 25 to 30 percent have documented evidence of any cost reductions due to these plans (Foster Higgins, 1994; Mercer, 1994).

There has also been little systematic evaluation of investments in information technology for benefit administration. Most benefit managers in large organizations report that benefit record keeping and reporting would not be feasible without computer applications (Broderick & Boudreau, 1991; KPMG Peat Marwick, 1988). However, experience with more sophisticated applications has thus far not resulted in much consensus about their cost effectiveness or other effects. A recent Conference Board report (1993) found that many managers have concerns about the development and implementation costs of expert system applications meant to help employees understand their benefit options and to make selections among them. In particular, they noted that such applications were used effectively by only a small portion of their workforces (such as engineers already familiar with similar applications).

A recent study of the use of expert systems in assisting employee decisions about flexible benefit options (Hannon, Milkovich, & Sturman, 1990) reported that expert systems increased employee satisfaction with benefits by as much as 20 percent, and also increased understanding of benefit options and their value. On the downside, employees were no more likely to choose the options the expert system recommended as most appropriate to their situation than they were without computer assistance, making employer cost control uncertain. Thus an employer's short-term returns on the costs of developing the expert system are questionable if there are other, less expensive options available for assisting employee decision making. But the long-term educational benefits added by expert system use should also be considered.

The discussion of benefit cost control has thus far focused on health care and the wisdom of investments in computer technology for benefit administration. Yet Table 2 shows that employer costs for retirement and paid time off, though less than costs for health care, are also significant. Costs in both these areas are related to wage and salary growth so that employer control of headcount and base payroll growth will also affect dollars spent on retirement and paid time off. Employers have also moved more retirement dollars from defined contribution to defined benefit plans, a move believed to control future retirement costs. Some flexible benefit plans allow employees to trade off other types of benefits for more or less paid time off. Despite the fact that employer expenditures in these areas are discretionary, there has been little evaluation of, or research and speculation about, ways in which employers can control benefit costs in either area. Also, over the last five years, some employers have begun contracting out aspects of benefit administration, such as regulatory discrimination testing, defined contribution plan record keeping, and many of the tasks involved in managed health care. There has been little evaluation of the cost effectiveness of such contracting. Increasing workforce diversity, business globalization, and the need to view employee benefits as part of a total compensation package and as a strategic contribution to the organization all suggest that further scrutiny is warranted.

MAJOR RESEARCH FINDINGS ON EMPLOYEE BENEFITS

Evidence suggests that organizational performance outcomes such as profits, market share, and stock performance are influenced by human resource decisions (Pfeffer, 1994; Noe, Hollenbeck, Gerhart, & Wright, 1994), including decisions regarding high performance work systems (Huselid, 1995; MacDuffie, 1992; Womack, Jones, & Roos, 1990) and employee compensation

(Gerhart & Milkovich, 1990). These decisions most likely affect organizational performance through their influence on employee attitudes, motivation, and behaviors (e.g., attraction, retention, and performance). But do benefit decisions also influence employee behaviors and organizational performance? The large expenditures made by employers on benefits suggests that they believe the answer to be "yes" (although their opinions can differ from their actions). Similarly, favorable tax treatment and the consequent revenue losses (over $70 billion annually [Mitchell, 1992]) also attest to the federal government's belief in the importance of employer-provided benefits. Nevertheless, the evidence to support the influence of benefits on employee and organizational outcomes is not especially clear, and there is ample evidence that employers receive a relatively poor return on their benefits investments. In fact, Lincoln Electric, a company often written about and discussed at length as a model of success, offers virtually no employee benefits (no paid sick leave, no paid health insurance, etc. [Harvard Business School, 1975]).

In addition to focusing on retirement and savings and medical benefits, this section also focuses on two research questions about employee benefits in organizations: "Do employees understand and are they aware of the value of their benefit packages?" and "Can employers link benefit outcomes to either employee behaviors or organizational performance?"

Employee Understanding and Valuation of Benefits

Drawing on psychological theories of motivation, such as expectancy theory (Lawler, 1971), benefit researchers assume that employees must understand their benefits if benefits are to motivate their behaviors and achieve compensation objectives. Moreover, the HR management literature suggests that the success of many of the approaches employers take to controlling benefit costs, such as managed health care or flexible benefit programs, depend heavily on employees' understanding (Biggins, 1992).

Empirical research, however, suggests that current employees and job applicants often have a poor understanding of the value of fringe benefits. Nor do employees and applicants have a good understanding of how to make benefit choices that are most cost effective for themselves (Hennessey, Perrewe, & Hochwarter, 1992). For example, one study asked employees to estimate both the amount contributed by the employer to their medical insurance and what it would cost the employees to provide their own health insurance; employees underestimated both cost and market value. Among those with family coverage, the mean estimate of employer cost was only 38 percent of the employer's actual cost, and the average estimated market value was only 31 percent of what an employee would have to pay as an individual (Wilson, Northcraft, & Neale, 1985).

Other evidence on employee understanding of benefits comes from a study by Sturman and Boudreau (1994), which found that employees who are given the choice between two health care coverage plans often chose the "wrong" one, that is, "wrong" in the sense that the employees' out-of-pocket costs were higher than necessary given their past medical claim experience. Specifically, only 60 percent of employees made the optimal choice (despite the fact that with two options, random choices would yield 50% optimal choices). Further, mean annual out-of-pocket costs were $450; if each employee had made the optimal choice, mean out-of-pocket costs would have been $109 (or about 25%) less.

The understanding of benefits among job applicants, especially those fresh out of school, is not much better (for a summary see Hennessey, 1989). One study of MBA students found that 46 percent believed that benefits costs added 15 percent or less to an employer's base payroll. Not surprisingly, benefits were dead last on the MBAs' list of priorities used in making job choices (Huseman, Hatfield, & Robinson, 1978). Another study found that when graduating college seniors were given a choice between two options (a salary increase and employer-paid medical/life insurance), and were told that these two options had the same pre-tax value, the average student tended to choose the salary increase. The salary increase was favored even though it had an after-tax value much lower than the employer-paid medical/life insurance and would result in lower take-home pay (Davis, Giles, & Feild, 1985).

Why would job applicants make what seems like an obvious mistake? It may be that salary information is more easily understood than benefit information. Also, applicants and employees may pay little attention to benefits until they need to use them (e.g., as age increases and health problems arise or retirement draws near). In the case of campus recruiting, students exchange a good deal of labor market information with one another, and it is probably easier to exchange and make comparisons using salary rather than benefit information. Recruiters themselves may be partly to blame. At least two studies have found that recruiters substantially underestimate the importance of some forms of benefits, especially medical insurance, to graduating college students (Posner, 1981; Davis, Giles, & Feild, 1985). Perhaps as a consequence, recruiters neglect benefits in the recruiting process. After all, many recruiters are recent graduates themselves and may not have reason to be concerned about benefits.

These results suggest the relative unimportance of benefits in job choice decisions, but they must be interpreted with caution. There is also research suggesting that job attributes can be ranked low in importance, not because they are unimportant per se, but because all employers are perceived to be about the same on that attribute (Rynes, Heneman, & Schwab, 1983). If some employers offered noticeably poorer benefits than others, the importance of benefits in job choices could increase. The recent trend toward downsizing in many large firms has led to less campus recruiting by some, and smaller firms have stepped into fill this gap.[11] Since smaller firms typically offer fewer benefits than larger firms, graduating students may now be seeing greater differences in benefits packages. Similarly, the fact that employers have taken a variety of actions to bring benefit costs and growth under greater control (e.g., shifting of medical costs to employees and retirees, limitations on health care provider choice, reversions of pension assets, etc.) may mean that some of the conclusions from previous studies are out-of-date and newer data will yield different conclusions.

In any case, if one believes that increasing employee understanding about benefits increases the likelihood that benefits will have positive outcomes for the organization, the existing research makes it clear that employers have their work cut out for them. What can employers do? Researchers have examined the impact of changes in communication and plan design on employee understanding of benefits. In the area of communications, one study found that employees' awareness of benefit value was significantly increased by communicating information via memoranda, question-and-answer meetings, and detailed brochures (Hennessey, Perrewe, & Hochwarter, 1992). The increased awareness, in turn, contributed to significant increases in employee satisfaction with benefits.

However, it is important to note that increased employee knowledge of benefits can have a positive or negative effect on employee satisfaction with benefits, depending on how lucrative the benefit package is. Not surprisingly, higher out-of-pocket costs for employees are associated with lower overall benefit satisfaction (Dreher, Ash, & Bretz, 1988). Less obvious perhaps is the fact that the correlation between cost and satisfaction may be most negative among employees with the best understanding of benefits (Dreher, Ash, & Bretz, 1988). In other words, employees will be least satisfied with their benefits if their out-of-pocket costs are high and they are well-informed. Obviously, good communication is helpful if you have a good story to tell, but not so helpful otherwise.

Research on employee understanding of benefits has taken advantage of the increasing number of employers switching to more flexible approaches to benefit plan design and administration. Most flexible benefit (or cafeteria) plans permit employees some discretion in choosing the types and amounts of benefits they want for themselves. Typically, employees have a certain number of credits or dollars that they can allocate. An employee might choose fewer vacation days and receive more take-home pay or less vacation to help fund a more comprehensive medical insurance choice. Other plans include flexible spending accounts; these permit pre-tax contributions to cover health care expenses (e.g., deductible or coinsurance payments). Although research on flexible benefit plans is still very limited, one study (Barber, Dunham, & Formisano, 1992) found that employees' self-reported understanding of the value of their benefit package increased significantly after the implementation of flexible benefits. This increase in employee understanding may have been due in part to other changes accompanying flexible benefits, for example, added benefit communication and training or the added incentives for employees to learn more about their benefits in order to make informed choices.

Benefits, Employee Behavior, and Organizational Performance

"Can employers link benefit outcomes to either employee behaviors or organizational outcomes?" In general, the answer is, "probably not with much confidence." There is little theory or research linking benefits to employee behaviors. Research mostly examines links between benefits and different measures of employee satisfaction, and between benefits and an employer's ability to attract and retain employees. Some theories have been proposed to explain how benefits and employee performance might be linked, but virtually no theory or research links benefits and organizational performance.

Benefits and Employee Satisfaction

Employee satisfaction with multiple aspects of work, especially pay satisfaction, is believed by many researchers to influence employee turnover, absenteeism (Motowidlo, 1983; Weiner, 1980) work motivation, and performance (Lawler, 1971). Thus, in adding to pay and job satisfaction, employee satisfaction with benefits might influence employee behaviors. Drawing on discrepancy models of job satisfaction (Locke, 1969, 1976), most research on employees' satisfaction with benefits assumes that their levels of satisfaction are determined by the size of the "discrepancy" between what they perceive the value of their benefits to be and what they think that value should be. Since the evidence discussed earlier indicates that employees may underestimate the value of their benefits, the discrepancy model predicts that employers will receive less than the full value of their benefit dollars in terms of returns on employee satisfaction and related behaviors.

Models of benefit satisfaction also incorporate concepts from equity theory (Adams, 1965; Goodman, 1974; Heneman, 1985). Equity theory predicts that employees' assessments of the value of their benefits are significantly influenced by comparisons of their actual benefits against those of others in similar positions inside or outside the organization, against those of others in similar demographic groups, or against their own history of benefits. Most of the research relevant to equity and employee benefit satisfaction examines the relationships between differences in employee demographics (age, marital status, family status, gender, and income level) and differences in employee preferences for specific forms of benefits. This research assumes that if employees receive more of a benefit form they prefer, they will be more satisfied. A recent review of research on employee compensation (Gerhart & Milkovich, 1992) suggests that generalizable findings from research on benefit preferences are few: given a choice among benefit forms, older workers prefer more benefit dollars in pensions, women prefer more paid time off, and the number of dependents is related to preferences for health care. Recent research (Barringer & Mitchell, 1994; Miceli & Lane, 1991) suggests that the list of employee differences studied might be worth expanding to include differences in employee risk aversion (especially the effects of age and income levels on health care choices), the number of sources employees have for benefit coverage, and employee demands for leisure or family time.

Research *does* support the existence of benefit satisfaction as an independent dimension of pay satisfaction (Scarpello, Huber, & Vandenberg, 1988). The most widely used measure of benefits satisfaction comes from the Pay Satisfaction Questionnaire (PSQ) (Heneman & Schwab, 1985). The PSQ reliably measures four facets of pay satisfaction: level, benefits, raises, and structure/administration (Judge, 1993). Although the PSQ benefit scale is useful in gauging overall benefits satisfaction, it contains only four very general items. Therefore, it does not provide much information on why an employee is or is not satisfied with benefits. Benefit satisfaction has also been shown to be related to pay satisfaction (Berger, 1984). But there is surprisingly little evidence relating benefits satisfaction to more general employee attitudes and behaviors.

Benefits and Employee Attraction and Retention

Do benefits influence employee decisions to join and remain with an organization? The evidence reviewed earlier suggests that applicants and employees rank benefits low in importance relative to most other job attributes, perhaps because they tend to underestimate their value or because they perceive little variance among employers in benefit offerings. Therefore, benefits may not have much effect on attraction unless an organization differs in a significant and noticeable way from its competitors.

Greater variance in benefit packages among organizations competing in the same labor markets may be a more recent phenomenon. As discussed earlier, employer cost control efforts have led to greater variance in the ways that benefits are designed and administered. Also, proportionately more job creation is now generated by smaller firms or service sector firms in which benefit packages have typically not been as generous as in the manufacturing sector. As a result, new research examining the relationship between benefits and employee attraction may find different results. For example, in a 1992 study of 352 U.S. banks, Williams and Dreher (1992) found that variance across employers in some aspects of benefit packages influenced both the number of applicants for bank teller jobs and the time it took to fill these jobs. Specifically, the overall level of resources devoted to benefits (as measured by the percentage of total payroll devoted to benefits) was positively related to the number of applicants. Also, the amount of flexibility in employee benefit choices (as measured by the presence or absence of a flexible benefit plan) and the amount of paid time off was positively associated with less time needed to fill jobs. However, the results of one study are hardly conclusive.

On the other hand, benefits, especially retirement and medical insurance, do seem to have a significant impact on employee retention, especially as employee length of service increases. There is solid theory and research evidence on the influence of retirement plans on employee retention. Drawing on agency theory, Gustman, Mitchell, and Steinmeir (1994) suggest that pension decisions should be framed as a long-term implicit contract between the employee and the employer. Under such a contract, the value of an employee's direct pay and pension rises with length of service. This is because employers are interested in recouping substantial hiring and training costs by reducing employee turnover early in their tenure. Gustman, Mitchell, and Steinmeir also suggest that employers use pension plans to attract certain types of employees, namely those who are "stayers" as opposed to "movers." Empirical studies by Mitchell (1982) and Ippolito (1987) provide some support for these proposals, showing that, all else equal, the turnover rates of workers covered by pensions plans are about one-half those of workers not covered by such plans.

Gustman, Mitchell, and Steinmeir point out some caveats about the evidence on pension mobility effects, however. First, the pension benefits lost by quitting a new job and taking another may, on average, be offset by only a 2 to 3 percent increase in cash compensation over the remainder of a person's working career (Allen, Clark, & McDermed, 1993). Second, and more perplexing, according to at least some research, defined contribution plans, which do not penalize employees for mobility, appear to deter employee mobility to the same degree as defined contribution plans, which do impose a penalty for mobility.

Finally, Gustman, Mitchell, and Steinmeir discuss the evidence on the impact of pensions on retirement. Lazear (1979) has argued that pensions are used by employers as a way to encourage high length of service employees to retire after the point at which their earnings significantly exceed productivity. According to Gustman, Mitchell, and Steinmeir, the evidence supports this proposition, both when one looks at the "spike" in core pension benefits at retirement age[12] and when one considers the widespread use of early retirement programs to reduce employment levels.

It is not clear that medical benefits have as significant an impact as pensions on employee retention, despite the fact that in the United States medical insurance is strongly linked to employment. Indeed, 94 percent of covered American workers receive their coverage through their employer or a family member's employer (Employee Benefit Research Institute/Gallup Poll, 1991). Also, employers vary in the quality of the medical coverage they offer. Several studies have found that among displaced workers who had health insurance through their previous employers, about one-sixth had no coverage on their new jobs, and those who did not find new jobs were much less likely to have coverage

(Podgursky & Swaim, 1987; Herz, 1991; Mitchell, 1992). Recent studies suggest that the lack of health care portability does increase employee retention. For example, Monheit and Cooper (1994) found a positive relationship between higher employee retention (or lower worker mobility) and the likelihood of losing health coverage when switching jobs. Also, in a study of the effects on worker mobility of regulation enabling employees to get medical insurance at employer rates for up to 18 months after leaving their job (Consolidated Omnibus Reconciliation Act or COBRA regulations), Gruber and Madrian (1994) found that COBRA did increase worker mobility. From the employer's perspective, then, more portable health coverage could decrease employee retention.

Benefits, Employee Performance, and Organizational Performance

Employee benefits have been notably independent of both employee and organization performance. There are some exceptions, for example, pensions in which payments are tied to years of service or retirement plans in which plan contributions depend on organizational profits. But for the most part, outstanding performers do not receive better benefits (more health insurance, more vacation time) than average performers. And employee benefits do not vary year to year with the organization's financial performance.

However, some models drawn from agency theory have been proposed to explain how pensions could affect employee effort and performance. As described earlier, many employers design employee compensation systems so that pay increases with years of service. If it is correct to assume that employee earnings exceed productivity both early and late in their tenure, then employees have an incentive to remain with the employer, especially during the early portion of their careers. To avoid the loss of this earnings windfall, employees will put forth at least enough effort to avoid dismissal. Employers will find this approach to motivation most useful in cases where performance is otherwise difficult to monitor (Hutchens, 1986, 1987). However, Gustman, Mitchell, and Steinmeir (1994) point out that it is hard to disentangle the reasons for employees' higher earnings later in their careers because other explanations (e.g., human capital) can explain the same phenomenon as can the agency cost approach.

In a recent review of the literature on pension portability and labor market efficiency, Stuart Dorsey (1995) points out that implicit labor contract models predict that such benefits as less portable pensions can enhance overall firm productivity by increasing employee retention and maintaining reasonable employee performance levels, especially among employees whose skills and jobs are well matched or in whom the employer has a large training investment. Though Dorsey admits that the empirical evidence supporting these models if far from conclusive, he suggests that, "policy makers [including employers] need to consider the possibility that requiring greater pension portability will have adverse productivity effects" (p. 289).

The research relating benefit levels or practices to organizational performance is extremely limited, but there is one model linking profit-sharing retirement plans to organizational performance. Here, an agency theory approach is used to propose that employee and employer interests are aligned by using an outcome-based contract that links employee pay to profits. However, reinforcement theory from psychology suggests that rewards have the most impact on behavior if they are received immediately. This, of course, does not happen in retirement plans. Consistent with reinforcement theory, Kruse (1993) found that the use of cash profit-sharing plans was associated with better organizational performance, but he did not find such an effect for deferred (or retirement) profit-sharing plans.

There are, however, some circumstantial reasons to believe that benefit expenditures may influence organizational performance. For example, changes in regulated accounting standards have made some types of pension plans and retiree health care expenses a liability that employers must report on their balance sheets. Have these changes had an effect on organizational finances or reputation? In early 1993 General Motors (GM) announced a $20.8 million reduction in net income to comply with new accounting standards for retiree health care reporting. Standard & Poor's reacted to GM's announcement by downgrading GM debt from A-minus to BBB-plus. Research on other dramatic HR changes (e.g., major layoffs or restructuring) has suggested that they can influence corporate "reputation" and stock value (Abowd, Milkovich, & Hannon, 1989). Other research suggests that the way an organization mixes base pay and bonuses is tied to changes in selected financial ratios (Gerhart & Milkovich, 1990). Since benefits represent a substantial portion of total compensation costs in many organizations, changes in the benefits portion may also influence the financial performance of companies.

RESEARCH AND POLICY DIRECTIONS

Benefits have become increasingly important to employees, employers, and the U.S. public. The cost of benefits has grown so high that the federal government and employers are involved in ongoing struggles to manage and control expenditures. At the same time, the provision of benefits by the government and employers has become more salient to the average voter and employee.

Research on employee benefits is catching up with the public interest in benefits, but still has a long way to go. The increased scrutiny of benefits by government and employers has been accompanied by changes in employer benefit plans, providing researchers an opportunity to examine theories about how benefits influence employee attraction, retention, and performance. The changes also provide opportunities to examine the impact of variations in benefit plan design and administration on costs, employee satisfaction, and behavior. When considered together with the changes occurring in other areas of the compensation package, the role of benefits in that package merits further examination. Now is the time for researchers to integrate economic, sociological, psychological, and management perspectives to advance research on benefits and compensation. Researchers must also forge partnerships with HR professionals to define benefit measures, develop research models, test existing theory, and contribute to effective total compensation management.

For their part, employers and HR professionals can take advantage of changes in benefit design and administration by systematically collecting the information needed to evaluate the impact of benefit costs and performance. Do flexible benefit plans really help to reduce costs?; do they increase employee understanding of benefit choices?; do they increase employee attraction and retention? Are there individual or demographic differences among employee benefit preferences and choices that are also associated with satisfaction, cost, and other employee behaviors? What are the most effective ways of negotiating with community health care providers to produce a health care package that satisfies employees at reasonable cost? Which benchmarks are most effective for comparing benefit and total compensation packages offered by competing organizations? It is currently difficult for most employers to do good short-term benefit planning, let alone longer term strategic planning, and to develop benefit policies with the information currently available within their organizations.

Finally, researchers, employers, and HR professionals need to inform each other on issues of national health care and pension plan-retirement reform. The national interest provides all parties an opportunity to examine and compare national—and international—models of compensation and benefits, and assess their effects on employer costs, employee and organizational performance, and national welfare.

NOTES

1. Many temporary or contract workers are hired through agencies or are self-employed. In such cases, the agency or the workers are responsible for mandated payments under Social Security and Medicare. The definition of temporary or contract workers is being reviewed by the U.S. Department of Labor and the Internal Revenue Service due to concerns that some full-time employees are presently classified as temporary or contract workers in order to lower employer benefit costs.

2. In defined benefit pension plans, the employer promises employees a specific benefit payment on retirement and is responsible for assuring that the required funds are available when needed. In defined contribution pension plans, the employer promises only a specific payment to employees during their employment. Employees are responsible for investing these payments for their retirement.

3. This section draws heavily on material from Beach (1975, pp. 19-20), Ehrenberg and Smith (1988, pp. 336-342), and Noe, Hollenbeck, Gerhart, and Wright (1994, pp. 619-622).

4. Internal labor markets are defined here in terms of their openness to the external labor market. When employees can enter any job in the organization the internal labor market is fully open. When employees are hired only into a small number of entry-level jobs and promotion from within is used to fill all other jobs, the internal labor market is fully closed.

5. Ippolito (1995) points out additional reasons for the increase in the number of defined contribution plans (especially 401K) plans, including: structural employment shifts away from manufacturing sectors where defined benefit plans are most commonly found, and the likelihood that firms that would never have offered defined benefit plans elected to offer 401K plans when the government made them possible.

6. The legality and tax free status of performance-linked benefits under ERISA regulations is an open question.

7. Mandated employer payments for unemployment insurance and workers' compensation are partially under employer control, but represent a small portion of total mandated benefit payments.

8. See, for example, issues in *Compensation and Benefits Review* (Saranac, NY: American Management Association); *W.F. Corroon Alert* (St. Louis, MO: W.F. Corroon); *The Wyatt Compensation and Benefits File* (Washington, DC: The Wyatt Company).

9. There are many nuances relevant to defining managed care, but, broadly, managed care includes: employees' higher contributions to medical care costs, employer negotiations with providers to obtain basic care at a specified price, and more supervision of employee medical treatment via primary providers, second surgical opinions, and case management. The Health Maintenance Organization (HMO) is an example of managed care.

10. Two cost drawbacks with flexible plans are their administrative costs (especially start-up) and potential adverse selection. Software packages and standardized flex plans developed by consultants offer some help with administrative costs. Adverse selection refers to the fact that employees are most likely to choose benefits that they expect to need the most. Therefore, an employee who expects to have many medical problems will choose the maximum coverage, an employee who expects to have a lot of dental work chooses maximum dental coverage, and so forth. Thus each person ends up making choices that maximize employer expenditures. This also makes it difficult, especially for smaller companies, to estimate what plan benefits costs will be. Adverse selection can be controlled by placing caps on coverage amounts, by higher pricing for benefits liable to adverse selection, and by limiting employee choice among options to prevent choices that pose a high risk of adverse selection.

11. This information was provided by Tom Devlin, Director of Career Services, Cornell University.

12. Gustman, Mitchell, and Steinmeir in their Figure 1, report that the value of retirement benefits in the early 1980s increased each year prior to retirement by an amount equal to about 15 percent of annual direct pay. However, at normal retirement age, this jumped to 24 percent per year, and after normal retirement age, the pension accrual actually became negative (at least prior to the 1967 Age Discrimination in Employment Act).

REFERENCES

Abowd, J.M., Milkovich, G.T., & Hannon, J.M. 1989. *The effects of human resource management decisions on shareholder value.* Working paper no. 89-20, Center for Advanced Human Resource Studies, School of Industrial and Labor Relations, Cornell University, Ithaca, NY.

Adams, J.S. 1965. Inequity in social exchange. In L. Berkowitz (Ed.), *Advances in experimental social psychology* (pp. 272-283). New York: Academic Press.

ACA NEWS (1994, May). Health care reform strategies. pp. 22-24.

Allen, S.G., Clark, R.L., & McDermed, A.A. (1993). Pension bonding and lifetime jobs. *Journal of Human Resources, 28,* 463-481.

Balkin, D., & Gomez-Mejia, L.R. (1984). Determinants of R&D compensation strategies in the high tech industry. *Personnel Psychology, 37* (4), 635-650.

Barber, A.E., Dunham, R.B., & Formisano, R.A. (1992). The impact of flexible benefits on employee satisfaction: A field study. *Personnel Psychology, 45* (1), 55-76.

Barocas, V.S. (1992). *Strategic benefit planning. Managing benefits in a changing business environment.* New York: The Conference Board.

Barringer, M., & Mitchell, O.S. (1994). Workers' preferences among company-provided health insurance plans. *Industrial and Labor Relations Review, 48* (1), 141-152.

Barton, P.A. (1994, May). New age of benefits. Employer benefits role is changing from "paternalism" to "partnership." *ACA NEWS,* 20-21.

Beach. D.S. (1975). *Personnel: The management of people at work.* New York: Macmillan.

Beam, B.T., & McFadden, J.J. (1992). *Employee benefits.* Homewood, IL: Irwin.

Bennett, M.A. (1994, August). Managed care. Health care reform moving forward with or without government action. *ACA NEWS,* 20-21.

Berger, C.J. (1984). *The effects of pay level, pay values and employee benefits on pay satisfaction.* Unpublished manuscript, Purdue University Krannert School of Management, LaFayette, IN.

Billet, T. (1984). An employer's guide to preferred provider organizations. *Compensation Review, 16* (4), 58-62.

Biggins, P. (1992). Flexible/cafeteria plans. In J.D. Mamorsky (Ed.), *Employee benefits handbook* (3rd ed.). Boston, MA: Warren, Gorham, & Lamont.

Broderick, R.F. (1987). Pay policy and business strategy: A question of fit. In R. Niehaus (Ed.), *The human resource planning society's research symposium* (pp. 43-58). New York: Plenum Press.

Broderick, R. & Boudreau, J.W. (1991). The evolution of computer use in human resource management: Interviews with ten leaders. *Human Resource Management, 30* (4), 485-508.

Carroll, S.J. (1987). Business strategies and compensation systems. In L. Gomez-Mejia & D. Balkin (Eds.), *New perspectives on compensation* (pp. 343-355). Englewood Cliffs, NJ: Prentice-Hall, Inc.

Conference Board. (1993). *Benefit communication: Enhancing the employer's investment.* Report Number 10-35. New York: The Conference Board.

Coopers and Lybrand. (1994). *Compensation and benefits planning for 1994.* New York: Coopers and Lybrand.

Cox, T.H., & Blake, S. (1991). Managing cultural diversity: Implications for organization competitiveness. *Academy of Management Executive, 5* (3), 45-56.

Davis, K.R., Giles, W.F., & Feild, H.S., Jr. (1985). Compensation and fringe benefits: How recruiters view new college graduates' preferences. *Personnel Administrator, 30,* 43-50.

Dorsey, S. (1995). Pension portability and labor market efficiency. *Industrial and Labor Relations Review, 48* (5), 276-292.

Dreher, G.A., Ash, R.A., & Bretz, R.D. (1988). Benefit coverage and employee cost: Critical factors in explaining compensation satisfaction. *Personnel Psychology, 41,* 237-254.

Dyer, L., & Blancero, D. (1992). Workforce 2000: A delphi study. Working paper no. 92-10. Center for Advanced Human Resource Studies, School of Industrial and Labor Relations, Cornell University, Ithaca, NY.

Dyer, L., & Holder, G.W. (1988). A strategic perspective on human resource management. In L. Dyer (Ed.) *ASPA-BNA Series: Human resource management evolving roles and responsibilities* (pp. 1.1-1.35). Washington, DC: Bureau of National Affairs.

Ehrenberg, R.G., & Smith, R. (1988). *Modern labor economics: theory and public-policy.* Glenview, IL: Scott, Foresman, and Company.

Ellig, B.R. (1981). Compensation elements: Market phase determines the mix. *Compensation Review*, 3rd Quarter, 30-38.

Employee Benefit Research Institute (1994). Characteristics of the part-time work force. Analysis of the March 1993 Current Population Survey. *EBRI Special Report*. Issue Brief Number 149. Washington, DC: Employee Benefit Research Institute.

_____ . (1990). *Fundamentals of employee benefit programs*. Washington, DC: Employee Benefit Research Institute.

Employee Benefit Research Institute/Gallup Poll. (1991). *Public attitudes on health insurance, 1991*. Report Number G-26. Washington, DC: Employee Benefit Research Institute.

Fagenson, E.A. (Ed.) (1993). *Women in management. Trends, issues, and challenges in managerial diversity*. Newbury Park, CA: Sage Publications.

Fernandez, J.P., with Barr, M. (1993). *The diversity advantage. How American business can outperform Japanese and European companies in the global marketplace*. New York: Lexington Books.

Fombrun, C., Tichy, N.M., & Devanna, M.A.. (1984). *Strategic human resource management*. New York: John Wiley and Sons.

Foster Higgins (1994). *1994 Survey of flexible benefit plans*. New York: Foster Higgins.

Gerhart, B., & Milkovich, G.T. (1990). Organizational differences in managerial compensation and financial performance. *Academy of Management Journal, 33* (4), 663-691.

_____ . (1992). Employee compensation: research and practice. In M.D. Dunnette & L.M. Hough (Eds.), *Handbook of industrial and organizational psychology* (3rd ed.) (pp. 538-539). Palo Alto, CA: Consulting Psychologists Press, Inc.

Gomez-Mejia, L.R., & Balkin, D.B. (1992). *Compensation, organizational strategy, and firm performance*. Cincinnati, OH: Southwestern.

Goodman, P.S. (1974). An examination of referents used in the evaluation of pay. *Organizational Behavior and Human Performance, 12*, 170-195.

Goodstein, J.D. (1994). Institutional pressures and strategic responsiveness: Employer involvement in work-family issues. *Academy of Management Journal, 37* (2), 350-382.

Gruber, J., & Madrian, B.C. (1994). Health insurance and job mobility: The effects of public policy on job-lock. *Industrial and Labor Relations Review, 48* (1), 86-102.

Gustman, A.L., Mitchell, O.S., & Steinmeier, T.L. (1994). The role of pensions in the labor market: A survey of the literature. *Industrial and Labor Relations Review, 47*, 417-438.

Hannon, J.M., Milkovich, G.T., & Sturman, M.C. (1990). The feasibility of using expert systems in the management of human resources. Working paper no. 90-04. Center for Advanced Human Resource Studies, School of Industrial and Labor Relations, Cornell University, Ithaca, NY.

Harris, C.I. (1993, Spring/Summer). Outsourcing benefits administration: The make or buy decision. *ACA Journal*, 32-39.

Harvard Graduate School of Business (1975). *The Lincoln Electric Company*. Case 376-028. Boston, MA: Harvard Business School Publishing.

Hay-Huggins (1994). *1993 Hay/Huggins benefits report*. Philadelphia, PA: Hay Huggins.

Heneman, H.G., III. (1985). Pay satisfaction. In K. Rowland & G. Ferris (Eds.), *Research in personnel and human resource management* (volume 3, pp. 115-139). Greenwich, CT: JAI Press.

Heneman, H.G., III, & Schwab, D.P. (1985). Pay satisfaction: Its multidimensional nature and measurement. *International Journal of Psychology, 20*, 129-141.

Hennessey, H.W., Jr. (1989). Using employee benefits to gain a competitive advantage. *Benefits Quarterly, 5* (1), 51-57.

Hennessey, H.W., Jr., Perrewe, P.L., & Hochwarter, W.A. (1992). Impact of benefit awareness on employee and organizational outcomes: A longitudinal field examination. *Benefits Quarterly*, Second Quarter, 90-96.

Herz, D.E. (1991). Worker displacement in the 1980s. *Monthly Labor Review, 114*, 5, 3-9.

Hills, F.S., Bergmann, T.J., & Scarpello, V.G. (1993). *Compensation Decision Making* (2nd ed.). Fort Worth, TX: The Dryden Press.

Huselid, M.A. (1995). The impact of human resource management practices on turnover, productivity, and corporate financial performance. *Academy of Management Journal, 38* (3), 635-672.

Huseman, R., Hatfield, J., & Robinson, R. (1978). The MBA and fringe benefits. *Personnel Administrator, 23* (7), 57-60.

Hutchens, R. (1986). Delayed payment contracts and a firm's propensity to hire older workers. *Journal of Labor Economics, 4*, 439-457.

Hutchens, R. (1987). A test of Lazear's theory of the delayed payment contract. *Journal of Labor Economics, 5*, Part 2, S153-170.

Ippolito, R. (1987). Why federal workers don't quit. *Journal of Human Resources, 22*, 281-293.

———. (1995). Toward explaining the growth of defined contribution plans. *Industrial Relations, 34* (1), 1-20.

Judge, T.A. (1993). Validity of the dimensions of the pay satisfaction questionnaire. *Personnel Psychology, 46*, 331-355.

Kavanagh, M.J., Gueutal, H.G., & Tannenbaum, S.I. (1990). *Human resource information systems: Development and application.* Boston, MA: PWS-Kent Publishing Company.

KPMG Peat Marwick (1988). *Computer usage in human resources: A competitive advantage.* Dallas, TX: KPMG Peat Marwick.

Kruse, D.L. (1993). *Profit sharing: Does it make a difference?* Kalamazoo, MI: W.E. Upjohn Institute.

Lawler, E.E., III. (1971). *Pay and organizational effectiveness: A psychological view.* New York: McGraw-Hill.

———. (1981). *Pay and organization development.* Menlo Park, CA: Addison-Wesley Publishing.

———. (1990). *Strategic pay. Aligning organizational strategies and pay systems.* San Francisco, CA: Jossey-Bass.

Lazear, E.P. (1979). Why is there early retirement? *Journal of Political Economy, 87* (6), 1261-1284.

Lewin, D., & Mitchell, D.J.B. (1994). *Human resource management: An economic approach* (2nd ed.). Cincinnati, OH: Southwestern.

Locke, E.A. (1969). What is job satisfaction. *Organizational Behavior and Human Performance, 4*, 309-336.

———. (1976). The nature and causes of job satisfaction. In M.D. Dunnette (Ed.), *Handbook of industrial and organizational psychology* (volume 2, pp. 1297-1349). Chicago, IL: Rand McNally.

MacDuffie, J.P. (1992). Beyond mass production: Organizational flexibility and manufacturing performance in the world auto industry. Working paper. University of Pennsylvania, The Wharton School, Philadelphia, PA.

Mercer, W.M. (1994). *The 1993 survey of cafeteria plans.* Los Angeles, CA: William M. Mercer.

Miceli, M.P., & Lane, M.C. (1991). Antecedents of pay satisfaction: A review and extension. In K. Rowland & G. Ferris (Eds.), *Research in personnel and human resource management* (volume 9, pp. 235-309). Greenwich, CT: JAI Press.

Milkovich, G.T., & Newman, J.M. (1993). *Compensation.* Homewood, IL: Irwin.

Milkovich, G.T., & Mahoney, T.A. (1976). Human resources planning and PAIR policy. In D. Yoder & H.G. Heneman, Jr. (Eds.), *ASPA handbook of personnel and industrial relations: Planning and auditing PAIR* (volume VI, pp. 2.1-2.30). Washington, DC: Bureau of National Affairs.

Milkovich, G.T., & Wigdor, A.K. with Broderick, R., & Mavor, A. (Eds.) (1991). *Pay for performance. Evaluating performance appraisal and merit pay.* Washington, DC: National Academy Press.

Mitchell, D.J.B. (1992). Social insurance and benefits. In D. Lewin, O.S. Mitchell, & P.D. Sherer (Eds.), *Research frontiers in industrial relations and human resources* (pp. 587-625). Madison, WI: Industrial Relations Research Association.

Mitchell, O.S. (1982). Fringe benefits and labor mobility. *Journal of Human Resources, 17*, 286-298.

Morrison, E.M. (1994, Autumn). Health care benefit design and the generations of managed care. *ACA Journal*, 34-45.

Monheit, A.C., & Cooper, P.F. (1994). Health insurance and job mobility: theory and evidence. *Industrial and Labor Relations Review, 48* (1), 68-85.

Motowidlow, S.J. (1983). Predicting sales turnover from pay satisfaction and expectation. *Journal of Applied Psychology, 68*, 484-489.

Noe, R., Hollenbeck, J.R., Gerhart, B., & Wright, P.M. (1994). *Human resource management: Gaining a competitive advantage.* Burr Ridge, IL: Irwin.

Paul, R.D., & Grant, D.B. (1993, Winter). The next generation of benefits plans: What the past says about the future. *ACA Journal*, 6-17.

Pearce, J. (1993). Toward an organizational behavior of contract laborers: Their psychological involvement and effects on employee co-workers. *Academy of Management Journal, 36* (6), 1082-1096.

Pfeffer, J. (1982). *Organizations and organization theory.* Boston, MA: Pitman.

―――――― . (1994). *Competitive advantage through people.* Boston, MA: Harvard Business School Press.

Podgursky, M., & Swaim, P. (1987). Health insurance loss: The case of the displaced worker. *Monthly Labor Review, 110* (4), 30-33.

Posner, B.Z. (1981). Comparing recruiter, student, and faculty perceptions of important applicant and job characteristics. *Personnel Psychology, 34*, 329-339.

Rabin, B.R. (1994, Summer). Assessing employee benefit satisfaction under flexible benefits. *Compensation and Benefits Management*, 33-41.

Rosenblum, J., & Hallman, G.V. (1991). *Employee benefit planning.* Englewood Cliffs, NJ: Prentice Hall, Inc.

Rynes, S.L., Heneman, H.G., III, & Schwab, D.P. (1983). The role of pay and market pay variability in job application decisions. *Organizational Behavior and Human Performance, 31*, 353-364.

Salisbury, D.L., & Super Jones, N. (Eds.). (1994). *Pension funding and taxation: Implications for tomorrow.* Washington, DC: Employee Benefit Research Institute.

Saunders, N.C. (1993). The U.S. economy: Framework for BLS projections. *Monthly Labor Review, 116* (11), 11-30.

Scarpello, V., Huber, V., & Vandenberg, R.J. (1988). Compensation satisfaction: Its measurement and dimensionality. *Journal of Applied Psychology, 73*, 163-171.

Sturman, M., & Boudreau, J. (1994). Out-of-pocket costs and flexible benefits decisions: Do employees make effective health care choices? Working paper no. 94-05. Center for Advanced Human Resource Studies, School of Industrial and Labor Relations. Cornell University, Ithaca, NY.

Thomas, R. (1990, March-April). From affirmative action to affirming diversity. *Harvard Business Review*, 107-117.

U.S. Chamber of Commerce Research Center (1994). *Employee benefits, 1993.* Washington, DC: Chamber of Commerce.

Watson, W.E., Kumar, K., & Michaelsen, L.K. (1993). Cultural diversity's impact on interaction process and performance: Comparing homogeneous and diverse task groups. *Academy of Management Journal, 36* (3), 590-602.

Werner, N. (1980). Determinants and behavioral consequences of pay satisfaction. *Personnel Psychology, 33*, 741-757.

Williams, M.L., & Dreher, G.F. (1992). Compensation system attributes and applicant pool characteristics. *Academy of Management Journal, 35* (3), 571-595.

Wilson, M., Northcraft, G.B., & Neale, M.A. (1985). The perceived value of fringe benefits. *Personnel Psychology, 38*, 309-320.

Womack, J.P., Jones, D.T., & Roos, D. (1990). *The machine that changed the world.* New York: MacMillan Publishing.

Wyatt Data Services (1994). *The 1993/1994 survey report on variable pay programs.* Fort Lee, NJ: Wyatt Data Services/ECS.

GENDER GAPS IN BENEFITS COVERAGE

Janet Currie

Gender differences in wages are well documented—the female to male wage ratio is about .66 in the United States, and only about half of this wage gap can be explained by differences in observable characteristics of workers such as their age, education, and labor market experience (Smith & Ward, 1989; Goldin, 1990). Much of the remaining difference is associated with the fact that men and women tend to hold different jobs (Treiman & Hartmann, 1981; Groshen, 1988)—the vast majority of men and women work in jobs that are over 70 percent one-sex, and it is estimated that 60 percent of American working women would have to change occupations in order to achieve a gender-neutral distribution of persons across occupations (Fields & Wolff, 1991; Bianchi & Rytina, 1986).

However, the previous chapter highlighted the fact that non-wage compensation (benefits) now accounts for between 30 to 40 percent of labor costs in Western industrial countries. Hence, it is natural to ask whether gender gaps in benefits coverage exist, and if so, whether they have implications for human resource management and in particular for efforts to attract the best workers regardless of gender?

In a world in which, given total compensation, it was possible for a worker to find a job with any desired combination of wages and benefits, one could attribute all of the observed gender gaps in benefits coverage to the optimizing choices of workers, and there would be no need for either policymakers or employers to be concerned about them. There are two reasons to suspect that observed benefits choices may in fact be suboptimal. The first is that, as the previous chapter showed, the largest growth in benefits as a fraction of compensation occured over a period when the composition of the workforce was far different than it is today. Since 1980 the labor force participation rate of women with preschool children has continued to increase from 45.1 to over 57 percent; the number of female-headed households has also continued to grow. To the extent that there is "institutional lag" benefits packages may not meet the needs of these workers.

Second, Ureta and Light (1993) show that in the past, it may have been rational for employers to invest less in the retention of women workers, because these workers were more likely to leave the firm for reasons that were unobservable at the time of hire. But in a more recent birth cohort, they find that it is no longer difficult to identify female non-quitters—hence there is no justification for using "femaleness" as a screening device among young workers. To the extent that some employers rely on outdated screening devices, women workers may be denied access to jobs with characteristics that they find desirable.

In either case, the aim of this chapter is to examine the empirical evidence regarding the extent to which gender differences in benefits packages appear to reflect employee preferences. In order to address this question, the chapter first lays out the differences between the benefits packages received by male and female workers, and relates these differences to one of the most salient differences between men and women: the fact that in general women continue to bear primary responsibility for "household production." The second part asks whether men and women appear to value similar packages differently. The third part gets to the heart of the matter, and assesses the extent to which gender gaps and benefits packages seem to reflect the voluntary sorting of men and women into different jobs. The limited evidence available suggests that firms that wish to attract and retain female employees can achieve some success by altering their benefits packages. In particular, conditional on worker characteristics such as age and education, more flexible leave and vacation provisions, and access to on-the-job training are linked to reduced turnover among female employees.

DO MEN AND WOMEN RECEIVE SIMILAR BENEFITS PACKAGES?

One way to answer this question would be to add up employer costs for each component of the benefits package, and ask whether employers spend the same amounts on men and women. There are two drawbacks to this approach however. First, detailed information of this kind is not available for a representative sample of U.S. workers (Antos, 1983). Second, benefits packages may differ in terms of their composition, as well as in terms of their cost to employers. Hence, this section will begin with an analysis of whether men and women are equally likely to receive six types of benefits: pensions, health insurance, paid sick leave, paid vacations, disability, and training. Legally required benefits are discussed below.

Of these benefits, pensions, vacations, and health care account for the largest share of employer costs. The Bureau of Labor Statistics (1994a) reports that in 1993 vacations, health care, and pensions accounted for 3.2, 6.7, and 3.0 percent of payroll, respectively, while sick leave and disability together accounted for 1.1 percent. The category "other benefits," which includes employee education, accounted for only .2 percent. These figures imply average hourly expenditures of $.54, $1.14, $.52, and $.04 in addition to an average hourly wage of $12.14. The total cost of benefits as a percentage of payroll was 28.9 percent, of which 9.4 percent was legally required payments. Although expenditures on sick leave, disability, and training are small relative to total benefit payments, examining this relatively broad package will help us to address the link between benefits packages, worker valuations, and occupational segregation.

Composition of Benefits Packages

Pensions are perhaps the most studied element of the benefits package. They are not only a relatively "big ticket" item, they also have important uses as retention devices as discussed in an earlier chapter in this volume. Many authors have pointed out that on average, women are less likely to be enrolled in private pension plans than men (Beller, 1981; Even & Macpherson, 1990; Galarneau, 1991; Hersch & White-Means, 1991; Kotlikoff & Wise, 1987; Lazear & Rosen, 1987; Moore, 1987; Woodbury & Huang, 1991). In the United States, 55 percent of male employees were enrolled in a pension plan in 1988, compared to only 45 percent of female employees; the gap in pension coverage was even larger in Canada where 51 percent of male workers were covered compared to 37 percent of female workers (Even & Macpherson, 1994).

However, these raw differences in coverage rates do not take account of the fact that labor market characteristics of male and female workers differ. Because men and women tend to have different characteristics on average, differences in non-wage compensation can arise even when the same benefit formulas are applied to both groups, as the Equal Employment Opportunity Commission's rules require.[1]

Table 1 shows male-female differences in the means of some characteristics of workers and jobs that have been shown to be closely associated with levels of compensation. The table focuses only on full-time, full-year workers, since part-time workers are much less likely to have benefits coverage.[2] The table breaks workers down by marital status and number of children, since these variables may affect workers' valuations of benefits packages, as discussed below.

Table 1. Worker Characteristics by Gender, Marital Status, and Presence of Children

| | Married, Separated, Widowed | | | | Single, Divorced | | | |
| | Children | | No Children | | Children | | No Children | |
	Male	Female	Male	Female	Male	Female	Male	Female
Age	37.3	35.5	45.0	42.3	36.2	35.0	31.2	33.7
Years of Education	13.5	12.8	13.0	12.9	12.4	12.8	13.2	13.4
Tenure on the Job	8.6	6.0	12.1	8.0	9.3	5.5	5.2	5.3
Fraction Non-White	.07	.13	.06	.08	.03	.21	.09	.11
Fraction Union Worker	.21	.08	.22	.10	.23	.12	.22	.13
Fraction Hourly Worker	.48	.60	.47	.54	.60	.58	.60	.55
Firm Size < 100	.28	.33	.28	.35	.40	.31	.38	.32
Firm Size 500+	.51	.41	.50	.41	.39	.45	.38	.44
# Observations	2399	1266	1618	1274	62	242	1208	980

Source: Currie, 1993. Computations are from the May 1988 Current Population Survey.

Table 1 indicates that female workers tend to be younger and to have much less tenure in their jobs than male workers, unless they are single and childless. Married women workers are less educated, while single women workers are more educated than their male counterparts. Finally, female workers are more likely to be nonwhite than male workers, especially if they are single parents.

Turning to characteristics of the job, we see that female workers are much less likely to be unionized, and much more likely to be hourly workers than male workers. Both being salaried and being unionized increase the probability that benefits are received, other things being equal (Freeman, 1981). Married women workers are also more likely to be in small firms, and less likely to be in large firms than married male workers—though these firm-size relationships are reversed among single workers.

Differences in average firm size for men and women are likely to be particularly important. Smeeding (1983) calculates that the difference between what employees would have to pay in the market for benefits purchased individually and what employers pay averages about 32 percent of the employer's cost. The difference is biggest for the largest firms, reflecting scale economies in the purchase of benefits. Hence, it is not surprising that large firms have more generous benefits as shown in Table 2.

Hence, Tables 1 and 2 suggest that based on personal characteristics and on job characteristics, one would expect women to be paid less and to have inferior benefits packages relative to men. They also suggest that we might expect the gaps to be greatest among married workers, since the differences in characteristics are greatest among this group.

These hypotheses are explored in Table 3, which shows mean wages and the fraction of workers who receive each of four benefits for the same eight worker groups. Once again, only means for full-time workers are shown. In this table, conventional defined contribution and defined benefit pension plans have been grouped together with 401k plans since the latter are an increasingly important type of pension coverage.[3]

Table 2. Employee Benefits in Large vs. Small Firms

	Firms with < 100 Emp.	Firms with >= 100 Emp.
% of Employees Covered by		
Pensions	45	78
Paid Vacations	88	97
Health Insurance	71	82
Paid Sick Leave	53	65
Disability Insurance	21	41
Job Related Educational Assistance	36	69*

Source: Bureau of Labor Statistics, 1994b, 1994c. An asterisk indicates that the source is BLS (1990).

Table 3. Wages and Benefits by Gender, Marital Status, and Presence of Children

| | Married, Separated, Widowed | | | | Single, Divorced | | | |
| | Children | | No Children | | Children | | No Children | |
	Male	Female	Male	Female	Male	Female	Male	Female
Hourly Wage	13.0	8.5	13.0	8.9	11.4	9.0	10.1	8.8
Has Pension/401(k)	.67	.54	.70	.54	.52	.54	.48	.51
Has Health Insurance	.87	.69	.86	.72	.79	.81	.77	.79
Has Sick Leave	.72	.73	.72	.72	.63	.72	.60	.71
Has Disability	.67	.50	.65	.49	.68	.51	.58	.53

Source: Currie, 1993. Tabulations based on the May 1988 Current Population Survey.

180

Table 3 indicates that while women are paid less than men in all four groups, only among married workers are women less likely to receive pension coverage or health insurance coverage. Single women workers are actually *more* likely than single male workers to have sick leave, while male workers are more likely than female workers to have disability benefits regardless of marital status. These differences suggest that much of the raw gap in benefits coverage may be explained by worker characteristics, such marital status. The results regarding paid sick leave are consistent with those of Trzcinski (1991). She finds using a survey of small businesses that the probability that a firm offers paid sick leave rises with the fraction of employees who are female.

In a study of the benefits packages received by workers who took part in the RAND Health Insurance study, Leibowitz (1983) found that in addition to more generous sick leave provisions, 21 percent of the women had paid vacations compared to 9 percent of the men. However, this difference was not statistically significant once education and experience were controlled for. Since the incidence of vacations increases with the education and experience of the worker, this result suggests that the women in her sample had more human capital than the men on average. Hence, it is difficult to extend these results to other samples.

Reed and Holleman (1994) examine the incidence of paid vacations, health coverage, and life insurance for a sample of young workers from the National Longitudinal Survey of Youth (NLSY). The average age of the workers in their sample is 22, and only 23 percent of them are married. Although they do not report the average number of children, it is likely that many of these people were childless. In this sample they find that women were actually slightly more likely than men to have all three benefits, a finding that is consistent with the results shown in Table 3. Together, these findings suggest that while gender gaps in benefits coverage are relatively small among single workers, among married workers, women are less likely to have pensions and health insurance, and more likely to have paid sick leave and paid vacations.

While a similar breakdown by marital status is not available for training, Lynch (1992) uses a sample of young workers from the National Longitudinal Survey of Youth (NLSY) to document gender gaps in access to training programs, as shown in Table 4. This information is incomplete as respondents were questioned only about spells of training that lasted at least four weeks (though they did not have to be full time). A positive feature of the NLSY data is that it is possible to distinguish between training received on the job (a benefit), and training received off the job and presumably paid for by the employee. Table 4 shows that this distinction is important. Although men and women were approximately equally likely to have received any training, 5.8 percent of males received training on the job compared to only 3.4 percent of females. Conversely, only 13 percent of men received off the job training compared to 17 percent of women.

Table 4.   Gender Gaps in Training

	White Males	White Females
# with on-the-Job Training	77	37
# with Off-the-Job Training	177	185
# Apprenticed	41	9
Duration On-the-Job Training	34.6	24.7
Duration Off-the-Job Training	43.5	39.5
Duration of Apprenticeship	74.8	18.9
Sample Size	1320	1090

Source: Lynch, 1992. Data is from the National Longitudinal Survey of Youth. In order to be included in the sample, workers had to have valid wage data in both 1980 and 1983, but no restrictions were placed on their hours of work.

A more formal way to test the hypothesis that gender gaps in benefits coverage are explained by worker characteristics is to estimate linear probability models of the probability of being covered by each benefit on the complete set of worker characteristics. Logit models produce similar results. A regression that includes a variable equal to one if the worker is female and zero otherwise, yields an estimate of the average effect of "femaleness" on the probability of benefits coverage, holding all other observable characteristics constant. Models that allow the effect of femaleness to vary with the worker's characteristics (in order to determine whether the penalty associated with being female is smaller for younger workers, for example) can also be estimated.

The results of following these estimation procedures are summarized in Table 5 for full-time workers. The first row shows that even after controlling for all observable characteristics, women are on average 5 percent less likely to receive pension coverage, 8 percent less likely to have health insurance, 3 percent more likely to have sick leave, and 11 percent less likely to have disability coverage.[4] Lynch (1992) presents similar estimates showing that among young workers, men are 2 percent and 1 percent more likely to receive on-the-job training and to be apprenticed, respectively, and 3 percent less likely to receive off-the-job training.

The second row of Table 5 shows gender gaps for a particular group of workers—young (25 to 34 years old), single, high school educated workers in firms with between 20 and 99 employees. The gaps are similar to those for the average worker, except that among these young workers there are no significant gender gaps in health coverage, and female workers are even more likely than men to receive sick leave. Row 3 indicates that, as we might expect on the basis of Table 3, gender gaps in pension and health coverage are twice as big among married workers. A comparison of rows 3 and 4 shows that the gender gap in pensions is larger for older workers, probably because average levels of job tenure have been increasing over time among women. Rows 3 and 5 show that gender gaps in benefits coverage among married workers are similar, whether or not workers have children, although married women with children are even less likely

Table 5.   Gender Gaps in Benefits Coverage,
for Workers with the Same Characteristics

Type of Benefit	Pension	Health	Sick Leave	Disability
1. Average Gap for all Workers	-.05	-.08	.03	-.11
2. Gap for Baseline Worker	-.05	...	07	-.10
3. Same as 2 but Married	-.09	-.16	.08	-.12
4. Same as 3 but 55-64	-.14	-.16	...	-.09
5. Same as 3 but 2 Children	-.10	-.20	.05	-.11
6. Same as 5 but University ed.	-.09	-.20	...	-.14
7. Same as 5 but Large Firm	-.01	-.08	.08	-.08

Source: Currie, 1993. The baseline estimates refer to 25 to 34 year old workers with a high school education who work in firms with 20 to 99 employees. Estimates are based on the Benefits Supplement to the May 1988 Current Population Survey. Dots indicate that there is no statistically significant difference between men and women.

than comparable men to have health insurance. And while women are still more likely than comparable men to have sick leave, the gap is narrowed among workers with children. A comparison of rows 5 and 6 indicates that gender gaps are similar among university educated workers and workers with high school educations. The main exception is that among university educated workers, there is no gender gap in the probability of sick leave. Finally, row 7 indicates that large firms have dramatically smaller gaps in the probability of pension, health, and disability coverage, although women in these firms are still more likely than men to have sick leave.

The regressions underlying Table 5 do not control for one important job characteristic: the worker's wage. This is because wages and benefits are part of the same package and are chosen simultaneously by the worker. Hence it is not appropriate to "explain" benefits using wages or vice versa. In fact, economic theory suggests that, other things being equal, workers should be willing to trade off benefits and wages. That is, there ought to be a negative relationship between the generosity of benefits and wages when all other characteristics of the job are adequately controlled for (cf. Brown, 1980; Leibowitz, 1983; Rosen, 1986; Smith & Ehrenberg, 1983).

In practice, however, there tends to be a strong positive relationship between wages and the generosity of benefits coverage.[5] One reason is that given a progressive tax system, higher wage workers are more likely to want to have a portion of their benefits in the form of untaxed benefits (Woodbury & Huang, 1991).

Nevertheless, in most data sets the wage is the best measure we have of the "quality" of the job: good jobs tend to have both high wages and generous benefits. Hence, we might wish to add wages to a benefits equation as a proxy for job quality. When this is done, the coefficient on "female" in the equation for pension coverage becomes statistically insignificant, so that among men and women with the same wages there are no differences in the probability of pension coverage. The male/female difference in the probability of health coverage drops to 5 percent, and the difference in the probability of disability coverage falls to 6 percent. However, controlling for wages, women are 6 percent more likely to have sick leave than men. Hence, differences in the probability of sick leave and disability coverage tend to offset each other.[6]

One reason that employers might prefer to offer women sick leave rather than disability, is that under the federal Pregnancy Discrimination Act of 1978, employers must cover maternity-related conditions under existing disability plans. Alternatively, it may be the case that women are less likely to be disabled on the job and hence value sick leave more highly than disability.

In summary, this section shows that there are significant gender gaps in the probability of receiving various kinds of benefits that persist when observable characteristics of workers and firms are controlled for. Moreover, these gaps vary systematically with worker and firm characteristics, although they become much smaller when wages are controlled for.[7]

Gender Gaps in the Employer Cost of Benefits

The next question that arises is whether men and women receive benefits that are similar in terms of generosity, given that they do receive the benefit. Several authors have addressed the question of whether the same pension promise is likely to be worth more to a man or to a woman. Wise and Kotlikoff (1987) and Moore (1987) argue that because women live longer on average, a given pension will be worth more to a woman than to a man. However, Lazear and Rosen (1987) argue that in addition to actuarial considerations, the employer cost of pension plans depends on the average salary and average tenure of workers in different groups.

In the first stage of their analysis they use nationally representative data from the 1979 Current Population Survey (CPS) to estimate the average tenure and salary of male and female workers of retirement age. They find, somewhat surprisingly in view of the numbers shown earlier, that the expected tenure at retirement is very similar for men and women. However, despite this similarity in expected years of tenure at retirement, they found that the expected salary of a white female worker was only 64 percent of the expected salary of a white male worker at retirement. This large gap in salary suggests that there will be a large gap in the value of pensions paid to male and female workers, since pensions are generally based on salaries paid in the last few years before a worker retires. The gaps in salary between male and female African-American workers were smaller: at retirement a typical African-American woman earned 82 percent of what the typical male earned.

In the second part of their analysis they ask how typical male and female workers would fare in retirement using detailed information about the pension plans of 172 large corporations from the Bankers' Trust *Corporate Pension*

Plan Study (1980). They find that among whites who receive pensions, the typical female worker's pension is worth 78 percent of the typical male worker's, while among African Americans it is worth 92 percent of the typical male worker's. Hence, the inequality in wages is partially offset by the higher actuarial value of the women's pensions and also by the fact that most plans reward tenure on the job as well as final salary. These results suggest that the main reason that a given pension promise is worth less to a woman than to a man, is that women are more likely to be in low-wage jobs. Hence, it is not surprising, that controlling for wages, women are as likely as men to receive pension coverage, as discussed earlier.

Less information is available regarding the relative generosity of health plans, although some data is available in the May 1988 CPS. Among those covered, married women are only half as likely as married men to have a plan that covers their spouse and children. However, this figure could reflect choices made by women themselves if women and children are covered under spouses' policies. Another index of plan generosity is whether the employer pays the full cost of the health plan. Eighty-five percent of married men report that the employer pays for "some" or "all" of their plan, while only 67 percent of married women make the same claim. But married women are much more likely to report that they do not know whether the employer pays or not: 30 percent of married women are in this category compared to 12 percent of married men. Hence, the difference in reported generosity could be an artifact of the missing data. There were few differences among single people in these reports of plan generosity.

Hersch and White-Means (1991) employ an alternative strategy and use data on the percentage of industry wages that are spent on health benefits (as reported in U.S. Chamber of Commerce, 1989) to impute a value of health insurance coverage to each worker in the CPS. They also impute a value for pension coverage using the worker's salary, along with the average value of pension benefits as a percentage of wages in the worker's industry. They find that these two benefits together are worth $1.08 to a white male, $.65 to a white female, $.87 to a black male, and $.70 to a black female. These figures are not directly comparable to those cited earlier, because in addition to the inclusion of health benefits, they reflect the fact that women are less likely to receive pensions and health coverage than men. However, at .61, the ratio of female to male benefits among whites is almost identical to Lazear and Rosen's estimate of the ratio of *expected* pension wealth among whites of .62. This similarity between the figures for health plans and pensions together and those for pensions alone implies that women are not concentrated in industries with less available or less generous health plans.

Finally, the Bureau of Labor Statistics (1994b, 1994c) reports that there are only small differences in the generosity of plans offered by large and small firms. Among small firms, 37 percent of individuals had their own health care wholly covered by their employers compared to 39 percent among larger firms, while 19 percent of small firm employees had dependents care fully paid for by employers compared to 24 percent of large firm employees. BLS (1993b) estimates also suggest that conditional on being covered, employees of large and small firms bear similar out-of-pocket costs. Hence, it seems that women are unlikely to have systematically less generous plans, even though they tend to be concentrated in smaller firms.

Turning to sick leave, women in the May 1988 CPS are slightly more likely to report that they receive leave with full pay, but they report a smaller mean maximum number of days: for example, married women report an average of 61 days compared to 87 days for married men. However, the standard deviations are also large (54 days for both married men and women) which reflects a great deal of heterogeneity in the plans. However, once again, there are some differences by firm size, which suggests that women may actually get fewer days than men on average. The BLS (1993a, 1994c) reports that small firms offer an average of 7.7 days paid sick leave after one year, and 10.2 days after 10 years. In contrast, large firms offer 9 days after one year and 17 days after 10 (BLS, 1990).

A final piece of information about benefits costs can be gleaned from Table 4, which showed that conditional on receiving formal on-the-job training or being apprenticed, women were in systematically shorter, and presumably therefore cheaper, programs.

In summary, there is some evidence with regard to pensions that the same pension promise is worth less to a woman than to a man. However, almost all of the difference is accounted for by the fact that women are likely to have lower wages at retirement. The evidence with regard to the employer costs of other benefits is sketchy, but does not offer much support for the view that benefits received by women are less generous than those received by men, when they are in fact received. A possible caveat is that to the extent that women are concentrated in small firms, they may receive somewhat less generous benefits coverage. Still, variations in generosity appear to be of second-order importance relative to the question of whether the benefit is offered or not.

Legally Required Payments

There is little empirical evidence regarding the effects of legally required payments on gender gaps in benefits coverage. But since one-quarter of all benefits payments are legally required, some discussion of their likely effects is important. At first blush, legislated payments, which include social security, unemployment insurance, and worker's compensation, would appear to be equalizing since the law is gender-blind.

But if female employees tend to value these benefits differently than male employees, then increasing the share of compensation taken in this form can be expected to have complicated effects. For example, actuarial considerations suggest that other things being equal, increases in the generosity of social security will make work more attractive to women than to men. Similarly, since women are at higher risk of losing their jobs, more generous unemployment insurance may also tend to make work attractive. However, it is not obvious what effect increases in female labor supply would have on the tendency of men and women to sort into different jobs. Presumably both men and women would be more likely to enter jobs without pension coverage, or with unstable employment, than before. It is also unclear how much of the increase in required payments would be offset by reductions in wages or other benefits. For example, Fishback and Kantor show that employers were able to pass a significant fraction of costs due to worker's compensation onto employees in the form of lower wages (Fishback & Kantor, 1994).

Other types of legislative interventions into compensation packages may inadvertently exacerbate gender differences in benefits coverage by exempting small firms (Trzcinski & Alpert, 1990). Since women are overrepresented in small firms, these measures tend to leave many women uncovered. The Family and Medical Leave Act of 1993 falls into this category since employers with fewer than 50 employees are exempted from the law. BLS (1994) reports that in 1992 only 18 percent of small firms offered unpaid maternity leave, while only 8 percent offered unpaid paternity leave.

EMPLOYEE VALUATIONS OF BENEFITS PACKAGES

If data about employer costs of benefits packages are sketchy, then data about employee valuations of benefits packages are even scarcer. Yet this is an essential piece of the puzzle. The arguments laid out earlier in this volume suggest that an important reason for the growth of benefits as a fraction of total compensation is that certain benefits can be provided by employers more inexpensively than they can be purchased by employees in the marketplace. Hence, the substitution of benefits for wages can make both employers and employees better off. However, in practice some employees are likely to value certain benefits more highly than others. How can we tell whether these differences in tastes are systematically related to gender?

One answer is to see whether women are systematically more likely than men to turn down offered benefits. The May 1988 CPS asked workers both whether their firm offered pension and health coverage and whether they were covered (comparable information is not available for other benefits). Table 6 compares these values. For convenience, coverage numbers are reproduced from Table 3. Table 6 shows that gaps in offered coverage are much smaller than gaps in actual coverage. For example, married women with children are 13 percent less likely to have pension coverage than men in the same category, but they are only 8 percent less likely to work at a company with a pension plan. These women are 18 percent less likely to have health insurance coverage, but only 5 percent less likely to be at a firm that offers a health plan.

Table 6. Offers vs. Takeup of Benefits by Gender, Marital Status, and Presence of Children

	Married, Separated, Widowed				Single, Divorced			
	Children		No Children		Children		No Children	
	Male	Female	Male	Female	Male	Female	Male	Female
Pension Offered	.74	.66	.76	.65	.60	.66	.61	.67
Pension Coverage	.67	.54	.70	.54	.52	.54	.48	.51
Health Offered	.92	.87	.92	.86	.86	.86	.84	.86
Health Coverage	.87	.69	.86	.72	.79	.81	.77	.79

Note: See Table 3.

In order to explore why men and women are not equally likely to be covered under offered pension plans, I examined the gender gap in coverage for those with 10 years of experience or more. Federal law would have required that the vast majority of these employees be vested under the offered plan (Hoopes & Maroney, 1992). For the "married with children" group discussed earlier, women were 7 percent less likely to be covered by a plan, and 5 percent less likely to be in a job that offered a pension plan.

Hence, about half of the overall gender difference in pension coverage can be attributed to differences in tenure. However, among the group with 10 years of experience or more, the gender difference in pension coverage appears to be mainly due to the fact that women are less likely to be in jobs that offer plans. The probability that a plan is offered is in turn closely related to the wage—once the wage is controlled for, there is no significant difference in the probability that a pension is offered.

Even and Macpherson (1994) offer a complementary analysis of pension offers and participation rates among men and women. They find that between 1979 and 1993, male offer rates rose by 2.2 percentage points while female offer rates rose by a huge 18.4 percentage points. However, participation rates fell over the same time period by 11.1 percentage points for men and 17.3 percentage points for women. The net effect was that male coverage fell 4.9 percentage points while female coverage rose 8.3 points over this period. Some of this decline in participation is due to the increasing importance of 401k plans, which have lower participation rates than traditional plans (Even & Macpherson, 1994).[8] In any case, the numbers suggest that more than half of the women who were offered plans, did not find participation attractive.

The difference between health coverage and the availability of a health plan can be further examined using the responses to a question addressed to respondents who were not covered even though their employers had a plan. Female respondents in this situation were about 10 percent less likely than male respondents to answer that they were ineligible for the plan, and 12 percent more likely to answer that they were covered by another plan. Only about 10 percent of married men and women, and 19 percent of single men and women said the offered plan was too expensive. Hence, the large gender differences in health coverage among married workers appear to be largely due to voluntary choices on the part of women who do not value the coverage because they are already covered under their husband's plans.[9] Given that some people are covered by plans that are completely paid for by their employers, and thus have little incentive not to take up offered coverage, these figures probably represent an underestimate of the number of workers with duplicative coverage that is of little value to them.

Perhaps the most discussion of possible gender differences in the valuation of benefits has occurred with respect to paid sick leave. Current gender roles dictate that it is most often women who take time off from work to care for newborn or sick children, elderly parents, and other family members. Conventional wisdom has it that married women and single women with children often use their own sick days for this purpose if other types of paid family leave are not available (Trzcinski, 1991). Hence, women might value leave provisions more highly than men. There is, however, little direct evidence on this question, although some work has been done regarding the value of maternity leave.

Using data from the United States (the NLSY) and United Kingdom (the National Child Development Survey) Waldfogel (1994) shows that women who take maternity leave and return to the same firm, suffer much smaller wage losses than women who leave the firm when they give birth and later move to another. Since it is possible that women are more likely to take maternity leave when they have high wages (rather than vice versa), she also estimates models that control for whether or not the firm offers maternity leave.[10] The latter model suggests that an American woman's wages are 4 percent higher if she is able to take maternity leave and return to the same firm after the birth. Previous research suggests that these women's wages might eventually catch up to what they would have been without the interruption (Mincer & Polachek, 1978). But, a leave policy that enables a woman to stay with her employer is likely to be worth a considerable amount to a female employee in terms of avoidance of lost wages.

Gruber (1994) takes a somewhat different approach and examines the extent to which wages for women of child-bearing age fell when several states mandated that firms provide maternity leave in the late 1970s and early 1980s. He finds that wages adjusted almost completely, and that there was little loss of employment among this group, which suggests that women are willing to pay at least the employer's cost in order to obtain this benefit.[11]

Finally, Reed and Holleman (1994) show that in their sample of young workers, both men and women are less likely to leave their jobs if they have paid vacations, other things being equal. However, the coefficient is twice as big for female workers as for male workers, suggesting that women value this benefit more highly than men.

Little information is available on the question of whether men and women might value disability plans or training programs differently. It is worth noting, however, that there may be interactions between valuations of different types of benefits. For example, if there is no leave plan, and a woman knows that she may be forced to leave her employer in the next few years because of family responsibilities, then she may not value firm-specific training or pension coverage very highly.

ARE GENDER GAPS THE RESULT OF OPTIMAL MATCHING?

The first and second sections of this chapter show that there are gender gaps in benefits coverage, and that it may also be true that men and women tend to value some benefits differently. These two phenomena are quite likely to be related to each other and to the fact that men and women tend to hold different jobs. The question posed in this section is whether gender differences in the composition of compensation packages reflect optimizing choices of workers, rather than an inability to find employment with desired compensation packages?

It is possible that, conditional on their observable characteristics, men and women tend to be in different jobs because they choose jobs with characteristics, including benefits packages, that they value. Since women typically bear primary responsibility child rearing, it makes sense that women might choose jobs with characteristics that were compatible with this role (Becker, 1985). Leave provisions could be viewed as one such characteristic.

However, Table 5 provides relatively little support for the hypothesis that gender gaps in benefits coverage are primarily due to choices made by women who wish to specialize in household production. First, young, single, childless women (the baseline) are about as likely as women generally to be offered pension coverage, but they are less likely to be offered health coverage, and about equally likely to have disability coverage. Yet, they are twice as likely as the average woman to have sick leave. It is possible that this last result reflects worker preferences (i.e., that women are more likely than men to take sick leave regardless of marital status[12]), but if so, this preference would not appear to have anything to do with women's roles as wives and mothers. The gender gaps in benefits coverage (and wages) are especially noteworthy for this group given that there is no significant gender difference in tenure on the job.

Second, married women 25 to 34 suffer greater gaps in benefits coverage and wages than single women, whether or not they have children. If women with children can be expected to be most intensively involved in household production then this observation is inconsistent with the "specialization in household production" theory outlined earlier.

Third, a comparison of gender gaps among married, university educated workers with children to gender gaps among similar workers with only a high school education shows that for most individual benefits, the gender gap is just as large among the highly educated. Since more educated women have made greater investments in human capital and can be shown to have a greater commitment to market work (and arguably have somewhat different tastes) this observation also appears to be inconsistent with the theory that gender gaps are primarily a reflection of worker preferences.

If gender gaps do not reflect worker preferences, a possible explanation is that some employees cannot find employers who offer the desired benefits packages. Take as a starting point, Lynch's (1992) observation that employers are less likely to offer on-the-job training to young women than to young men. She also shows that young women are more likely than young men to seek off-the-job training. This finding strongly suggests that women who are frustrated in their attempts to obtain training from their employers seek training at their own expense. Lynch (1991) documents the fact that women who received on-the-job training were significantly less likely to leave their employers than women who received no training, while those who received off-the-job training were significantly more likely to leave. And, as discussed previously, Reed and Holleman found that paid vacation provisions had a greater negative effect on turnover among women than among men. Similar analyses have yet to be undertaken for other fringe benefits.

The hypothesis that women are leaving employers who do not offer them the same opportunities as are offered to men fits nicely with Loprest's (1992) finding that although young women change jobs as frequently as young men, their wages grow only half as quickly with job changes. That is, young women appear to be changing jobs when it is less advantageous for them to do so. To the extent that valuable workers are lost to the firm, this kind of turnover is costly to firms as well as to workers.

DISCUSSION AND CONCLUSIONS

The evidence reviewed in this chapter shows that there are gender gaps in benefits coverage, and that there may also be gender-related differences in the way that employees value similar benefits packages. However, it seems unlikely that the observed gaps primarily reflect differences in employee preferences. Instead, the evidence suggests that some turnover among young women results from an inability to find jobs that offer satisfactory benefits, at least in terms of training opportunities and paid leave/vacation time. This turnover is costly to employees, since the wages of young women do not rise as quickly with job changes as those of young men. It is also likely to be costly to employers.

A possible solution to the problem of offering benefits packages that will attract able workers regardless of gender (and other personal characteristics that influence tastes) is to offer flexible benefits (e.g., cafeteria plans). A survey by the Employer's Council on Flexible Compensation found that the number of major employers adopting these plans had grown from eight in 1980 to 800 in 1989 (Pilenzo, 1989). One of the primary reasons given for offering such a plan is the need to meet the needs of a changing workforce, which includes increasing numbers of working women, employees with working spouses, and working single parents (Johnson, 1986).[13]

A recent Hewitt Associates Survey of 472 employees found that flexible benefits plans were effective in attracting and retaining employees (Lissy, 1993). And the Employer's Council survey cited earlier found that 87 percent of the women and 61 percent of the men who participated in flexible plans said that the plan had influenced their decision not to seek job changes (Pilenzo, 1989).

On the other hand, cafeteria plans have drawbacks from the point of view of employers. They may be costly to administer, and employers may lose leverage with insurance carriers if they cannot promise a certain number of enrollees; they encourage adverse selection; and the tax code's restrictions on creating benefit plans that favor the highly compensated may mean that in fact it is not possible to allow employees a free hand in designing a benefits package.[14] Moreover, the definitive study linking the adoption of such plans to a reduction in turnover among women (and other groups) has not yet been executed.

Hence, the findings reported in this chapter are best viewed as preliminary and suggestive. Human resource managers who find that their firms are having difficulty attracting or retaining female employees should consider the possibility that relatively small changes in the composition of benefits packages, such as opening training programs to women or offering more flexible leave policy, could have a positive effect on recruitment and retention.

NOTES

1. It is not obvious what effect rules will have on the probability that a pension is offered. Suppose that in the absence of regulation, firms would pay women smaller monthly benefits. The EEOC policy will not necessarily raise costs since the firm can pay a benefit that is the weighted average of what it would have paid to men and women. However, this pension promise will be worth less to men, than one that was based on actuarial considerations.

2. Of course, part-time workers are also more likely to be female. By focusing on full-time workers, the analysis implicitly assumes that women who select part-time work "voluntarily" sacrifice benefits in order to obtain more flexible hours. Full-time, full-year workers are defined here as those who work 35 hours per week or more, at least 50 weeks per year (where weeks per year includes weeks of paid vacation).

3. Although these numbers are based on the 1988 CPS, the most recent evidence available, from the 1993 CPS Employee Benefits Survey, suggests that there has been little change. For example, in 1993, 56 percent of men had pension coverage compared to 57 percent in 1988, while

the comparable figures for women were 47.9 percent in 1993 and 45.1 percent in 1988 (Even & Macpherson, 1994). Surveys of employee benefits have been conducted in 1983, 1988, and 1993.

4.   The regressions underlying Table 5 included marital status, number of children, a dummy variable for nonwhite, four age categories (25 to 34, 35 to 44, 45 to 54, 55 to 64), four educational categories (some high school, high school, some college, and university degree), and five firm size categories (20 to 99, 100 to 499, 500 to 999, 1000+, and don't know). The models in rows 2 through 5 included interactions of the female dummy with all these variables. Including dummy variables for union and hourly workers did not affect the results reported here (see Currie, 1993 for the full set of regressions).

5.   Montgomery, Shaw, and Benedict (1992) do however find a one-for-one tradeoff between the present value of *lifetime* wages and pension coverage.

6.   These regressions are shown in Currie (1993) and are based on the May 1988 Current Population Survey. Lazear and Rosen (1987) report similar results for pension coverage using the 1979 CPS.

7.   Currie and Chaykowski (1995) report similar results for Canada. They find using contract-level data that bargaining units with a high proportion of female workers are less likely to have pension coverage and more likely to have leave provisions, even when the wage is controlled for in an instrumental variables framework. They also show that the gender gap in pension coverage exists in individual-level data and persists when wages are controlled for, although it becomes much smaller.

8.   These plans have shown tremendous growth over the past 10 years. Whereas in 1983 only 4.4 million employees reported participation in a 401k, by 1993, 43 percent of all workers offered pension plan had a 401k plan as the primary plan (Even & Macpherson, 1994).

9.   This discussion also raises the possibility that some women turn down offered pension coverage because they are covered by their husband's plans. ERISA requires that survivor benefits be offered.

10.   Waldfogel also estimates instrumental variables models using whether or not the firm has a maternity leave program as an instrument for whether the woman took such leave.

11.   If the labor supply of married women were perfectly elastic, then employers would bear all of the costs. However, most estimates of the labor supply of married women suggest that it is reasonably elastic.

12.   For example, Leibowitz (1983) reports that in her data, 5.1 percent of women employed full time lost work time due to illness in May 1978 compared to only 3.4 percent of men. However, men had lengthier absences for each incident. The BLS (1993c) reports that among workers with jobs who were not a work in November 1993, 29 percent of the men were ill compared to 35 percent of the women.

13.   Other reasons given for the adoption of these plans include educating employees about their benefits, and cost management.

14.   The problem is that low-wage employees prefer cash to benefits, while high-wage employees are likely to prefer benefits for tax reasons.

REFERENCES

Antos, J. (1983). Analysis of labor cost: Data concepts and sources. In J.E. Triplett (Ed.), *Measurement of labor costs* (pp. 153-181). Chicago: The University of Chicago Press.

Banker's Trust Company (1980). *1980 study of corporate pension plans*. New York: Banker's Trust.

Becker, G. (1985, January). Human capital, effort, and the sexual division of labor. *Journal of Labor Economics, 3*, s33-s58.

Beller, D. (1981, July). Coverage patterns of full-time employees under private retirement plans. *Social Security Bulletin, 44*, 3-29.

Bianchi, S., & Rytina, N. (1986, February). The decline in occupational segregation during the 1970's: Census and CPS comparisons. *Demography, 23* (1).

Brown, C., Hamilton, J., & Medoff, J. (1990). *Employers large and small.* Cambridge MA: Harvard University Press.

Brown, C. (1980, February). Equalizing differences in the labor market. *Quarterly Journal of Economics, 96,* 113-134.

Bureau of Labor Statistics. (1990, June). *Employee benefits in medium and large firms, 1989.* Washington DC: U.S. Dept. of Labor, Bulletin 2363.

————. (1993a). *Employee benefits in medium and large private establishments, 1991.* Washington, DC: U.S. Dept. of Labor, Bulletin 2422.

————. (1993b, Dec). *Payouts from employee benefit plans.* Washington, DC: U.S. Dept. of Labor, Bulletin 2436.

————. (1993c, Dec). *Employment and earnings.* Washington, DC: U.S. Dept. of Labor.

————. (1994a, June 16). *Employer costs for employee compensation–March 1994.* Washington: U.S. Dept. of Labor, preliminary report.

————. (1994b, Sept 30). *Employee benefits in medium and large private establishments, 1993.* Washington: U.S. Dept. of Labor, preliminary report.

————. (1994c, May). *Employee benefits in small private establishments, 1992.* Washington, DC: U.S. Dept. of Labor, Bulletin 2441.

Currie, J. (1993). Gender gaps in benefits coverage. National Bureau of Economic Research Working Paper *v*4265, Cambridge MA, January.

Currie, J., & Chaykowski, R. (1995). Male jobs, female jobs, and gender gaps in benefits coverage in Canada. In S.W. Polachek (Ed.), *Research in labor economics.* Greenwich, CT: JAI Press.

Even, W., & Macpherson, D. (1990, May). The gender gap in pensions and wages. *Review of Economics and Statistics, 72,* 259-265.

————. (1994a, Spring). Gender differences in pensions. *The Journal of Human Resources, 29* (2), 555-587.

————. (1994b). Why has the decline in pension coverage accelerated among less educated workers? Mimeo, Dept. of Economics, Miami Univeristy, December.

Fields, J., & Wolff, E. (1991, Fall). The decline of sex segregation and the wage gap. *Journal of Human Resources, 26,* 608-622.

Fishback, P., & Kantor, S. (1994). Did workers pay for the passage of worker's compensation laws? NBER Working Paper *v*4947, December.

Freeman, R. (1981). The effect of unionism on fringe benefits. *Industrial and Labor Relations Review, 34,* 489-509.

Galarneau, D. (1991, August). Women approaching retirement. *Statistics Canada: Perspectives,* 28-39.

Goldin, C. (1990). *Understanding the gender gap.* New York: Oxford University Press.

Groshen, E. (1988). The structure of the female/male wage differential: Is it who you are, what you do, or where you work? Working Paper *v*8708, Federal Reserve Bank of Cleveland, May.

Gruber, J. (1994, June). The incidence of mandated maternity benefits. *American Economic Review, 94* (3), 622-641.

Hersch, J., & White-Means, S. (1991). Employer-sponsored health and pension benefits and the gender/wage gap. Mimeo, Department of Economics, University of Wyoming, October.

Hoopes, T., & Maroney, K. (1992). Summary of federal legislation affecting private pensions. In J. Turner & D. Beller (Eds.), *Trends in pensions 1992.* Washington DC: Government Printing Office.

Johnson, R. (1986). *Flexible benefits: A how-to guide.* Brookfield, WI: International Foundation of Employee Benefit Plans.

Kotlikoff, L., & Wise, D. (1987). The incentive effects of private pension plans. In Z. Bodie, J. Shoven, & D. Wise (Eds.), *Issues in pension economics* (pp. 283-339). Chicago: University of Chicago Press.

Lazear, E., & Rosen, S. (1987). Pension inequality. In J. Shoven & D. Wise (Eds.), *Issues in pension economics* (pp. 341-359). Chicago: University of Chicago Press.

Leibowitz, A. (1983). Fringe benefits in employee compensation. In J.E. Triplett (Ed.), *Measurement of labor costs* (pp. 341-394). Chicago: University of Chicago Press.

Light, A., & Ureta, M. (1992, April). Panel estimates of male and female job turnover behavior: Can female nonquitters be identified? *Journal of Labor Economics, 10* (2), 156-181.

Lissy, W. (1993, May-June). Currents in compensation and benefits. *Compensation and Benefits Review.*

Loprest, P. (1992, May). Gender differences in wage growth and job mobility. *American Economic Review, 82* (2), 526-532.

Lynch, L. (1991, May). The role of off-the-job vs. on-the-job training for the mobility of women workers. *American Economic Review, 81* (1), 151-156.

————. (1992, March). Private-sector training and earnings. *American Economic Review, 82* (1), 299-311.

Mincer, J., & Polachek, S. (1974, March/April). Family investments in human capital: Earnings of women. *Journal of Political Economy, 82*, s76-s108.

Montgomery, E., Shaw, K., & Benedict, M. (1992, February). Pensions and wages: An hedonic price theory approach. *International Economic Review, 33* (1), 111-128.

Moore, R. (1987). Are male-female earnings differentials related to life-expectancy-caused pension cost differences? *Economic Inquiry, 35.*

Pesando, J., Gunderson, M., & McLaren, J. (1991, August). Pension benefits and male-female wage differentials. *Canadian Journal of Economics, XXIV*, 536-550.

Pilenzo, R. (1989). Benefits priorities in an era of change. *Business, work, and benefits.* Washington, DC: Employee Benefits Research Institute.

Reed, R., & Holleman, J. (1991, June). Do women prefer women's work? Mimeo, Department of Economics, University of Oklahoma.

Rosen, S. (1986). The theory of equalizing differences. In *The handbook of labor economics.* New York: North Holland.

Smeeding, T. (1983). The size distribution of wage and nonwage compensation: Employer cost versus employee valuation. In J.E. Triplett (Ed.), *Measurement of labor costs* (pp. 153-181). Chicago: The University of Chicago Press.

Smith, R., & Ehrenberg, R. (1983). Estimating wage-fringe tradeoffs: Some data problems. In J.E. Triplett (Ed.), *Measurement of labor cost* (pp. 347-369). Chicago: University of Chicago Press.

Treiman, D., & Hartmann, H. (1981). *Women, work and wages: Equal pay for jobs of equal value.* Washington, DC: National Academy Press.

Trzcinski, E., & Finn-Stevenson, M. (1991, May). A response to arguments against mandated parental leave. *Journal of Marriage and the Family, 53*, 445-460.

Trzcinski, E., & Alpert, W. (1990). Leave policies in small business. Final Report prepared for the U.S. Small Business Administration, Office of Advocacy, October.

Trzcinski, E. (1992). The provision of maternity-related medical leave. Paper prepared for the American Economic Association Meetings, January 3-5, New Orleans.

Waldfogel, J. (1994). The family gap for young women in the US and UK: Can maternity leave make a difference? Mimeo, Kennedy School of Government, Harvard University, Cambridge MA, May.

Woodbury, S., & Huang, W.-J. (1991). *The tax treatment of fringe benefits.* Kalamazoo, MI: W.E. Upjohn Institute.

SECTION II

THE CHANGING EXTERNAL ENVIRONMENT

REGULATION OF THE HRM FUNCTION

Barbara A. Lee and Donna Sockell

The United States has a unique system of regulating the relationship between an employer and its workers. The concept of "system" must be applied loosely, for, when compared with the employment and labor relations regulatory framework of many other developed (and developing) nations,[1] the U.S. "system" may appear inchoate and, to some observers, chaotic as well. Despite the panoply of federal and state laws, judicial opinions, regulations, and common law doctrines that regulate the employment relationship, and despite the fact that laws, particularly at the federal level, have been enacted to address a perceived social problem (such as employment discrimination) rather than as components of an overall scheme of employment regulation, the "system" has evolved into a relatively stable set of guidelines for employers. This chapter will roughly sketch those guidelines and their application to various aspects of the human resource management function, both in workplaces with and without formal employee representation by unions.

THE REGULATORY FRAMEWORK

Laws and agency regulations exist at both the federal and state level, and frequently seek to control the same type of employer conduct. For example, several federal laws prohibit employment discrimination; all states and the District of Columbia prohibit employment discrimination under state law as well. When state and federal laws affect the same type of employer conduct, it must be determined whether the federal law preempts state law. In some cases (such as the regulation of collective bargaining under the National Labor Relations Act [NLRA] or in the area of occupational safety and health [OSHA]), federal law is supreme and preempts state law. In these two areas of employer conduct, the courts have found that Congress intended to "occupy the space;" thus, state efforts to regulate the "space" that Congress has already claimed are unavailing. For other areas of the law, however, the courts have allowed federal and state laws covering the same matters to coexist, ruling that Congress did not manifest an intent, either directly or indirectly, to preclude state regulation.[2] This has occurred most notably with regard to nondiscrimination laws.

Although federal statutes and regulations interpreting these statutes are important, equally (or perhaps more) significant is the body of case law that has developed to interpret these laws. For some laws, such as the Fair Labor Standards Act (FLSA), most issues of statutory interpretation were resolved some time ago, although litigation remains over the application of the laws to particular fact situations. For other laws, however, interpretation shifts over time and in response to social or political trends. This has been particularly true of the National Labor Relations Act and the agency that applies this law, the National Labor Relations Board (NLRB). Furthermore, unless the U.S. Supreme Court has ruled on a particular issue of statutory interpretation, a federal law may be interpreted and applied in inconsistent ways by various federal appellate courts.

State law may present an even greater challenge for employers because it may change more quickly, is more vulnerable to judge-made law for common law claims (under contract and tort theories), and may vary sharply from one state to the next. Employers operating in more than one state must, therefore, not only stay current with federal law developments, but with changes in state statutory and common law in each state in which their employees are based.

The body of law that regulates employment relations can be divided into at least six categories. Some laws fit more than one category, and the categories overlap somewhat. Nevertheless, for the sake of simplicity and given space limitations, we have organized the various statutes and legal doctrines into the categories identified in Table 1. Each of these categories and their underlying doctrines are briefly discussed.

Limitations on Motivation for Decisions

This category contains the largest number of laws and legal doctrines, and their number is matched by their complexity. Title VII of the Civil Rights Act of 1964, as amended by the Civil Rights Act of 1991, is probably the best known of the nondiscrimination laws, although it is not the earliest such law.[3] Other federal and state laws listed in Table 1 add a variety of classifications of protection against nondiscrimination. Prohibitions against age discrimination

Table 1. Selected Laws and Legal Doctrines that
Regulate the U.S. Employment Relationship

Motives for Employment Decisions

Federal

Title VII of the Civil Rights Act of 1964, 42 U.S.C. sec. 2000e-2 *et seq.*
Civil Rights Act of 1866, 42 U.S.C. secs. 1981, 1983, 1985
Age Discrimination in Employment Act of 1967, 29 U.S.C. secs. 621-634
Equal Pay Act, 29 U.S.C. sec. 206
Americans With Disabilities Act, 42 U.S.C. secs. 12101-12213
Rehabilitation Act of 1973, 29 U.S.C. sec. 794
Employee Polygraph Protection Act of 1988, 29 U.S.C. sec. 2002
National Labor Relations Act, 29 U.S.C. secs. 141 *et seq.*

State

Nondiscrimination laws, whistleblower laws, smoking laws, common law exceptions to at will
employment, protection for political activity, use of polygraphs

Legal Obligation to Provide Benefits

Federal

Family and Medical Leave Act of 1993, 29 U.S.C. sec. 2601 *et seq.*
Employee Retirement Income Security Act, 29 U.S.C. secs. 1001-1461; 26 U.S.C. secs. 401-418
Vietnam Era Veterans Readjustment Assistance Act, 38 U.S.C. sec. 2021 *et seq.*

State

Laws regulating workers' compensation, unemployment benefits

Workplace Standards

Federal

Fair Labor Standards Act, 29 U.S.C. secs. 201 *et seq.*
Occupational Safety and Health Act, 29 U.S.C. secs. 651 *et seq.*
Drug Free Workplace Act of 1988, 41 U.S.C. secs. 701-702
National Labor Relations Act, 29 U.S.C. secs. 141 *et seq.*

State

Laws regulating health and safety for public employees; state wage and hour laws

Notice

Federal

Worker Adjustment and Retraining Notification Act, 29 U.S.C. sec. 2101
Immigration Reform and Control Act of 1986, 8 U.S.C. sec. 274(a) *et seq.*

State

State laws regulating drug and/or AIDS testing, use of arrest records, access to personnel files

Employee Representation

Federal

National Labor Relations Act, 29 U.S.C. secs. 141 *et seq.*

State

Laws enabling public employees to bargain collectively

Tort Theories

State

Defamation, intentional/negligent infliction of emotional distress, fraud, prima facie tort, invasion
of privacy, negligence

have eliminated mandatory retirement for most workers, and separations due to reductions-in-force have frequently been challenged under this law. The Americans With Disabilities Act of 1990 protects a new category of "qualified" individuals with disabilities, and has required some employers to reassess the way that work is configured and performed.[4]

Although employment-at-will has been the prevailing legal doctrine since the publication of an influential legal treatise in 1877,[5] state courts have been chipping away at this doctrine since the 1960s, shifting their concern from the freedom of employers to contract to an attempt to equalize somewhat the imbalance of power between employers and unrepresented employees. Significant erosions of this doctrine have occurred in every state, although the extent of the erosion varies by state. In general, exceptions to at-will employment have taken four forms:

1. contract exceptions (employee handbooks, implied-in-fact from employer behavior or past practice, or oral promises that are held to bind the employer);[6]
2. "public policy" exceptions, in which a court derives public policy from state constitutions or laws that limits the reasons for which an employee may be discharged (for example, exercising a legal right [worker's compensation claim], fulfilling a legal duty [jury service], or reporting unlawful or dangerous conduct [whistleblowing]);[7]
3. "covenant of good faith and fair dealing," in which a state court declares that, even if no written or oral contract exists, an implied-in-law contract (as opposed to implied-in-fact, as in the first example) is in effect that requires the employer to treat the employee fairly and in good faith;[8]
4. statutes requiring just cause for discharge (such as Montana's Wrongful Discharge From Employment Act).[9]

All of these exceptions are created at the state level, usually by the courts, but occasionally by state legislatures (in the case of state laws protecting whistleblowers or the Montana statute cited above). Because these exceptions are judge-made, the status of at-will employment can shift rapidly when one significant court opinion is released, particularly by a state's highest court. For that reason, employers should follow legal developments related to employment at the state level as carefully as those at the federal level.

The National Labor Relations Act,[10] a federal law, prohibits an employer from taking adverse action against a worker, whether unionized or not, who takes collective action for mutual aid and protection or who engages in other activities related to union membership or advocacy.

The collective effect of these laws is to require employers to be very clear about the *reasons* for any employment decision, whether the employee perceives the decision as negative or positive, in case a challenge to that decision is later filed. Documentation of the reasons, and a reasonable justification for the decision, are critical to a well-managed human resource function. Employer motive may be difficult to establish for an individual challenging the decision; it should not be difficult for the *employer* to establish if it is called on to do so. Other implications of this category of laws and doctrines will be addressed in a later section of this chapter in the context of specific human resource functions or actions.

Legal Obligation to Provide Benefits

Although federal laws create a framework for benefits provided through workers' compensation and unemployment, state laws establish the amount of benefits, the circumstances under which benefits may be obtained, the qualifications for receiving or continuing to receive benefits, and the duration of benefits.

Workers' compensation is a no-fault insurance system that requires employers to pay the medical costs ensuing from a work-related injury as well as benefits to replace a proportion of the worker's wages while she or he cannot work. In exchange for these benefits, the laws prohibit employees injured at work from suing their employers under tort theories (such as negligence or infliction of distress).[11] Although workers' compensation laws differ somewhat by state, all states have created tests to determine whether a work-related injury is compensable. Typically, the injury must (1) be in the course of employment (not during a commute or at home), (2) have arisen out of employment (and not an activity unrelated to the work), (3) be an injury that prevents the individual from working, and (4) be the result of an accident rather than an intentional wrong committed by another employee or the employer.

Unemployment laws generally specify eligibility for benefits (usually based on a specified number of weeks of employment, availability for work, and the reason for the loss of employment). Employers typically are required to contribute to a state-controlled unemployment insurance fund based on their "experience rating," a calculation of the frequency of employment loss in their industry and, often, for that organization as well.[12]

Family leave laws, most notably the federal Family and Medical Leave Act,[13] guarantee workers 12 weeks of unpaid leave per year for the serious health condition of the employee or so that the employee can care for a newborn or newly adopted child or for a family member who is ill. Many states have adopted their own family leave laws as well, and since the federal law does not preempt state laws the interplay between state and federal family leave laws can raise challenging issues of eligibility for leave, how certain types of leave are "counted" for state or federal law purposes, and whether leave under both types of laws can be "stacked" rather than running concurrently. The laws generally require employers to grant the leave and, under most circumstances, to reinstate the employee to the same or an equivalent position, barring legitimate business reasons that would make reinstatement impossible.

The federal Employee Retirement Income Security Act (ERISA)[14] regulates pensions and "employee welfare benefits" provided by the employer. Major provisions include reporting requirements (to employees and to several federal agencies), vesting requirements, and regulation of annuity options on retirement.

Workplace Standards

The Fair Labor Standards Act,[15] a federal law, specifies the minimum wage and overtime provisions with which employers must comply for "nonexempt" employees (employees who meet the statute's definition and do not fit any of the exceptions). Individuals who meet the statutory and regulatory definition of administrative, professional, or managerial employees are exempt from the law's overtime and minimum wage provisions (although the minimum wage is rarely an issue for exempt employees). The law also includes recordkeeping requirements. Recent litigation has focused on the scope of the law's definition of "employee," particularly with regard to workers who may be regarded as independent contractors.

The federal Occupational Safety and Health Act (OSHA)[16] regulates health and safety standards in a wide array of industries. It is applicable only to private sector workers, although most states have passed similar laws for public sector workers in that state.[17] The law gives the Secretary of Labor the authority to promulgate specific safety and health standards, and also imposes a general duty on employers to maintain a workplace that is, "free from recognized hazards that are causing or are likely to cause death or serious physical harm."[18] Regulations require employers to train workers as to the hazards of the substances they work with or around,[19] and the law also imposes substantial recordkeeping requirements.[20] OSHA provides for civil fines for companies that violate the law as well as modest criminal penalties for managers or officers who willfully violate the law. Workers have a statutory right to file complaints about safety violations with the Department of Labor, and are protected from retaliation if they do so.

Notice

The federal Worker Adjustment and Retraining Notification Act (WARN) requires employers who plan to lay off or discharge 100 or more workers for financial reasons to provide these workers or their representatives (such as a trade union) with 60 days notice prior to the separation.[21] A few exceptions are provided for organizations that need to keep their plans confidential as they attempt to arrange financing for their business or for those organizations that were not aware of the need for the layoff 60 days before it occurred.[22]

Businesses found to have violated the law may be required to provide workers with back pay for the notice period.

The Immigration Reform and Control Act (IRCA)[23] affects employees only indirectly, but may provide a disincentive for employers to hire individuals who appear to be recent arrivals in the United States, a potential violation of the nondiscrimination laws. Employers may violate the laws against discrimination on the grounds of national origin if they assume without verification that a "foreign-looking" applicant or an applicant who speaks English with an accent is ineligible to work in the United States. The law requires an employer to obtain from all individuals, at the time of hiring, documentation that indicates that the individual is in the country legally and has the legal right to work in the United States. Authorization to work can be established by the presentation of a valid social security card or a birth certificate showing birth in the United States or U.S. nationality. Identity can be established by a driver's license with a photograph, a passport, or a resident alien card with a photograph. IRCA does not prohibit the hiring of noncitizens; it simply requires the employer to verify that noncitizens have the proper immigration status to entitle them to work in the United States.

Employee Representation

The National Labor Relations Act (NLRA) confers the right on individuals, who meet the definition of employee, to organize collectively and to bargain with the employer through representatives of their own choosing.[24] Although the entitlements of this federal statute do not provide employees with the right to influence or bargain over all workplace decisions, employee representatives may lawfully demand that management bargain over any issue embraced by the phrase, "wages, hours, and other terms and conditions of employment."[25]

Tort Theory

Common law tort theories, such as defamation or intentional infliction of emotional distress, are frequently appended to other types of employment claims, such as wrongful discharge or discrimination. Defamation (an oral or written communication that harms an individual's reputation or exposes her to ridicule) may be claimed in the context of performance evaluations, discussion of employee work problems, determinations of reasonable accommodation, or the provision of references to prospective employers of former employees.[26] A claim of intentional or negligent infliction of emotional distress may be added to a lawsuit challenging a discharge.[27] Invasion of privacy claims may result from locker searches, workplace surveillance, nonfraternization or anti-nepotism policies, or "honesty (integrity) testing" practices.[28]

Tort claims are particularly serious for employers because the jury hearing the case may award the employee both compensatory and punitive damages. While compensatory damages are designed to reimburse the employee for economic losses occasioned by the employer's allegedly illegal behavior, punitive damages often bear no relationship to the employee's actual loss. Punitive damage awards occasionally exceeding one million dollars are not uncommon in tort cases involving employment issues.

The common law of agency is being applied with greater frequency to workplace disputes. For example, the operation of agency law may result in employers being held liable for unauthorized activities by managers or supervisors that are asserted to result in racial or sexual harassment, whether or not the employer knew of or ratified that behavior.[29] The same agency law theory applies to violations of the NLRA.[30]

With this brief framework in place, we will turn to a discussion of how these laws apply to various components of the human resource management function.

REGULATION OF THE HRM FUNCTION

Selection and Placement

Most challenges to recruitment, selection, hiring, and placement decisions attack either the alleged motives of the employer for making the challenged decision (such as failure to hire or to promote) or the manner in which the decision was carried out. Nondiscrimination laws prohibit the employer (or an employment agency or other entity acting on behalf of the employer) from using status criteria (such as age or sex) to screen employees or to hire them. Furthermore, selection or placement tests that tend to screen out individuals by status characteristics (such as physical strength tests for women candidates) may violate Title VII, the ADA, or state nondiscrimination laws.[31] The Equal Employment Opportunity Commission (EEOC) has developed guidelines for determining when selection tests or other selection criteria have a "disparate impact" on groups protected by the nondiscrimination laws: a gap of more than 20 percent between the passing rate for the majority group and that of the minority group will usually support the legal presumption that discrimination may have infected the selection device.[32] This presumption may be rebutted by the employer's proof that the selection device is valid (that it predicts knowledge or skills that are necessary for the job) and that it is consistent with business necessity.[33]

Although only those employers who receive federal funds[34] (and in some states state funds), as well as public employers, are required to practice affirmative action in hiring and promotion, many other employers have voluntarily assumed the obligation to do so. Affirmative action, a doctrine of considerable controversy, requires the employer to consider race, sex, or ethnic origin as one of several "qualifications" when making a hiring, promotion, or other employment decision. Employers wishing to practice affirmative action must first evaluate the underrepresentation of various categories of protected groups in their workforce, analyze the representation of these groups in the qualified labor force, and then develop an affirmative action plan with goals (but not quotas) and timetables for achieving parity.[35] Protected class status cannot be used as the sole criterion, however, for an employment decision, and courts have ruled that doing so violates the law.[36] But using race or sex (the two most frequently used status categories in affirmative action) as one of several "plus" factors has been approved by the U.S. Supreme Court,[37] although the current political debate about affirmative action in the U.S. Congress and in the press may result in changes to or abolition of affirmative action.[38]

As noted earlier, IRCA regulates the hiring process and requires the employer to verify that the applicant selected for the position is legally entitled to work in the United States. The employer must require the successful applicant to produce evidence of his or her identity and authorization to work. Employers who exclude applicants because they "appear" foreign, speak with a foreign accent, or because they were not born in the United States, without inquiring into their immigration status, may be liable for violating the nondiscrimination laws.

In addition to potential discrimination claims, employers may face tort claims from disgruntled applicants or current employees. Defamation is probably the most frequently used tort theory, and these claims often arise in connection with a reference (usually oral) given by a former employer or co-worker to a prospective employer. The claim would be made against a former employer when the former employee is not hired (or is discharged) by the next or prospective employer.[39] Although states have created a "qualified privilege" that will protect an individual or employer from liability for defamation if the information was communicated in good faith to an individual with a business-related reason to receive it,[40] the application and scope of the privilege must be determined at trial and is thus not a deterrent to litigation by disappointed job applicants. For this reason, many organizations have developed a policy of giving very limited information about a previous employee (e.g., name, title, dates of employment) to a prospective employer. Other employers require the former employee to sign a release that authorizes the company to provide certain information to the prospective employer. Although releases cannot guarantee freedom from litigation, they are useful to employers if they are sued, for a signed release suggests that the employer provided the information at the former employee's request and did not seek to interfere with his or her future employment. In some states the doctrine of "compelled self-defamation" has been used to find employer liability. In this doctrine the former employer gives the employee an allegedly defamatory reason for the discharge (for example, theft or insubordination); when a prospective employer asks the former employee why he or she left the former position, the employee is faced with the choice of either misrepresenting the reason (which could be grounds for subsequent termination from the new position) or communicating the allegedly defamatory reason for discharge to the prospective employer. Even though the former employer has not communicated any information to the prospective employer, liability may attach because the former employer indirectly harmed the former employee by providing the allegedly defamatory information that was eventually communicated to a third party by the applicant.[41]

Common law contract claims may arise if promises made to an applicant, either orally or in an employment manual, are not kept. For example, courts in some states have ruled that oral promises involving job security may be contractually binding.[42] Promises made in employment manuals, particularly those that guarantee progressive discipline before discharge or guarantee that no discharge will be made without just cause, have also been found to bind employers contractually.[43] The use of disclaimers, both on employment applications[44] and in employee handbooks,[45] has been recommended by various courts if the employer does not wish oral promises or statements made in handbooks to have contractual significance. These disclaimers must be very explicit, however. They must make it clear that: (1) no one (except a named individual or position) has the authority to modify an employee's at-will employment status; and (2) statements made orally or in the employment manual have no contractual force and create no legal rights for employees. Employers in those states in which handbooks have been found to be contracts have thus been faced with the difficult choice of either treating their handbooks like contracts (and incurring potential legal claims for noncompliance) or risking alienating their employees (and possibly inviting organization by a trade union) by making it very clear that the employees have no job security and cannot rely on the employer's policies for their protection.

Another contractual issue related to hiring is the use of arbitration clauses. Employers, particularly in the insurance and securities industries, have been requiring newly hired or current employees to enter agreements in which they promise to use arbitration to resolve any dispute with their employer. Although the U.S. Supreme Court has ruled that a union cannot waive the rights of its members to challenge employment decisions under the civil rights laws,[46] the court later ruled in *Gilmer* vs. *Interstate/Johnson Lane Corp.*[47] that an agreement in which an *individual* employee waived his right to sue by entering an agreement to arbitrate did not violate federal law. Although most federal courts have followed *Gilmer* in subsequent challenges to the enforceability of arbitration clauses when an employee files a claim of discrimination or harassment under the nondiscrimination laws, the U.S.

Court of Appeals for the Ninth Circuit recently ruled that the agreement must specify which legal protections the employee is agreeing to waive before such a waiver will be enforceable.[48]

A final area of potential legal liability related to hiring may be implicated when an employee acts in a way that harms a nonemployee. The civil liability for the harm caused by the employee (usually physical assault or murder, but crimes of dishonesty are also grist for this theory) is shifted to the employer under a doctrine known as "negligent hiring." The victim (or the victim's heirs) argues that, had the employer checked into the employee's past work or life history, behavior similar to the behavior that harmed the victim would have been discovered. Organizations whose employees are not confined to a particular location (such as truck drivers,[49] property managers or maintenance staff in residential complexes, or outside sales personnel) are particularly vulnerable to this claim. Given the strict privacy laws of some states, it may be difficult for employers to obtain information on prior misconduct; furthermore, the disability discrimination laws preclude inquiries about previous (or current) psychiatric illnesses. Claims brought under this theory are difficult to defend and often create a sizable public relations problem for the employer.

Rewards

Compensation

Challenges to workplace rewards (compensation and certain benefits) typically attack the motive for these decisions. Compensation decisions may be attacked as inequitable in terms of the employee's status (race, sex, age). Although both state and federal nondiscrimination laws require individuals doing the same job to be paid equally,[50] most courts have rejected the claim that the law requires employers to follow the doctrine of comparable worth in making compensation decisions. Comparable worth requires the employer to determine the "value" of each position to the organization by conducting a job evaluation that assigns points for various job characteristics (such as the consequences of error, degree of supervision, complexity of tasks, etc.).[51] Although unions representing public employees in several states have attempted to convince federal courts that comparable worth is required by Title VII, their efforts have been unavailing.[52] Several states, such as Minnesota and Iowa, and the province of Ontario, Canada, have legislated comparable worth either for public employees (Minnesota and Iowa) or for all employees (Ontario). Public sector unions with large proportions of female members have also made some inroads to equalize pay for similarly "valued" occupations that are sex-segregated. Most compensation policy at the organization level, however, is linked to performance and market issues rather than being shaped by legal doctrine.

The Fair Labor Standards Act (FLSA), a federal law, sets minimum pay and requires, for certain categories of employees, that overtime pay be given for hours worked past 40 per week. For most employers the minimum pay requirement is not an issue because their employees are paid substantially more than minimum wage. But interesting issues have arisen with regard to which employees are included in the law's protections for overtime work as well as questions about what "work" means.

The FLSA includes exemptions for three categories of workers: administrative, executive, and professional employees.[53] Regulations interpreting this part of the law create both "long" and "short" tests for making these determinations. The tests focus on how much the individual is paid, the nature of the individual's primary duty or duties, the amount of independent judgment or discretion exercised by that individual, and the degree to which the individual's work is shaped or dictated by management.[54]

As organizations become more dependent on technology, they have also increased their dependence on individuals who can manage that technology, diagnose problems, and resolve them. Some employers place employees "on call" during their off-work hours so that they can return to work if an emergency occurs. Questions have arisen as to whether the employee is actually working during "on call" time and whether a wage is due for that time. Although the courts have not been entirely consistent, many have ruled that if the employee can engage in rest or recreational activities during the "on call" time (for example, by wearing a pager or by calling in periodically), his or her activity is not sufficiently restricted by the employer to constitute "work" and thus no additional pay is due.[55]

Whether or not an individual who receives compensation is an employee at all may pose complex legal issues, particularly for those organizations that use the services of consultants, short-term or temporary contract workers, or other nonstandard work arrangements. The status of independent contractors has raised issues both for FLSA purposes and under the Internal Revenue Code. Under the FLSA the individual must fit the definition of "employee."[56] Given the brevity of the statutory definition, courts have turned to the common law concept of "employee" to resolve this issue. In *Brock* vs. *Mr. W Fireworks, Inc.*,[57] the court identified five criteria that courts have used to determine whether an individual is an employee or an independent contractor.[58]

Benefits

Although most employers are not required by law to provide their workers with medical insurance, pensions, or other benefits, many employers believe that offering a wide range of benefits attracts and retains high quality workers. Most benefits provided by an employer in the private sector are regulated by the federal Employee Retirement Income Security Act of 1974 (ERISA).[59] The law is complex and cannot be described, even succinctly, in this chapter, but its scope extends to two broad categories of benefits: pensions and "employee welfare plans."[60]

Pensions generally fall into one of two categories: defined benefit plans in which the amount of the retirement benefit is specified in advance, and defined contribution plans in which each participant has an individual pension account, and the eventual retirement benefit depends on the amount of the contribution and any growth in the account attributable to investment income. Employee welfare plans include group medical insurance, disability insurance, severance pay arrangements, supplementary unemployment benefits, and other benefits, but not vacation programs.[61] ERISA contains many reporting and disclosure requirements, both to the federal government and to employees participating in the covered benefit plans. Voluntary retirement programs are also regulated by ERISA and the law requires employers to provide certain options for married participants with regard to survivors' annuities. Given the complexity and scope of ERISA, employers should consult experienced benefits professionals or legal counsel before beginning or modifying a program of employee benefits.

Leaves of Absence

The federal Family and Medical Leave Act (FMLA)[62] requires employers who have employed 50 or more employees within a radius of 75 miles for each working day during each of 20 or more weeks in the preceding year to grant up to 12 weeks of unpaid leave in any 12-month period. Events that qualify for this leave include:

1. The birth of a child and its care during the first year.
2. The adoption of a child or placement in the employee's home of a foster child of any age.
3. The care of the employee's spouse, child, or parent with a serious health condition.
4. The serious health condition of the employee.

Employees who take a family or medical leave under this law are entitled to reinstatement to an equivalent position when they return to work. The employer must also maintain health benefits to which the worker was entitled prior to the leave.

Most issues arising under the FMLA involve whether the employee has a "serious health condition" as defined in the act, and by whom this information is to be determined.[63] Most claims under this recent law have involved employers' refusals to reinstate workers returning from FMLA leave; the law permits the employer to refuse reinstatement only to a "key employee" and then only because "substantial and grievous economic injury" to its operations will ensue if the employee must be reinstated.[64]

Given the newness of both the FMLA and the Americans With Disabilities Act (ADA), it is not yet clear how these two laws will interact. A worker is entitled to FMLA leave for his or her own serious health condition only when unable to work; the reasonable accommodation provisions of the ADA may permit workers with disabilities to request additional leave beyond the statutory 12 weeks. In order to qualify under the ADA, however, the worker must be able to perform the essential functions of the position. Several years and substantial litigation will very likely be required before the interplay between these two laws is resolved.

Working Conditions

This large category of workplace issues involves a correspondingly large number of legal doctrines, including the requirement of a harassment-free work environment, nondiscriminatory dress and conduct codes, restrictions on off-duty conduct (such as using controlled substances or dating a co-worker), leaves of absence, the use of confidential employer information, and health and safety issues.

Harassment

Federal and state nondiscrimination laws require employers to maintain a work environment that is free of harassment or discrimination on the basis of a variety of protected class characteristics (race, sex, national origin, religion, color, age, marital status, disability, liability for military service, and, in eight states, sexual orientation).[65] Although racial, age, and sexual orientation harassment are serious problems in some workplaces, sexual harassment has received the most attention in recent years, in part because of the allegations made by Professor Anita Hill during the confirmation hearings for Supreme Court Associate Justice Clarence Thomas. According to the EEOC, unwelcome sexual advances, requests for sexual favors, and other verbal or physical conduct of a sexual nature constitute sexual harassment when:

1. submission to such conduct is made either explicitly or implicitly a term or condition of an individual's employment;
2. submission to or rejection of such conduct by an individual is used as the basis for employment decisions affecting such individual; or
3. such conduct has the purpose or effect of unreasonably interfering with an individual's work performance or creating an intimidating, hostile, or offensive working environment.[66]

Harassment by a manager or supervisor that affects an employee's terms or conditions of employment (called *quid pro quo* harassment) will virtually always result in employer liability, even if the employer was not aware of the harassment.[67] Harassment that creates a hostile or offensive working environment will usually result in employer liability unless the employer can demonstrate that it was unaware of the misconduct and could not have learned of the conduct. In *Meritor Savings Bank* vs. *Vinson*,[68] the U.S. Supreme Court ruled that a claim of hostile environment sexual harassment was actionable under Title VII; in 1993 the court ruled that the plaintiff need not prove any economic or psychological damage in order to establish a sexual harassment claim.[69] In that case, the court ruled that a plaintiff must demonstrate that the conduct was so severe or pervasive as to create "an objectively hostile or abusive work environment—an environment that a reasonable person would find hostile or abusive."[70] The court did not address whether the "reasonable person" or the "reasonable woman" standard should apply, an issue of some significance, given the differences between men and women with regard to their attitudes toward sexual behavior.[71] Because of the intense scrutiny that courts give sexual harassment claims, employers should, at a minimum, make sure that they have a strong policy against harassment, a reporting mechanism with multiple channels so that targets of harassment are not required to report alleged harassment to a harassing supervisor, prompt and effective investigative and remedial practices, training of, at a minimum, supervisors and managers in detecting and preventing harassment, and a monitoring system that allows the organization to minimize the opportunities for harassment to occur and to respond promptly and appropriately when harassment does occur. In addition to litigation by targets of sexual or other forms of harassment, employers may face lawsuits by individuals who were disciplined or discharged as a result of a harassment complaint and investigation.

Restrictions on Off-Work Conduct

Although employers may require employees to be drug-and alcohol-free while at work,[72] and may impose a code of conduct during work time, seeking to regulate off-work conduct may result in litigation. For example, although the use of controlled substances is illegal, 18 states have either outlawed or significantly restricted the manner in which employers may conduct drug testing.[73] In addition, liability for invasion of privacy, battery, intentional or negligent infliction of emotional distress, and other claims may ensue if the testing procedures do not protect the employee's privacy or if the proper chain of custody procedures are not used to ensure the integrity of the sample. Some state courts have found a privacy right for employees of private sector companies in state constitutions that would prohibit random drug testing for all but "safety-sensitive" positions.[74]

Although the use of controlled substances is unlawful, other types of behavior that employers sometimes seek to regulate, such as dating or working at second jobs, is not. For example, in *Rulon-Miller* vs. *International Business Machine Corp.*,[75] a state appellate court ruled that an IBM manager's decision to discharge an employee because she was dating the employee of a competitor violated her right to privacy and also violated IBM's own privacy policies, a breach of an implied contract. Other courts, however, have upheld nonfraternization or similar restrictions on dating co-workers or competitors.[76]

Dress and Grooming Codes

Although courts have generally upheld a private sector employer's right to regulate the appearance of its employees, it cannot act in a discriminatory fashion in so doing, and the required uniform must not expose the worker to unlawful conduct. For example, in *EEOC* vs. *Sage Realty*,[77] the employer required a female lobby attendant to wear a very revealing costume, which resulted in persistent sexual harassment by visitors to the building. Several courts have found that requiring women, but not men, to wear uniforms, despite the fact that they performed the same job, constituted sex discrimination.[78] Public employers who forbid the wearing of facial hair have generally sustained constitutional challenges to these regulations,[79] but if an employee can demonstrate that being required to shave exacerbates a race-related skin condition, the regulation may be found to have a discriminatory impact.[80] No-beard regulations have sustained challenges when the purpose of the regulation was safety rather than a uniform appearance.[81]

Regulation of Trade Secrets and Competition

Employers have used contract law and the common law of agency to require employees not to disclose trade secrets or other proprietary information that they learn on the job. Most controversial have been noncompetition agreements in which an employer requires the employee, as a condition of being hired or retained, to sign an agreement not to work in the industry within a certain geographic area for a certain period of time after resignation or discharge. These "restrictive covenants" have been upheld by courts if the time period and the geographic area are reasonable to protect the employer's business interests.[82] If, however, the contract language would virtually preclude the employee from engaging in his or her trade or profession, the covenants have either been unenforceable or courts have modified their terms.[83]

Trade secrets are protected by common law and, in about half the states, by state statute as well. Former employees who reproduce, either from memory or from copies of plans or formulas, their former employer's product or process risk substantial liability; however, if the product or process's components could be discovered through reverse engineering (discovering a product's components by disassembling it), an employer may have considerable difficulty prevailing in a lawsuit charging a former employee with misappropriation of a trade secret.[84]

Health and Safety

The federal Occupational Safety and Health Act (OSHA)[85] requires employers to maintain a workplace that is free of recognized hazards that could cause injury or death. In addition to this general duty, the law empowers the Secretary of Labor to promulgate specific health and safety standards with which the employer must comply. The law is enforced by the Occupational Safety and Health Administration, a unit of the U.S. Department of Labor.[86]

Approximately 50 workplace standards have been promulgated by the Secretary of Labor; nearly 4,000 other "consensus" standards were adopted shortly after the law became effective in 1971. Industry challenges to standards have slowed their adoption; the U.S. Supreme Court has been called upon on several occasions to determine whether OSHA must use cost-benefit calculations in developing the standard. Current jurisprudence requires OSHA to determine that the standard is economically and technologically feasible, that the old standard that is to be replaced poses a significant risk to employees' health, and that the new standard is reasonably necessary to protect employee health.[87]

Employers must report accidents that result in lost work time and must keep extensive records of compliance with OSHA standards. Recordkeeping violations, as well as lack of compliance with OSHA standards, can result in civil fines and criminal penalties. In addition, some states are turning to criminal law to prosecute corporate officials who willfully exposed employees to dangerous chemicals; manslaughter theories have been used with some success in several states.[88]

In addition to OSHA, federal and state environmental laws regulate employer conduct with regard to certain chemicals and other potentially dangerous substances. Certain industries, such as trucking and the nuclear power industry, are governed by special laws that regulate worker safety and health.[89]

Employers whose workers are exposed to substances that may cause birth defects or other problems for the workers' unborn children have, on occasion, attempted to restrict women of childbearing age from jobs involving such exposure. Although the employers' concern for the health of the workers' children, and their wish to avoid legal liability for the child's exposure to these substances is understandable, excluding only women from jobs in which they are exposed to fetotoxins is unlawful. In *United Auto Workers* vs. *Johnson Controls*,[90] the U.S. Supreme Court ruled unanimously that excluding women of childbearing age, but not men, from jobs involving exposure to fetotoxins was intentional sex discrimination, and rejected the employer's argument that legitimate business concerns (avoidance of future liability) justified the discrimination. This interplay between the nondiscrimination laws and the safety of workers and their unborn children presents difficult policy issues for employers—issues that, for the most part, the Supreme Court did not address.

This section has surveyed a wide array of legal restrictions on working conditions. If employees are represented by a trade union, then the collective agreement will very likely contain provisions that limit the employer's discretion in regulating working conditions. Terms and conditions of employment, which includes conditions of work, are a mandatory subject of negotiation for those employers whose employees are represented by a union certified by the National Labor Relations Board or by a state body enforcing a public sector collective bargaining law.

Exit

Employees typically are separated from employment by voluntary resignation, layoff, retirement (a form of voluntary resignation), or discharge. Assuming that the separation is voluntary, the major legal issues involve the enforceability of any waiver or release that the employee signed and noncompetition clauses (discussed earlier). Legal challenges to "voluntary" retirements usually attack the voluntariness of the retirement, often under the Age Discrimination in Employment Act.

Layoffs may be regulated by a collective bargaining agreement. If not, the employer is free to use any business-related criterion to select workers for layoff (e.g., relative performance, centrality of the position to the organization, and availability of the individual's skills in other parts of the organization), as long as the reason for selection is not related to a status characteristic such as age, race, gender, and so on, or is not limited in some way by employer policy or past practice. A recent review of age discrimination claims that followed a reduction in force concluded that employers with evidence of relative performance differences between employees selected for layoff and those retained were usually successful in obtaining summary judgment or dismissal of the lawsuit. But if the plaintiff could present evidence of age-related statements by supervisors or could show that their position was filled by a younger worker, they could at least avoid dismissal of the case, although they often had difficulty proving discrimination (see Lee, 1995).

Discharge, the "capital punishment" of the employment relationship, can be challenged under numerous theories. Workers who are represented by a union typically contest their discharge through the contractual grievance procedure present in virtually all collective bargaining agreements. There are certain legal theories, however, that allow individuals covered by a collective agreement to bypass the contractual grievance procedure if they wish to file claims with enforcement agencies (in the case of alleged discrimination)[91] or in court (in the case of allegations of wrongful discharge based on public policy).[92] Most discharged workers who are not organized file either a discrimination claim (if they believe that discrimination infected the discharge decision) or a wrongful discharge claim, using either contract or tort (public policy) theories.

Discrimination theories available to employees challenging a discharge have been described earlier. Individual plaintiffs must show intentional discrimination by the employer; because direct evidence of discrimination is rarely available, plaintiffs typically compare their work performance, attendance, or other records to the records of "comparable" employees who were not discharged and who do not share the plaintiff's status (race, sex, etc.). Documentation of performance problems and consistent treatment of similar employees are essential if an employer is to defend successfully such discrimination claims. Even if an employer later discovers additional information to support a discharge that was not available to the employer at the time the decision was made, this "after-acquired evidence" will not substitute for a legitimate business reason for the discharge should an employee claim that the discharge was discriminatory.[93]

Wrongful discharge theories encompass either contract or tort claims. Contract claims may be based on a company handbook that appears to promise that discharge will be only for just cause. As noted earlier, clear and prominent disclaimers that warn employees that the handbook does not create contractual rights are essential to avoid such claims.[94] The tort of wrongful discharge, a theory not uniformly embraced by all states, asserts that the reason for the discharge violates public policy. As noted earlier, allegations that the discharge was a result of performing a legal duty (jury duty), exercising a legal right (filing a workers' compensation claim), refusing to violate a law (perjury), or whistleblowing raise a public policy theory of wrongful discharge. Professionals who allege that they were discharged for refusing to violate a professional code of ethics have, in some states, successfully pursued wrongful discharge theories based on public policy.[95]

In addition to discrimination and wrongful discharge theories, employees contesting a discharge may assert other tort claims, such as intentional infliction of emotional distress, defamation (particularly if the employer provides a negative reference to a prospective employer), fraud, intentional interference with contract, or negligence. Plaintiffs using these theories are usually attacking the manner in which the discharge was effected, rather than the decision itself.

REGULATION OF UNION-MANAGEMENT RELATIONS

Each of the human resource management functions discussed previously is dramatically affected by an ongoing collective bargaining relationship and, to some extent, by the existence of a union organizing drive. The broad array of union effects on all forms of unionized employees' remuneration, internal and external mobility, job requirements and work rules, job retention and employee discipline and discharge, job satisfaction, and even firm productivity and profitablity, among other things, is amply reviewed elsewhere.[96] It is also noteworthy that these aspects of the employment relationship in the unionized environment also have a hand in shaping characteristics of the employment relationship in the nonunion environment.[97]

Since union effects on how employees are used and treated in the firm are substantial, it is important that managers are aware of how the labor management relationship is shaped by unionization law. Labor tribunals' interpretations of the National Labor Relations Act (NLRA)[98] set the parameters on just how managers may act in the face of union attempts to organize or represent employees at a workplace. Below, we review the general constraints and requirements on management's conduct imposed by law in the following areas: organizing, setting up employee participation plans, negotiating a contract, and living under a contract (contract administration).

Organizing

Eligibility for Union Membership

The starting point for grasping the impact of the regulation of the union-management relationship on managers is to recognize that not all employees are eligible to unionize within the act's protections. Managers may challenge the right of individuals who do not meet the definition of employee to form or join unions or to be in bargaining units determined by the National Labor Relations Board (NLRB).[99]

Although the statute does not precisely identify just who is an employee entitled to the act's protections, it does list classes of workers who fall outside of the act's reach, such as agricultural laborers, domestic servants, supervisors, and independent contractors.[100] By statutory interpretation, managers (defined as those individuals who are in a position to "formulate, effectuate, and determine" employer's policies)[101] and confidential secretaries who possess a "labor relations nexus"[102] are also excluded.

It is especially noteworthy that the act explicitly confers the right to unionize to "professional employees."[103] Professional employees are defined as those individuals who engage in work that is "predominantly intellectual...as opposed to routine...involving the consistent exercise of discretion...that cannot be standardized in relation to a given period of time...requiring knowledge of an advanced type...."[104] Interestingly, labor tribunals have had to struggle to accommodate the coverage of these individuals with the exclusion of supervisors and managers who often possess similar characteristics. Recent developments in labor law suggest that many professional employees once afforded unionization rights, such as college faculty and nurses, increasingly may be viewed as supervisors and managers, and therefore be denied coverage by the law.[105] As a result, the eligibility of professional workers to unionize will likely dwindle.[106]

Conduct During Organizing Drives

When a group of eligible workers seeks to organize a union, a number of constraints are imposed on employers' conduct. The justification for constraining management's conduct is to protect or facilitate employee free choice for or against union representation. In order to enable employees to register a "free and untrammelled" choice in elections, decribed as "laboratory conditions,"[107] limitations are imposed on what managers can say during an organizing campaign, the conduct of interrogations, the promulgation of no-solicitation and no-distribution rules, the granting of employee benefits and employee discharges, and plant closures, to name but a few.

Employer Speech

The act protects an employer's right to campaign against the union during an organizing drive, as long as such speech does not contain "a promise of benefit" (if employees reject the union) or "a threat of reprisal" (should employees support the union).[108] Thus, managers/employers may offer honest predictions of the likely consequences of unionization, but may not intimidate or coerce employees into non-support of the union by threatening them. It is noteworthy, however, that there is often a fine line between an honest prediction and a threat, and labor tribunals have long struggled with drawing this distinction on a case-by-case basis.

In terms of disseminating propoganda, on the other hand, the law has been in a state of flux. Although campaign misrepresentations that are substantial departures from the truth and likely to have a substantial effect on election outcomes were once grounds for setting aside election outcomes,[109] today such misrepresentations are allowed liberally. In fact, managers (and unions) may legally propogandize employees, as long as such misrepresentations do not involve the falsification of legal documents.[110]

Interrogations

Typically, managers have a significant interest in knowing who supports a union, and why. This interest has often prompted them to question employees about their union sympathies, referred to as interrogations. Although such interrogations were once viewed as unlawful, per se,[111] labor law has moved in the direction of liberalizing the conditions under which such interrogations can take place legally. In general, casual questioning of employees in a background free of union hostilities or unfair labor practices is acceptable, although somewhat greater restrictions have been placed on the interrogation of employees who have not yet openly declared their union sympathies, in contrast to those who are open and active union supporters.[112]

No-Solicitation and No-Distribution Rules

All organizing campaigns involve some attempt by employees to gather support for the union, and often involve the circulation of campaign materials. Managers may legally prevent employees from soliciting support for the union and distributing information on company property during working time and in work areas, provided that this rule is applied to all forms of solicitation.[113] On the other hand, with limited exceptions managers may not deprive employees of the right to solicit support for the union during nonwork time and in nonwork areas when they are properly not working. Among nonemployees or outside organizers, management is given the legal right to bar such individuals from company premises at all times, provided that reasonable alternative access to employees is available. Recent cases have narrowed this exception to highly unusual circumstances, such as logging camps.[114]

Employee Benefits and Employee Discharges

In effect, the law requires that managers conduct "business as usual," when faced with a union organizing drive. As a result, managers may not seek to sway employees' votes by granting them wage or benefit increases (or otherwise improve employees' terms and conditions of employment), regardless of whether such benefits are not contingent on election outcomes.[115] Similarly, although managers retain the general right to discharge or discipline employees during an organizing campaign, they may not discriminate against an employee because of his or her union sympathies.[116] Thus, managers may not discharge an employee just because he or she actively supports the union. In cases where the motivation for the discharge is truly mixed, or "dual" (that is, there are legitimate and illegitimate or discriminatory reasons for the discharge), managers must show that the discharge would have occurred absent the employee's union activities or protected conduct.[117]

Plant Closures

Public policy has long established the right of an employer to close his business entirely in the face of an organizing drive or for any other reason. However, an employer may not close a part of his business or a plant in an effort to chill unionization in the remaining part of his business (e.g., other plants).[118] In addition, management is forbidden to close a business because it is or is becoming unionized and then reopen that business in a nonunion setting (referred to as a "runaway shop").[119]

Employee Participation Plans

New forms or programs of labor-management cooperation outside of the traditional bargaining context have grown increasingly popular under the rubric of enlightened personnel policies or sophisticated union avoidance strategies. Regardless of whether these plans are instituted prior to an organizing drive, in response to an organizing drive, or in the face of an already organized workforce, there are important constraints on their legality and management's role in their operation.

In light of the legacy of company unions, which public policy has long sought to curb, management may not establish and deal with employees in programs that qualify as labor organizations regardless of whether management's motivation for instituting the plan is benign with respect to unionization. In the unorganized context, an organizing union will be successful in blocking the operation of employer-instituted programs if such structures "deal," but do not necessarily bargain, with management over any issue embraced by the phrase, "wages, rates of pay, hours of employment, or conditions of work."[120] Given that the overwhelming majority of these programs cover at least one issue covered by that phrase, it is extremely difficult for management to devise and implement an employee participation program that will escape legal sanction in the face of an unfair labor practice charge of employer domination of a labor organization.

In the organized setting management is similarly proscribed from establishing programs that qualify as labor organizations if they are outside of union control. Were management to set up such a plan and deal with employees in that forum, it would be found guilty of abrogating its duty to bargain only with the union, that is, the exclusive representative of employees. The same would be true even if the program were solely the idea of and created by a group of employees.[121]

These seemingly tight restrictions on the legality of employee participation programs and new attempts at labor-management cooperation appear to be at odds with a strong national sentiment favoring experimentation with cooperative efforts to increase employee morale and productivity.[122] As a result, labor tribunals have expressed a desire to find a way of legitimizing at least some of these programs.[123] To date, however, the NLRB has been unable to accommodate this desire with any of its recent decisions, although it has continued to express its wish to allow such programs to exist.[124] It is unclear whether the current legal framework will ever enable employee participation programs to flourish in the United States, absent significant changes in the statute governing union management relations.[125]

Collective Bargaining

Once a union has won a majority of votes in a certification election, it becomes the exclusive representative of all employees eligible to vote in that election. Contract terms negotiated by the union, therefore, cover the terms and conditions of employment among all members of the bargaining unit regardless of whether these employees voted in favor of the union or chose to be union members. Management's obligation to bargain collectively with the union includes both process and substantive requirements, which are often intermingled.

Process requirements. Management must bargain with the union in "good faith." While the duty to bargain in good faith is not well-defined in the NLRA, case interpretations of the law indicate that this duty amounts to a subjective state of mind requirement: management and union must bargain with "the intent of reaching an agreement."[126] Although the statute explicitly indicates that this "obligation does not compel either party to agree to a proposal or require the making of a concession,"[127] concessionary behavior, the offering of proposals, and the willingness to meet and confer, among other things, are factors that will be considered by labor tribunals in determining whether the "totality" of a party's conduct indicates that it has met its duty to bargain.[128]

It is also noteworthy that the law requires that management provide information to the union that is reasonably necessary for the union to carry out its representation function.[129] Management is also required to deal exclusively with the union, as any circumvention of the bargaining agent (such as dealing with other groups of members of the bargaining unit) will be viewed as a derogation of the duty to bargain.

From a process perspective it is also important to note that management is deprived of the right to make unilateral changes in any terms and conditions of employment that fall within the scope of statutory duty to bargain, even if these changes benefit members of the bargaining unit (for example, management may not unilaterally increase wages or benefits).[130] To understand the breadth of this limitation, however, it is necessary to explore the substantive requirements of the duty to bargain.

Substantive requirements. Management must, at the union's request, bargain with the union over any issue embraced by the statutory phrase, "wages, hours, and other terms and conditions of employment."[131] The array of such issues, known as mandatory subjects of bargaining, is vast. Any configuration of remuneration (e.g., hourly pay, salary, commissions, merit pay, overtime, and incentives), benefits, hours of work, break time, holidays, vacations, and so on is subject to the mandatory bargaining obligation. The "other terms and conditions of employment" portion of the scope of the mandatory bargaining obligation has been interpreted to encompass most other aspects of the employment relationship (such as, manning requirements, workload, union security, discipline and discharge procedures, and safety considerations, among others).[132] As stated earlier, management may not make unilateral changes in any of these areas, unless it has bargained to impasse over them with the union.

Although the universe of mandatory subjects is broad indeed, there are nonetheless a number of subjects of bargaining that lawfully fall outside of the mandatory bargaining obligation. These items, referred to as permissive subjects of bargaining, include internal union matters (such as a contract clause requiring a pre-strike ballot of employees),[133] issues deemed to have only a slight or insignificant impact on employees' interests (such as benefits to retirees),[134] and issues that are viewed as falling within the scope of management's prerogatives to change or alter the scope of a firm's operations (such as the decision to merge, close a plant, or institute production process changes).[135]

According these issues permissive status is significant from management's and labor's perspectives for three reasons. First, bargaining over these subjects is purely voluntary, as the scope of the compulsory duty to bargain does not extend to them. Second, both parties are denied the right to insist on these issues to the point of impasse. In other words, the right to strike or lockout over demands on permissive issues is not allowed. Because the parties are denied the right to use their full economic muscle with which to extract concessions on permissive issues, these issues are less likely than mandatory subjects to appear in labor contracts.[136] Finally, management may make unilateral changes in permissive issues without consultation with the union, provided that it has not ceded this right in the contract. Thus, management is afforded substantial control over these issues.

Recent case law has expanded the array of permissive issues falling within management's domain, thereby reducing the scope of collective bargaining and affording management a greater degree of control over the enterprise. Partial plant closures, classified inconsistently in the past, are now clearly a permissive subject of bargaining as long as management justifies these decisions based on general profitablity concerns rather than to reduce labor costs, per se.[137] Indeed, similar analyses are applied, in general, to other decisions that have important effects on employees' job interests, such as work consolidation, relocations, and automation, even if these decisions do not involve changes in the scope of a firm's operations.[138] Thus, while management is obligated to bargain over a vast array of mandatory subjects, the scope of these subjects has diminished in recent years.

Contract Administration

Once management has been successful in achieving a contract with the union, its bargaining obligation and its relationship with the union does not cease.

The parties must now deal with one another on day-to-day living under the contract, aided by a grievance procedure. Grievance procedures, present in virtually all contracts, are institutionalized mechanisms for resolving disputes over the application and interpretation of collective bargaining agreements. How the parties define the term "grievance" in the contract will determine the issues which may be pursued through the procedure.

Although the grievance procedure is a private method of dispute resolution, there are important legal constraints on that process. First, management (or the union) retains its obligation to bargain in good faith during contract administration. Second, if the grievance procedure culminates in grievance arbitration as its final step,[139] management cannot refuse to arbitrate an unsettled claim.[140] In addition, the union is denied the right to strike over a dispute during contract administration, provided that the issue is arbitrable. Interestingly, the union is denied this right even if the contract does not contain a "no-strike" pledge, evidencing public policy's strong preference for the peaceful resolution of disagreements during the life of a labor contract.[141]

Third, an additional area of important regulations on the contract administration process concerns the status of arbitral awards. Demonstrating public policy's respect for the process, when the parties have agreed to arbitrate, the courts will not review an arbitration award; doubts about whether an issue is arbitrable will be resolved in favor of arbitrability and an arbitrator's award is not subject to review on its merits.[142]

Despite this deference to arbitral awards, challenges to the sanctity, privacy, and finality of the process have been posed by the morass of other human resource regulations external to the collective agreement discussed in earlier sections of this chapter. Because contractual disputes over safety may involve OSHA, discrimination issues may involve Title VII or the ADA, and plant closure issues may involve the WARN Act (to cite but a few examples), arbitrators may not have sole jurisidiction over cases they are asked to decide. Each agency with which an arbitrator has overlapping jurisdiction must decide whether it wishes to defer to the arbitrator's award, render the award to be immune from review, retain its right to review the arbitrator's award, or decide the case de novo. Although regulatory agencies and the court system have reached different conclusions in this regard,[143] the current trend nonetheless appears to be toward greater deference to arbitral awards.[144]

Summary

There are indeed dramatic effects on the human resource management function posed by unions and labor law. From the perspective of the law on union-management relations, constraints on management's conduct of its human resource functions are imposed at the outset of organizing activity and continue through a successful campaign, the contract negotiation process, and contract adminstration. As recent developments noted in this chapter illustrate, however, the law appears to be evolving toward greater management flexibility and latitude in dealing with its workforce during an organizing campaign or in an established bargaining relationship by denying the right of many professionals to unionize, liberalizing allowable employer (and union) speech, interrogations, and no-soliciation rules (during organizing campaigns), promoting more cooperative employee-management relations outside of the traditional bargaining context, contracting the scope of the mandatory bargaining obligation, and increasing the deference to arbitral awards even though issues of external law may be involved in certain workplace disputes (during the contract administration process). However, since the law governing union-management relations is judge-made and is subject to different interpretations over time (with changes in the composition of labor tribunals), management is well-advised to keep abreast of new developments in the law that will affect its human resource management policies and practices.

IMPLICATIONS FOR POLICY AND PRACTICE

This chapter has surveyed a wide variety of legal restrictions on the employment relationship. Although the laws and court opinions address a variety of subjects under many different theories, their implications for human resource management practice are less complex than they might seem.

First, if a union represents employees, adherence to the collective bargaining agreement and compliance with the numerous statutory requirements and case precedents is crucial. Given the large body of law developed by the NLRB on a case-by-case basis (rather than through regulatory rule making, which is a more typical regulatory approach), employers whose workers are represented by a trade union should ensure that they have staff who understand both the law and the dynamics of a unionized workplace. Supervisory and managerial training, adherence to written policies and unwritten past practice, and thorough documentation of all performance problems are essential. Most important, open communication channels with union leaders and frequent discussions of mutual concerns, while not legally required, are essential to successful union-management relations.

Second, for employers whose workers are not represented by a union, the careful development of policy and consistent treatment, when possible, of employees is critical to litigation avoidance and to consequent success if litigation occurs. Clear standards of conduct and performance, well-trained supervisors and managers who understand the employer's policies and apply them consistently, and support from top management for a workplace free from harassment and discrimination will reduce the probability of a legal challenge to an employment decision, and will enable the employer to successfully defend those challenges that are litigated.

This chapter has provided a snapshot of the current state of the law regulating the human resource function in the United States. But the law is a dynamic institution that shifts often, sometimes subtly and sometimes abruptly. The real challenge for business executives and human resource managers, therefore, is to keep abreast of the changing landscape of statutory, case law, and common law theories, and to understand how they interact, how they occasionally conflict, and their implications for the practice of human resource management.

NOTES

1. For a summary of the employment regulation systems of several Western nations, see Blanpain (1990).
2. For a general discussion of the federal preemption doctrine, see Cox (1954).
3. Title VII prohibits employers from making employment decisions on the basis of race, gender, religion, color, or national origin. Additional categories of protection, such as marital status, liability for military service, or sexual orientation, exist under some state nondiscrimination laws.
4. For a thorough review of issues related to the accommodation of individuals with disabilities, see Rothstein (1992).
5. See Wood (1877). The employment-at-will doctrine permits an employer to discharge a worker who is not represented by a trade union and not covered by an individual employment contract for a good reason, a bad reason, or no reason. For a discussion of this doctrine and a critique of Wood's treatise, see Feinman (1976).
6. See *Woolley* vs. *Hoffmann LaRoche*, 491 A.2d 1257, 499 A.2d 515 (N.J. 1985) (handbook as contract); *Foley* vs. *Interactive Data Corp.*, 765 P.2d 373 (Cal. 1988) (implied-in-fact contracts); and *Shebar* vs. *Sanyo Business Systems* 544 A.2d 377 (N.J. 1988) (oral promise enforceable as contract).
7. See, for example, *Lally* vs. *Copygraphics*, 428 A.2d 1317 (N.J. 1981) (workers' compensation); *Nees* vs. *Hocks*, 536 P.2d 512 (Ore. 1975 (jury service); and *Melchi* vs. *Burns International Security Services, Inc.*, 597 F. Supp. 575 (E.D. Mich. 1984) (whistleblowing).
8. *See, for example, Fortune* vs. *National Cash Register Co.*, 364 N.E. 2d 1251 (Mass. 1977).
9. Mont. Code Ann. secs. 39-2-901 to 39-2-914 (Montana Wrongful Discharge from Employment Act of 1987).
10. 29 U.S.C. secs. 141 *et seq.*
11. For a discussion of the no-fault system and its effect on employer liability under tort theories, see Epstein (1982).
12. For an overview of the operation of unemployment law, see Hamermesh (1977).
13. 29 U.S.C. secs. 2601 *et seq.*
14. 29 U.S.C. secs. 1001-1461 (nontax provisions) and 26 U.S.C. secs. 401-418 (tax provisions).
15. 29 U.S.C. secs. 201 *et seq.*
16. 29 U.S.C. secs. 651 *et seq.*
17. See, for example, the New Jersey Public Employees Occupational Safety and Health Act, N.J.S.A. sec. 34:6A-25 *et seq.*
18. 29 U.S.C. sec. 654(a)(1).
19. 29 C.F.R. sec. 1910.1200.
20. 29 U.S.C. sec. 657(c).
21. 29 U.S.C. sec. 2101.
22. 29 U.S.C. sec. 2102.

23. 8 U.S.C. sec. 274(a) *et seq.*
24. 29 U.S.C. sec. 157.
25. 29 U.S.C. sec. 158(d).
26. For a discussion of the application of defamation law to employment decisions, see Green and Reibstein (1992).
27. See, for example, *Agis* vs. *Howard Johnson Co.*, 355 N.E.2d 315 (Mass. 1976) (no requirement of bodily injury to state emotional distress claim).
28. See, for example, *K-Mart* vs. *Trotti*, 677 S.W.2d 632 (Tex. App. 1984)(locker search); *Rulon-Miller* vs. *International Business Machine Corp.*, 208 Cal. Rptr. 524 (Cal. App. 1984)(nonfraternization policy).
29. See, for example, *Karibian* vs. *Columbia University*, 14 F.3d 773 (2d Cir. 1994).
30. See 29 U.S.C. sec. 152(13) (1974).
31. See, for example, *Griggs* vs. *Duke Power Company*, 401 U.S. 424 (1971).
32. EEOC Guidelines on Uniform Selection Practices, 29 C.F.R. sec. 1607.4(D).
33. Civil Rights Act of 1991, codified at 42 U.S.C. sec. 2000e-2(k)(1)(A).
34. Executive Order No. 11,246 (1965), as amended by Executive Order 11,375 (1968).
35. *Steelworkers* vs. *Weber*, 443 U.S. 193 (1979).
36. *Wygant* vs. *Jackson Board of Education*, 476 U.S. 267 (1986).
37. *Johnson* vs. *Transportation Agency*, 480 U.S. 616 (1987).
38. For criticisms of affirmative action, and proposals for modifying or abolishing the doctrine, see Bloch (1995), also Steele (1995).
39. See, for example, *Frank B. Hall & Co.* vs. *Buck*, 678 S.W.2d 612 (Tex. App. 1984).
40. In order to assert a qualified privilege, the employer must demonstrate that the individual who made the statement believed in good faith that it was true, that the statement was made for a business purpose, that the statement was limited to the business interest of the speaker or receiver, that the statement was made under appropriate circumstances, and that the statement was communicated only to those with a business reason to hear it. Restatement (Second) of Torts, secs. 599, 600, 603-605.
41. See, for example, *Lewis* vs. *Equitable Life Assurance Society*, 389 N.W.2d 876 (Minn. 1986).
42. *Shebar* vs. *Sanyo*, 544 A.2d 377 (N.J. 1988).
43. See, for example, *Woolley* vs. *Hoffmann-LaRoche*, 491 A.2d 1257, 499 A.2d 515 (N.J. 1985); see also *Toussaint* vs. *Blue Cross and Blue Shield of Michigan*, 292 N.W.2d 880 (Mich. 1980).
44. See, for example, *Reid* vs. *Sears, Roebuck and Co.*, 790 F.2d 453 (6th Cir. 1986).
45. *Woolley* vs. *Hoffmann LaRoche*, 491 A.2d 1257, 499 A.2d 515 (N.J. 1985).
46. *Alexander* vs. *Gardner-Denver*, 415 U.S. 36 (1974).
47. 111 S. Ct. 1647 (1991).
48. *Prudential Insurance Co. of America* vs. *Lai*, 42 F.3d 1299 (9th Cir. 1994).
49. *Malorney* vs. *B&L Motor Freight, Inc.*, 496 N.E.2d 1086 (Ill. App. 1986).
50. The Equal Pay Act contains four exceptions to the requirement that jobs requiring the same skills, effort, responsibility, and working conditions be paid equally. The exceptions are: a merit pay system, a piece-rate system, pay linked to a bona fide seniority system; and "any factor other than sex," which has been interpreted to mean that positions that the external labor market values less than others may be paid at a lower rate, even if women are overrepresented in the less-valued positions and men are overrepresented in the positions that the market values more highly.
51. For a discussion of the comparable worth doctrine and an account of its operation in Minnesota, see Evans and Nelson (1984), Gold (1984), and Hill and Killingsworth (1989).
52. See, for example, *AFSMCE* vs. *Washington*, 770 F.2d 1401 (9th Cir. 1985).
53. 29 U.S.C. Sec. 213(a)(1).
54. See, for example, *Dalheim* vs. *KDFW-TV*, 918 F.2d 1220 (5th Cir. 1990).

228   BARBARA A. LEE and DONNA SOCKELL

55. See, for example, *Bright* vs. *Houston Northwest Medical Center Survivor, Inc.*, 934 F.2d 671 (5th Cir 1991).

56. The law defines "employee" as "any individual employed by an employer." 29 U.S.C. sec. 203(e)(1).

57. 814 F.2d 1042 (5th Cir. 1987).

58. The criteria are: (1) the degree of control exercised by the alleged employer; (2) the extent of the relative investments of the alleged employer and employee in the business; (3) the extent to which the alleged employee's opportunity for profit and loss is determined by the employer; (4) the skill and initiative required for performing the job; (5) the permanency of the relationship.

59. 29 U.S.C. secs. 1001-1461 (nontax provisions) and 26 U.S.C. secs 401-418 (tax provisions).

60. For a concise overview of ERISA's provisions, see Coleman (1993).

61. 29 C.F.R. sec. 2510.3-1(b)(3)(i).

62. Pub. L. 103-3 (1993).

63. 29 C.F.R. secs. 825.114 and 825.305-307.

64. 29 C.F.R. secs. 825.216-218.

65. Discrimination on the basis of sexual orientation is prohibited by state law in California, Connecticut, Hawaii, Massachusetts, Minnesota, New Jersey, Vermont, Washington, and in the District of Columbia, as well as by ordinance in over 50 cities.

66. 29 C.F.R. sec. 1604.11.

67. See, for example, *Bundy* vs. *Jackson*, 641 F.2d 934 (D.C. Cir. 1981).

68. 477 U.S. 57 (1986).

69. *Harris* vs. *Forklift Systems*, 114 S. Ct. 367 (1993).

70. 114 S. Ct. at 370.

71. For a discussion of this issue, see *Ellison* vs. *Brady*, 924 F.2d 872 (9th Cir. 1991).

72. See the Drug Free Workplace Act of 1988, 41 U.S.C. secs. 701-702.

73. *Hennessey* vs. *Coastal Eagle Point Oil Co.*, 129 N.J. 81 (1992)

74. See, for example, *Hennessey* vs. *Coastal Eagle Point Oil Co.*, 129 N.J. 81 (1992); see also *Luedtke* vs. *Nabors Alaska Drilling, Inc.*, 768 P.2d 1123 (Alaska 1989).

75. 208 Cal. Rptr. 524 (Cal. App. 1984).

76. See, for example, *Patton* vs. *J.C. Penney Co.*, 719 P.2d 854 (Or. 1986).

77. 507 F. Supp. 599 (S.D.N.Y. 1981).

78. See, for example, *O'Donnell* vs. *Burlington Coat Factory Warehouse*, Inc., 656 F. Supp. 263 (S.D. Ohio 1987). But requiring male, but not female, attorneys to wear a tie was not sex discrimination in *Devine* vs. *Lonschein*, 621 F. Supp. 894 (S.D.N.Y. 1985), *aff'd*, 800 F.2d 1127 (2d Cir. 1986).

79. See, for example, *Kelley* vs. *Johnson*, 425 U.S. 238 (1976).

80. See, for example, *Bradley* vs. *Pizzaco of Nebraska, Inc.*, 7 F.3d 795 (8th Cir. 1993).

81. See, for example, *Fitzpatrick* vs. *City of Atlanta*, 2 F.3d 1112 (11th Cir. 1993) (city could require firefighters to be clean-shaven because of the need to use respirators in their work).

82. See, for example, *Torbett* vs. *Wheeling Dollar Savings and Trust Co.*, 314 S.E.2d 166 (W. Va. 1983).

83. See, for example, *Timenterial, Inc.* vs. *Dagata*, 277 A.2d 512 (Conn. Super. Ct. 1971).

84. See, for example, *Schulenberg* vs. *Signatrol, Inc.*, 212 N.E. 865 (Ill., 1965).

85. 29 U.S.C. secs. 651 *et seq.*

86. For a comprehensive review of the law's requirements, see Moran (1989).

87. *Industrial Union Dept., AFL-CIO* vs. *American Petroleum Institute*, 448 U.S. 607 (1980).

88. See, for example, *Briggs* vs. *Pymm Thermometer Corp.*, 537 N.Y.S. 2d 553 (N.Y. App. Div. 1989) and *People* vs. *O'Neil*, 550 N.E.2d 1090 (Ill. App. Ct. 1990). For a discussion of this issue, see Bixby (1991).

89. For a summary of various laws regulating worker safety and health, see Blosser (1992).

90. 111 S. Ct. 1196 (1991).

91. *Alexander* vs. *Gardner-Denver Co.*, 415 U.S. 36 (1974).
92. *Lingle* vs. *Norge Division of Magic Chef*, 486 U.S. 399 (1988).
93. *McKennon* vs. *Nashville Banner Publishing Co.*, 513 U.S. 352 (1995).
94. *Woolley* vs. *Hoffmann-LaRoche*, 499 A.2d 515 (1985).
95. *Pierce* vs. *Ortho Pharmaceutical*, 417 A.2d 505 (N.J. 1980).
96. For an excellent review of these effects, see Freeman and Medoff (1981, 1984).
97. The impact of union wage determination on the wages of nonunion workers has been described as the spillover or threat effect. For an excellent empirical treatment of interplay between human resource policies in the unionized and nonunion firm, more generally, see Ichinowski, Delaney, and Lewin (1989).
98. The act governing labor relations is an amalgam of statutory language enacted and amended in 1935, 1947, 1959, and 1974. The act is typically referred to as the NLRA or the Labor-Management Relations Act.
99. The National Labor Relations Board, a panel of five political appointees with five-year terms, was established by the National Labor Relations Act (1935) to administer and enforce the provisions of the statute governing union-management relations. Acting through its General Counsel, the NLRB prosecutes unfair labor practices and holds elections to determine whether employees will be represented by a union. If employers and unions (or a group of employees) fail to agree on who should be eligible to vote in such elections (or become members of the bargaining unit), the NLRB will determine the scope of the bargaining unit upon the conclusion of a hearing.
100. See 29 U.S.C. sec. 152(3) (1974).
101. See *NLRB* vs. *Bell Aerospace Company*, 416 U.S. 267 (1974).
102. See, for example, *Westinghouse Elec. Corp.* vs. *NLRB*, 398 F. 2d 669 (6th Cir. 1968).
103. See 29 U.S.C. sec. 152(12) (1974).
104. Id.
105. See *NLRB* vs. *Yeshiva University*, 444 U.S. 672 (1980); *NLRB* vs. *Health Care and Retirement Corp. of America*, 114 S. Ct. 1778 (1994).
106. Although the intention of the Supreme Court in both cases cited at note 105 was to confine its holdings to only those professionals at issue, the logic underlying these holding may be extended to large classes of professional workers. For a discussion of this point, see Sockell and Delaney (1995).
107. The term "laboratory conditions" was coined in *General Shoe Corp.* 77 N.L.R.B. 124 (1948).
108. See 29 U.S.C. sec. 158(c) (1974).
109. See *Hollywood Ceramics Co.*, 140 N.L.R.B. 221 (1962); also see, *General Knit of California, Inc.*, 239 N.L.R.B. 1687 (1978).
110. See *Midland National Life Insurance*, 263 N.L.R.B. 127 (1982); also see, *Shopping Kart Food Market*, 228 N.L.R.B. 1311 (1977).
111. For a discussion of the evolution in the treatment of interrogations, see Sockell and Delaney (1987).
112. See *Rossmore House*, 269 N.L.R.B. 1127 (1984), *aff'd*, 760 F.2d 1006 (9th Cir. 1985).
113. That, in general, employees may not be prohibited from soliciting union support during nonwork time, in nonwork areas, when they are properly not working was established by the landmark case, *Republic Aviation* vs. *NLRB*, 324 U.S. 793 (1945). Several exceptions to this general rule have been carved out for atypical workplaces, including hospitals, department stores, and restaurants. See, for example, *May Department Stores*, 59 N.L.R.B. 976 (1944), *enf'd as mdf'd*, 154 F. 2d 533 (8th Cir. 1946), *cert. den.*, 329 U.S. 725 (1946).
114. The central case providing the method of determining the rights of employers to bar outside organizers from his or her property is *NLRB* vs. *Babcock & Wilcox Co.*, 351 U.S. 105 (1956). For a recent application of that case, in which employers are given even greater rights to bar such access, see *Lechmere, Inc.* vs. *NLRB*, 112 S. Ct. 841 (1992).

115. See *NLRB* vs. *Exchange Parts Co.*, 375 U.S. 405 (1964).

116. See 29 U.S.C. sec. 158(a)(3) (1947).

117. *A Division of Wright Line*, 251 N.L.R.B. 150 (1980).

118. *Textile Workers* vs. *Darlington Manufacturing Co.*, 380 U.S. 263 (1965).

119. The case law identifying just what constitutes a runaway shop is reviewed thoroughly by Morris (1983).

120. This phrase is excerpted from the definition of labor organization included in the statute. See 29 U.S.C. sec. 152(5).

121. See the Supreme Court's analysis in *Emporium Capwell Co.* vs. *Western Addition Community Organization*, 420 U.S. 50 (1975).

122. For example, that there is this strong national sentiment in favor of cooperation is suggested by President Clinton's establishment of the Commission on the Future of Worker Management Relations (also known as the Dunlop Commission), early in his presidency. The specific charge to this commission is to find ways to "enhance work-place productivity through labor-management cooperation and employee participation." For the entire mission statement of this commission, see *Daily Labor Report* (March 25, 1993).

123. It is noteworthy that several Circuit Courts of Appeal have long held a more generous view of the legality of cooperative programs. See, *Chicago Rawhide Mfgr. Co.* vs. *NLRB*, 221 F.2d 165 (7th Cir. 1955); *Hertzka & Knowles* vs. *NLRB*, 503 F.2d 625 (9th Cir. 1974). These holdings are contrary to the approach taken by the NLRB and do not necessarily accord with the Supreme Court's views. For a discussion of this point, see Sockell (1984).

124. See, *Electromation, Inc.*, 309 N.L.R.B. No. 163 (1992) *enforced Electromation* vs. *NLRB and Teamsters*, 35 F.3d 1148 (7th Cir. 1994); *E.I. du Pont & Co.*, 311 N.L.R.B. No. 88 (1993).

125. For an excellent discussion of this point, see Member Raudabaugh's separate concurrence in *Electromation*, cited at note 124.

126. See, for example, *NLRB* vs. *Reed & Prince Mfg. Co.*, 205 F.2d 131 (1st Cir. 1953), *cert. den.*, 346 U.S. 887 (1953).

127. 29 U.S.C. sec. 158(d) (1974).

128. See *Borg-Warner Corp.*, 128 N.L.R.B. 1035 (1960).

129. See, for example, *Aluminum Ore Co.* vs. *NLRB*, 131 F.2d 485 (7th Cir. 1942).

130. See *NLRB* vs. *Katz*, 369 U.S. 736 (1962).

131. This substantive obligation can be found in section 8(d) of the statute. 29 U.S.C. sec. 158(d) (1974).

132. For a detailed review of the issues viewed to be mandatory subjects of bargaining, see Gorman (1976).

133. *NLRB* vs. *Wooster Div. of the Borg-Warner Corp.*, 356 U.S. 342 (1958).

134. *Allied Chem. & Alkali Workers Local 1* vs. *Pittsburgh Plate Glass Co.*, 404 U.S. 157 (1972).

135. A discussion of the array of "management" decisions classified as permissive may be found in Sockell (1986).

136. For an empirical study supporting this argument, see Delaney and Sockell (1989).

137. *First National Maintenance Corp.* vs. *NLRB*, 452 U.S. 666 (1981).

138. See, for example, *Otis Elevator Company*, 269 N.L.R.B. 891 (1984), *Dubuque Packing*, 303 N.L.R.B. 386 (1991).

139. The vast majority of all grievance procedures culminate in grievance arbitration.

140. *Textile Workers Union* vs. *Lincoln Mills of Alabama*, 353 U.S. 448 (1957).

141. The denial of the right to strike over an arbitrable grievance exists even when the parties have failed to execute a "no-strike" pledge in their collective bargaining agreement. *Local 174, Teamsters* vs. *Lucas Flour Co.* 369 U.S. 95 (1962). It is noteworthy that this denial of the right to strike does not hold in cases in which the subject of the grievance is not arbitable. This legal doctrine is explained by two Supreme Court holdings: *Boys Market, Inc.* vs. *Retail Clerk's Union,*

Local 770, 398 U.S. 235 (1970); *Buffalo Forge Co.* vs. *United Steeelworkers of America*, 428 U.S. 397 (1976).

142.   See three case known as the "Steelworkers Triliogy:" *United Steelworkers of America* vs. *American Mfg. Co.*, 363 U.S. 564 (1960); *United Steelworkers of America* vs. *Warrior & Gulf Navigation Co.*, 363 U.S. 574 (1960); *United Steelworkers of America* vs. *Enterprise Wheel & Car Co.*, 363 U.S. 593 (1960). In addition, federal courts may refuse to defer to an arbitration award if they believe that the arbitrator acted beyond the scope of his or her authority or because the outcome of the award is contrary to important public policy goals.

143.   The NLRB, for example, has maintained a fluctuating policy of deferral to arbitral awards, beginning with the approach that it would only defer to such awards if three conditions were met: the proceedings were fair and regular, all parties agreed to be bound by the arbitrator's award, and the arbitrator's opinion was not clearly repugnant to the policies of the Act. See *Spielberg Manufacturing Co.*, 112 N.L.R.B. 1080 (1955). Since that time, the NLRB has swung widely between deferral and nondeferral. For claims involving Title VII, on the other hand, nondeferral has been the clear policy. See *Alexander* vs. *Gardner-Denver Co.*, 415 U.S. 36 (1974).

144.   See, for example, *Olin Corporation*, 268 N.L.R.B. 573 (1984). It is also noteworthy that the language of the Civil Rights Act of 1991 appears to suggest that Congress would prefer employment discrimination claims to be resolved in alternative dispute forums, rather than by the court system. This preference is at odds with the Supreme Court's prior approach, giving individuals (with discrimination claims) their "day in court," regardless of whether they have received adverse decisions in other adjudicatory forums (such as arbitration). See *Alexander* vs. *Gardner-Denver Co.*, supra, note 143. Space limitations preclude us from reviewing additional challenges to the finality of arbitral awards posed by union breaches of its duty of fair representation.

REFERENCES

Bixby, M. (1991). Workplace homicide: Trends, issues, and policy. *Oregon Law Review, 70*, 333.

Blanpain, R. (1990). *International encyclopedia for comparative law*. Deventer: Kluwer.

Bloch, F. (1995, March 1). Affirmative action hasn't helped blacks. *Wall Street Journal*, p. A-14.

Blosser, F. (1992). *Primer on occupational safety and health*. Washington, DC: Bureau of National Affairs.

Coleman, B.J. (1993). *Primer on ERISA* (4th ed.). Washington, DC: Bureau of National Affairs.

Cox, A. (1954). Federalism in the law of labor relations. *Harvard Law Review, 67*, 1297.

Delaney, J.T., & Sockell, D. (1989, July). The impact of the mandatory-permissive distinction on collective bargaining outcomes. *Industrial and Labor Relations Review, 42* (4), 556-583.

Epstein, R.A. (1982). The historical origins and economic structure of workers' compensation law. *Georgia Law Review, 16*, 775.

Evans, S.M., & Nelson, B.J. (1984). *Wage justice: Comparable worth and the paradox of technocratic reform*. Chicago: University of Chicago Press.

Feinman, J.M. (1976). The development of the employment at will rule. *American Journal of Legal History, 20*, 118.

Freeman, R.B., & Medoff, J.L. (1981). The impact of collective bargaining: Illusion or reality? In *U.S. industrial relations 1950-1989: A critical assessment* (pp. 47-97). Madison, WI: IRRA.

_____ . (1984). *What do unions do?* New York: Basic Books.

Gold, M.E. (1983). *A dialogue on comparable worth*. Ithaca, NY: ILR Press.

Gorman, R.A. (1976). *Basic text on labor law, unionization and collective bargaining* (pp. 498-509). St. Paul, MN: West Publishing Co.

Green, R.M., & Reibstein, R.J. (1992). *Employer's guide to workplace torts*. Washington, DC: Bureau of National Affairs.

Hamermesh, D.S. (1977). *Jobless pay and the economy.* Baltimore, MD: Johns Hopkins Press.

Hill, M.A., & Killingsworth, M. (1989). *Comparable worth: Analyses and evidence.* Ithaca, NY: ILR Press.

Ichniowski, C., Delaney, J.T., & Lewin, D. (1989). The new human resource management in U.S. workplaces: Is it really new and is it only nonunion. *Relations Industrielles, 44* (1), 97-119.

Lee, B.A. (1995). Legal pitfalls of downsizing. *Human Resource Management Review.*

Moran, R.D. (1989). *OSHA handbook* (2d ed.), Washington, DC: Government Institutes.

Morris, C.J. (Ed.). (1983). *The developing labor law* (2nd ed,. pp. 223-226). Washington, DC: BNA Books.

Rothstein, L.F. (1992). *Disabilities and the law.* Boulder, CO: Shepard's/McGraw Hill.

Sockell, D. (1984, July). The legality of employee participation programs in unionized firms. *Industrial and Labor Relations Review, 37* (4), 541-556.

Sockell, D. (1986, October). The scope of mandatory bargaining: A critique and a proposal. *Industrial and Labor Relations Review, 40* (1), 19-34.

Sockell, D., & Delaney, J.T. (1987, October). Union organizing and the Reagan NLRB. *Contemporary Policy Issues, 5,* 29-31.

Sockell, D., & Delaney, J.T. (1995, February). *HCRCA: The rise or fall of nurses' unions.* Unpublished manuscript.

Steele, S. (1995, March 1). Affirmative action must go. *New York Times,* p. A19.

Wood, H.G. (1877). *Master and servant* sec. 134. Albany, NY.

CHANGING MARKET ECONOMIES AND HUMAN RESOURCE MANAGEMENT

Calvin D. Siebert and Mahmood A. Zaidi

In recent decades market economies have experienced structural changes that some have deemed revolutionary. These changes, which are ongoing, include the internationalization of market competition, technological change which has influenced the optimum scale of production, and changes in the financial area. Along with these changes there have been massive shifts in consumer preferences from traditional standardized commodities to value-added products expressed in the form of goods and services of high intrinsic quality. This means that consumers are becoming less price conscious as they strive for "quality" and uniqueness in their goods and services.[1]

At the same time, many macroeconomic changes have occurred that have had significant microeconomic implications.[2] For example, there has been a change from a fixed exchange system to one in which exchanges are allowed to float. This has resulted in swings in the exchange rate among the leading countries in the world and has had significant repercussions on the international division of labor. Long periods of high unemployment, in the European countries in particular, have led to efforts for less regulation and more flexibility in the labor markets of these countries. Very rapid growth in the Asian Pacific rim countries has led to a restructuring of global competitive forces. All these changes have led to calls for flexible labor markets in order to better adapt to the changing business environment. This, in turn, has led to calls for changes in human resource management in order for firms to better adjust to changing market conditions.

The purpose of this chapter is to delineate these market changes in more detail and set forth, to the extent possible, their implications for human resource management. Since these changes in market economies are ongoing, we will not be able to specify the ultimate form to which human resource management will evolve. We will, however, be able to set forth some of the directions in which it is progressing.

CHANGES IN INTERNATIONAL COMPETITION AND THE FIRM'S EXTERNAL ENVIRONMENT

Change in international competition and the external environment can have a profound impact on the management of firms and, thus, human resource management. Although the pace of worldwide economic integration increased during the 1980s, the movement toward greater international competition is not a new phenomenon. The world economies have progressed toward more openness for a number of decades. With the elimination of capital controls in the 1950s and 1960s and the computer revolution in transferring ownership claims, financial markets have become global for the industrial economies of the world. With the slow but sure lowering of tariffs and nontariff barriers to trade from their high points in the 1930s, world trade in goods and services has expanded tremendously. As Troy has pointed out, the recent passage of international trade agreements such as NAFTA and GATT has been a significant factor in increasing international competition (Troy, 1997). Worldwide trade has, in fact, grown more rapidly than the level of output in the world economy; the world has truly become a global economy. As a result, firms feel competitive pressure not only from other firms within their industry in a particular economy, but are in competition with firms a continent away. Monopoly and oligopolistic positions of firms have eroded in this type of environment.

Such competition forces firms to operate as efficiently as they can, to cut costs where they can and to introduce rapidly new technology. To gain a competitive edge firms attempt to improve product quality and/or expand product range flexibility. These pressures lead firms toward flexible specialization which tends to reduce the scale of operations. Competitive pressures lead firms to resist more strongly union wage demands and opt for more labor market flexibility (Kochan, Katz, & McKersie, 1986; Sussex, 1992). It appears that these competitive pressures have been more successful in forcing nonunion firms to adopt flexible job designs than in unionized environments (Ichniowski, Delaney, & Lewin, 1989). However, regardless of the firm's union or nonunion status, the pressures force firms to change working conditions and organizational structures. Human resource management techniques are necessarily having to evolve. Undoubtedly changes will differ across firms, industries, and countries. This means that in some firms and industries there will be greater teamwork and more worker involvement in decision making ("Stalking the New Consumer," 1989, pp. 54-62; Therrien, 1989). It is worth noting here, though, that both nonunion and union workplaces are just as likely to adopt employee participation plans (Ichniowski, Delaney, & Lewin, 1989).

Another factor in the global convergence of organizational structures is the continued expansion of the multinationals. For various economic and strategic reasons, firms find it advantageous to have subsidiaries in many countries. For example, Japanese firms have manufacturing operations in the United States and Europe as well as Japan. U.S. firms have subsidiaries in many different countries around the world. Indicative of the extent of globalization of the marketplace is an example provided by Reich (1991). From each $20,000 an American spends on a General Motors Pontiac Le Mans, only 40 percent remains in the United States: "About $5,000 goes to South Korea for routine labor and assembly operations, $3,500 to Japan for advanced components (engines, transaxles, and electronics), $1,500 to West Germany for styling and design engineering, $800 to Taiwan, Singapore, and Japan for small components, $500 to Britain for advertising and marketing services and about $100 to Ireland and Barbados for data processing."[3] These types of international interactions enhance the competitive pressures among the firms in the global economy. These firms learn and imitate each others' marketing techniques and production procedures as well as their organizational structures.[4]

An important contribution to increased international competition has been the phenomenon of rapid economic growth of the Asian Pacific rim countries. Countries such as South Korea, Taiwan, Hong Kong, Singapore, Thailand, and Malaysia have had growth rates between 5 and 10 percent per year over several decades. Even Mainland China has joined the parade in the past decade or so. Of course the country that led the parade was Japan, which went from a low-income country to a leading industrial economy in the world in less than three decades. It went from a country in which "made in Japan" connoted poor quality to being a leader in the quality of its products. As a result, the United States and other industrial countries have had a difficult time competing with Japan in world markets.[5]

There have been numerous attempts to explain this transformation. Common factors in all these Asian Pacific countries have been their outward-looking export promotion policies and their high saving rate relative to the United States. However, other reasons have been given to explain the transformation of these countries into rapid growth, quality-oriented production centers. Particularly in the case of Japan, different human resource management methods have been cited as a factor in explaining its large productivity increases while, at the same time, leading the world in the quality of its products (Blinder, 1990). Some have emphasized that W. Edwards Deming's management techniques were embraced in Japan even while they were being rejected in the United States. At the heart of Deming's system is an emphasis on quality improvement and cooperation within the firm.

Some have emphasized other features of Japanese human resource management in their analysis. For example, Gordon (1982) emphasized the lifetime employment system and the bonus payment as explanations of why the Japanese labor market behaves differently than the United States labor market. He found that nominal wages in Japan were much more flexible than nominal wages in the United States, resulting in more stable employment. Much of this wage flexibility can be explained by Japan's semiannual variable wage bonuses. If firms are profitable workers gain a large bonus, while if firms do poorly bonuses are small or nonexistent. Such a payment scheme increases workers sense that if they work hard and allow or suggest productivity-increasing innovations in production techniques they, as part of the group, will gain.[6] Long-term attachments between workers and firms are formalized in the lifetime employment system and mandatory retirement at age 55. The lifetime employment system allows firms to amortize their specific and general human capital investment in their workers.[7] The seniority wage, or nenkō system, relates earnings to length of service and not to work performance. Cooperation in the workplace is emphasized. It is interesting to note that while in Japan a hierarchical rather than equalitarian system represents the ideal in social relations, this system does not operate in the workplace. Glazer (1976) argues that outside of China, the Japanese factory or company is the most egalitarian in the world. There is little distinction of dress between white-collar and manual workers. In contrast to the formal level of address used outside the company, an informal, familiar level of speech is used within the factory. Managers and workers receive almost the same benefits, for example, access to sick pay, sports clubs, and vacation resorts. Hofstede (1993) has also found that the Japanese culture adheres to the theory of "PM leadership," which he defines as a preference of citizens to maintain social stability and place more emphasis on collectivism. All this goes a long way to explaining the lack of conflict in Japanese labor relations.

The success of the Japanese economy and firms within the economy has led some U.S. firms to try to emulate the Japanese system of human resource management. During the 1980s Deming, the prophet without honor in his own country, was hired to provide seminars on his management techniques in the United States. As a result, the workplace in many firms has been reorganized in a more equalitarian craft-like way (Dreyfuss, 1989). In recent years American firms have been able to challenge Japanese firms in the marketplace as more and more Japanese firms have had difficulty selling overseas. While a large part of Japanese firms' difficulties in recent years has been the appreciation of the yen relative to the dollar and other currencies, some must have resulted from the restructuring of foreign firms.

THE IMPACT OF CHANGES IN TECHNOLOGY

Tylecote (1995) proposes the theory that technology has progressed in waves since the beginning of the industrial period. Each of these waves lasts approximately half a century. A dominant technological style is associated with each new wave. As new innovations accumulate, a point is reached were a new method for the production of goods and services emerges. This new techno-style eventually becomes the rational or common sensible way for firms to organize their production process. Tylecote argues that the last major style to begin and end in the industrial period was the Fordist style. This techno-style is typified by the assembly line production process and lasted from about 1915 to 1975. Tylecote claims that the latest style, which he terms the information and communications technology (ICT) style, can be characterized by flexible manufacturing systems (FMS). FMS incorporate advanced manufacturing technologies which allow for increased customization and quality in goods and services. Table 1 presents a comparison between Tylecote's Fordist and ICT styles.

The introduction and diffusion of advanced manufacturing technology will, it is argued, lead to vast organizational changes and have major implications for human resource management. Advanced manufacturing technology is computer-controlled or microelectronics-based equipment used in the design, manufacturing, or handling of a product. Typical applications include computer-aided design equipment, computer-aided engineering used to optimize manufacturing, flexible machinery centers, robots, automated transport

Table 1. Change of Technological Paradigm

Fordist	ICT
Energy-intensive	Information-intensive
Design and engineering in drawing offices	Computer-aided design
Sequential design and production	Concurrent engineering
Standardized	Customized
Rather stable product mix	Rapid changes in product mix
Dedicated plant and equipment	Flexible production systems
Automation	Systemation
Single firm	Networks
Hierarchical structures	Flat horizontal structures
Departmental	Integrated
Product with service	Service with products
Centralization	Distributed intelligence
Specialized skills	Multi-skilling
Government control, sometimes ownership	Government information, coordination and regulation
Planning	Vision

systems, and automated storage and retrieval systems. (For the impact of computer-aided design, see Spinanger, 1992.) Such systems will require mental or problem-solving skills rather than physical skills. The systems will also result in greater independence among work activities, thus requiring flexible, multiskilled employees (Fong & Hill, 1992). Some argue that firms will require a high retention rate of well-trained workers because of greater investment in capital per worker and this may result in a stronger partnership between management and labor (Robinson, Oswald, Swinehart, & Thomas, 1991; Vickrey & Campbell, 1991).

These changes in technology allow for more customized production, moving away from mass assembly-line production toward a more craft-like production process. With such applications come pressure for "flexible specialization" and finding changing market niches. An emphasis is also placed on change rather than stability in workplace relations, job content, and so on (Piore & Sabel, 1984). Such changes allow firms to cater to consumer's shifts from traditional standardized commodities to a taste for "quality" and uniqueness in the firm's goods and services.[8] Computers allow for increased use of such flexibility without much if any increase in costs (Pepper, 1989). However, it is probable that this will be more true for some industries than others. Perez (1986) identifies industries that can capitalize on advanced manufacturing technologies as carrier branch industries. For example, the auto industry was a benefactor to technological advances in oil refining and utility services during the early twentieth century. Undoubtedly, there will be some industries or firms within particular industries that will be better suited to benefit from advances in microelectronics. In these industries, quality and uniqueness of the product will allow higher prices to be charged.

Such flexibility, of course, undermines the long-term relationship inherent in collective bargaining relationships. Pressure for flexible specialization argues for a reduction in the firm's scale of operations (Cohen & Zysman, 1987). Functions within the firm such as payroll, accounting, and maintenance can be outsourced to outside service vendors. Peak production can be farmed out to subcontractors. Core employment within the firm can be reduced by using part-time or temporary employees and private consultants. Efforts to remain flexible to respond to changing market conditions are reinforced by the uncertainty created by possible gyrations in exchange rates.[9]

As a result of these changes, human resource practices and policies will have to change. For example, temporary workers, "telecommuters," and workers at small supplier firms have been more difficult to unionize than permanent workers at large enterprises (Mangum, Mayal, & Nelson, 1985). As stated earlier, those firms that do adopt these new production methods will need to provide more training for their workers. As Ashenfelter and LaLonde explain, the firms must believe that the employment relationship will continue in order for them to invest in training (Ashenfelter & LaLonde, 1997). This seems to imply that long-term employment relationships will need to exist in these firms in order for the new production techniques to be successful. All these changes mean that small firms and employing entities will grow relative to larger firms and units. The relationships between big firms and big unions will be undercut. A return to an emphasis on craft unions rather than industrial unions may be necessary if unions are to remain a viable option in this brave new world. The movie and TV industry is an example of an industry where unions organized along craftlines have remained relatively strong.

This analysis paints a picture of vast organizational change as the advanced manufacturing technology penetrates more and more industries. However, a recent study for the Organization for Economic Cooperation and Development (OECD) by Vickrey and Campbell argues that the changes may not be that dramatic and the organizational adjustment not that traumatic. In their study, they not only surveyed the literature in the field but made a number of on-site visits in the United States, Japan, and Europe. They admit that advanced manufacturing techniques are employed by firms for one or a mix of three strategic reasons: to attain productivity gains by reducing labor input; to improve product quality; or to expand product range flexibility, that is, to attain "economies of scope" rather than "economies of scale." They go on to argue that the direction of organizational change may be quite different depending on whether the firm's principal aim is "process" rationalization or "product" flexibility (also, see Willman, 1987). Their research findings suggest that in countries such as the United States and the United Kingdom, where Taylorism may be more fully entrenched, the use of the new technology may be primarily aimed toward process change. As a result, the organizational consequences of the changes in job content and worker autonomy may be less pronounced than if the technology is used to attain "economies of scope," that is, greater product range flexibility.

There may be worker resistance to organizational change, particularly if organizational change occurs independently of technological change. The export of the Japanese approaches of just-in-time and total quality control to other national settings, for example, has clear implications for the organizational status quo. Existing management and union structures may be threatened by the decentralization of responsibility for quality matters, which encourages more direct participation and joint problem solving.[10]

Vickrey and Campbell (1991) argue that technology does not necessarily determine organization. Some have argued that the new technology inevitably leads to de-skilling of the workforce, with de-skilling being a conscious management strategy to increase control over the production process. On the contrary, researchers have found an upgrading of skills, rather than a de-skilling effect from advanced manufacturing technology (see Daniel, 1987 as a representative example). A second argument some have made is that efficient use of the new technology is incompatible with the Taylorist organizational paradigm of hierarchical control and a high division of labor. The new technology requires greater teamwork and worker involvement in decision making, reduction in direct labor, and an increase in indirect labor inputs. According to Vickrey and Campbell, such changes are less dependent on the technology than on the organizational response to it. The empirical studies convincingly show that the same technology is compatible with a wide variety of organizational patterns, and that such factors as the existing organizational culture, plant size, and national setting are the important determining variables. (For a discussion of this issue, see Ben-Ner, Montias, & Neuberger, 1993.) Indeed, Vickrey and Campbell's site visits showed differences in organizational adjustments among different nations to the introduction of the new technology. Also, there appear to be differences in adjustment to the new technology at the local, regional or industrial level. (For a more extended discussion see, for example, OECD, 1986, 1989). For example, trade unions reactions to technological change may depend on whether the union is organized along craft or industrial lines or on the type of bargaining relationship with management. They note that firm specific differences in applications exist within the same industry for a number of reasons, including differing acceptance of new technology by management. Vickrey and Campbell, however, do admit the situation is still evolving and that the final chapter has not yet been written.

Concurring somewhat with Vickrey and Campbell, Tylecote (1995) argues that each time a technological shift has occurred, problems have arisen in the world economy because of certain mismatches with the old systems. Tylecote contends that microeconomic mismatches result in problems for some firms because their organizational structures are unsuited for or are unwilling to adopt the new techno-style. Other authors in this volume have also noted the problems that might be caused by this type of mismatch. For example, Levine points out that, "New technologies open up new possibilities for higher productivity, but often fail to increase performance" (Levine, 1995). Levine goes on to say that this has led managers to realize that the "old ways" are not necessarily the best ways. Levine also comments on the difficulty that firms have had in implementing Total Quality Management (TQM) programs. These firms place statistical process control (SPC) charts on the production line in order to increase quality. However, because the firms fail to change other parts of the system, particularly reward structures, the use (or nonuse) of these charts fails to produce higher quality products. Appelbaum and Berg highlight studies by Lynch and Zemsky (1995) and others who report that the use of team production and employee participation schemes are diffusing slowly across the United States, indicating a reluctance by U.S. firms to adopt the new techno-style (Appelbaum & Berg, 1997). Tylecote (1995) also calls attention to macroeconomic mismatches that occur. The major example he gives of this type of mismatch is the lack of qualified personnel which arises because of the technology shift. Lillard and Tan (1992) found that the value of some worker's skills may be depreciating by as much as 10 percent per year as new technologies are introduced. Lee and Sockell report that many firms have become so dependent on some workers' technical knowledge of the production system, that they are requiring these employees to wear pagers and remain on call (Lee & Sockell, 1997). These facts seem to lend support to Tylecote's arguments.

The new technology will cause important adjustments in human resource management practices and policies. It will undoubtedly change worker-management relationships.[11] Whether that means a movement toward more craft unions or substantial reduction in union activity is not clear. In the United States, firms starting afresh (for example, Japanese producers in the United States) that apply the new technology do not include unions as a part of the organizational plan. However, in older firms such as in the automobile industry, the technology has been introduced with less organizational change (Katz, 1985, 1987). This is also true in many European countries. A critic may argue that these industries and firms have not fully integrated the new technology and its organizational implications into their operations. In any case, we conclude that the situation is still evolving and that changes should follow an evolutionary course rather than a revolutionary one. The cumulative effect of continuous technological change will lead to more and more institutional change over time, that is, changes in the organization of firms and human resource practices.

IMPACT OF FINANCIAL MARKETS

Changes in financial theory in the 1950s led to the view of the firm as a malleable portfolio of assets. Traditional caution concerning corporate debt-to-equity ratios were considered unnecessary. Using portfolio adjustments, stockholders could adjust for the risks associated with high debt equity ratios of particular firms. This led to large increases in debt financing of the corporate operation. The use of debt as a share of corporate financing relative to equity increased throughout the 1970s. It continued into the 1980s, ultimately leading to the "junk bond" financing binge characteristic of that decade. This view of the corporate organization as simply a collection of financial assets within a portfolio reduced the continuity of ownership. Owners of the corporation had no long-term interest in the operations of the firm. If the short-term performance of the firm as measured by stock values did not match their aspirations, the stock owners would simply sell the firm's stock and move to the ownership of another firm. Of course the ability of stockholders to move their ownership does not mean they are willing to so in all cases. In a number of cases, in recent years, stockholders, particularly if they are on the board of directors, have become involved in changing management if they think the company is not performing well. In addition, there have been corporate raiders who have searched for companies whose stock is priced below what they think is its intrinsic value. They buy controlling interest in the corporation, resturcture it, merge it with other firms, and/or sell off parts of it.

In such an atmosphere managers have little incentive to take a long-run view of firm operations. Actions tend to be judged on how quickly they will impact the bottom line. Such an attitude biases management away from long-term stable industrial relations, if such relations are conducted at the employer-union level. Corporate investment in human resources is downplayed not only because the payoff on such an investment is long term, but also because such investments, unlike investments in physical assets, do not appear on the balance sheet. Rather, they appear as current costs on the income statement and, thus, cut into current profits. In fact, it seems that most firms place little faith in the ability of human resource policy investments to contribute to the bottom line. From a recent survey, Levine cites the perceived importance managers place on 19 different performance measures (Levine, 1995). The three human resource performance measures included in the survey: employee satisfaction, turnover, and training expenditures, were ranked 17th, 18th, and 19th, respectively, in importance. But as Levine points out later in his book, declines in training expenditures and employee satisfaction, plus rising turnover, are really heralding a decline in the firm's human assets, which will undoubtedly lead to worse future financial performance for the firm. A recent study indicates that an inverse relationship seems to exist between collective bargaining and the stock value of the firm (Abowd, 1989). As wage increases are negotiated by the unions, the value of the firm may decrease. That is, a reduction in profit occurs as labor cost (expense) increases, resulting in a lower stock value for the company. However, the goodwill resulting from a stable employer-union relationship and an investment in human capital may not lead to an increase in stock price for the firms as they are intangible assets and are not easily conducive to the assignment of monetary value. Of course, as Ashenfelter and LaLonde suggest, the fact that more able employees seek out employers that provide superior training opportunities should be of monetary concern for firms (Ashenfelter & LaLonde, 1997).

It might be thought that corporate shareholders could see through the veil of false accounting, but in practice this does not appear to be the case.[12] Management is under great pressure to obtain short-term labor costs savings. If management does not, the board of directors may replace it with a management team that does. This helps explain the wave of corporate downsizing that has hit many corporations in the past decade or so.[13] Many observers may view such behavior as an American aberration, or at any rate, an Anglo-Saxon phenomenon. However, corporate downsizing had been occurring in Europe and more recently in Japan. Other countries' national employer-union bargain systems have not yet been eroded as much as the American system has. However, the financial model of the firm is clearly spreading to all market economies. As it does, efforts by the management of the firms to take a long-term view will be further and severely compromised.

Another financial change that, although external to firms, has had a significant impact on the decision making of firms is the movement from a fixed to a flexible exchange rate system. During the post-World War II period until 1971, the world's industrial countries operated under a fixed exchange rate system centered around the United States. Under this system, firms in various countries could sell their products at known and unchanging exchange rates.[14] Multinationals could make their investments in various countries based on economic considerations, such as location of supplies of labor, raw materials, and markets, but that all changed with the advent of flexible exchange rates in 1971. Now firms had to consider long-term movements in the exchange rates as part of their investment strategy. This would not have caused many problems if the exchange rates had remained relatively stable. Unfortunately this is not what happened. For various reasons, which we do not have space to analyze here, there have been massive long-term changes in exchange rates, particularly between the United States and the other industrial countries.

In particular, the dollar, after initially falling in value about 25 percent relative to other currencies in the 1970s, appreciated nearly 80 percent in the first half of the 1980s. Thus the cost of goods produced in the United States increased in the world market by over 75 percent. This had a number of significant repercussions, both short run and long run, in the world economy. First, it made the recession of the early 1980s in the United States deeper than it would have been as U.S. exports fell. Many companies in the automobile, steel, and related industries found themselves in or near bankruptcy (Hoerr, 1988; Mills & McCormick, 1985; Steiber, 1980). It allowed the Japanese auto industry to gain a stronger foothold in the U.S. market, and it led multinationals in the United States to move their investments overseas to get out from behind the wall of the strong U.S. dollar.

In addition to adjustments in the world industrial structure, the massive appreciation of the dollar also had repercussions on the labor market front. The cost squeeze that many U.S. international firms found themselves in led to a more determined position on unions and union demands for wage increases to keep up with the cost of living. Many firms dropped the COLA's in their union contracts and attempted to renegotiate contracts before they expired (Hoerr, 1988; Mills & McCormick, 1985; Steiber, 1980). With bankruptcy as a possible option, many unions found themselves with few alternatives but to accept the changes proposed by the firms (Jones, 1992). In the nonunion sectors the same pressures were being felt and the adjustments could be made more quickly.

During this period the restructuring and downsizing of firms began and continues even today. Firms reduced their labor force in order to become more productive and alleviate the cost squeeze. Human resource management techniques changed in this context. Firms reduced their labor force, in many cases, not by massive layoffs, but by offering early retirement incentives as well as by attrition (Hill & Dwyer, 1990; Jones, 1992). As the downsizing continued in the 1990s more firms found it necessary to resort to layoffs. Firms in the computer industry such as IBM, Hewlett-Packard, and others, as well as the giants in the auto industry, have followed this pattern. For example, the automobile industry today can produce its output with about a third less employees than it would have required two decades ago. This, of course, has led to increases in labor productivity. However, these increases in labor productivity have not all been passed on in real wages. Real wages have not risen as much as labor productivity has in the United States during the 1980s.[15]

Just as the first half of the 1980s saw the massive appreciation of the dollar, the latter half and beyond experienced a massive depreciation of the dollar, particularly against the Japanese yen and the German Mark, the strongest of the European currencies. Again the large movement in the exchange rate had many global economic repercussions. As the dollar depreciated, firms in foreign countries found they were being priced out of the United States market. For example, as the yen appreciated, Americans found Japanese-produced goods more and more expensive. To maintain their competitive position, the Japanese firms were forced to reduce their profit margins. The Japanese also found themselves being attacked more and more by U.S. firms with charges of dumping, that is, selling products in the United States below the prices charged in Japan. To alleviate the problem, the United States became the focus of investment by foreign multinationals as these firms attempted to maintain their foothold in American markets (O'Brien, 1992).

At the same time, there have been economic repercussions in Japan. Recently, Japan has had its first full-scale recession in the post-World War II period. In the past, Japan only had what were termed growth recessions. As a result, the famous lifetime employment system in Japan is beginning to break down at an even faster pace than has already been documented. There have been some actual layoffs of workers in the large multinational Japanese firms which employed the system of lifetime employment contracts.

In sum, the massive swings in the exchange rate among several of the industrial countries have had profound economic consequences in their restructuring of global economic activity. It has reinforced the general tendency toward greater labor market flexibility that has been occurring in the past couple of decades. As firms had to become more flexible in moving their operations from country to country to defend themselves against the swings in the exchange rate, so too have there been changes in human resource management to promote more labor market flexibility. For example, in order to gain greater flexibility, firms, instead of hiring permanent employees, have hired private consultants, part-time employees, and subcontracted some work (Noe, Hollenbeck, Gerhart, & Wright, 1994; Spinanger, 1992). Whether it be the erosion of the system of lifetime labor contracts in Japan or the reduction of union power in the United States, the functions of human resource management have changed and will continue to change in the future.[16]

INDUSTRIAL RESTRUCTURING

All the changes in international competition, technology, and financial markets have led to industrial and corporate restructuring. Another force for change in industrial structure has been the high unemployment during the 1980s and 1990s in many industrial countries. During the 1950s and 1960s most European countries had unusually low unemployment rates. In fact, many of these countries had labor shortages and had to import guest workers from southern Europe, northern Africa, and the Middle East. However, most of the European countries moved from low unemployment countries (1-4%) to high unemployment countries (8-15%) in the 1980s and beyond. Much has been written to attempt to explain this seemingly permanent change in the level of European unemployment.[17] A leading explanation for the high rate of unemployment has been structural problems in the labor markets. This has led to an effort at increasing labor market "flexibility" by reducing hiring and firing costs, limiting union power, improving retraining and, in general, increasing wage flexibility.[18] Whether such changes will improve unemployment is still an open question since not many countries have enacted all the proposed structural changes. The United Kingdom has probably gone the furthest in instituting the structural changes so far with little beneficial effects on unemployment (Bean, 1994, p. 615). If the proposed changes were made, one can see that they would require significant revisions in human resource management practices with respect to layoffs and wage setting. Because there are, in the current environment, large costs to hiring and firing permanent workers, more firms are attempting to gain flexibility by hiring more temporary workers, part-timers, and subcontractors.

The response of corporations and labor to all these enumerated changes in market conditions has been varied. The impact of these changes and pressures, as noted earlier, has been particularly acute in the slow growing, high labor cost, high unemployment countries of North America and Western Europe.[19] This has led to a number of new corporate strategies as firms have attempted to respond to changing market forces. A typical response has been attempts by various industries to raise import barriers and lobby for other forms of assistance.[20] However, increased protection creates a number of problems. Protection for one industry through higher tariffs on the goods it produces can lead to higher costs for other industries which use these goods as inputs in their production processes. Also, since GATT, in most cases, does not allow increases in tariffs, protectionism efforts have had to take the form of nontariff barriers (NTBs), such as quotas and voluntary export restraints. These measures restrict the *volume* of imports but leave room for increased *value* of imports and for new suppliers to enter the market. Another way to get around the tariff walls, quota restrictions, and long-term adverse exchange rate movements is investment in production facilities within protected markets.

A second response has been to substitute capital for labor through automation. This has allowed firms to save labor costs by laying off redundant workers and at the same time increasing the quality of their goods. These tend to be high volume organizations, and Lawler (1991) contends that this type of environment is more conducive to Total Quality Management (TQM) programs. TQM programs require off-line, non-decision making, participation programs to be effective. Nonunion employees feel considerable pressure to join these groups and have far less say about their participation in the groups than unionized workers. A third strategy has been diversification. Firms that are pessimistic about the long-term prospects for their industry invest funds in other lines of business. This led to the conglomeration binge of the 1980s (see "Smeltdown at Armco," 1988).

A fourth response has been for producers to move away from bulk, mass-produced, standardized goods toward goods and markets where price is less of a factor. This strategy stresses quality and flexibility of response to changes in demand and concentrates on market niches. (For a discussion of this point, see Bartlett & Yoshihara, 1988.) It means, for example, production of special steel, designer clothing, luxury cars, and so on. The computerization of industry has allowed such flexibility. The rewards are high if successful, but the risks are great. This leads to a fifth strategy; that is, high labor cost firms that are producing labor intensive products subcontract the labor intensive part of the production out to domestic or international firms with low labor costs, whichever is most cost efficient. Domestic subcontracting to firms and workers with significantly lower wages and less favorable working conditions has typically occurred in Italy and Japan, but is also occurring in the United States despite the government's efforts to weed out these so-called sweat shops. The high risks resulting from flexible response to changes in demand and concentration on market niche results in a sixth strategy in which firms attempt to reduce such risks by diversification through international subcontracting. Location of activities such as design, marketing, and manufacturing become a prime consideration. The willingness to move operations globally increases worldwide competition, eroding profitable market niches and locations.

Labor's response to changing market conditions and the strategies of business firms to cope with them have been varied. In some cases labor has cooperated with the business strategies and in other situations labor has played a more adversarial role (van Liemt, 1992b). In almost all cases labor has supported attempts to increase trade barriers, or at the very least not reduce them. These efforts have slowed but not stopped the long-run movement toward free trade and reduced nontariff barriers (NTBs) which has been occurring since the 1930s. As noted earlier, firms can circumvent trade barriers or long-term adverse movements in the exchange rate by building manufacturing plants or subcontracting operations behind the tariff or exchange rate walls.

This has led to a second strategy on the part of organized labor. Labor has attempted to restrict the mobility of capital to make it more difficult for employers to locate in low labor-cost countries or move operations to countries behind the exchange rate and tariff barriers. However, the increased financial openness in recent years has promoted movement in the opposite direction— toward more capital mobility. Some countries, such as Japan and South Korea, however, do retain some external capital barriers. A third option for labor has been an attempt to promote international labor standards and multinational bargaining campaigns. Labor has, for example, tried to have minimum working conditions written into trade liberalization laws, such as the recently passed NAFTA agreement.

The role of labor has been weakened in recent years due to lowered trade union density and the poor employment situation in many countries. As a result, the strategies of reducing capital mobility and increasing trade barriers have not been too successful. This leaves few alternatives other than adjusting to the pressures of the changing market economies. In practice this has meant cooperating with employers to achieve higher productivity and enhance flexibility, adaptability, and quality of production. Firms want a skill profile of employees that matches their changing needs as well as more flexibility in the tasks employees perform. Japan is frequently cited as the leading example where labor-management cooperation has been the greatest. As noted earlier, a significant portion of Japanese workers have had the job security of the lifetime employment system. Japanese labor has accepted a far greater degree of pay flexibility as a result of the bonus system which accounts for about 25 percent of its total compensation. The assumed competitive success of the Japanese firms has led employers in North America and Europe to attempt to emulate them. It is interesting to note, however, that in a study by Cooke (1994) it was found that work teams increased the effectiveness of variable compensation plans to increase productivity in nonunion workplaces, but decreased their effectiveness to increase productivity in unionized settings.

Another way firms have attempted to increase labor flexibility is in their use of temporary, part-time, and subcontracted workforces (Belous, 1989). It might be possible that some of these firms are bending the rules as to how they classify "employees," because of the increase in employment cases dealing with this issue (see Lee & Sockell, 1997). It has been argued that the use of more temporary and subcontracted workers leads to a dual labor market with a highly paid core workforce which has full benefits, and a peripheral workforce which is poorly paid and has limited benefits. The widening gap between the wage rate, including benefits, of the skilled workforce and lower skilled wage earners in the United States has been cited as evidence of this as well.[21] This dichotomy, however, neglects the fact that some of the peripheral workers are highly specialized professionals and that some subcontractors have their own core and peripheral workers. As a result, the subcontracting pyramid, on the labor side, displays a hierarchy of quality of work, wages, and working conditions, rather than a dual employment system.

ALTERNATIVE APPROACHES

The market forces that have been described here are moving world labor markets in an atomistic direction toward more management and labor market flexibility. Labor market flexibility is necessarily a multidimensional issue. It includes dimensions such as conditions of employment, labor costs, work practices and work patterns, rules and regulations relating to the labor market, external and internal mobility, and education and training. Market forces are influencing all these dimensions to varying degrees and, as such, modifying human resource management policy and practices in the firm.

How much the balance of labor-management relations will shift over time as a result of these economic forces is a matter of conjecture. While it is no doubt true that different countries will be affected differently, the tendencies toward nonunion workforces, which have most keenly been felt in the United States, will develop elsewhere, even if current trends are ambiguous. As the international competition of firms increases, it will become increasingly difficult for firms not to compete on the basis of labor costs, thus pressuring firms in all countries to develop some nonunion workplaces (e.g., Japanese nonunion transplants in the United States). Undoubtedly, it will depend on the degree of centralization of the industrial relations structure, the degree of unionization, and the level at which bargaining takes place, that is, at the national, regional, or enterprise level. As Figure 1 shows, there is a positive correlation across countries between the degree of unionization and level of bargaining. Countries that have a high degree of unionization tend to bargain more at a national or industrial level while countries with lower degrees of unionization tend to bargain at local or enterprise level. There also appears to be a higher degree of unionization in countries that have a highly centralized industrial relations structure. Countries that have a highly centralized industrial relations structure, a high degree of unionization, and where bargaining takes place at a national level (countries such as Austria, Sweden, and Norway), labor and unions may be able to maintain their power in the face of economic forces detailed in this paper. In countries such as the United States, Canada, and the United Kingdom,

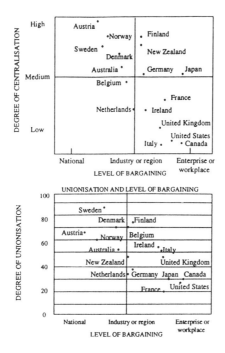

Source: Bean (1985).

Figure 1. Centralization of Structure and Level of Bargaining

in which there is a low degree of centralization and in which much of the bargaining is done at the local level, the reverse may be true. This conjecture is reinforced by the fact that countries with a high degree of unionization and a centralized industrial relations structure have a social partnership, industrial relations tradition. In these countries, which include Germany and Sweden, there is greater state involvement in the maintenance of the existing structure (Vichrey & Campbell, 1991). On the other hand, countries with a decentralized industrial relations structure have an adversarial labor-management tradition. In the latter countries, which include the United States and the United Kingdom, the labor-management relationship is market based rather than state supported and in these countries there have been reductions in the unionization rate (Vichrey & Campbell, 1991).

Many countries have institutions surrounding the workplace that slow the shift in the balance of labor-management relations implied by the market forces enumerated above. First, legal barriers may be erected that will prevent management from following market-based incentives toward a reduction of union power or reduce the incentives to do so. An example of such a legal barrier is Australia's arbitration system, under which the issue of union representation is a court decision, not an employer matter. However,

Australian unions have found it difficult to penetrate some of the newer sectors of the economy and to prevent industrial restructuring. Canada's slower rates of union erosion in the 1980s than that of the United States seems to reflect tight legal controls and the encouragement of public sector unionization. It should be noted, however, that a switch in government can lead to changes in legal structures, as the British case clearly illustrates.

Second, social barriers to overt attempts to eliminate or marginalize unions may be present. The German and Dutch cases seem to be examples of such social pressures. But this social pressure may change from being supportive of labor power to being antiunion, as the American case illustrates.

Third, market forces can be accommodated by enterprise-sensitive bargaining, such as in the case of Japan. In Japan the bonus system provides a variable element of pay reflecting company economic conditions. If pay reflects enterprise conditions, managers have less incentive to follow a nonunion strategy. Even so, Japanese union density has declined significantly.

The changes in the economic environment enumerated in the paper are not only affecting the interactions between organized labor and management but will also influence human resource practices in the nonunion sectors of the economy, which, in countries such as the United States, France, and so on, encompass the major portion of the economy. Their responses will vary across countries, across industries, and even from firm to firm within particular industries. Following Sengenberger (1992), we can group these human resource practice changes under two principal headings: lowering costs, especially labor costs; and increasing the capacity for innovation. These groupings are not mutually exclusive, but are a useful way to categorize the many changes taking place.

Management has tried to reduce costs by operating on both the numerator and the denominator of unit labor costs, that is, labor costs divided by output. Unit labor costs can be controlled by reducing or slowing the rate of increase in wages and benefits. Many times this is done on the understanding that such wage concessions are necessary to save the plant or firm from economic difficulties.

Unit labor costs can also be contained by increasing labor productivity, that is, improving the efficiency with which labor is used. This is done in a number of ways. The most obvious way to increase labor productivity is through increased use of capital or more productive capital in the production process. But there are other ways to increase labor productivity through more efficient allocation of labor. These include the following:

1. Extending operating hours (e.g., reintroducing weekend work) or arranging so-called capital-oriented work scheduling, that is, arranging flexible working hours more in line with production needs.
2. Introducing various kinds of non-standard forms of employment such as part-time work, subcontracting, and the use of all-salaried workforces (Levine, 1995).

3. Changing government regulations to allow more flexible operation of firms. This could include changes in tax laws as well as exemptions from certain labor protection regulations.
4. Relocation of production plants to areas and countries with lower labor costs. This could include outsourcing of production and so on.

An alternative to competing on the basis of lower cost is an increase in a firm's or industry's ability to adapt to changing market conditions and to innovate to meet changing market demands. This allows firms to compete by introducing products and processes quickly to changing market demand. To meet these demands, the firms, or some parts of the firms, may have to depart from a mass production regime. It involves incorporating what Womack, Jones, and Roos (1990) characterized as "lean production." These changes include:

1. Breaking down the conventional barriers and demarcation lines between managers and workers and incorporating joint decision making by workers and managers. It should be noted that problems have arisen promoting this strategy as firms have become so dependent on some workers' technical knowledge that they require them to remain on-call with no compensation, in essence interfering with their private lives (Lee & Sockell, 1997).
2. It involves the extension of group work and the reduction of job classifications. Workers are encouraged to develop multiple skills which makes them more versatile and allows them to adjust to changing conditions more rapidly.
3. Vocational training of workers is emphasized. This may require joint efforts on the part of firms to share costs and risk of investing in human capital which may be of general value in the labor market. (For further development of these arguments, see Sengenberger, 1992.)

As can be seen from the above cataloging of firms' responses to the changing market conditions, the strategies have been quite varied. At one extreme, firms may choose to compete for larger shares of standardized products produced by low-wage workers carrying on relatively simple tasks. Labor is seen in static, passive terms as merely a cost factor, like the cost of land. At the other extreme, firms may choose to tailor production to high value-added, high quality products. Here the role of labor is perceived in much more active, dynamic terms, as a partner in the production process. If the initiative, commitment, and cooperation of the workers in the production process is harnessed, the firm's strategies can be profitable depending on the circumstances. Of course, varying combinations of the two extreme strategies will also be employed.[22]

SUMMARY AND CONCLUSIONS

In this chapter we have delineated the market changes that have been occurring in recent decades and how these forces have impacted on human resource management. The picture is necessarily a complex one. We have found that there has been a wide range of responses to changing market conditions. Our view has much in common with Kerr, Dunlop, Harbison, and Meyers's (1960) picture of the evolution of industrial relations within economies. (For an update and further discussion, see Kerr, 1983.) In their view industrial society converges on what they called pluralistic industrialism in which influence is shared formally or informally by political leaders, management, and organized labor. The relative power of these groups would vary over time and place. They saw the system as always moving, always changing, never reaching a final equilibrium. In recent decades, however, it appears market forces are gaining the upper hand and organized labor's influence has been on the decline. In this chapter we enumerated a number of these influences that have continued the evolution of industrial society and human resource management practices.

One of the major forces for change has been the increased international competition and the globalization of the marketplace. The reduction of barriers and the elimination of capital controls has led firms to perceive themselves as competing not locally or nationally but internationally. This has led to continued expansion of multinationals. Firms have opted to compete not only in the product market where they have focused on improved product quality and product range flexibility but also on the human resource management front. This has led to resistance to union wage demands, attempts to opt for more labor market flexibility along the lines of W. Edward Deming's management techniques.

Technology is another force for change. There has been a move from the Fordist-Taylorist techno-style to the information and communications technology style. The latter system is characterized by flexible manufacturing systems. Flexible manufacturing systems incorporate advanced manufacturing technologies which allow for increased customization and quality in goods and services. This means moving away from mass assembly line production techniques in the Fordist system toward more craft-like production processes that require more flexibility in human resource management. Will this lead to a movement toward craft unions and workers becoming more a part of the management team? How this evolves is still an open question. In any case, it appears the new system will differ from industry to industry and will require more skill, not less skill, on the part of the workers.

A third force for change has been in the financial area. Here an emphasis on short-run bottom line results have led management to downplay investment in human resources since the payoff on such investment is long term. Many of the more highly skilled jobs, such as accounting, can be out-sourced. On the global scale the movement toward flexible exchange rates has created greater uncertainty in the management of firms. As a result of massive changes in exchange rates companies have had to diversify internationally. This has led to more global competition and pressures on firms to modify their human resource practices to compete.

All the changes in international competition, technology, and financial markets have led to considerable industrial and corporate restructuring. In the paper we note that since the leading explanation of the high rate of unemployment in Europe and Canada has been structural problems in the labor market, there has been a call for greater labor market flexibility by reducing hiring and firing costs, limiting union power, and increasing wage flexibility. Such changes would require significant revisions in human resource practices with respect to layoffs and wage setting.

The response of labor and management to all these forces has been varied. In the last section of the paper we note the response will differ between countries and from industry to industry. The response will vary depending on the degree of centralization of the industrial relations structure, the degree of unionization, and the level at which bargaining takes place. As in the Kerr and his colleagues's (1960) model, the system of industrial pluralism is still evolving but during the current time frame forces for market flexibility appear to be in ascendancy.

ACKNOWLEDGMENT

We would like to thank Beth Miller and John Mavers for excellent research assistance in the preparation of this paper.

NOTES

1. For an overview of how these changes impact human resource management, see Williams (1993). For further analysis of how human resource management and economics interact, see Mitchell and Zaidi (1990a, 1990b).

2. For a fuller analysis of how macroeconomic wage and price setting impacts industrial relations, see Mitchell and Zaidi (1992).

3. For a discussion of how international trade theory has changed to explain these new patterns of global specialization, see Harris (1992).

4. For a discussion on how firms are forming alliances with international companies in order to gain a competitive advantage, see Doz, Hamel, and Prahalad (1986).

5. For a fuller discussion of ecomonic competition among nations, see Porter (1990). For an argument that we need to move beyond narrow economic nationalism concerns, see Reich (1991).

6. However, a recent study shows that bonus systems do not necessarily generate greater productivity than conventional merit systems (see Schwab & Olson 1990).

7. Of course the importance of the lifetime practice should not be over emphasized. The lifetime employment practice does not cover a large percent of Japan's nonagricultural workforce and these benefits only apply to certain firms in the Japanese economy (Cole, 1972). As Houseman

and Abraham (1993) note, males are the main recipients of the benefits of this policy. It should also be mentioned that researchers have been tracking the gradual decline of this policy for several years (Cole, 1972). Some analysts predict that Japan's rising unemployment rate will cause even greater erosion of the lifetime employment system. In April 1995 Japan's unemployment rate climbed to 3.2 percent, its highest level ever. Analysts predict that the rate will climb to 4.3 percent by April 1996 (Pollack, 1995).

8.   Feigenbaum (1994) reports that it is "affordable quality" in which consumers are most interested.

9.   The uncertainty created by external factors can also have an adversarial affect on management-union relations. See Piore and Sable (1984) and Kochan and Katz (1983).

10.   Unions are responding to increased competition by incorporating "Quality of Work Life" (QWL) programs into their contracts. These programs focus on increased participation in decision making by workers (Williams & Watts, 1986).

11.   For a discussion on technology's adverse impact on the union-management relationship, see Sussex (1992).

12.   See Levine (1995) for a discussion of the limitations of financial results in predicting future performance.

13.   For further discussion of the impact of downsizing on the financial performance of a firm, see references cited in De Meuse, Vanderheiden, and Bergmann (1994). This study also shows that the financial performance of the firms worsened rather than improved following the announced layoffs. However, some studies (e.g., Worrell, Davidson, Wallace, & Sharma, 1991) found that firms need not be concerned about the affects of announcements of layoffs for restructuring reasons, not related to financial distress, on stock prices.

14.   It is true that the Bretton Woods system, as it was known, allowed for changes in exchange rate in cases of fundamental disequilibrium. Such changes were often accompanied by balance of payments and financial crises in the countries involved. It is nevertheless true that such exchange rate adjustments occurred very infrequently in most countries, if at all. In any case, throughout the period the bellwether U.S. dollar remained fixed at $35 per ounce of gold.

15.   During the 1980s the economy-wide real wage rose about 6 percent while labor productivity increased nearly 15 percent.

16.   For a discussion in the popular press on how human resource management has become more flexible in responding to the changing demands of the market, see Norton (1993).

17.   See Bean (1994) for a recent survey. Also, see Layard, Nickell, and Jackman (1991) for an explanation and possible solutions to the problem. Mitchell and Zaidi (1992) develop a model which attributes the high unemployment to the wage price determination processes. In this model, which appears in Erickson, Kimbell, and Mitchell (1997), a high unemployment rate (NAIRU) would result if both labor and management targets for real wages and profit margins were high.

18.   The flexibility companies have to adjust labor inputs to slack demand and to the new technologies differ substantially across countries as explained by Houseman (1997). She notes, for example, that countries such as the United States and the United Kingdom impose relatively few restrictions on layoffs and that companies in Europe and Japan impose many restrictions on layoffs but use alternatives to the layoffs for adjusting labor inputs.

19.   This section borrows heavily from van Liemt (1992b) and Sengenberger (1992). For more detailed industry studies, see van Liemt (1992a).

20.   For a discussion of the impact of imports and exports on collective bargaining, see Mishel (1986).

21.   Herman and his colleagues (1992) identify the union-nonunion wage gap as $18.25, union, versus $13.48, nonunion. Jarrell and Stanely (1984) demonstrate that the union wage premium is partially explained by the higher skill levels of union workers. For a discussion of changing wage patterns in the labor market, see Bhagwati and Kosters (1994) and the references cited in it.

22. For an excellent discussion of the way in which HR policies can be productively combined, see Ichniowski, Shaw, and Prennushi (1993). Here the authors discuss the ways in which cultural, trust-based, and technical complementaries are adjusted in order to achieve maximum performance for the firm.

REFERENCES

Abowd, J.M. (1989). The effect of wage bargains on the stock market value of the firm. *American Economic Review, 79* (4), 774-800.

Abowd, J.M., Milkovich, G.T., & Hannon, J.M. (1990, February). The effects of human resource management decisions on shareholder value. *Industrial and Labor Relations Review*, 203-236.

Appelbaum, E., & Berg, P. (1997). Work reorganization and flexibility in job design. In D. Lewin, D.J.B. Mitchell, & M.A. Zaidi (Eds.), *The human resource management handbook*. Greenwich, CT: JAI Press.

Ashenfelter, O., & LaLonde, R. (1997). Economics of training. In D. Lewin, D.J.B. Mitchell, & M.A. Zaidi (Eds.), *The human resource management handbook*. Greenwich, CT: JAI Press.

Bartlett, C., & Yoshihara, H. (1988). New challenges for Japanese multinationals: Is organization adaptation their achilles heel? *Human Resource Management, 27* (1), 19-43.

Bean, C.R. (1994, June). European unemployment: A survey. *Journal of Economic Literature, XXXII* (2), 573-619.

Bean, R. (1985). *Comparative industrial relations*. Sydney: Croom Helm.

Belous, R.S. (1989). *The contingent economy: The growth of the temporary, part-time and subcontracted workforce*. Washington, DC: National Planning Association.

Ben-Ner, A., Montias, J.M., & Neuberger, E. (1993, June). Basic issues in organizations: A comparative perspective. *Journal of Comparative Economics, 17* (2), 207-242.

Bhagwati, T., & Kosters, M. (1994). *Trade and wages: Leveling wages down?* Washington, DC: The American Enterprise Institute.

Blinder, A.S. (1990). Introduction. In A. Blinder (Ed.), *Paying for productivity: A look at the evidence*. Washington, DC: The Brookings Institution.

Cohen, S.S., & Zysman, J. (1987). Manufacturing matters. In *The myth of the post-industrial economy* (p. 156). New York: Basic Books.

Cole, R.E. (1972). Permanent employment in Japan: Facts and fantasies. *Industrial and Labor Relations Review, 30* (1), 615-630.

Cooke, W.N. (1994). Employee participation programs, group-based incentives, and company performance: A union-nonunion comparison. *Industrial and Labor Relations Review, 47* (4), 594-609.

Daniel, W. (1987). *Workplace industrial relations and technical change*. London: HMSO, Economic and Social Research Counsel, Policy Studies Institute, ACAS, and Francis Pinter Publishers Ltd.

De Meuse, K.P., Vanderheiden, P.A., & Bergmann, T.J. (1994, Winter). Announced layoffs: Their effect on corporate financial performance. *Human Resource Management, 33* (4), 509-530.

Dercksen, W. (1994). *Internationalization, policy competition and industrial relations*. Mimeograph, Utrecht University, The Netherlands.

Doz, Y., Hamel, G., & Prahalad, C.K. (1986, October). Strategic partnerships: Success or surrender? Paper given to conference on Cooperative Strategies in International Business, Wharton School, Rutgers University.

Dreyfuss, J. (1989, August 14). Reinventing IBM. *Fortune Magazine*, pp. 31-35, 38, 39.

Ebel, K.H. (1985, March). Social and labour implications of flexible manufacturing systems. *International Labour Review, 124* (2), 133-196.

Erickson, C.L., Kimbell, L.J., & Mitchell, D.J.B. (1997). The macro side of human resource management. In D. Lewin, D.J.B. Mitchell, & M.A. Zaidi (Eds.), *The human resource management handbook*. Greenwich, CT: JAI Press.

Feigenbaum, A.V. (1994). How total quality counters three forces of international competitiveness. *National Productivity Review, 13* (3), 327-330.

Fong, P.E., & Hill, H. (1992). Government policy, industrial development and the aircraft industry in Indonesia and Singapore. In G. Van Liemt (Ed.), *Industry on the move; Causes and consequences of international relocation in the manufacturing industry*. Geneva: International Labor Organization.

Glazer, N. (1976). Social and cultural factors in Japanese economic growth. In H. Patrick & H. Rosovsky (Eds.), *Asia's new giant: How the Japanese economy works* (pp. 813-896). Washington, DC: Brookings Institution.

Gordon, R.J. (1982, March). Why U.S. wage and employment behavior differs from that in Britain and Japan. *The Economic Journal, 92*, 13-44.

Harris, R.G. (1992). New theories of international trade and the pattern of global specialization. In G. van Liemt (Ed.), *Industry on the move: Causes and consequences of internal relocation in the manufacturing industry*. Geneva: International Labor Office.

Herman, E.E., Schwarz, J.L., & Kuhn, A. (1992). *Collective bargaining and labor relations* (pp. 274-275). Englewood Cliffs, NJ: Prentice-Hall..

Hill, R.E., & Dwyer, P.C. (1990, September). Grooming workers for early retirement. *HR Magazine*, pp. 59-63.

Hoerr, J.P. (1988). *And the wolf finally came*. Pittsburgh, PA: University of Pittsburgh Press.

Hofstede, G. (1993). Cultural constraints in management theories. *Academy of Management Executive, 7* (1), 81-94.

Houseman, S.N. (1997). External and internal labor market flexibility: An international comparison. In D. Lewin, D.J.B. Mitchell, & M.A. Zaidi (Eds.), *The human resource management handbook*. Greenwich, CT: JAI Press.

Houseman, S.N., & Abraham, K.G. (1993, May). Female workers as a buffer in the Japanese economy. *American Economics Review, 83* (2), 45-51.

Ichniowski, C., Delaney, J.T., & Lewin, D. (1989). The new human resource management in US workplaces: Is it really new and is it only nonunion? *Relations Industrielles, 44* (1), 97-119.

Ichniowski, C., Shaw, K., & Prennushi, G. (1993, July). *The effects of human resource practices on productivity* (Draft). Columbia Graduate School of Business.

Jarrell, S.D., & Stanley, T.D. (1984). A meta-analysis of the union-nonunion wage gap. In R.B. Freeman & J. Medoff (Eds.), *What do unions do?* New York: Basic Books.

Jones, K. (1992). Structural adjustment in the United States steel industry. In G. Van Liemt (Ed.), *Industry on the move; Causes and consequences of international relocation in the manufacturing industry*. Geneva: International Labor Organization.

Katz, H.C. (1985). *Shifting gears: Changing labor relations in the US automobile industry*. Cambridge, MA: MIT Press.

————— . (1987). Automobiles. In *Collective bargaining in American industry* (pp. 13-53). Lexington, MA: D.C. Health.

Kerr, C. (1983). *The future of industrial societies*. Cambridge, MA: Harvard University Press.

Kerr, C., Dunlop, J.T., Harbison, F.H., & Meyers, C.A. (1960). *Industrialism and industrial man: The problems of labor and management in economic growth*. Cambridge, MA: Harvard University Press.

Kochan, T.A., & Katz, H.C. (1983). Collective bargaining, work organizations, and worker participation: The return to plant-level bargaining. In *Papers and Proceedings at the Spring Industrial Relations Research Association* (pp. 524-529).

Kochan, T.A., Katz, H.C., & McKersie, R. (1986). *The transformation of American industrial relations* (Ch. 3). New York: Basic Books.

Layard, R.G., Nickell, S.J., & Jackman, R.A. (1991). *Unemployment: Macroeconomic performance and the labour market.* Oxford: Oxford University Press.

Lawler, E.E.. III. (1991). Total quality management and employee involvement: Are they compatible? *Academy of Management Executive, 2* (3), 68-76.

Lee, B., & Sockell, D. (1997). Regulation of the HRM function. In D. Lewin, D.J.B. Mithcell, & M.A. Zaidi (Eds.), *The human resource management handbook.* Greenwich, CT: JAI Press.

Levine, D.I. (1995). *Reinventing the workplace: How business and employees can both win.* Washington, DC: Brookings Institution.

Liemt, G. Van (1992a). *Industry on the move: Causes and consequence of international relocation in the manufacturing industry.* Geneva: International Labor Office.

————. (1992b). Economic globalization: Labour options and business strategies in labour cost countries. *International Labour Review, 131* (4-5), 453-470.

Lillard, L.A., & Tan, H.W. (1992). Private sector training: Who gets it and what are its effects? In R. Ehrenberg (Ed.), *Research in labor economics* (volume 13, pp. 1-62). Greenwich, CT: JAI Press.

Lynch, L.M., & Zemsky, R. (1995). Briefing on the first findings of The EQW National Employer Survey. Washington, DC.

Mangum, G., Mayal, D., & Nelson, K. (1985, July). The temporary help industry: A response to the dual internal labor market. *Industrial and Labor Relations Review,* pp. 599-611.

Mills, D.Q., & McCormick, J. (1985). *Industrial relations in transition* (pp. 276-297). New York: John Wiley & Sons.

Mishel, L. (1986, October). The structural determinants of union bargaining power. *Industrial and Labor Relations Review,* pp. 90-104.

Mitchell, D.J., & Zaidi, M.A. (Eds.). (1990a). *The economics of human resource management.* Oxford: Basil Blackwell.

————. (1990b). Macroeconomic conditions and HRM-IR practice. *Industrial Relations, 29* (2), 164-188.

————. (1992). International pressure on industrial relations: Macroeconomics and social concertation. In T. Theu (Ed.), *Participation in public policy making* (pp. 60-72). New York: Walter de Gruyter.

Noe, R.A., Hollenbeck, J.R., Gerhart, B., & Wright, P.M. (1994). *Human resource management: Gaining a competitive advantage.* Homewood, IL: Richard D. Irwin, Inc.

Norton, E. (1993, January). Small, flexible plants may play crucial role in US manufacturing. *The Wall Street Journal,* pp. A1-A2.

O'Brien, P. (1992). The automotive industry: The permanent revolution. In G. Van Liemt (Ed.), *Industry on the move; Causes and consequences of international relocation in the manufacturing industry.* Geneva: International Labor Organization.

OECD. (1986). *Labour market flexibility.* Report by a High-Level Group of Experts to the Secretary-General. Paris: OECD.

————. (1989). Japan at work: Markets, management and flexibility. Paris: OECD.

Pepper, J. (1989, April). Sweet success in sales automation. *Working Woman,* pp. 59-62.

Perez, C. (1986). Structural changes and assimilation of new technologies in the economic and social system. In C. Freeman (Ed.), *Design, innovation and long cycles in economic development.* London: Frances Pinter.

Piore, M.J., & Sabel, C.F. (1984). *The second industrial divide.* New York: Basic Books, Inc.

Pollack, A. (1995, May 31). Japan's jobless rate reaches 3.2%, its highest level ever. *New York Times.*

Porter, M.E. (1990). *The competitive advantage of nations.* Cambridge, MA: Harvard University Press.

Reich, R. (1991). *The work of nations.* New York: Alfred A. Knopf.

Robinson, R.M., Oswald, S.L., Swinehart, K.S., & Thomas, J. (1991, November-December). Southwest industries: Creating high performance teams for high technology production. *Planning Review,* pp. 10-14, 47.

Schwab, D.P., & Olson, C.A. (1990, February). Merit pay practices: Implications for pay-performance relationships. *Industrial and Labor Relations Review, 43* (3), 237-255.

Sengenberger, W. (1992). Intensified competition, industrial restructuring and industrial relations. *International Labour Review, 131* (2), 139-155.

Smeltdown at Armco: Behind the steelmakers long slide. (1988, February 1). *Business Week*, pp. 48-50.

Spinanger, D. (1992). The impact on employment and income of structural and technological changes in the clothing industry. In G. Van Liemt (Ed.), *Industry on the move; Causes and consequences of international relocation in the manufacturing industry*. Geneva: International Labor Organization.

Stalking the new consumer. (1989, August 28). *Business Week*, pp. 54-62.

Steiber, J. (1980). Steel. In G.G. Somers (Ed.), *Collective bargaining: Contemporary American experience* (pp. 151-208). Madison, WI: Industrial Relations Research Association.

Sussex, E. (1992). The impact of structural change on trade unions. In G. Van Liemt (Ed.), *Industry on the move; Causes and consequences of international relocation in the manufacturing industry*. Geneva: International Labor Organization.

Therrien, L. (1989, November 13). The rival Japan respects. *Business Week*, p. 108.

Troy, L. (1997). The twilight of old unionism. In D. Lewin, D.J.B. Mitchell, & M.A. Zaidi (Eds.), *The human resource management handbook*. Greenwich, CT: JAI Press.

Tylecote, A. (1995). Technological and economic long waves and their implications for employment. *New Technology, Work and Employment, 10* (1), 3-18.

Vickrey, G., & Campbell, D. (1991). *Managing manpower for advanced manufacturing technology*. Paris: Organization for Economic Co-operation and Development.

Williams, A. (1993). *Human resources management and labour market flexibility*. Aldershot: Avelury.

Williams, R., & Watts, G. (1986). The process of working together: CWA's/AT&T's approach to QWL. *Teamwork*, pp. 75-88.

Willman, P. (1987). *Technological change, collective bargaining, and industrial efficiency*. Oxford: Oxford University Press.

Womack, J.P., Jones, D.T., Roos, D. (1990). *The machine that changed the world*. New York: Rawthorne Associates.

Worrell, D.L., Davidson, W.N., III, & Sharma, V.M. (1991). Layoff announcements and stockholder wealth. *Academy of Management Journal, 34* (3), 662-678.

Zaidi, M.A. (1994). Challenges for human resource management and industrial relations: An economic approach. In R. Berndt (Ed.), *Management-Qualität Contra Rezession und Krise*. Berlin and Heidelberg: Springer-Verlag.

THE MACRO SIDE OF HUMAN RESOURCE MANAGEMENT

Christopher L. Erickson, Larry J. Kimbell, and Daniel J.B. Mitchell

What linkage can there be between macroeconomics—which looks at the economy as an aggregate—with the field of human resource management, a firm-level (micro) area of study? At first blush, it might seem that no significant connection could exist, because of the macro-micro gap. Despite appearances, however, there are linkages, as we will show. But the linkages that are to be found are not exclusively those involving the traditional topic of macroeconomics, that is, business cycles. Rather, they are located at the basic idea of macroeconomics, that things look different collectively than they do at the level of the individual or firm. This notion has special resonance in a decentralized economy, such as that of the United States.

America's numerous firms and human resource decision makers are far removed from the collective consequences of their decisions. Unlike the situations in smaller, more corporatist European states, there are few mechanisms that promote consideration of aggregate behavior in the United States. And there are few micro incentives for U.S. human resource managers to modify their behavior for macro reasons.

DIFFERENCES IN MICRO AND MACRO PERSPECTIVES

The fact that macroeconomics is generally tied to the business cycle is an indication of the need for a special understanding of collective outcomes in the economy. No one at the micro level wants business cycles; everyone would prefer to have an economy that grew steadily at full employment. Yet the cumulative effect of micro-level behavior—including human resource practices regarding hiring, firing, and pay setting—results in cycles. Other micro behaviors in the human resource area also can produce undesired collective consequences.

The Means of Adjustment

One of the first lessons in "Economics 1" is the equilibrating role played by the prices, depicted as the intersection of demand and supply curves. The position of the curves may vary, but equilibrium—in the sense of demand = supply—is assured by price adjustments. If there is an unexpected glut of apples, the price of apples falls, discouraging farmers from entering or continuing in the apple business. As apple prices fall relative to those of other crops, the production of other crops becomes more attractive to farmers and they depart the apple sector. Similarly, as apple prices fall relative to those of other fruits, consumers buy more apples. Supply falls, demand increases, and the apple market quickly "clears." An important element in clearing or equilibrating the apple market is the ability of apple prices to move *relative* to other prices.

But what if there were a glut of virtually everything, that is, what if there were what we commonly call a recession? The price of everything cannot fall relative to everything else, because there is nothing else.[1] Hence, an important equilibrating mechanism that seems to work at the micro level becomes impotent at the macro level. Aggregate behavior, in short, is likely to result in fluctuations of real activity—in surpluses and shortages—which a market-by-market micro study is unlikely to reveal. Market-by-market analysis assumes there is an equilibrating substitution effect, for example, bananas for apples; macro analysis points out the absence of that effect.[2]

External Effects

Just as economic analysts who approach the macro economy exclusively from a micro perspective may fail to anticipate outcomes, so, too, may the micro-level actors fail to see (or care about) the full consequences of their collective behavior. Even within standard micro analysis, such cases—in which actors fail to appreciate (internalize) "externalities"—are common. Consider the classic case of fishermen who "overfish" certain waters, collectively depriving themselves of their livelihood over time.

Each fisherman acts optimally in ignoring the very small effect that removing the marginal fish from the sea has on future fish reproduction. For individual fishermen to restrain their own catches would be senseless, since competitors would bring in the avoided fish. There is what macroeconomists like to term a "coordination failure;" all fisherman would be better off if they banded together and policed a limit on their catches. Absent some external regulator, however, collective restraint is hard to accomplish and self-restraint absent such a coordinator is in no one's individual interest.[3]

At the macro level there are several important examples of coordination failures. In the simplest case, imagine that in 1933—the bottom of the Great Depression—all economic actors had been persuaded to act as if they were back in 1929, the peak of the 1920s boom. Consumers would have gone out and spent at 1929 levels, thus stimulating the economy. And they would have had the income to do so since employers would have hired back the unemployed, knowing that renewed consumer spending would justify the hiring. Investors, seeing the demand pressure, would have resumed adding to the nation's capital stock. By acting as if it were 1929, the actors would effectively have made it so again.

The fact that such collective action would in theory have restored the economy did not produce a cure for the Great Depression, however. Despite exhortation from national leaders to act confidently ("The only thing we have to fear is fear itself!"), despite parades and cheery official messages, unemployed consumers could not spend. Consumers could not be persuaded to act as if it were 1929, nor could producers and investors. It would have been folly for a consumer who was unemployed or threatened with unemployment to pretend that he or she had a 1929 income. Similarly, it would have been folly for employers or investors to pretend there was no depression.

In the next section, therefore, our key concern is how micro behavior in the human resource area may produce collective results different from the understanding achieved at the micro perspective. What may be good for all is not necessarily accomplished by normal micro incentives. Such situations have implications for public policies which affect human resource practice, implications which practitioners may have difficulty perceiving.

INDIVIDUAL VERSUS COLLECTIVE PERSPECTIVES: EXAMPLES

Consider the reaction of the business community to labor regulations that inflict a cost on employers. More specifically, consider the proposal to require all business to provide health insurance (such as emerged from the Clinton administration in 1993). Or consider changes in the attitudes of workers' compensation tribunals so that worker claims are more easily accepted and compensated, causing employer premium costs to rise. Finally, consider regulations limiting the ability of employers to lay off or dismiss employees in the face of economic downturns or poor individual performance.

We know politically what the reactions of employers are in response to such proposals, developments, and regulations: opposition. Mandated benefits are an anathema to business leaders in the United States as the debate over the Clinton health plan showed. Even employers who would have had their health care costs cut by the plan were reluctant to support it, fearing a "foot in the door" would lead to other mandates in the future.

Such reactions are not confined to the federal level or even to the United States. Rising workers' compensation premiums triggered legislative crises in California during the recession of the early 1990s, as local firms asserted that their escalating workers' compensation costs were worsening the state's business climate and destroying jobs. In Europe in the 1980s, limits on employer ability to lay off or dismiss workers led to calls by employers to improve the "flexibility" of the labor market along American lines by reducing or eliminating such protective constraints. With increased flexibility, the argument went, more jobs would be created (Brodsky, 1994; Emerson, 1988; OECD, 1989, 1994; Treu, 1992).

Viewed from the firm perspective, all of these positions make sense. Mandates add to labor costs. If labor costs go up, firms will hire fewer workers. Cut regulation or avoid mandates and more jobs will be created. But taken collectively, the arguments lose some (perhaps all) of their strength.

The Severance Cost Example

Consider seniority-based entitlements. Examples are the European-style job security regulations that require permission from authorities to lay off workers with designated levels of job tenure or otherwise impose costs of involuntary termination as tenure rises. Taiwanese law requires severance pay bonuses based on seniority for involuntary dismissals. Related elements of labor market institutions can be found in the United States under unemployment insurance (UI) where eligibility is linked to seniority and layoffs can lead to higher employer UI premiums. Less formally, American wrongful discharge litigation verdicts show sympathy to long-service employees.

All of these examples add a cost to hiring and retention of employees. We refer to these examples as the "cost of severance" since they all have effects similar to the impact of a mandated severance pay system where the severance bonus is paid only in the case of involuntary termination and increases with tenure on the job (Erickson & Mitchell, 1996). What is the ultimate consequence of mandated severance? We can view the answer in a sequence of steps involving just the costs, the costs and the benefits, and the specifics of a seniority-based entitlement.

To the individual employer in, say, the widget industry, the answer to the ultimate consequence question is clear. "If my firm didn't have to pay these costs," an employer might say, "its labor costs would be lower than its immediate competitors; it could undersell them in the widget market, and it would therefore have an incentive to add workers." For the individual firm being hypothetically excused from the mandate, the employment effect involves both market share and possible widening of the market if widget prices are reduced. But note that if the costs are imposed on *all* employers in the widget industry, the *relative* labor cost effect is removed.

Immediate competitors are all disadvantaged by the mandate's cost. If the entire industry were excused from the mandate, there would be no market share effect for any individual firm. But if the mandate had applied just to the widget industry, there might be some substitution effect in favor of widgets were the mandate dropped.[4] The market share effect to the individual firm is gone but the market widening effect remains, leading to some employment effect but a smaller one than share + widening would produce. If *all* employers in *all* industries were subject to the mandate, and if all were then excused from the mandate, even the widening effect could be reduced or even reversed. The precise net effect as seen by the individual employer would depend on differences in the mandate's cost across industries and products.[5]

There is a parallel here between the apple glut case versus the general glut (recession) case discussed earlier. Relative effects tend to be lost as aggregation is increased. Apple gluts can be eliminated by substitution effects of a relative price decline. But all-economy gluts cannot be cured by relative price changes since all prices cannot drop relative to one another.

Beyond the loss of the relative effect, a full analysis must take account of both demand and supply effects. At the simplest level, the cost impact has some analogies with the effect of a payroll tax on wages and jobs. As Figure 1 shows, the standard analysis suggests that a tax rate T imposed on employment will be partly absorbed by the wage, which drops from W_1 to W_2, thus lessening the adverse employment impact.[6] The more inelastic the supply curve, the more the burden of the tax is shifted to labor via the wage and the smaller is the employment effect, that is, the smaller is the drop from E_1 to E_2.

There is a literature estimating the burden-shifting impact of payroll taxes, and related mandated benefit costs going back at least to the early 1970s. Some studies have concluded that the burden is almost entirely shifted to labor (which would mean *no* residual jobs effect). Others have found partial shifting. The proposal for a mandated health care plan by the Clinton administration resulted in estimates that between two-thirds and three-fourths of the cost would be shifted back to labor. Estimates across countries or of other types of programs have generally also found large elements of shifting (Aaron & Bosworth, 1994, p. 263; Brittain, 1971, 1972a, 1972b; Erickson & Mitchell, 1995; Feldstein, 1972; Gruber, 1992; Gruber & Krueger, 1990; Hamermesh, 1979; Holmlund, 1983; Krueger, 1994; MacRae & Macrae, 1976; Moffit, 1977; U.S. Congress, 1980, p. 4; U.S. Congressional Budget Office, 1993, p. 3; U.S. President, 1994, pp. 148-149; Vroman, 1974).

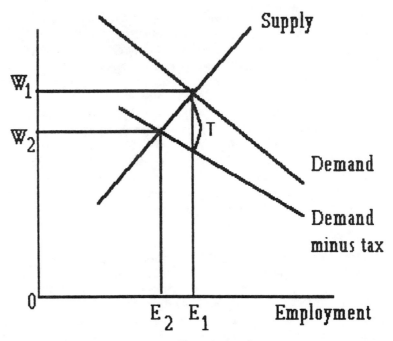

Figure 1.   Effect of Payroll Tax

So we learn that even in the pure cost case, it matters whether the cost is viewed from the individual firm perspective or in aggregate. Just adding up what the impact would be of a tax on each firm *only* does not provide a good indication of the impact of a tax on all employers. Simple adding up results in a fallacy of composition.[7] In general, the employment impact is attenuated from the aggregate perspective relative to the individual micro perspective.

Now consider adding another element to the notion of a tax or mandate, the potential benefit to accrue to workers. Suppose the tax or mandate results in a worker-specific benefit. For example, when an employee is covered by social security taxes, he or she receives added benefits by working that do not accrue to nonworkers.[8] The added benefit, taken by itself, tends to increase labor supply despite the fall in wages shown on Figure 1. In effect, the supply curve of that figure tends to shift to the right, further reducing the adverse employment effect shown. (E_2 is closer to E_1 as the supply curve shifts to the right.)

In fact, workers do put some value on added health insurance, pensions, or other such benefits which may be mandated or included in a social security system. Such benefits may not be perfect substitutes for cash, however. To the extent the benefits are valued by workers below the cash equivalent, the labor supply effect will not totally offset the cost effect in reducing employment. But in an extreme case where the benefit and cash are perfect substitutes, say a mandate that employers pay a 5 percent cash bonus on top of the basic wage, there will be no employment effect at all.[9] Indeed, if employers can provide certain benefits cheaper than workers can buy them individually—because of tax advantages, administrative economies of scale, or avoidance of adverse selection—$1 of benefits might be worth *more* than $1 of cash.

Generally, in cases where workers value benefits over cash, employers would be expected to offer the benefits voluntarily. In some situations a mandated system might be cheaper than a privately developed one. Those who promote mandated single-payer health insurance plans of the Canadian variety argue that by cutting the paperwork of employer-by-employer plans, the costs of the system are reduced.[10] The mandate might reduce labor costs (wage + mandated payment) relative to what employers could achieve through decentralized private insurance. The labor supply curve would shift to the right to a point where $E_2 > E_1$. We are not providing an actual evaluation of health plans here; just pointing to the need to consider collective (macro) effects in judging the impact of mandated employee benefits.

Would more "flexible" labor markets reduce European unemployment? The micro answer is "of course." But the macro answer—sadly—is "it depends." There are models in which mandating inflexibilities such as requiring just cause for dismissals will raise productivity. For example, if workers particularly value just-cause dismissal protections, employers should offer such "insurance" as a benefit. But if an individual firm were to consider making such an offer, it might be discouraged by the potential adverse selection problem. A disproportionate number of low productivity job seekers might be attracted. In contrast, an economy-wide mandate requiring all employers to offer the protections would eliminate adverse selection, possibly boosting morale and productivity[11] (Levine, 1989). But even if there are net costs, the mandate's ultimate effect depends on whether wages can absorb the costs of the mandated inflexibilities.

Union-Sector Examples

Another chapter in this volume deals with the marked decline of private sector unionization in the United States and other countries. The gap between micro and macro perspectives can be applied equally to issues surrounding union decline. Research in the 1980s opened new perspectives on the economic impact of unions. Some research indicated that unions raise productivity—contrary to management perceptions—by creating alternative channels for employee "voice." They create these channels through enforceable grievance and arbitration procedures and through direct bargaining over issues of concern to workers (Freeman & Medoff, 1984, chap. 11-12).

However, even those researchers who have argued for the existence of a positive union productivity effect have also found that the higher wage and benefit costs of unionization more than offset the positive productivity gains. Unions shift profits into wages. Thus, management rationally seeks to avoid unionization based on micro-level incentives, for example, profit maximization.

For the sake of argument, let us concede the positive productivity effect and then ask what is the impact collectively if management succeeds at the micro level in reducing the unionization rate? There are two answers at the macro level which we can term "economic" and "political." The economic effect is loss of the added output that union-related productivity increases would have created. But with lower unionization profits would be up and wages would be down, so the issue becomes more one of distribution of income than level of output.[12]

The political answer is somewhat different. Absent unions, employee voice may still be expressed by employees, although through the political and juridical channels. Congress and state legislatures may become *ersatz* unions, mandating a variety of benefits. Examples in the 1980s and 1990s have included continuation-of-benefits legislation, advance notification of plant closings and mass layoffs, and family leave entitlements. One state—Montana—has enacted arbitration of discharges as an entitlement for nonunion workers (Krueger, 1991). Others are considering such proposals. Social issues may make their way into detailed regulation through the political channel. For example, California enacted a law in 1994 forbidding employers from requiring that women wear dresses rather than pants suits to work.

Apart from Congress and state legislatures, lawyers can also become channels for expressing employee voice. Wrongful discharge litigation developed in the 1970s as a legal challenge to the at-will employment doctrine. And older programs (workers' compensation and EEO) can be used as de facto grievance mechanisms. As the median baby boomer crosses the age 40 line, is it surprising that age discrimination complaints are on the rise?

Clearly, all of these phenomena are an anathema to U.S. employers, yet they result from actors—especially employers—in the economic and political systems following their micro incentives. Might the management community, not to mention "society," be better off if the expressions of employee voice were handled by union-management mechanisms rather than legislatures and courts? That is inherently a macro question (although not a topic of traditional macroeconomics) which a decentralized society cannot readily address.

Under decentralized decision making, it is not just the management community that may have difficulty internalizing macro issues. Unions, too, have the same problem. Public opinion is important to unions, both politically and in shaping organizing campaigns. Several studies suggest that unions garner the most media attention by striking, but strikes are often perceived negatively by the public (Erickson & Mitchell, 1996). Decisions to strike are made locally, however, and the negative externalities on the overall union movement are not significant factors in those decisions. While the AFL-CIO could in principle be a forum for internalizing otherwise external strike effects, in practice it has little authority over its affiliates.

Examples from Public Policy

Public policies dealing with unemployment come in two basic forms: demand and supply. On the demand side, there is the traditional monetary and fiscal policy aimed at raising the number of jobs available. The supply side generally involves attempts to modify the characteristics of the unemployed, particularly through training programs. While it is easy to imagine instances in which either or a mix of both approaches is appropriate, much depends on the model of labor market processes envisioned.

Supply side efforts are typically evaluated at the micro level. For example, a training program might be evaluated by comparing the experiences of unemployed persons who went through the program with similar controls. If those in the treatment group exhibited better labor market performance, for example, if they found jobs faster or earned more, the training program might be viewed as effective. A further step might be to compare the discounted future earnings streams of the treatment group and the control group and weigh the gains in earnings against program costs in some kind of cost/benefit analysis.

Suppose we imagine a labor market consisting of 950 jobs and 1,000 job candidates. At the end of the day, the unemployment rate will be 5 percent. The question is which job seekers will end up among the unlucky 50 jobless. Presumably when jobs must be rationed, employers make screening decisions which put the unlucky 50 at the end of the queue. A training program might be quite effective in providing job candidates with attributes that would bump them up high enough in the queue so that they are selected for employment.

The treatment might range from cosmetic pointers ("Look the interviewer in the eye!") to an accretion of job skills. A micro comparison of the treatment group and a control group might well find the training program worthwhile. *And yet the macro results will still be a 5 percent unemployment rate*, given our queuing model (Thurow, 1979).

Clearly, a different model of the labor market might produce different conclusions. Sometimes the argument for training is that there is simply a "mismatch" between jobs and candidates which can be remedied. For example, if there were 1,000 jobs and 1,000 candidates, but some candidates lacked skills, the day might end with, say, a 5 percent unemployment rate *and* a 5 percent vacancy rate. With training to eliminate the mismatch, the vacancies might be filled by the unemployed. Sometimes it may be assumed that if skills are upgraded, jobs will be created in some variation of Say's law. That is, jobs are not fixed at 1,000 and—as in *Field of Dreams*—"if you train them new jobs will come."

The key point is that there is likely to be *some* element of job rationing and queuing and *some* displacement of the untrained by the trained. A pure micro perspective misses this displacement and overestimates training success. The macro perspective provides a clearer view of the bottom line, reduction in aggregate unemployment, though the effect of any given training program on this bottom line is difficult to measure in practice.[13]

MACRO REGULARITIES AND THE QUESTIONS THEY POSE

Although macroeconomics has a theoretical side, its historical background was in observed empirical evidence (often viewed as a social problem), particularly in the labor market. As noted earlier, economists tend to emphasize prices as adjustment mechanisms for markets which bring demand and supply into balance. But the issue of unemployment seems to suggest that wages are not playing that role in the labor market. So, too, does the observation of periods of persistent labor shortage, although these have received less attention in the literature.[14] The failure of labor market clearing in a commonsense usage of that term, suggests that: (1) wages are inflexible (i.e., if wages were flexible, the labor market would clear, but they aren't), or (2) wages are flexible but the labor market doesn't clear anyway, or (3) wages are inflexible but even if they weren't, the market wouldn't clear. There have been similar debates about price inflexibility but it is fair to say that wages have received more attention (Blinder, 1991).

The fact that macro theory developed in the 1930s when unemployment was *the* problem, and that the United States—a major supplier of macro theorists—has had more years of seemingly high unemployment than labor shortage, has led to a focus on theories which "explain" persistent labor surpluses. It would be interesting to speculate on what macro theory would look like had it first developed in the 1960s in certain European countries when labor shortages sucked in immigrants, or more recently in Hong Kong, Singapore, or other "Asian miracle" countries with their chronic labor shortages.

Unemployment

Employers could insulate workers from layoffs and unemployment—if they wished to do so—through wage fluctuations. Instead of reducing jobs by 5 percent, why not retain jobs and reduce wages by 5 percent? Here the arguments are similar to those earlier. Workers would perceive wage cuts as "unfair" and loyalty and morale would decline. Maybe, once the recession was over, the demoralized workers would leave, taking their employers' "investment in employees" with them. Or "insiders" (incumbent workers) would conduct covert sabotage. In all of these approaches, wage rigidity creeps in, weakening whatever market clearing effect downwardly flexible wages might have.

Wage Nominalism and Downward Wage Rigidity

The downward wage rigidity part of this story poses another challenge for micro-to-macro theory of human resource practices. In most models what should matter to workers is the *real* wage, not the *nominal* (Mitchell, 1993). A rational worker should care about the purchasing power of his or her paycheck, not the abstract number of "dollar" accounting units it contains. Yet there is considerable evidence of wage "nominalism" in labor markets.

For example, when workers are found to be earning too much under job evaluation plans, their wage rates commonly are "red circled."[15] That is, their nominal wage is preserved—but frozen—until other workers' pay catches up. This preservation of the nominal wage, but not the real, is apparently thought to be fair and acceptable to the overpaid employees. Note that the time frame over which the overpayment problem will be corrected is uncertain under this approach; it depends on how fast external nominal wages rise and the degree to which the external market influences the internal.

Consider the common complaint during periods of high inflation by human resource managers that merit pay systems are corrupted because the general pay adjustment becomes large relative to the merit portion. In nominal terms, this assertion is true, but in real terms it need not be. Consider a worker during a period of, say, 3 percent inflation who receives a general pay increase of 4 percent and a merit increase of 5 percent. With compounding, the nominal increase is 9.2 percent ($[1.04] \times [1.05] = 1.092$) and the real increase is 6 percent ($1.092/1.03 = 1.060$). Now suppose the inflation rate were instead 6 percent, the general pay increase were 7 percent, and the merit adjustment was 5 percent, producing a nominal increase of 12.35 percent ($[1.07] \times [1.05] = 1.1235$) but the same 6 percent real adjustment ($1.1235/1.06 = 1.06$). In nominal terms, 5 percent is a smaller proportion of 12.35 percent than of 9.2 percent ($5/12.35 = 40\%$; $5/9.2 = 54\%$). So the manager's complaint appears to be correct in nominal terms. But in real terms the two situations are the same; the worker has received a 6 percent real adjustment of which 5 percentage points are merit and 1 percentage point is general.

As yet another nominalist example, consider union concession bargaining. When union concession bargaining broke out in the 1980s, a typical concession involved a freeze of the basic wage, not a nominal wage cut. Nominal zero seemed to be a barrier, although some cuts did occur. Yet the real impact of a nominal wage freeze (a zero) varies with the external price inflation rate.

If workers and employers "thought" in Consumer Price Index (CPI) units, rather than nominal monetary units, nominal zero would have no particular significance. But thinking in nominal terms persists, despite the ready availability of the CPI to help pay setters chart the price inflation rate. Why do wage setters think in terms of "dollar" units rather than CPI units?

One possible answer is that they don't, despite the examples mentioned earlier. One could point to the use of escalator clauses in union contracts as a counterexample. Yet most union workers do not have escalators and virtually no nonunion workers have them. Probably no more than 5 percent of the workforce had a formal link between the CPI and wage setting in the early 1990s, not an impressive proportion.[16] And few escalators that do exist give simple proportionate pay increases, that is, a 1 percent wage increase for each 1 percent increase in the CPI. Instead, escalators are encumbered with complex formulas, often limiting their protection against inflation, and are commonly expressed in cents per hour per CPI index point terms rather than in percentages.[17]

While there is some recognition of inflation's implication for wage setting, the evidence is that it is imperfect, lagged, and varies with the rate of inflation. (Countries experiencing hyperinflation tend to use escalation of wage and other contracts more extensively than those with modest inflation rates.) The nominalist phenomenon, which characterizes all markets (not just labor markets), seems to be a product of sticky standards of value.

Successful standards, even if imperfect, tend to become dominant and become difficult to change because of the need to retain "compatibility." Examples are spoken languages, manners, DOS, VHS, speeds of phonograph records, and so on. Money was a standard of value (although imperfect) long before (also imperfect) price indexes came along. It seems to be hard to change from the money standard and there would be penalties for any employer to switch to a real perspective when the rest of the world did not.

Note that the issue of real and nominal wage rigidity is closely linked to the question—discussed earlier—of the impact of mandates (benefits, jobs security) on employment. If nominal wages are rigid, then a wage cut such as was shown in Figure 1 cannot occur. The initial effect of a costly mandate would be reduced employment. However, in a world in which nominal prices and wages generally rise, the cost shift to labor shown in Figure 1 could occur gradually through a temporary period in which wages did not rise or rose more slowly than "normal." If real wages are rigid, as European macroeconomists tended to argue for their countries in the late 1970s and early 1980s, then cost shifting—even in the long term—is difficult and mandates are likely to lower employment permanently.

Labor Shortages and Upward Wage Rigidity

Generally, to the extent labor shortages are treated in the economics literature, the approach has been micro. For example, the long-term nursing shortage (which may have ended in the 1990s), was examined in terms of the standard employer monopsony model. Nurses were limited primarily to the health care field, according to this view, and hospitals and other health care providers could collude to hold down wages. Each provider would then experience vacancies in the sense that an added job applicant would be eagerly employed since each nurse cost less than her marginal revenue product. But no disequilibrium was involved; with collusion the shortage was a profit-maximizing, stable condition.[18]

An alternative view of labor shortages—sometimes found in noneconomic discussions of national "need" is often "refuted" by economists on conventional micro grounds. The United States did not have, say, an engineering shortage in the 1970s or 1980s, even though Japan or the USSR or some other competitor had more engineers per capita. If employers needed more engineers, they would bid up the wage until demand equaled supply, according to this view.

These examples refer to labor markets for particular occupations. However, there have been periods and places in which shortages were general (macro) and seemed to persist. Mention has already been made of the Asian miracle countries. But examples can be found in the American context. During World War I, employers seemed to compete for labor based on progressive personnel practices; the wage increases they did provide did not clear the market (Jacoby, 1985). Subsequent wartime periods also produced shortages, although the story is muddied in some cases by legal wage controls.[19]

During the late 1960s a labor shortage developed without wage controls in place. Various symptoms could be spotted in the labor market including employer willingness to lower hiring standards and provide training to the unskilled (Okun, 1970). Unemployment rates fell, quit rates increased, strikes rose in frequency, and workers became more prone to reject contracts negotiated on their behalf by union officials and to demand still more.

Such episodes suggest that theories which depend on worker notions of fairness to explain wage rigidity are more applicable to downward rigidity than upward. It is hard to see workers protesting the receipt of generalized wage increases on grounds of fairness. Would such wage increases lower morale and loyalty? And if employers are worried about losing their investment in employees—an influence sometimes cited to explain downward wage rigidity—would not they quickly raise wages to retain their investment during shortage periods? The evidence suggests, that employers are reluctant to changes wages, *either up or down*, and that the efficiency wages, implicit contracts, and other stories that have developed to explain wage rigidity are not complete explanations.[20]

The Regional Example

At the national level, where relative wage effects are lost, it is possible to adopt the argument—considered earlier—that wage flexibility would not be especially useful since relative wage effects are lost. However, this approach is not valid at the regional level. In periods during which labor shortages have appeared in some parts of the country, but not others, there has been some bidding up of relative wages, as in the northeastern states during the mid-1980s. Yet the bidding up is modest and does not seem sufficient to clear the market. In the northeast case, for example, the labor shortage seemed to end with the stock market crash of 1987, which soured the financial services industry, rather than through some kind of national wage realignment.

The relative imperviousness of wages to regional conditions was especially notable in the 1980s and 1990s in California, as the state went from a defense-spending boom to a post-cold war bust. Despite the shift from rapid job growth to job loss after 1990, the California-to-U.S. wage ratio showed a gradual upward trend during 1983-1993 with little evidence of a boom-to-recession effect. At most, there was some leveling off of the ratio in the early 1990s (Mitchell, 1994). The regional evidence is consistent with a quantity-adjusting labor market. If there are not enough jobs to go around, job seekers leave the region.

In short, wage determination mechanics, although they can be empirically described, are not well explained in a theoretical sense. It is not that explanations cannot be cooked up. It may be, in fact, that the research problem is too many cooks and too few empirical tests capable of validating or refuting the various models.

CAN HUMAN RESOURCE PRACTICES HELP OR HURT THE MACRO ECONOMY?

Certain macro theories blame labor market disequilibria on human resource practices, mainly wage inflexibility. But traditional economic reasoning—which tends to be based at the micro level—also provides an "out" for practitioners. They are only behaving rationally, based on the incentives they have, according to the various theoretical models of wage setting that have developed. It is a pity that their collective action causes macro problems, but—depending on your ideological fix—either (1) that is the way God intended it in this best of all possible worlds; there is nothing to be done but to wait for the painful quantitative adjustments to occur, or (2) the government should fix the problem, perhaps by diddling with interest rates or public works or tax cuts, or—not so many years ago!—by nationalizing everything and running an economy that deliberately keeps everyone employed.

However, during the 1980s it was suggested that there was a human resource fix available through the adoption of profit or gainsharing. It had been noted earlier—much earlier—that profit sharing could be viewed as a kind of *ersatz* pay flexibility in the sense that profits tend to be procyclical. In good times, profits grow and profit-sharing bonuses increase. In bad times, the reverse occurs. But the Weitzman (1984) proposal—discussed more fully in another chapter—added a further theoretical element.

Profit Sharing and Gainsharing as a Cyclical Fix

Human resource managers view profit sharing and similar gainsharing plans as micro-level incentive systems *for employees* which are designed to stimulate productivity. There have been waves of popularity and disrepute for profit sharing during this century, most of which seem related to social currents and management fads rather than hard evaluation of the productivity effect (Mitchell, Lewin, & Lawler, 1990). Still, there is some evidence of a positive productivity effect of profit sharing in the economics literature (Kruse, 1993; Weitzman & Kruse, 1990).

The Weitzman proposal stands the usual human resource view on its head. It views profit sharing as an incentive plan *for employers* that gives them an incentive to behave in the collective good by expanding and stabilizing employment. (Note that the former notion means that the job expansion effect must overcome the productivity effect which tends to reduce jobs.) Since employers—as we have stressed throughout this chapter—do not, in fact, have an incentive to worry about macro consequences of their behavior, the Weitzman plan assumes that government would have to subsidize widespread use of profit sharing, probably through a tax break. Weitzman assumed that wages are rigid but was agnostic concerning the reasons. These issues are discussed in another chapter.[21]

Is Human Resource Management Moving Away from a Cyclical Fix?

There was much discussion in the 1980s of a move toward "pay for performance." However, it was unclear whether—despite the rhetoric—there was, in fact, a large movement in the direction of such programs. As is often the case in management fads, much relabeling occurred. Thus, merit pay plans (which have been around for a very long time and often are not well linked to employee or group behavior in practice) were suddenly tagged "pay for performance." While some observers may have seen the pay for performance movement as an unsubsidized move to a more stable Weitzman-style economy, such a proposition is dubious. Most of the plans that were lumped with profit sharing under the pay-for-performance label—piece rates, bonuses, employee stock ownership—do not have Weitzman properties. And one could just as easily cite moves toward human resource practices which potentially were destabilizing at the macro level.

Growth of a more contingent style of employment could be potentially destabilizing. In the past, macroeconomists noted a procyclical productivity effect on employment. During downturns, employers seemed to hang on to workers (causing measured productivity to fall or fall below trend). During upturns, the reverse would happen; employment would expand more slowly than output. The result was a net tendency to reduce the sensitivity of employment to the business cycle, potentially providing a stabilizing effect by insulating worker incomes from booms and busts. Of course, the micro motivation for such insulating practices would not include whatever positive macro effects there might be. Usually, it has been argued that certain workers were viewed as "overhead" by employers or otherwise costly to lay off, resulting in the procyclical productivity phenomenon. That is, it was explained by micro-level incentives.

In a contingent economy workers are not viewed as overhead to be retained but as variable factors to be readily hired and fired. If employers—due to increased uncertainty in product markets from exchange rates, deregulation, or whatever—shift to contingent employment policies, business cycle trends could be amplified. The notion of a "white-collar recession" became popular in the early 1990s, suggesting such movement toward contingency was occurring among a traditionally protected occupational group. If so, it could be the case that future booms and busts will be aggravated as employee incomes are left less insulated from business cycle tendencies.

Human Resource Trends and the Long-Term Macro Economy

Over the long haul, at the macro level, the major concerns are underlying trends in productivity, per capita income, and the noncyclical element of unemployment rather than the business cycle.[22] In the United States and other countries there seemed to be a slackening of productivity growth in the early 1970s. Partial recovery appeared in the 1980s in the official numbers, but long-term productivity trends in the United States did not return to post-World War II growth paths.[23] The question arises as to the role human resource practices played in these trends and the role they could play in improving the outlook.

Some radical economists argued in the early 1980s that the productivity growth slump was the product of labor-management frictions (Weisskopf, Bowles, & Gordon, 1983). By the early 1990s, however, a more mainstream view focused on deficiencies in the educational system and the need for job-related training. In addition, there was concern with fostering cooperative and participative styles of employee-management and union-management relations. Such issues are dealt with in other chapters. But there are some collective (macro) aspect of participation, training, and skill acquisition that are difficult to handle at the level of the firm. Those aspects involve norms, standards, and credential recognition.

It has been argued that micro-participative systems operate more successfully in economies where certain norms of practice reinforce them. One element of participatory systems has been an effort to downplay major status differences between worker and manager. Sometimes this effort shows up in symbolic gestures such as elimination of reserved parking for managers and a common employee-executive cafeteria. But it has been argued that compressed pay scales might also be needed to reinforce status reductions and that such compression could be reinforced if all firms practiced it.

The reinforcement effects are externalities, however, so that the requisite norms may not develop (Levine & Tyson, 1990). If an individual firm tries to compress its wage distribution relative to the outside market, its higher-wage employees may take jobs elsewhere. Only if all firms practice compression can any one of them sustain it.

With regard to training and skill acquisition, European models are often cited as having certain desirable attributes. Some countries levy a pay-or-play training tax on payrolls; firms either spend a designated portion of payroll on worker training or they pay an equivalent tax to support training programs. Such systems may resolve the micro dilemma of employer unwillingness to invest in general skill training since it is difficult to recoup the investment.[24] It has also been argued that the government could play a role by providing standards and credentials for both training and schooling experiences on which all employers could rely. Standards are difficult to establish based on micro incentives although employers collectively benefit from them.

The climate of labor-management relations could be expressed in terms of wage determination in ways which affect long-term unemployment, the so-called "natural" rate of unemployment or non-accelerating inflation rate of unemployment (NAIRU). Figure 2 provides a wider analysis at the macro level, drawing on the Mitchell-Zaidi (1992) model of the determination of the "natural" rate of unemployment. Consider a situation in which wages tend to be above market-clearing levels and in which labor's bargaining position— whether viewed as individual or collective bargaining—is influenced by the unemployment rate (U). Assume also that in the long run, wage setters overcome wage nominalism.

The unemployment rate weakens labor's bargaining position, other things equal, so that its target W/P, wages divided by a price index (the real wage), tends to be lower at higher unemployment rates. This labor-market relation is shown by downward-sloping line LL in Figure 2. In the product market, firms mark up prices P over their labor costs W so that P/W represents the target profit margin. Other things equal, high unemployment (economic slackness) will reduce the ability to maintain high profit margins so target P/W will be lower at higher as unemployment rates. But P/W is simply the inverse of W/P and is graphed in Figure 2 as *upward*-sloping line PP.

Clearly, the inverse of target P/W from the product market must equal target W/P in the labor market for equilibrium to prevail, as at U^* in Figure 2. U^* is the natural rate of unemployment because it harmonizes labor and product market targets. If U falls temporarily below U^*, workers will try to obtain a higher W/P in the labor market and firms in the product market will try to obtain a higher P/W (lower W/P). It is not possible for W/P and P/W to go up simultaneously. A wage-price spiral will therefore

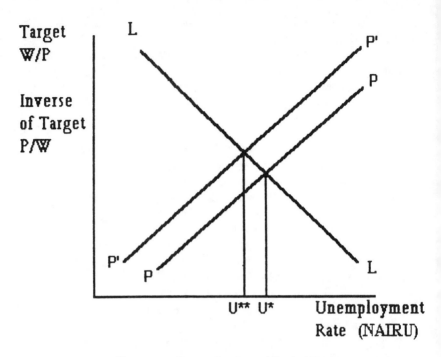

Figure 2.   Determination of the NAIRU

accelerate at point to the left of U^* in Figure 2. Conversely, to the right of U^*, a zone of disinflation exists.

At U^*, whatever rate of inflation currently exists will tend to continue. Assuming the macro authority (the central bank) is content with current inflation rate, it will follow policies to hold unemployment at level U^*. And departures from U^* will be unsustainable in the long run.

Note how, once again, the macro perspective differs from the micro. In a micro view, the effects of a push up of the real wage would be evaluated in principle by summing up the impact of wage increases along labor demand curves. The macro view, in contrast, requires analysis of product as well as labor market behavior, along with that of the central bank.

Note, also, that the model provides an additional channel whereby HR practices—which may affect productivity—might affect national welfare. Higher productivity, in Figure 2, would show up as an upward movement of the product market curve (say from PP to $P''P''$) since profit targets could be achieved at lower markups.[25] Such a move both raises productivity and lowers the NAIRU. Not only is output/worker raised, but more workers are employed on a long-term basis. Note, in contrast, that the micro perspective suggests that productivity increases would displace workers, not produce more jobs.

MODELING POSSIBLE HUMAN RESOURCE MANAGEMENT EFFECTS

So far, we have noted that human resource practices may have externalities (positive or negative) which are felt at the macro level. In this section we attempt simulation of selected practices, using one large-scale macro model. Our purpose is to illustrate the complexities involved when human resource management is viewed at the macro level rather than to argue that a particular model necessarily produces the correct predictions. The model we use for illustrative purposes is that provided by the WEFA Group, which we believe reasonably represents the many-equation models used by economic forecasters.[26]

In using the model we seek to determine what indirect effects might be expected from a change in micro behavior, that is, effects that would not be considered by micro policymakers. We undertake four experiments. *First*, we step up the degree of wage flexibility in response to demand/supply conditions of the labor market. Such a change might reflect adoption of various pay for (firm) performance plans, for example, profit sharing, or simply more responsive wage decisions. In the union sector it might represent a move to shorter-duration labor-management contracts. *Second*, we change the NAIRU and consider the consequences. A change in the NAIRU might reflect better job matching by employers, provision of more training for the hard-to-employ by employers, or perhaps—if the Weitzman share economy argument is correct—adoption of more profit sharing.

A *third* experiment involves adoption by employers of greater use of contingent workers so that workers are more readily added or subtracted from payrolls in response to short-run fluctuations in labor demand and labor costs are made more flexible. Finally, a *fourth* experiment involves improvement in the growth rate of labor productivity, perhaps associated with more training, greater use of employee participation in decision making, or use of incentive plans which reward individual or group effort.

Although we present the results of the experiments in numerical terms, the reader is cautioned not to take the results literally. The point is simply to show that some changes matter "little" while others matters "more."

Wage Flexibility

Like most forecasting models, the WEFA model contains a "Phillips curve"-type equation relating wage inflation to the gap between the actual unemployment rate and the NAIRU, as well as terms linked to lagged price inflation.[27] Making wages more responsive to demand/supply conditions therefore involves increasing the coefficients of the current and lagged unemployment gaps. In the experiment described below, the coefficients were doubled. The objective was to determine how such greater responsiveness of wages would translate into employment growth.

To perform the experiment, the growth of labor force participation was raised sufficiently to add about 1 percentage point of unemployment throughout a six-year period. Wage equations tend to show relatively little responsiveness of the nominal wage to excess supply (compared to classical assumptions or auction market behavior). In this case, the impact of adding a percentage point of unemployment was to reduce the nominal wage by 3.4 percent over 6 years.[28] This effect includes the direct impact of unemployment and the indirect feedback through the price inflation channel. Hence, a doubling of the responsiveness of wages still produces only modest adjustments compared with an auction market. The key impacts are summarized below:

Doubling wage responsiveness in the face of chronic additional 1 percent of unemployment produces at the end of 6 years:

1. An additional drop of the nominal wage compared to the base case by 3.1 percent.
2. An additional drop of consumer prices compared to the base case by 4.0 percent. (Hence, the real wage is *raised* by about 0.9%.)
3. The lower price inflation cuts nominal interest rates by about 0.6 percentage points raising housing starts by about 7 percnet.
4. Real GDP is increased by 1.2 percent.
5. Employment increases by about 1 percent. Although the real wage actually rose, the reduction in inflation and interest rates permitted better real economic performance.

Should these results be taken as exact? As noted earlier, literal numerical predictions are not the goal. The point is that the channels of linkage between a change in human resources policy look very different at the macro level compared with the micro. Micro wage setters would not, for example, consider the effects of their behavior on inflation, interest rates, and housing starts. Greater wage flexibility does seem to provide real benefits although it would take a very substantial change in current behavior to obtain dramatic results.

Decreasing the NAIRU

Could human resource management practices alter the NAIRU? As noted, various policies from more extensive training to more widespread profit sharing have been cited as potential devices that could reduce the NAIRU. Yet much depends on the economic climate in which NAIRU reduction is accomplished. Reducing the NAIRU by itself does not create more jobs; it simply opens up the *potential* for more job creation without inflation.

Using the WEFA model, we reduced the NAIRU by one percentage point and tracked the results for a three-year period. Since nothing was directly done to stimulate the economy, the results were modest:

1. Price inflation was reduced by about 0.5 percent/year at the end of the period. Because of the direct impact on wage adjustments, wage inflation was reduced slightly more (about 0.7%), so that the real wage fell slightly.
2. Lower inflation produced somewhat lower long-term interest rates (about-0.5 percentage points on a 30-year Treasury bond) which modestly raised housing starts by about 5.6 percent by the end of the period.
3. Real GDP grew by about 0.5 percent as a result, compared with the base period, and the unemployment rate was about 0.2 percentage points lower.

In short, reducing the NAIRU has some side benefits but these arise primarily through lessened inflation. To exploit the benefits, some demand expansion would have to be provided through monetary or fiscal policy. Nonetheless, even the modest benefits would not be internalized by the human resource decision makers whose policies influenced the NAIRU's level.

Increased Contingent Employment

The primary risk of a more contingent form of employment is that a potential employment stabilizer is lost. Workers are hired/fired immediately as demand swings. The added instability of employment could be translated, through the consumption mechanism, into an amplification of the demand shock. Since there is no ongoing relationship between employer and employee, it might be assumed that employers also vary the wages they pay contingent workers. With high turnover, a lower wage could simply mean that when one worker left, a new one was hired at a lower wage than that of the previous employee.

Although in theory, there is a greater risk of macro instability with more contingency, our experiment did not find much impact. In the experiment we made two modifications of the model. First, we made wages more flexible than the base case, as in our first experiment. That is, we doubled the responsiveness of wage inflation to unemployment. Note that through the inflation channel, as the first experiment showed, this added wage flexibility could speed the adjustment process, that is, it could add rather than subtract macro stability. However, our second adjustment made consumption more quickly dependent on income. If there is instability associated with contingency, it would likely come about by loss of wage income—as contingent workers were laid off—showing up quickly as a drop in consumer demand.

The base WEFA model assumes that consumption is a function of permanent income rather than current income. Permanent income is defined as a weighted average of income over a three-year period. If workers in fact consume out of current income—which we defined by cutting the three-year period in half to six quarters—it is possible that economic shocks could be amplified.

After making these adjustments, however, the added instability was quite small, indeed negligible. A $10 billion export shock, for example, produced a multiplier of 1.67 after seven quarters in the base case. In the contingency experiment, the multiplier rose only to 1.69.[29] Such a small effect meant that other key variables such as inflation, interest rates, and unemployment were barely affected. In this case, although a change in human resource policy— more contingency in employment—could have macro consequences which would be ignored by micro decision makers, the model suggests that the macro consequences would in fact be quite small.

Faster Productivity Growth

Training and cooperation are often seen by human resource practitioners as possible boosters of productivity. There is some ambiguity as to whether such practices should be viewed as primarily having a one-shot effect, or whether there is something to the notion of "continuous improvement." As an experiment, we added an additional 0.5 percent to the nonfarm business productivity growth rate for three years. Although this increment seems modest, it would be a major accomplishment if it could be achieved.

Such a change—productivity higher by about 1.5 percent at the end of the three-year period—should, as a first approximation, boost the output of the nonfarm business sector proportionally. Since some output is generated outside the nonfarm business sector—chiefly in government—the effect on real GDP would be diluted to perhaps 1.2 percent (about $70 billion in 1987 dollars). However, the WEFA model does not capture the direct effect; instead it focuses on the anti-inflation impact of reducing unit labor costs. The result after three years is an inflation reduction of about 0.3 percent, leading to a modest boost in real output and a reduction of unemployment by about 0.3 percentage points. That is, productivity gains, apart from directly leading to more output and income, produce an anti-inflation "bonus" of modest proportions.

Clearly, the model misses some important by-products of the boost in output which would be captured by the private decision makers. However, as in previous examples, the positive impact of reduced inflation is not captured at the micro level. Indeed, in the experiments described earlier, the impact of human resource policy on inflation was often the unappreciated link between micro and macro. This observation is not new and, in fact, has been the justification at various times for "incomes policies," real wage insurance, and similar proposals[30] (Tarantelli, 1986).

CONCLUSIONS

There is a notable gap between macro and micro perceptions of human resource policies and their impact. By itself, this observation is not surprising. There is a notable gap between macro- and microeconomics, especially if macro is taken to mean the kind of analysis done by professional forecasters. And the old idea that where you stand determines what you see applies. The perception gap becomes acute in a large, decentralized society such as the United States. It is difficult for employers in such a society to see their interest as going beyond reduction of regulatory constraints.

Of course, merely making that observation does not provide a guide to appropriate policy. There may well be important indirect, macro-level effects to consider. But are our models of these effects sufficient to provide precise guides to policy? Clearly not. We cannot prove, for example, that it is better to "be aware" of macro complications without being sure what they are and how they play out than it is to put on micro blinders. However, it does appear that problems such as chronic unemployment, health care costs and access, and income inequality are not likely to be solved simply by employers acting on their own. Surely, if they could be solved that way, they would have been long ago.

ACKNOWLEDGMENT

The authors thank Nelson Pedrozo for his assistance in some of the WEFA model simulations.

NOTES

1. Purists will immediately note we have left out the international sector. U.S. prices could fall relative to foreign, either directly or via exchange rates, thus increasing real net exports. They would also note that the real value of money would increase if all prices drop, given a constant money supply, perhaps producing a stimulating effect of increased real wealth. Our purpose in the text is not to assert these other effects do not exist but rather to note that a very important balancing wheel for micro markets—the adjustment of relative internal prices—is absent at the macro level.

2. Note that if markets—especially labor markets—are prone to adjust in quantity terms rather than price (wage) terms, then employers and employees will adapt (Thurow, 1979). Human resource practices are different because of the quantity-adjusting feature of labor markets than they would be if labor markets always cleared by changes in wages. For example, the degree to which an employer protects employees from the risk of unemployment (through job security mechanisms) becomes an element of human resource management strategy.

3. Economists, faced with the problem of the fishermen, generally suggest the ultimate solution would be extension of property rights. If some entity owned fishing rights, it would see to it that overfishing would not occur through some sort of licensing, policing, or simply doing

the fishing itself through wage-earning employee fishermen. However, granting property rights is not always possible. In the case of some of the traditional macro failures such as recessions, it would be necessary to have one entity which "owned" the entire economy.

4. We are neglecting possible interfirm differences in the cost impact of mandates.

5. For example, if a mandate was especially costly for part-time workers, those industries that used such workers extensively, for example, fast-food restaurants, would be most affected. This complaint was often registered by such employers regarding mandated health insurance; since such insurance involves a fixed cost regardless of hours worked, the percentage labor cost increase (assuming no labor cost absorption by employees) would be greater for employers with many part timers in their workforces.

6. Note that the issue of cutting the nominal wage (a matter we take up separately below) need not arise if nominal wages are generally increasing. A reduced rate of nominal wage increase in a climate of generally rising wages can be equivalent to the wage cut shown in Figure 1. We take up this issue more fully below.

7. The fallacy of composition is often cited by economists. One economics dictionary defines it as follows: "In economics, the whole is often more than the sum of its parts. For example, an individual may decide to save more and consume less, and succeed; but if many people in the economy decide to save more, they may altogether save less because of the adverse effect of reduced consumption on national income" (Knopf, 1991, pp. 111-112).

8. In the U.S. system social security is a defined benefit pension in which more work quarters and higher pay generally raise the eventual pension benefit. Obviously, the system is complex in practice and this added benefit need not always be present. For example, a low-wage spouse might not gain from work because the benefit achieved is less than the entitlement already provided by the spouse's work activity.

9. The economic prediction would be that each $1 in bonus would reduce wage payments by $1. Workers would receive the same take home pay, but slightly less than 5 percent (.05/1.05 = 4.8%) would be labeled "bonus" instead of "wage." We neglect interactions of such a hypothetical mandated bonus with benefit plans such as pensions which are often based on the "wage."

10. Under an employer-by-employer system, plans will try to shift worker health costs to other plans under which they may be eligible, for example, coverage under a spouse's plan. Such cost shifting creates administrative expense.

11. Under one model, a mandate that firms provide just cause before being able to fire employees could lower the unemployment rate, if the macro unemployment rate affects workers' rate of effort. The intuition is that without the mandate, the choice of harsh severance policies by some firms will increase hiring rates at these firms and thus decrease the expected duration of unemployment for all workers. This may have an effect on the motivation of workers employed elsewhere, which results in a high equilibrium unemployment rate. Mandating that firms can't follow such harsh severance policies therefore reduces equilibrium unemployment, but at the cost of higher expected duration of unemployment (Levine, 1989; Shapiro & Stiglitz, 1984). While the assumptions in this model may not be valid, the surprising conclusion does illustrate how a more macro view can change perceptions based only on a micro perspective.

12. As usual, we are neglecting other considerations here to make the point that the macro perspective looks different than the micro. For example, investment might be linked to profit rates so that in the longer term, squeezed profits might produce lower output. Anything is possible, absent a carefully specified model. Also, the union voice/productivity discussion has usually been in the context of partial unionization. If the unionization rate went to 100 percent, it would be necessary to make assumptions about whether unions simply pushed up nominal wages, leading to price increases that would offset the distributional effects, or whether they would push up real wages. In that case, there could be an impact on the natural rate of unemployment.

13. There have been other arguments in economics for departing from the usual textbook view that decentralized price-guided decision making is best. For example, Weitzman (1974, 1977)

notes instances based on the high costs of error or considerations of income distribution in which departure from such decision making is best. Our argument here, however, is based mainly on the issue of important interconnections and consequences which may be hidden at the purely micro level.

14.   Less attention has been paid to shortages than surpluses because by themselves shortages are not viewed as a social problems. Indeed, apart from the inflationary link often made to shortages, a labor shortage seems ideal for employee welfare. Jobs are plentiful, choices abound, and any frictions between employer and employee can be readily resolved with voluntary job changes. Moreover, as employers desperately search for labor, they bring in disadvantaged workers who might otherwise be rationed out, provide training they would otherwise not, and upgrade the labor force.

15.   Under job evaluation, jobs are evaluated to determine their value to the firm. In formal systems, points are assigned for particular job attributes and the points are then converted to monetary units.

16.   As of late 1994 the U.S. Bureau of Labor Statistics reported that 18 percent of the 8.1 million workers under "major" private and state and local union-management contracts had escalators. Estimates for non-major contracts (those covering fewer than 1,000 workers plus federal union workers are not available). If we assumed that non-major workers had the same coverage by escalators as major workers, and that no nonunion workers had such coverage, about 3 percnet of wage earners would be covered. Nonunion coverage is quite rare. Federal postal workers do have escalators. Hence, taking 5 percent as an overall estimate seems likely to be at the upper limits of the probable range.

17.   Cents-per-hour formulas give the same absolute across-the-board adjustment to high and low paid occupations. Thus, wage compression will occur during periods of inflation. Thinking in nominal monetary units rather than percentage terms is another expression of wage nominalism.

18.   It might be noted that there was some evidence that by the early 1990s, the nursing shortage had been alleviated, in part due to efforts at health care cost containment and rising nursing salaries. The monopsony explanation for shortage has also been used for school teachers.

19.   Although the government intervened in labor markets during World War I to settle strikes, it did not impose wage controls.

20.   The fact that there is reluctance to raise or lower nominal wages does not necessarily mean that the resistance is symmetrical. Nominal wage increases are clearly less difficult than cuts.

21.   One simple way of looking at the Weitzman plan is to view the share (s) of profits (p) going to workers under profit sharing as if it were a profits tax, so that $(1 - s)p$ remains with the firm's owners. As a first approximation, a firm maximizing $(1 - s)\, p$ will behave the same— including hiring the same amount of labor—as a firm maximizing p. However, since the share bonus has some value to workers, Weitzman assumes that the bonus will partly substitute for the regular wage, leaving the wage lower. With a lower wage, firms will expand labor purchases, leading to a drop in unemployment. In addition if all firms seek to expand employment, a chronic labor shortage will develop. Firms will have unfilled vacancies and—in business downturns—will "lay off" vacancies rather than real jobs. Thus, according to the Weitzman proposal, the economy will end up with both lower unemployment and greater job stability. Presumably, firms collectively would be better off in a more stable economy operating at lower unemployment. But—absent a tax break or other subsidy—insufficient profit sharing will be adopted pursuant to micro incentives to produce the desirable "share economy" effect.

22.   There is discussion in macro literature concerning whether it is appropriate to view the business cycle as simply oscillation around an underlying trend or whether there is a "unit root" phenomenon at the macro level. Obviously, some business cycles have long-lasting effects through the political channel, for example, the Great Depression produced the social security system and other institutional changes which could have long-term consequences.

23.   There are some questions about productivity measurement—especially in manufacturing—associated with the adoption of "hedonic pricing" and the evaluation of computer output. If anything, these adjustments bias up the measured trend in productivity in the 1980s and 1990s.

24.   The issue is more complex since workers might be willing to work at lower wages—in effect pay de facto tuition—to acquire general skills. Lower wages up front, or other contractual arrangements, could resolve the general skills problem in theory.

25.   For every 1 percent rise in productivity, real wages can rise by 1 percent (the price-wage markup can fall by 1%) without affecting the relative shares of capital and labor. The resulting lower unemployment (greater real economic activity) would actually raise the absolute share of profits even as the relative share remains unchanged.

26.   The WEFA model contains 810 behavioral equations and identities.

27.   The equation is based on the difference between the actual unemployment rate and the NAIRU over 8 quarters, various lags on a moving average of private, nonfarm productivity change, expected inflation (with various lags) and a minimum wage change term.

28.   The wage index used is the Employment Cost Index for wages and salaries in the private, nonfarm sector.

29.   Large multi-equation models tend to oscillate indefinitely after a shock is introduced. We report in the text the first round impact rather than the continuing oscillation. In both the base and the experimental cases, the export shock effect diminished to essentially zero after about five years.

30.   Incomes policy is the European term for wage-price guidelines. Real wage insurance was a proposal of the Carter administration that would have provided a tax incentive for workers whose wages were kept in line with the administration's anti-inflation guideline. The proposal had many practical problems and was never enacted.

REFERENCES

Aaron, H.J., & Bosworth, B.P. (1994). Economic issues in reform of health care financing. In *Brookings papers on economic activity* (Micro, pp. 249-286).

Blinder, A.S. (1991, May). Why are prices sticky? Preliminary results from an interview study. *American Economic Review, 81*, 89-100.

Brittain, J.A. (1971, March). The incidence of social security payroll taxes. *American Economic Review, 61*, 110-125.

————— . (1972a, December). The incidence of the social security payroll tax: Reply. *American Economic Review, 62*, 739-742.

————— (1972b). *The payroll tax for social security*. Washington, DC: Brookings Institution.

Brodsky, M.M. (1994, November). Labor market flexibility: A changing international perspective. *Monthly Labor Review, 117*, 53-60.

Davis, S., & Haltiwanger, J. (1990). Gross job creation and destruction: Microeconomic evidence and macroeconomic implication. In *NBER macroeconomics annual: 1990* (volume 5, pp. 123-168). Cambridge, MA: MIT Press.

Diebold, F.X., Neumark, D., & Polsky, D. (1994, September). *Job stability in the United States* (Working paper no. 4859). National Bureau of Economic Research.

Eberts, R.W., & Montgomery, E.B. (1994). Employment creation and destruction: An analytical review. *Federal Reserve Bank of Cleveland Economic Review, 30* (3), 14-26.

Emerson, M. (1988). Regulation or deregulation of the labour market: Policy regimes for the recruitment and dismissal of employees in the industrialised countries. *European Economic Review, 32*, 775-817.

Employment Benefit Research Institute. (1994, July). *Baby boomers in retirement: What are their prospects?* (Issue Brief No. 151). Washington, DC: Employment Benefit Research Institute.

Erickson, C.L., & Mitchell, D.J.B. (1996, April). Information on strikes and union settlements: Patterns of coverage in a "newspaper of record." *Industrial and Labor Relations Review, 49*, 395-407.

_____ . (1995, Autumn). Labor market regulation, flexibility, and employment. *Labour, 9*, 443-462.

Feldstein, M.S. (1972, December). The incidence of the social security payroll tax: Comment. *American Economic Review, 62*, 735-738.

Freeman, R.B., & Medoff, J.L. (1984). *What do unions do?* New York: Basic Books.

Gruber, J. (1992, September). *The efficiency of a group-specific mandated benefit: Evidence from health insurance benefits for maternity* (Working paper no. 4157). National Bureau of Economic Research.

Gruber, J., & Krueger, A.B. (1990, December). *The incidence of mandated employer-provided insurance: Lessons from workers' compensation insurance* (Working paper 3557). National Bureau of Economic Research.

Hamermesh, D.S. (1979, April). New estimates of the incidence of the payroll tax. *Southern Economic Journal, 45*, 1208-1219.

Holmlund, B. (1983). Payroll taxes and wage inflation: The Swedish experience. *Scandinavian Journal of Economics, 85* (1), 1-15.

Jacoby, S.M. (1985). *Employing bureaucracy: Managers, unions, and the transformation of work in American industry, 1900-1945.* New York: Columbia University Press.

Knopf, K.A. (1991). *A lexicon of economics.* New York: Academic Press.

Krueger, A.B. (1991, July). The evolution of unjust-dismissal legislation in the United States. *Industrial and Labor Relations Review, 44*, 644-660.

_____ . (1994). *Observations on employment-based government mandates, with particular reference to health insurance* (Working paper no. 323). Princeton, NJ: Industrial Relations Section, Princeton University

Kruse, D.L. (1993). *Profit sharing: Does it make a difference?* Kalamazoo, MI: Upjohn Institute.

Levine, D.I. (1989). Just-cause employment policies when unemployment is a worker discipline device. *American Economic Review, 79*, 902-905.

Levine, D.I., & Tyson, L.D. (1990). Participation, productivity, and the firm's environment. In A.S. Blinder (Ed.), *Paying for productivity: A look at the evidence* (pp. 183-237). Washington, DC: Brookings Institution.

MacRae, C.D., & MacRae, E.C. (1976, June). Labor supply and the payroll tax. *American Economic Review, 66*, 408-409.

Mitchell, D.J.B. (1993, Winter). Keynesian, old Keynesian, and new Keynesian wage nominalism. *Industrial Relations, 32*, 1-29.

_____ . (1994, December). Wage pressures and trends. In *The UCLA business forecast for the nation and California* (pp. Nation 2.1-Nation 2.27). Los Angeles.

Mitchell, D.J.B., Lewin, D., & Lawler, E.E. (1990). Alternative pay systems, firm performance, and productivity. In A.S. Blinder (Ed.), *Paying for productivity: A look at the evidence* (pp. 15-88). Washington, DC: Brookings Institution.

Mitchell, D.J.B., & Zaidi, M.A. (1992). International pressures on industrial relations: Macroeconomics and social concertation. In T. Treu (Ed.), *Participation in public policy-making: The role of trade unions and employers' associations* (pp. 59-72). New York: de Gruyter.

Moffit, R.A. (1977, December). Labor supply and the payroll tax: Note. *American Economic Review, 67*, 1004-1005.

Oi, W.Y. (1962, December). Labor as a quasi-fixed factor. *Journal of Political Economy, 70*, 538-555.

Okun, A.M. (1970). Upward mobility in a high-pressure economy. *Brookings Papers on Economic Activity, number 1*, pp. 466-472.

Organisation for Economic Co-operation and Development. (1989). *Mechanisms for job creation: Lessons from the United States.* Paris: OECD.

―――――― . (1994). *The OECD jobs study: Facts, analysis, strategies.* Paris: OECD.

Shapiro, C., & Stiglitz, J. (1984). Equilibrium unemployment as a worker discipline device. *American Economic Review, 72,* 433-444.

Tarantelli, E. (1986, Winter). The regulation of inflation and unemployment. *Industrial Relations, 25,* 1-15.

Thurow, L.C. (1979). A job competition model. In M.J. Piore (Ed.), *Unemployment and inflation: Institutionalist and structuralist views* (pp. 17-32). White Plains, NY: M.E. Sharpe.

Treu, T. (1992). Labour flexibility in Europe. *International Labour Review, 131* (4-5), 497-512.

U.S. Congress, Senate Committee on Banking, Housing, and Urban Affairs, Subcommittee on Economic Stabilization. (1980). *Economic impact of payroll taxes.* Hearings of March 13. Washington, DC: U.S. Government Printing Office).

U.S. Congressional Budget Office. (1993, July). *Estimates of health care proposals from the 102nd Congress,* (CBO paper).

U.S. President. (1994). *Economic report of the President, February 1994.* Washington, DC: U.S. Government Printing Office.

Vroman, W. (1974). Employer payroll tax incidence: Empirical tests with cross-country data. *Public Finance, 29* (2), 184-200.

Weisskopf, T.E., Bowles, S., & Gordon, D.M. (1983). Hearts and minds: A social model of U.S. productivity growth. *Brookings Papers on Economic Activity, (number 2,* pp. 384-441).

Weitzman, M.L. (1977, Fall). Is the price system or rationing more effective in getting a commodity to those who need it most? *Bell Journal of Economics, 8,* 517-524.

―――――― . (1974, October). Prices vs. quantities. *Review of Economic Studies, 41,* 477-491.

―――――― . (1984). *The share economy: Conquering stagflation.* Cambridge, MA: Harvard University Press.

Weitzman, M.L., & Kruse, D.L. (1990). Profit sharing and productivity. In A.S. Blinder (Ed.), *Paying for productivity: A look at the evidence* (pp. 95-140). Washington, DC: Brookings Institution.

CONCLUSION

HUMAN RESOURCE MANAGEMENT:
KEY THEMES AND INTEGRATION

David Lewin, Daniel J.B. Mitchell, and Mahmood A. Zaidi

In the opening chapter, we noted that the field of management in general and human resource management in particular has been susceptible to fads or idea bubbles. That is, there is a long history of potentially useful ideas about human resource management being oversold or misapplied. Mindful of this historical tendency, we and the many contributors to *The Human Resource Management Handbook* have put before the reader numerous ideas and evidence about human resource management. We have challenged the reader to examine them critically. But as editors of the *Handbook* and as academics, we face the same challenge as do our readers. We will thus attempt in this closing chapter to identify and integrate key themes based on the ideas presented in the earlier chapters.

EMPLOYEE PARTICIPATION AND FLEXIBILITY IN THE ENTERPRISE

The idea that employees should be more heavily "involved" in workplace and organizational decision making has attracted much contemporary attention. It has been so widely supported in various academic and management circles that the danger of an idea bubble is present. But on closer consideration, the idea itself is underdeveloped and needs further definition. Without further development, participation borders on being meaningless and a fad.

Consider that once an individual is employed by an enterprise, he or she is "participating" in that enterprise in terms of performing work for pay. From the perspective of labor market exchange, all employees are therefore participating in work and in some workplace/organizational decisions. Indeed, even the unemployed—who are officially participating in the labor force as job seekers—may have some influence on wages and conditions inside the workplace.

What is really at issue here, then, is not the fact of employee participation in the enterprise but, rather, the extent or scope of participation. Following classical ideas about the design of work and the design of organizations, employees perform certain narrowly prescribed tasks. They do so individually, are supervised by a "boss" who, in turn (and with others), reports to a boss, and so on up the chain of command. These traditional practices are grounded in ideas/concepts of scientific management (Taylor, 1911), bureaucracy (Weber, 1947), and administration of the firm (Simon, 1957; Sloan, 1964). Such classical ideas—and the practices that came to be based on them—had and have in common a relatively restricted notion of employee participation. Under scientific management, participation was narrow and practiced individually.

Today these practices and the ideas on which they are based seem to many to be hopelessly dated—despite the fact that they contributed greatly to the economic advancement of firms, industries, and national economies during much of the twentieth century. Changes in consumer demand, competition, industry composition, technology, regulation, and other environmental variables have led to major, even dramatic, changes in the definition and design of jobs and organizations. Increasingly, the work required to be done to meet customer and competitive demands is complex, interdependent, and knowledge- (rather than physical effort) based. Similarly, the design of organizations that is required to meet contemporary customer and competitive demands emphasizes flatter, relatively more horizontal structures and arrangements than prevailed previously.

Nonetheless, organizations will vary in the degree to which they have these increasingly common characteristics. Taylorist practices may still be appropriate in some instances, particularly in countries which in their current stage of development resemble the United States in the early twentieth century. The lesson to be drawn is to avoid simply assuming that all forms of modern participation are helpful to all organizations—at least from the standpoint of productivity and profitability—regardless of circumstance. Alternatively, advocates of participation should be candid with their recommendations if they simply believe that participation is a Good Thing, regardless of its impact on firm performance.

USE OF TEAMS

A primary point of convergence of these ideas about the design of jobs and the design of organizations is in the use of teams. Today, team-based work and team-based organizations are in vogue. The historical precedent for such use of teams is, of course, the famous Hawthorne experiments (Roethlisberger & Dickson, 1939) out of which developed the idea of group norms. Those experiments, however, led to the use of industrial/psychological counseling programs and other "employee services" far more than they did to the use of teams for workplace and organizational decision making. The contemporary use of teams by business enterprises around the world appears to have been ignited by the successes of Japanese manufacturing firms in the 1970s and 1980s. These firms ostensibly used workplace teams and team leaders rather than supervisors to achieve product quality levels that surpassed those of competitor firms from other nations (notably the United States).

Total quality management (TQM) initiatives are often based on the concept of a semiautonomous or autonomous work team. Such initiatives seem to have stronger effects on the economic/financial performance of firms than other team-based participative arrangements, such as quality circles, quality-of-work-life improvement programs, works councils, and employee representation on company boards of directors. As Eaton, Voos, and Kim point out, some of these participatory arrangements are voluntary while others are mandated either by law or by management.

Levine strongly suggests that mandatory participation (an oxymoron?) initiatives are unlikely to succeed because they do not foster trust between employees and management. He also concludes, however, that employment security is a necessary (although not sufficient) condition for the success of any participatory initiative. This view, of course, is often seen as inconsistent with market capitalism and global competition—despite the Japanese example with its "lifetime" employment.

Presumably, the level of education of the workforce and the kind of socialization received also are important to the operation of teams. Some societies emphasize group norms and behaviors; others—notably the United States—have traditionally stressed individualism. It is interesting to note that in the United States, from elementary school to business school, conscious efforts are now being made to emphasize teamwork, an effort that will undoubtedly influence operations in the American workplace of the future.

SCOPE AND NATURE OF PARTICIPATION

Apart from the choice of a particular employee participation scheme by the firm, the scope of issues covered by such schemes is especially relevant. Some employee participation programs are narrowly focused, indeed, often one-issue focused, such as in the area of TQM. Other participation programs are broader in scope, and may involve employees in decision making or consultation about a wide range of issues including strategic-level issues. Support for use of such broader participation programs is provided by Kleiner and Ay, who document the positive effects of employee information-sharing programs on firm performance. They favor the use of two-way over one-way information-sharing programs.

Typically, the locus of responsibility for—or "ownership" of—employee nonfinancial participation programs rests with one unit, group, or champion in an enterprise. The locus of responsibility for employee financial participation programs may rest with another unit, group, or champion. Yet employees must derive tangible rewards from assuming more, new, and/or different decision-making responsibility through nonfinancial participation in the enterprise if they are to have an incentive to continue such participation (Levine, 1995; Mitchell, Lewin, & Lawler, 1990).

Consequently, the idea that employees should participate financially as well as nonfinancially in the business enterprise has spread widely in recent years. The leading employee financial participation programs, both in the United States and elsewhere, are stock ownership—not necessarily in the form of an ESOP—and profit sharing. Interestingly, both profit sharing and stock ownership programs have been practiced for decades by firms in the United States and abroad. Both of these financial participation arrangements (depending on the specifics of the plan) have in common certain macro-level rationale and incentives. For example, wealth sharing is sometimes a rationale and favorable tax treatment is sometimes an external incentive. At the micro level there is also a common rationale, that is, the motivation to engender enhanced employee and organizational performance.

Nevertheless, Kruse and Blasi observe that as a stand-alone financial participation program, employee stock ownership plans (ESOPs) do not appear to enhance the economic performance of firms with such plans compared to firms without them (see also U.S. General Accounting Office, 1987). That is, the evidence that just having an ESOP will improve productivity or profitability is weak. Perhaps this limited or zero effect results because stock prices and thus the market value of stock ownership are influenced by variables which are well beyond the control of the firm and its employees.

Profit-sharing programs appear at first glance to motivate and reflect more closely than ESOPs the "productive efforts" of firms and their employees. But Jones, Kato, and Pliskin do not find strong evidence that firms with profit-sharing programs have better economic performance than firms without such programs. (The evidence on this point varies from study to study.) Nonetheless, profit-sharing programs seem to have employment stabilization effects and might be useful if combined with Levine-type job security arrangements.

From a human resource management perspective, there are other important issues associated with the use of ESOPs, profit sharing, and certain other types of variable pay plans. The presence of such plans implies and is consistent with the notion of a (relatively) long-term employment contracting relationship. Unlike wages and salaries, which are paid out during short-term periods, the value of stock ownership and profit shares accrues over intermediate and long(er)-term periods. The clear implication of these plans is that the employee's attachment to the firm—and the firm's attachment to the employee—is an enduring one.

Today, however, this type of implicit employment contract is being severely questioned and, according to some, is receding. If this tendency is in fact the case, one would expect to observe decreasing use of ESOPs and profit-sharing plans by firms. However, the evidence for such a trend reveals both confirmation and contradiction. It appears that profit-sharing coverage rose in the early 1980s—notably in some union contracts—but in the late 1980s and early 1990s that tendency seemed to reverse. Strict ESOPs seem to have gradually increased but are less widespread than popular press accounts suggest. And there is a lack of good data on programs such as gainsharing, in part because such programs have no favored tax treatment and thus are not picked up in tax-related records.

PRINCIPALS AND AGENTS

From the micro-level perspective, use of programs such as profit sharing, gainsharing, ESOPs, sales commissions, and piece rates is based on principal-agent theory. Agency theory is one of the key contributions of the economic approach to human resources (Allen, 1996). Traditionally, the work of employees was monitored by supervisors (principals) who had a relatively narrow span of control—one supervisor for every six or so employees (agents). But where information is increasingly imperfect and the work to be performed is increasingly complex, it becomes more difficult (costly) for supervisors (principals) to monitor employees' (agents') work.

Therefore, firms may now have incentives to turn away from arrangements in which supervisors-principals monitor the work of employees-agents toward arrangements in which employees monitor their own work (and thus exercise principal and agent roles simultaneously). Under such arrangements, and following the reasoning advanced by Asch and Warner, traditional practices of pay for time worked or "pay for input" come to be deemphasized in favor of pay for results produced or "pay for output" through various financial participation plans.

However, and as also suggested by Asch and Warner, principal-agent theory can be invoked to support/explain several other compensation-related initiatives undertaken by firms. Among these is the use of pay premiums, or efficiency pay (wages), to motivate workers to monitor their work and reduce if not eliminate the incidence of shirking. Consequently, principal-agent theory may be useful as a starting point for the examination of changes in employee compensation practices, but it is not a parsimonious theory in that it can be used to invoke or support a variety of "new" and old compensation practices, including traditional merit plans.

FLEXIBILITY IN PAY

Recent initiatives by firms in the area of variable pay suggest a new desire for "flexibility" when it comes to rewarding employees. These initiatives provide insight into—and perhaps contradict—the long-standing observation that, contrary to the prediction of microeconomic theory, wages are downwardly inflexible. That is, wages do not appear to decline in the face of high unemployment (excess labor supply). The numerous extant explanations of wage rigidity are reported by Groshen and Schweitzer. But the reader may wish to consider that variable pay initiatives in the forms of ESOPs, profit-sharing plans, bonus plans, and stock option plans attest to the ability of firms to make contemporary employee compensation arrangements more variable/flexible. The wage rate (or salary) may be rigid but other, more variable elements of pay form part of the total compensation package.

Moreover, and as emphasized in this *Handbook*, new programs of employee financial participation in the firm are being accompanied by new programs of nonfinancial participation in the firm. Some empirical evidence indicates that such programs taken in combination or *packages* appear to enhance the economic performance of firms that adopt them. However, as is often the case in this field, not all studies are in agreement (Mitchell, Lewin, & Lawler, 1990).

RISK PREFERENCE

Employee financial and nonfinancial participation programs may turn out to be short-lived unless human resource management researchers devote more attention to the implication of these arrangements. In this regard, the concept of risk preference must be invoked. Consider that both financial and nonfinancial participation programs require employees to bear more risk than that which prevails in the traditional employment relationship.

Under financial participation, employees risk not receiving a profit share (or receiving a "low" share) or having shares of stock that decline in market value, or both. Such risks may be acceptable to employees if the portion of total compensation associated with financial participation or variable pay programs is relatively low (say 5%). But the risk may be less acceptable or even unacceptable when the portion is relatively high (say 25%). Similarly, under nonfinancial participation programs, employees risk not being able to perform certain newer complex tasks, not being able effectively to self-monitor their work, and not being able effectively to "manage" relationships with co-workers when work is performed in teams.

Again, such risks may be acceptable to the employee if the nonfinancial participation program deals relatively narrowly with workplace-level issues such as work flow, inventory management, or product quality. But the risk may be far less acceptable if the program calls for employee participation in policy or strategic level issues and/or requires most of the work to be done in fully autonomous teams. The risks to supervisors trying to operate in new systems in which they must delegate previously supervisory decisions to non-supervisors may be particularly high.

From the perspective of motivation theory, a financial or nonfinancial participation program should provide sufficiently large rewards and sufficiently challenging work to employees to motivate them to perform well and to reinforce such behavior over time. However, the risk preferences of employees and managers are likely to be asymmetrically distributed (the former generally having lower risk preferences than the latter). Thus, efforts at expanded participation may be limited, thwarted or overturned if employees come to believe that the risks they must bear under such initiatives are "too high."

FLEXIBILITY IN EMPLOYMENT

If firms are able to enhance their economic performance by adopting more flexible employee compensation and decision-making arrangements, they may also be able to enhance their economic performance by adopting more flexible employment arrangements. Perhaps no recent human resource management initiatives of firms have drawn as much attention as those based on the idea of flexible or contingent employment. As Belous observes, U.S. business enterprises have proceeded apace to reduce their "core" workforces and increase their "contingent" workforces—though there are varying estimates of the magnitude of such efforts.

Contingent employment takes many forms including, for example, temporary, part-time, contracted, and vendored work and workers. Typically, contingent employees are lower- (perhaps far lower) cost employees than core employees, with the former receiving lower pay and much lower benefits than the latter. In recent years many large publicly held firms have reduced their overall employment, especially the employment of core workforce members, while increasing their employment of contingent workers. Labor-cost containment appears to have been the dominant rationale for (re)structuring such employment arrangements.

However, some employers have long been prone to use the "flexible" or labor-cost containment practice of laying off workers in times of declining demand for products and services, and recalling/adding workers in times of increasing demand. Further, as Houseman observes, such practices have been far more typical of U.S. employers than employers abroad, such as in Western Europe and Japan. In many countries legal requirements and customs have in the past discouraged the use of layoffs as well as of temporary, part-time, and contract employees. More recently, however, under the impetus of increased global competition and declining economic performance, there has been pressure to reduce these disincentives. Firms in Western Europe, Japan, and other nations with traditions of permanent or continuous employment have initiated U.S.-style labor-cost containment practices, including layoffs.

But as noted by Appelbaum and Berg, employers may seek to enhance the economic performance of their firms either by reducing pay or by increasing the productivity of their current workforces. Such productivity-enhancing initiatives include older ones based on scientific management and the human relations school. Or, they may involve newer ones based on total quality management and employee financial and nonfinancial participation in the enterprise.

Many academics and traditional personnel managers have a preference for measures to improve employee productivity over labor-cost containment for the purpose of enhancing the economic performance of firms. However, those who lead and manage modern business enterprises, and who do so in increasingly competitive market economies, seem more inclined to pursue labor cost containment initiatives first. Productivity improvement initiatives come later, if at all.

But both sides need to reexamine their premises. Academics may be motivated by their tastes for ongoing employment relationships. Tenured professors surely enjoy them! On the other hand, downsizing for its own sake goes beyond rational analysis and is likely to be yet another bubble in the human resource field. Dispassionate analysis of options and likely outcomes is needed.

UNIONS, BARGAINING, AND DISPUTE RESOLUTION

As noted in the opening chapter, union representation is a form of employee participation in the enterprise. However, this type of participation is almost always opposed by employers and is commonly overlooked by human resource management scholars (though not by industrial relations scholars and labor economists). Employer opposition to economically oriented unions is understandable in as much as the objective of unions in this context is to shift economic returns from (owners of) capital to labor. Moreover, the dominantly adversarial character of union-management relations in the United States was shaped and sharpened by the underlying premises of the Wagner and Taft-Hartley Acts (Kaufman, 1996b). And, of course, the reverse is also true.

Many models of unionism have been advanced by scholars over the years, including the pre-Taft-Hartley social, uplift, reform, revolutionary, political, and economic models (Hoxie, 1921). In the United States and in some other parts of the world the economic model of unionism ultimately predominated. Collective bargaining and explicit contracting between employees and employers are at the heart of economically oriented unionism—also known as "business unionism" (Perlman, 1922).

STRIKES

Strikes are the most overt form of union-management conflict and the one most likely to be picked up in the media (Erickson & Mitchell, 1996). Of course, even adversarial union-management bargaining need not result in strikes. But the fact that strikes are recorded in the news media and official data may account for the detailed scrutiny which has been paid to them by academic researchers. Beginning with Hicks (1932), a large literature on the causes, dynamics, and consequences of strikes has developed.

For a while, the idea predominated that strikes were "mistakes" stemming from one or another party's lack of understanding of its opponent's position. More recently, strikes have been attributed to asymmetric or imperfect information available to the bargaining parties. Strikes are also ways in which information can be learned about the position of the opposing party. There are models that view strikes as rational short-term events—games—in larger, long-term joint utility maximization calculations by the parties to bargaining. And there are behavioral models that position worker militancy as the driving force behind strikes and which therefore focus on identifying the determinants of such militancy.

While the competition for ideas about strikes continues to be vigorous, the incidence of strikes in the United States has declined markedly in recent years, as documented by Gallagher and Gramm. They show that this decline is a structural shift by adjusting for the decline in employee unionism, changes in the industrial composition of the economy, and other changes in the nature of collective bargaining. The structure of collective bargaining—specifically the trend away from industry-wide and pattern bargaining toward decentralized firm-by-firm and plant-by-plant bargaining—is often claimed to be the key factor explaining the declining incidence of strikes in the United States. But the trend is also a clear manifestation of the decline of bargaining power among U.S. unions, beginning in the 1980s.

THIRD PARTY INTERVENTION AND DISPUTE SETTLEMENT

As noted, bargaining need not result in a strike; most contract negotiations are resolved without a strike and without reaching an impasse. But even when impasses do result, they need not be resolved by strikes (or lockouts). Instead, they may be settled through third party intervention utilizing techniques of mediation, fact-finding, arbitration, and combinations thereof. There are no legal requirements in the United States for private-sector unions and management to use third parties in attempting to resolve their bargaining disputes. In practice, mediation (in which the third party has no power to compel a settlement) is often used. A federal agency, the Federal Mediation and Conciliation Service, is explicitly directed to offer its mediation services where it thinks appropriate. Similar state agencies also exist.

In contrast, private-sector fact-finding is rarely used except in cases where the President declares a threatened or actual strike or lockout to constitute a national emergency under the Railway Labor Act or the Taft-Hartley Act. Interest arbitration (arbitration to settle disputes over the terms of a contract being negotiated) is rare—but not unknown—in the private sector. There is no requirement that private parties use arbitration but it can be found in professional sports (to settle the individual contractual terms of athletes) and occasionally in the steel industry, among others. In the public sector, there may be requirements that interest arbitration be used to resolve impasses. At the federal level the U.S. Postal Service is covered by such a requirement.

Interest arbitration is also present and regularly, if not widely, used in some state and local governments. Often, government employees do not have the right to strike—although strikes sometimes occur. Hence, arbitration is seen by legislators as the logical substitute in government for the private-sector right to strike. Devinatz and Budd show how public sector interest arbitration has shifted from a predominantly conventional form of dispute settlement—where the arbitrator typically produces a settlement somewhere between the parties' offers—to final-offer arbitration. In this form, the arbitrator must choose one of the two parties' final offers.

Final-offer arbitration is an example of academic influence in industrial relations, since it is premised on a model of how arbitrators and the parties react to particular institutional arrangements. Under conventional arbitration, the original logic went, the arbitrator will "split the difference" between the two positions. Knowing this, the parties will take extreme positions and thus be unlikely to settle the dispute without intervention—the so-called "chilling effect." Final-offer arbitration was thought to remove this tendency, since the payoff comes from offering the most reasonable settlement, not the most extreme. Ironically, more recent research suggests that a model in which arbitrators simply split the difference and have no preferences of their own is incorrect. (Indeed, if they had no preferences, how would they choose which settlement was more reasonable under final-offer arrangements?)

Empirically, arbitrated public sector bargaining settlements result in significantly higher pay rates than negotiated settlements. However, these pay differences are not large and, in addition, are statistically smaller when comparing arbitrated settlements with bargained settlements where interest arbitration is available but not used. But these findings refer to averages, and wide variations are possible in individual cases (Lewin, Feuille, Kochan, & Delaney, 1988).

From an analytical perspective, interest arbitration may be more important for its behavioral than its economic consequences. That is, interest arbitration may be conceptualized as a form of procedural justice. Under the procedure the parties to a negotiation who have reached an impasse may either praise or criticize the arbitrator for the results of settlement decisions, that is, for the distributive justice or injustice of the outcome.

Interest arbitrators have, except in rare cases, the power to impose settlements on the parties. But the parties' direct relationship will continue uninterrupted beyond the life of the imposed agreement. If one or the other party or both parties to this relationship are dissatisfied with certain outcomes (the distributive justice) of the arbitrated settlement, they can project their dissatisfaction onto the arbitrator and away from the other party. Such behavior can preserve and perhaps enhance the procedural justice of their own relationship.

Following this reasoning, bargaining impasses may be less likely to occur in future among the parties to this relationship because the relationship itself is viewed as relatively more procedurally just than before. Whether or not this or other consequences derive from the use of interest arbitration to settle labor-management disputes merits greater attention from behaviorally oriented researchers. However, the relative rarity of interest arbitration in the private sector suggests that the parties often do not see net benefits from adopting the procedure. If the procedure is imposed, as is often the case in public employment, the parties have two villains to blame for unfair settlements: the law and the arbitrator.

PUBLIC VERSUS PRIVATE SECTOR UNION MEMBERSHIP TRENDS

Public sector unionization has drawn a great deal of scholarly and practitioner attention in recent years because government is one of the few sectors where union membership has not fallen, both in the United States and many other developed countries. In the near-term future, moreover, and following Troy, it is likely that public sector union members will represent an even larger proportion of total union coverage. This prediction flows not because public sector unionization will grow further, but because private sector unionization is expected by Troy to continue to dwindle. Some observers judge employer (legal and illegal) opposition to unions and unfavorable government policy to be key factors in the decline of private sector unionization. In contrast, Troy cites declining employee support for unions and unfavorable product market competition as key factors.

But certain deeper questions and issues arise from Troy's conclusions. Consider, for example, that—as of yet—no theory of public sector unionization or union growth has been produced by researchers. What is usually said is that management resistance to unions is weaker in the public than in the private sector. But this hardly qualifies as a strong analytical statement, let alone a complete theory. Presumably, lack of a bottom line in public employment should be factored into any such model building.

Further, if it is the case that employees around the world systematically have a weaker preference for—or a stronger aversion to—unionization than members of predecessor generations, the question remains, "Why is this so?" Perhaps most intriguing, declining employee preferences for unionization do not necessarily mean declining employee preferences for other forms of representation in business enterprises. Earlier it was pointed out that unions are only one form of employee representation/participation in the enterprise. And the papers included in the first two sections of the *Handbook* may be read to mean that both employees and employers support the generalized notion of employee participation in the enterprise—even as they evidence a lack of support for unionism as a participatory form. Surely researchers are in a position to investigate further both employer and employee preferences, and the determinants of such preferences, for employee representation/ participation (Lewin, Kaufman, Fossum, & Verma, 1996).

In any event, employee preferences may change as the composition of the workforce changes. It is often assumed that the increased proportion of white-collar workers produced a climate less favorable to unions. (Note, however, the difficulties with this explanation when applied to the public sector.) Increased immigration of unskilled workers may have the opposite result. Hispanics have shown special interest in union representation, most prominently in the various Justice for Janitors campaigns of the Service Employees International Union (SEIU) but also in some instances in agriculture, local trucking, and construction. In important ways, the reform leadership of the AFL-CIO which ousted the old guard in 1995 owed its success to this development. The new AFL-CIO president, John Sweeney, who emerged from the internal revolt, was formerly president of the SEIU. And the success of the janitors campaign pushed him into prominence.

If in fact private sector unionization has declined around the developed world, it might have been expected that scholarly interest in unions would have also declined. But scholarly interest in unions and bargaining has, if anything, increased notably. Economics and industrial relations journals, not to mention political science, sociology, and labor history journals, are replete with articles modeling union and bargaining behavior. It may simply be that it is easier to obtain data on union contracts than on nonunion practices. If so, the wholesale abolition of much union-sector data collection and publication in 1995-1996 by the U.S. Bureau of Labor Statistics may put an end to this research. Be that as it may, what can be learned from the plethora of union-sector research available up to the mid 1990s?

SENIORITY, VOICE, AND INTERNAL UNION POLICY DETERMINATION

According to Addison and Chilton, one thing that has apparently been learned is that the union does not equally represent all of its members. Instead, the union represents a "median voter" worker who is typically older and more senior than the membership as a whole. As in any political process, it is the median voter who determines a majority-rules election. And it is these long-service workers who benefit most from bargained wage and seniority provisions because they are more likely than younger, less senior workers to be retained in the face of increased global competition or in economic recessions.

Another lesson that has been learned from contemporary research on unions and bargaining is that, by providing voice in the employment relationship, unions serve to reduce worker exit (quits). Union voice also lengthens employee job tenure, provides incentives for employers to invest in human capital (through training, for example), and—some argue—increases worker productivity. These productivity increases are sometimes claimed to be roughly equal to—or even to exceed—the cost increases resulting from collective bargaining. That is, unit labor costs under unions are unchanged (or even fall), with the consequence that unionized and nonunion firms can coexist within an industry.

Of course, there are problems with this view. If unions left costs unchanged, or even reduced them, it is hard to see why employers would resist unionization. Perhaps, however, unions have positive productivity effects in some instances (apart from those that go with simple raising of the wage and marginal revenue product), but this cost-lowering impact is more than offset by the pay impact. One might interpret employer efforts to create nonunion participation schemes in the 1980s and beyond as an attempt to obtain the benefits of unions without the costs. Indeed, the creation of now-illegal "company unions" (employer-dominated organizations) beginning around the era of World War I could be viewed in the same way.

UNION PAY IMPACTS

While the newer models are interesting, even intriguing, one wonders if they are as well supported empirically as the older view. Consider that the historically dominant economic model of union behavior, the monopoly model, had a simple prediction: unions would raise wages. Early on, which is to say during the 1950s and 1960s, empirical research on unions and bargaining using the monopoly model sought to measure the effects of unions on wages. The research was quite successful in this regard, producing varying estimates of the effects of unions on wages but typically finding these effects to be statistically significant.

Later, with the spread of employee benefit programs (pensions and insurance) and the availability of new data sets, researchers expanded their studies to examine the effects of unions on wages and benefits. Here, the findings showed larger and more significant effects than in the earlier "wages only" studies. Still later, researchers came to examine the effects of unions on firms' capital investments and expenditures on research and development, on firms' profitability, and on firms' market value.

In each case, the research can be summarized by saying that larger and more significant union effects were adduced than in previous studies. Taken as a whole, these studies can be read to constitute strong affirmation of the monopoly model of unionism and, even more, to be consistent with the decline of unionism in the United States and abroad during recent decades. That is, the rise in labor costs, particularly during the 1970s, created growing incentives for employers to avoid unions where possible in the 1980s and 1990s.

UNIONS IN THE FUTURE

Surely the question posed for unions and union leaders by the available research is whether or not a new model of unionization is needed if unions are to be a viable institution as the twenty-first century approaches. As noted earlier, an economic model, with the union as the exclusive representative bargaining over wages and conditions, is but one model of union activity. Perhaps a union movement grounded on concepts of employee service or social affiliation, rather than shifting economic returns from capital to labor, will be more attuned to the preferences of today's and tomorrow's employees. Note that this approach in some ways is a return to an earlier role of unions—as beneficial or "friendly" societies that provided the insurance services which were later taken over by employers.

Perhaps more use of interest arbitration, by reducing the risk and cost of strikes, would lessen management resistance to unions. Perhaps greater use of variable pay, such as profit sharing, would allow the job security union members seem to want to be more compatible with employer needs for flexibility in costs. Perhaps unions should reconceptualize their role as representing the employee interest in society, whether or not through collective bargaining. Such a conception would emphasize the political channel and representation in legal forums (Mitchell, 1993). Put another way, if a new model is not found, what Troy terms old unionism will wither, leaving unions as largely representatives of government employees.

DEALING WITH CONFLICT AT THE INDIVIDUAL LEVEL

From a human resource management perspective, it is also useful to recognize that unions and collective bargaining make manifest one of the most enduring aspects of the employment relationship, namely, the presence of conflict. Under business unionism in particular, grievance procedures evolved as the primary mechanism for resolving employment-related disputes occurring during the life of collective bargaining agreements. Virtually all union contracts contain such procedures, and almost all of those end in rights arbitration.

Of course, some grievances involve group complaints of one type or another rather than the complaints of a single employee. But we often think of grievance procedures as mechanisms whereby the individual can express his or her voice about adverse workplace decisions. When nonunion firms install grievance procedures, they almost always deal with individual problems. The alternative to a grievance system under a classical free labor market, of course, is simply exit.

In recent years, the recognition of conflict as endemic to the employment relationship has grown rapidly, as reflected in the adoption of grievance and grievance-like conflict resolution systems for nonunion employees. Yes, some nonunion firms use grievance procedures primarily to ward off employee unionization. Some firms have also been motivated to adopt such procedures by the growth of legal challenges brought by employees to the doctrine of employment-at-will. But, as Lewin points out, the dominant factors in the adoption of grievance procedures by nonunion firms include information-generation, problem solving, and procedural justice. Put differently, nonunion firms seem to adopt grievance procedures primarily for strategic reasons, and only secondarily to counter unions or ward off employee lawsuits.

As to the actual use of grievance procedures in nonunion firms, Lewin shows that these procedures are in fact used, though at roughly half the rates at which unionized employees use their grievance procedures. Nonunion employees are more likely to win their cases the higher the level of the procedures at which their grievances are settled. Finally, as in the union sector, most nonunion employee grievances are settled at the lower steps of the grievance procedures.

However, Lewin also finds that nonunion grievance filers (and their supervisors) apparently suffer unfavorable consequences compared to nonfilers (and their supervisors) after grievances are settled. The de facto penalties include lower job performance ratings, lower promotion rates, higher work absence rates, and higher turnover rates. To the extent that such consequences reflect management reprisals against employees who file grievances, they suggest that nonunion grievance procedures will be decreasingly used over time. Such outcomes run counter to the supposed strategic objectives of nonunion firms in adopting grievance procedures.

The most notable differences between grievance procedures in nonunion and unionized firms concern the representation of employees in the grievance process and the use of arbitration as the final step of the process. In unionized settings, union officials represent the employee at virtually every step of the grievance procedure (save perhaps the first step). But in nonunion settings, the use of a representative or agent—peer, outside counsel, ombudsperson, and so on—is far less pervasive and may occur only in the final steps of the procedure. Also in unionized settings, arbitration is virtually always the final step of the procedure. But only about one-fifth of nonunion grievance procedures provide for a decision by a third party (not necessarily an arbitrator) as the final procedural step.

In assessing whether or not the use of formal grievance procedures is a good idea or, instead, an idea bubble, much can be learned from historical analysis of grievance and rights arbitration systems in unionized settings. An important point in this regard, stressed by Bain, is that even under highly formalized grievance procedures, most grievances apparently are settled informally and never enter the official grievance system. Indeed, some authorities estimate that for each grievance that is reduced to writing and enters the typical grievance system, 10 others never do so. They are settled (or otherwise disposed of) informally in discussions between employees and their immediate supervisors (Lewin & Peterson, 1988).

The interesting question then becomes, "In firms with formal grievance systems, do these systems provide incentives for grievances to be surfaced and/ or settled informally when compared to firms without formal grievance systems?" While empirically challenging, this question is amenable to observational and participant-observation research. Such research has long been used to study informal organizations, group behavior, networks, and organizational cultures within business enterprises (Dalton, 1959; O'Reilly, 1989; Roy, 1952; Stephenson & Lewin, 1996).

Turning to the final and perhaps most formal stage of grievance settlement, namely, (rights) arbitration, Bain's historical analysis shows that this is a less well-settled process than appears at first glance. On the one hand, rights arbitration was initially conceived as an informal, open process in which the arbitrator assisted the parties—labor and management—to fashion an acceptable settlement. On the other hand and over time, the rights arbitration process has become more formal, legal-like, and time-consuming. Hence, the parties to arbitration, at least in unionized settings, have sought alternative dispute resolution (ADR) processes and methods which speed up and make less formal the standard arbitration process. Of course, labor relations is not the only field in which ADR is being tried as an alternative to more formal processes. In business disputes, even conventional arbitration is sometimes seen as preferable to—and less costly than—litigation in court.

EXIT, VOICE, AND ALTERNATIVES

Conceptually, as noted earlier, there is a market alternative to employee exercise of voice through a grievance procedure (whether in a unionized or nonunion setting), and that is to exit or quit the firm. This exit-voice dichotomy is at the heart of Hirschman's (1970) analytical framework, and many labor-market researchers have adopted his framework, although it was originally developed to explain consumer behavior. These researchers have generally concluded that, by providing a voice mechanism, unions significantly reduce the incidence of exit and significantly increase the incidence of voice (Freeman & Medoff, 1984). Voice is expressed through collective bargaining, processing of grievances, and less formal representation. Presumably, some of the same effects can operate through grievance procedures in nonunion settings. But recent research calls into question the assumed negative correlation between voice and exit in both unionized and nonunion settings (Lewin & Boroff, 1996).

Beyond the behaviors reflected in exit and voice, and as pointed out by Bemmels, employees may respond to workplace dissatisfaction in other ways, such as engaging in neglect or withdrawal through, for example, absenteeism. A more serious employee response to workplace dissatisfaction is destruction, which may involve acts of sabotage aimed at the firm or, by extension, acts of violence aimed at co-workers or oneself. Less serious, at least overtly, as a response to workplace dissatisfaction is "silence." Silence—suffering without officially complaining—is seen by several researchers as an alternative to exit, voice, and neglect (Boroff & Lewin, 1996).

In light of the many and varied responses that employees may demonstrate in response to workplace dissatisfaction, it is important to model and measure the factors shaping such responses. Bemmels employs an economic framework to show how the costs of various options influence employee choices of responses to workplace dissatisfaction. In addition, personal characteristics and cultural norms may influence the choice of responses in this regard. Intriguingly, Hirschman (1970) included loyalty as a key variable in his exit-voice framework, positing a positive relationship between loyalty and voice and thus a negative relationship between loyalty and exit. However, recent research on grievance filing activity by nonunion and unionized employees finds employee loyalty to be negatively correlated with the exercise of voice in both types of employment relationships (Lewin & Boroff, 1996).

In sum, research on dispute resolution in the employment relationship is shifting from a focus on unions and collective bargaining to a focus on conflict in the workplace—and perhaps especially to the incidence, determinants, and management of such conflict. At one time the study of workplace conflict might have been considered to be entirely separate from the study of (and management concern about) employee participation in the enterprise. From a different perspective, however, it is entirely possible to view conflict management and resolution as accompanying employee participation in the enterprise as central and perhaps intertwined foci of modern human resource management.

Employer initiatives to enhance employee participation in the firm and to structure more flexible employment arrangements are bound to induce various types of employee dissatisfaction and conflict in the employment relationship. A challenge to both scholars and practitioners, therefore, is to use the historical lessons drawn from union-management relations, strikes, and arbitration to shape new forms of dispute resolution in the workplace.

HUMAN RESOURCE MANAGEMENT

The phrase "human resource management" is of relatively recent origin, having been preceded by such phrases as personnel management, personnel administration, employee relations, human relations, and others. At one time, these phrases were often distinguished from "industrial relations" or "labor-management relations" and connoted *nonunion* administration. A firm might have a personnel department to deal with white-collar nonunion workers and an industrial relations department to deal with unionized blue-collar employees. Today human resource management has in common with its earlier (nonunion) predecessors the mutual reference to that part or function of the business enterprise that involves selecting, assessing, and rewarding employees. What, one may ask, is distinctive in modern usage about "human resource management?"

Some scholars and practitioners would answer this question by responding that human resource management connotes a more central and strategic role for the older personnel function. A comparison might be the way that the marketing function evolved from "sales" to occupy a central strategic role in the business enterprise. In effect, the contrast is with the Taylorist model in which the firm's various departments carry out orders originated from the top, but do not influence the nature of these commands. Since all functional areas of the firm now claim to enjoy some participation in strategy, what may be involved is a less Taylorist model in which influence is more diffused.

But has the management of people indeed become more strategically oriented in business enterprises? If so, then the corollary claim that "people are our most important asset" may have both conceptual and practical validity. The emergence of a large literature on human resource strategy tends to support this idea. So, too, does the ascension of senior human resource executives to top-level planning and decision-making bodies. Perhaps these developments indicate that the idea of strategic human resource management is more than an idea bubble (Cappelli & Singh, 1992; Lewin & Mitchell, 1995).

However, the evidence is not clear. One might cite the decline in the number of human resource managers that appeared in the 1990s as evidence of downgrading of the function. Human resource executives are quick to argue that the decline simply reflected a transfer of certain functions from their departments to line managers. But even if that is the case, it would suggest that the traditional role of the function—representing the employee interest—is being diminished.

SELECTION

In any case, there is little doubt that human resource management still begins with the selection (sourcing) of people to work for a business enterprise. When there are many jobs to be filled and many applicants to fill them, the psychological model of employee selection is especially relevant, as demonstrated by Ostroff and Rothausen. This model requires that predictors—for example, educational attainment, test scores, prior work experience, letters of reference, and so on—be correlated with criteria of job performance. Job performance might be measured by the number of products produced, value of sales made, documents word processed, and so on (Lewin & Mitchell, 1995).

When only a few jobs or perhaps even only one job is to be filled, the statistically based validation requirements of the psychological model of employee selection are inoperative. A more judgmental "clinical selection" process is used. Interestingly, clinical selection-type employee selection processes rely heavily on certain methods, notably interviews with job applicants. But research on the psychological model of employee selection indicates that interviews have relatively low statistical validity.

Whether employee selection involves filling many or few job vacancies, most selection processes, tools, and methods are aimed at assessing (predicting) the ability of individuals to perform the job(s) at hand. Yet in an era in which more and more jobs seem to require work to be performed in teams, one may question the larger organizational validity of individually oriented employee selection practices. Such tools do not often focus on how the individual will perform in a team setting. As noted earlier, many jobs are being redesigned to be performed in teams so that individually oriented employee selection practices may be misaligned with modern work requirements. Hence, it is notable that some industrial psychologists are focusing on identifying individuals' ability to work in teams.

To the extent that the workforce is becoming more contingent, traditional selection and prediction of performance assessment raises other issues as well. A contingent worker who is found to be unsuitable can be quickly dismissed and replaced at low cost to the firm. Thus, the need fully to predict or assess the performance of such workers may be lower than in the past. It would be a poor use of resources to assess workers who will shortly be gone in any event. Even if performance were accurately predicted, the cost of the assessment might not be amortized over the short duration of the job. In some cases, however, contingent workers are in sensitive jobs and thus their performance does need to be carefully predicted and/or closely monitored.

Where prediction of employee performance is continued in a contingent environment, it may well be performed by the suppliers of temporary help. Such temp agencies have reputations of providing reliable workers to protect. However, the type of selection practices that might be made by temporary help supply agencies could well be different from those traditionally made by employers. Questions of organizational fit are likely to be less important and the skills needed to perform a task, that is, use a particular word-processing program, may be more important. What is particularly important is the ability of the temporary employee to fit into many different types of organizations for short periods.

When selecting new (or promoting existing) "regular" employees, firms face a choice between those who may be productive immediately and those who may be productive later on. One approach in this regard is to (attempt to) select employees who can indeed be productive upon joining the firm, that is, "hit the ground running." Firms in certain industries, for example, financial services and management consulting, tend to follow this approach. Some occupational specialists, notably sales personnel, are also selected in this fashion.

Another approach is to select employees who will not be productive immediately, but who can be trained to be productive *eventually*. Firms in a variety of industries and industry segments, for example, consumer products and durable goods manufacturing, tend to follow this approach. The technology of the industry—broadly defined—should play a large role in determining the appropriate selection technique.

TRAINING

An especially important factor in firms' decisions about whether or not to provide training, and about its scope and duration, is the economic return to training. As shown by Ashenfelter and Lalonde, firms will not engage in employee training if they cannot at least recover the cost. To do so, the trained employee must remain with the firm for a sufficiently long period to permit the firm to recover those costs.

If the employee leaves the firm to go elsewhere before training costs are recovered, the firm is essentially bearing the burden of depreciation of investment in human assets. And if the training supplied is of the "general" type, the firm is effectively providing free training for other employers and its former employees. Consequently, labor economists often contend that a firm will only provide specific training to employees—the type of training that increases employee value to the firm in question—but not general training.

In practice, the distinction between general and specific training tends to blur. Anecdotally, one can point to vocational training programs—ranging from barber colleges to medical schools—in which employees pay for general training. And one can point to orientation programs for new employees in which much attention is paid to teaching specific knowledge, such as about the local or corporate culture (see below). But the general/specific distinction is not found in the standard personnel literature and one can point to contradictory anecdotes. For example, enrollees in executive MBA programs often have their tuition paid for by their employers despite the fact that MBA skills so acquired are general.

In short, there is good reason to believe that firms and employees share the cost of training. The firm pays a portion of the training costs directly and the employee "pays" via a wage or salary which is lower than would otherwise prevail if he or she was immediately productive upon hire by the firm. Disentangling the two shares of the costs of training is quite difficult as an empirical matter.

Organizational behavior specialists call attention to a type of training not typically within the purview of economists, namely, socialization (Feldman, 1980). Socialization refers to the process by which a firm inculcates (some would say indoctrinates) new employees with the dominant or core values and norms of the enterprise. For example, some firms require work to be performed in teams and require employees to self-monitor their work. Through such exercises, these firms provide an early socialization period to new employees by immersing them in the principles and practices of team-based work.

In some nations, such as Japan and Korea, the primary form of employee training and socialization is of the informal, on-the-job type. A new employee is typically assigned a mid-to-senior-level manager who serves as a counselor (mentor) and helps the employee to "learn the ropes." By contrast, in other nations, such as Germany, a new employee is formally designated an apprentice—may well have a certificate from a training school—and learns the ropes at a particular firm by following a senior or journeyman employee around.

In the United States and certain other nations, general training has historically been provided by public institutions, notably the public schools. Individuals who graduated from those schools were expected to be productive immediately upon hire by the firm. In the 1980s and 1990s, however, the ability of public schools to equip their graduates with the minimum or threshold capabilities to be productive upon initial entry to employment was severely called into question. Hence, much contemporary attention is understandably being focused on employer-provided training and the consequences of such training. To the extent that basic school skills are still stressed, there is renewed interest in junior colleges as the sources of such training—a kind of upward educational creep.

PERFORMANCE APPRAISAL AND REWARDS

Whether newly hired employees are immediately productive or productive later on, their job performance will be assessed at certain points after joining the firm. Traditionally, performance appraisal featured a one-one-one process in which a supervisor appraised the performance of a subordinate. But as Heneman and Von Hippel demonstrate, this conventional performance appraisal format is increasingly out of touch with modern job requirements, including team-based work. Consequently, performance appraisal formats and systems are shifting away from the conventional supervisor appraisal of a subordinate toward peer, subordinate, and even customer appraisals—so-called "360 degree" appraisal.

These new modes of performance appraisal are important in several respects. First, it is well known that conventional supervisor appraisals of subordinates are susceptible to perverse incentives which give rise to inaccurate ratings (Lewin & Mitchell, 1995). A common example is the pronounced tendency of supervisors to provide upward-biased appraisals of employees, in part because supervisors must live with employees in continuing relationships. Also a factor is that a supervisor who rates employees poorly may be blamed by superiors for either incorrectly selecting or badly managing them.

Second, there is evidence to show that peer-type performance appraisal systems tend to produce less biased—or at least lower—overall appraisals of employees than result from conventional performance appraisal systems. Stated differently, peers tend to be tougher than supervisors when it comes to evaluating employee job performance. Third, the attachment of customers to a particular firm tends to be weaker and shorter than the attachment of employees to the firm. Consequently, appraisals of employees rendered by customers may be least susceptible to upward bias among all types of performance appraisal formats and systems.

However, regardless of who does the rating, the issue of cost is an important consideration. Elaborate rating systems may require substantial time on the part of the rater—displacement. Some tradeoff must be made between full information and loss of productive working time. Customers, in addition, may not wish to spend a great deal of time rating someone else's employees (Ichniowski & Lewin, 1987).

Irrespective of the particular performance appraisal system that prevails in a firm, the appraisal results will be moot unless they are connected to the allocation of rewards. Expectancy theory highlights the rewards-performance linkage, and their is little doubt that the dominant use of employee performance appraisals in business enterprises is to allocate rewards—notably monetary rewards, including promotions. But does this process truly translate into "pay for performance?"

For many years the answer to this question was "yes." Differences in (measured) employee performance were used to justify differential economic rewards (merit pay) for employees. More recently, however, and as argued by Fossum and McCall, the ability of traditional "merit pay for individual performance" appraisal and compensation systems to motivate organization-wide performance has been called into question.

This questioning is occurring partly because work is increasingly being done in teams and groups. Also and fundamentally, it is occurring because employee performance appraisals taken alone or collectively do not necessarily "add up" to overall organizational performance. Indeed, in some firms, measured employee performance appraisals have risen while the firms' economic performance, measured by return on capital employed or assets, has declined (Murphy, 1991).

Moreover, the movement toward placing a larger proportion of employees' pay at risk (pay for output) and away from pay for time worked (pay for input) emphasizes overall organizational performance and deemphasizes individual employee performance appraisals. In entrepreneurial and start-up firms, annual individual performance appraisals are much less common than in more established firms. Monetary rewards for performance are focused on the organizational rather than the individual level in entrepreneurial and start-up firms, taking such forms as stock option plans and other variable compensation arrangements.

Also of note in the analysis of performance appraisal and rewards for performance is what Meyer, Kay, and French (1965) long ago labeled "split roles in performance appraisal." This phrase refers to the fact that employee performance appraisals are used for two main purposes. While, as noted earlier, employee performance appraisals have most often been used to allocate monetary rewards, they are also used—or are supposed to be used—to help employees remedy their job-related weaknesses (that is, to "develop" employees).

From this dual perspective, it may be argued that employee performance appraisals are overused for allocating rewards and underused for developing and coaching employees. One long-standing idea for dealing with this problem is to use the annual performance appraisal primarily to determine monetary rewards (merit pay adjustments). Intermediate performance appraisals can then be used primarily to coach and develop employees. Yet another idea is to use individual-level employee performance appraisals solely for the purpose of coaching and developing employees. Then, organizational-level incentives (in the form of profit-sharing, bonus, and stock option plans) can be used for the purpose of rewarding employees. However, such an approach leaves unresolved the issue of determining promotions.

EMPLOYEE BENEFIT PLANS

Conventional pay-for-performance systems result in differential rewards across individuals or—in the case of small-group piece rates and gainsharing—across groups. But other non-wage benefits often apply to all or most employees in the organization. Such benefits are not trivial today as their one-time name "fringes" seemed to imply. For large firms, especially unionized companies, such benefits may comprise 35-40 percent of total compensation. It seems strange that undifferentiated benefit plans are often found in companies emphasizing individual pay for performance. Perhaps for reasons of historical accident, perhaps because of tax incentives, such benefits serve as equalizers of pay.

At one time, the idea that benefits would constitute a major portion of employee compensation might have been regarded as a fantasy. While benefits such as pensions can be traced back to the nineteenth century, they began to be important only after World War II. Now, benefits—particularly pension and health plans (but also holiday, vacation, and leave plans)—have existed for so long that, as Broderick and Gerhart point out, they have come to be expected by new employees. And, existing employees expect their firms will continue to cover them.

PATTERNS OF SOCIAL RESPONSIBILITY

These employee expectations, as noted earlier, have been supported by tax laws that allows employers to deduct from operating income the cost of benefits while deferring or eliminating any income tax liability of the employee. Nevertheless, this "path-dependency" has been called into question by the benefit-cost containment initiatives undertaken by business enterprises in the 1980s and 1990s. Among the symptoms are cost sharing of health benefits with employees and declining coverage of employees by health care and defined-benefit pension plans. Also noteworthy is the rise of start-up entrepreneurial firms which are far less likely than established firms to offer either health care or pension plans.

Such labor cost containment initiatives recall to mind an important question in the development of market capitalism, namely, "To what extent should the business enterprise be used as an instrument of social policy?" In the United States especially, there has been a pronounced tendency to use the business enterprise to accomplish certain larger social or public purposes. These include income maintenance (through pension and disability plans), preservation of the family (through health care plan coverage of spouses and dependents), racial and ethnic integration (through EEO compliance and anti-adverse selection hiring programs), prevention of illegal drug use (through drug tests administered by firms), and even the reduction of smoking (through selection processes that prohibit the hiring of smokers).

Clearly, firms can be induced by tax subsidies—or forced by mandates— to offer various benefit plans. But there does seem to be a move by U.S. employers to shed some of the responsibilities that Congress has placed on them. There is, therefore, a new balance to be struck. The central government could assume the responsibilities that business does not shoulder directly, as has been the case with Social Security. But defeat of national health care proposals in the 1990s suggests that large-scale federal involvement in that field is unlikely to be adopted in the near term, if ever, in the United States.

If government doesn't do it, and business doesn't do it, responsibility reverts to individuals. There are some moves in that direction, such as Individual Retirement Accounts which allow employees to save on a tax-preferred basis if their employer does not provide a pension. In some cases, a compromise is struck whereby benefits are offered through the employment relationship but are made portable and left in important ways to the employee to administer. Tax-preferred savings plans, such as 401ks and 403bs, fall into this category, since it is generally up to the employee to determine how the funds should be invested from a menu of options.

BENEFITS AND PAY BY GENDER

Among the social-political objectives that have come to the fore, perhaps none sparked more controversy when originally proposed than the equalization of incomes among male and female employees. One would be hard pressed to identify a statistic more widely used than the ratio of female-to-male pay in the debate about employment discrimination, social policy, and economic progress. Yet, as Currie points out, this comparable worth debate is perhaps more appropriately directed at benefits than at take-home pay.

Various data sets show that men are more likely than women to receive training in the firm and to be covered by benefit programs. But these data sets were compiled during periods when male labor force participation outpaced female labor force participation, and tend to reflect an earlier dominance of male over female cohorts in the labor force. More recently, female labor force participation has grown rapidly while male labor force participation has fallen. Maternity leave plans rose in importance and were reinforced in 1993 when Congress mandated more general (unpaid) family leave. Thus it is possible that the day will come when male-female fringe benefit differentials are equalized.

HUMAN RESOURCE MANAGEMENT AS PROTECTOR OF THE EMPLOYEE INTEREST

Inevitably, the measures undertaken by firms to achieve larger social objectives devolve primarily on the human resource management function. That is one reason why the function is often seen as being primarily oriented toward compliance with governmental laws and directives. But the social role of human resource management dates back long before government policies of the post-World War II period. Well before that time, the personnel department was largely regarded as a spokesman for, and protector of, employee interests.

Of course, the top management of business enterprises fundamentally shaped this view of the personnel/human resource management function by counting among its key objectives the prevention of unionization among its employees. But with a decline in the union threat, that priority began to shift. In the 1990s the human resource function in business enterprises was called on to modify its traditionally dominant roles of protecting employee rights and complying with governmental directives. Instead, it was directed to restructure itself as a "business partner" (Kaufman, 1996a).

Whether and to what extent this idea will become more than an idea bubble will depend greatly on the development of new core competencies among human resource executives and professionals. Foremost among these will be the capability to design employee selection, training, appraisal, compensation and reward systems, and conflict management systems and programs which enhance overall organizational performance. This ability, in turn, will require human resource executives and professionals to enhance their understanding of—and gain threshold competency in—other key areas of the business enterprise, including strategy accounting, finance, marketing, and operations.

For a function that has traditionally focused on individual employee behavior and union behavior, these are formidable challenges indeed. Research by academics into best practice evidence can be helpful. But it is not clear how much the business partner notion extends beyond rhetoric in many firms. Is it yet another idea bubble?

The defeat of national health care plan proposals during the early 1990s in the United States has already been mentioned. An interesting question is raised by the behavior of human resource managers during that episode. Greater federal control of health care could have meant less control by private human resource managers. Arguably, the task of running a health insurance program is not central to most businesses. The business partner notion might therefore have suggested that human resource managers would have been pleased to shed the responsibility and leave the task to the government. But the fact that they did not generally support the plan may suggest a bureaucratic self-interest in maintaining traditional programs. Particularly in large firms, administration of health plans can involve great sums of money and ample supplies of subordinates. Further research into the reactions to those proposed plans within firms could be usefully undertaken by political scientists, management specialists, and others.

THE CHANGING EXTERNAL ENVIRONMENT

The final section of *The Human Resource Management Handbook* deals with the broadest level of human resource management analysis, namely, the external environmental level. A useful starting point in this regard is with public policies that shape the utilization of human resources at the level of the business enterprise. Virtually all nations provide some type of macro-regulation of micro-level human resources. The variation in such regulation is due in part to differences in economic and political systems across nations of the world.

In the United States relatively little federal government regulation of human resources existed until the 1930s. Prior to that time, regulation was primarily at the state level and tended to be limited in scope. During the Great Depression, federal New Deal laws were enacted to regulate private sector labor-management relations, the use of child labor, and the payment of minimum and overtime wages. Other laws passed during that era created programs of unemployment insurance and Social Security for privately employed workers.

By the 1950s the notion of using tax incentives to foster employer-provided benefits was firmly in place. Beginning in the 1960s another new era of human resource regulation emerged, with federal laws enacted to regulate private sector employment discrimination, workplace safety and health, and privately provided pension plans. More recent legislation has covered family leave, protection of the disabled against job discrimination, and employer prenotification of plant closings.

The dominant idea behind much, if not all, of this legislation has been to protect particular groups of workers or, in some cases, workers as a whole from the vicissitudes of the labor market. This idea is, of course, common among nations of the world. But its implementation in the United States inevitably raises tensions, given the strong traditions of a free labor market, individualism, suspicion of central government, and employment at will. Thus, it would be a mistake to view the U.S. system of human resource regulation as an integrated whole or the federal government as the sole enforcer of this system.

As Lee and Sockell point out, state governments share responsibility with the federal government for enforcing several federally enacted human resource regulatory statutes. And, virtually all U.S. states also have their own state-specific human resource laws and enforcement mechanisms. Further, at both the federal and state government levels, the courts often play a key role in interpreting the coverage and influencing the enforcement of human resource legislation.

IMPACT ANALYSIS

Given the piecemeal nature of U.S. human resource regulatory statutes and the multiplicity of governmental "actors" involved in their enforcement, what can be said about the effectiveness of the laws passed in the human resources field? As a whole, little can be said because research on human resource regulation focuses on analyses and assessments of individual laws, not the set of laws as a whole. When it comes to specific pieces of legislation, however, much of the research yields mildly to strongly negative assessments.

As examples, the Wagner/Taft-Hartley framework, or the manner in which it is enforced, is said by some researchers to hinder unionization and thwart collective bargaining. The Occupational Safety and Health Act is said to provide insufficient workplace inspections and penalties for violations to accomplish the purposes of this law. The minimum wage provisions of the Fair Labor Standards Act are said to reduce employer incentives to hire low-wage workers. The Employee Retirement Income Security Act is said to require profitable firms to subsidize the pension plans of unprofitable firms and even create perverse incentives for some firms to let their pension funds go bankrupt. Unemployment insurance is said to retard unemployed persons' search for work and to lengthen spells of unemployment. Social Security is said to provide overly generous benefits to today's retirees, perhaps reducing the overall rate of national saving, and to be likely to provide only meager benefits to future retirees. From a broader perspective, these claims call into question the continuance of human resource regulatory legislation beyond the period in which the problems originally addressed by such legislation were resolved or outgrown.

REGULATION AND ORGANIZATION DESIGN

In terms of the impacts of human resource regulation on the human resource management function in the firm, two effects are especially notable. First, human resource legislation spurs centralization of the human resource function. Uniform reporting requirements as well as internal and external audits associated with various public programs and regulations contribute to this centralizing tendency. Yet organization design theory suggests that organizational arrangements should be aligned with the firm's strategy (Chandler, 1962), and business enterprises seem increasingly to be advocating the decentralization of human resource management functions and responsibilities. Thus, there is perhaps a conflict between the regulatory imperatives and appropriate organizational design of firms.

Second, human resource regulation contributes strongly to the view that the human resource function is largely compliance-oriented. Yet earlier we noted that global competition, business deregulation, financial markets, and other forces are contributing to a view that the human resource function should become a business partner. Thus, in terms of both its effectiveness in achieving worker protection and its impact on the modern human resource function, the regulatory imperative raises questions. Is the long-standing regulatory model itself a slow-moving idea bubble now in the process of bursting?

INTERNATIONAL ASPECTS OF THE LABOR MARKET

Apart from human resource legislation, the hiring, training, utilization, assessment and compensation of the workforce are today often influenced by developments in international markets. Generally speaking, firms have four main sets of resources which they can utilize and manage in order to achieve their objectives. These are customers, capital (finance), technology, and human resources. In the 1980s and 1990s the boundaries of exchange in the markets for each of these resources became increasingly global, as demonstrated by Siebert and Zaidi. And each became an area of increased uncertainty, a major factor behind the push for more employer flexibility seen in many countries.

In the modern world a firm's customers may be distributed around the globe rather than confined to the geographic boundaries of the country or locality in which the firm is headquartered. Similarly, the expansion of capital and technology markets means that firms are not bound to "source" capital or technology solely from within the borders of their respective countries of origin. When it comes to human resources, firms are now able to search for, recruit, and hire employees from international labor markets, not just from national, regional and local markets.

Several issues arise for "labor" which is hired and utilized in an increasingly global and competitive environment. One of these is the displacement of workers from relatively high-paying jobs in advanced economies by workers in relatively low-paying jobs in developing economies. Manufacturing in North America and Western Europe has increasingly faced low-wage competition from Asia, Mexico, and other areas. Concerns have thus arisen that manufacturing wages in developed countries will drift lower and/or that jobs will be lost (Jacoby, 1995). Yet much the same concern was evidenced in the 1960s and 1970s when certain manufacturing jobs shifted from countries such as the United States and the United Kingdom to Japan.

An interesting observation, however, is the change in the Japanese manufacturing wage from one tenth of the American level (converted to U.S. dollars) in 1960 to a level above the U.S. wage by the mid-1990s. The United States and the United Kingdom were attracting major direct foreign investments by manufacturing firms from other advanced nations by the 1990s. In effect, the United States was no longer the most expensive place in the world to buy labor (Jacoby, 1995). These examples suggest that expanding global competition may well "raise rather lower all boats," even as it brings about a certain degree of worker displacement.

But in this case, no one is sure the past will be a guide to the present. China, with a labor force of over 600 million, presents a different order of magnitude that some of the other new competitors. As more and more of the Chinese economy is moved from subsistence peasant farming and from the nonmarket state sector, there may be impact on the U.S. workforce unlike previous experience. To some extent, U.S. trade with Mexico poses a similar uncertainty. Mexico is much smaller than China but it does have the advantage of geographic proximity to the United States. Proximity, by lowering transport and communication costs, to some extent substitutes for size of labor force.

One consequence of fears about indirect labor market competition through international trade with low wage countries has been a demand from developed countries for international labor standards of some type. At present, countries belonging to the International Labor Organization (ILO) are free to ratify its suggested standards. But countries often do not ratify standards—the United States has ratified relatively few—and even if its standards are ratified, the ILO has no enforcement authority. Thus, there have been calls for linking adherence to some set of "core" labor standards to access to international trade agreement privileges. Although there have been no serious calls for a global minimum wage, less developed countries fear that such standards might undermine their competitive positions. The issue of linking labor standards to access to markets in developed countries promises to be controversial for years to come (Erickson & Mitchell, 1996).

THE IMPACT OF TECHNOLOGY

As in the case of international trade, it is possible to attribute gloomy labor-market consequences to the spread of new technology. Technology has been blamed for the stagnation of real wages beginning in the early 1970s and for widening wage inequality. The argument is that new technology tends to favor more educated workers and displace traditional unskilled and semiskilled blue-collar workers. Computing technology is often cited as the source for such developments.

From an historical perspective, there is nothing new in fears about modern technology becoming a substitute for labor. But that does not mean that technology might not have adverse effects on the distribution of wages this time, even if did not have that effect before. Still, human resource researchers and practitioners, indeed, business leaders and policymakers, too, would do well to recall Schumpeter's (1947) dictum that the major threat to capitalism is too slow a rate of technological change and innovation.

MACRO PERSPECTIVES

"Macro" is often taken to be short for macroeconomics, that is, the study of the business cycle. Obviously, business cycles have implications for human resources, for example, layoff practices. However, the word "macro" can be taken in a more general sense to mean considerations of events external to the firm and the ways in which they are interconnected. What is perceived as the best policy from the firm (micro) level sometimes looks very different from the macro level.

To take a business cycle example, in an economic downturn it is often optimal from the firm's viewpoint to layoff workers. After all, demand for the firm's product has fallen, thereby requiring reduced labor input; eliminating the surplus labor will cut costs. However, if all firms collectively shed labor at the same time, they will intensify the economic downturn by reducing worker incomes and thus contribute to a further loss of profits. Yet it is not in any particular firm's interest to avoid layoffs because no single firm is large enough individually to affect the overall economic picture. If somehow all firms could coordinate their behavior and internalize the external effects of their individual behaviors, they might act differently (perhaps avoiding layoffs in this example).

As Erickson, Kimbell, and Mitchell point out, there are many examples in the human resource field in which the macro view is quite different from the micro. Although Troy would disagree, the decline in private-sector unions is arguably due in part to management policies of avoiding unionization or de-unionizing (as well as other factors). Since unions may cut into profits and reduce employer flexibility, such policies are easy to understand. But there is also evidence that the reduced level of employee voice through collective bargaining leads to the exercise of political voice. Management becomes constrained by laws, regulations, and court decisions in ways which may also be objectionable from the employer viewpoint. Since there is no forum for all employers to consider such macro issues and in which to make collective decisions, micro decision making is the rule and may lead to unintended consequences.

Management reactions to proposed changes in public policy may also be colored by the micro perspective. For example, a mandate to provide family leave, health care, pay minimum wages, or pay overtime premiums looks much more costly from the micro than the macro perspective. The question seen from the micro perspective is "What will be the consequence to my firm if my costs— say for health care—were raised, holding everything else constant?" But it is important, in answering that question, to recognize the fact that competitor firms will also have their costs raised, thus attenuating the impact. That is, everything will not be held constant. Further, economic theory suggests that many mandated costs are shifted back to labor through the collective actions of all employers and employees in the labor market.

All of these macro considerations suggest that the consequences of mandates are commonly much less dire than employers perceive. Perhaps that is why economists often have difficulty finding evidence of the employment consequences of mandates. Or when evidence is found, it rarely leaps from the raw data but instead requires subtle tools of analysis which often find small impacts.

In summary, the human resource field is often micro-oriented on both the practitioner and academic researcher sides. This result is understandable since much day-to-day work in the field involves small groups, evaluation of individuals, and interpersonal transactions. Business school curricula are more likely to feature material on how to be a group leader than on the implications of changing demographics for benefit plans. The point is not that one view— the macro or the micro—is better than the other; rather, it is that both perspectives are needed.

FINAL THOUGHTS

The idea that human resources can be used to achieve competitive advantage for business enterprises is an idea whose time has come. But as the introductory chapter pointed out, it is also the case that ideas in the field come and go. Many ideas have relatively little staying power; they are the bubbles or fads to which the field of management (including human resources) is so prone. And ideas and information of the kind presented in this *Handbook* are by no means the entire key to success as a practitioner in the field of human resources. Skills such as oral and written communications, team building, and negotiating are obviously important and do not naturally emerge from research studies (Hansen et al., 1996).

Still, we are convinced that the human resource function in the firm, whether performed in the formal human resource/personnel department or elsewhere, is an important element in the performance of the enterprise or organization. To achieve its potential, however, both practitioners and researchers must be able to draw information and concepts from outside the immediate field of human resources. For practitioners, this stricture means gaining familiarity with developments in other areas critical to the firm such as finance, marketing, and production. For academics, it increasingly means cross-disciplinary research. Not all ideas and concepts will turn out to be helpful. As elsewhere in economic life, there is a market test. But our review of the human resource field suggests that it can compete well, even vigorously, in the marketplace of ideas.

REFERENCES

Allen, S.G. (1996, August). Some principles of economics for human resource management. *Labor Law Journal, 47*, 549-554.

Boroff, K.E., & Lewin, D. (1996). Loyalty, voice and intent to exit a union firm: A conceptual and empirical analysis. *Industrial and Labor Relations Review, 50* (forthcoming).

Cappelli, P., & Singh, H. (1992). Integrating strategic human resources and strategic management. In D. Lewin, O.S. Mitchell, & P.D. Sherer (Eds.), *Research frontiers in industrial relations and human resources* (pp. 165-192). Madison, WI: Industrial Relations Research Association.

Chandler, A.P. (1962). *Strategy and structure*. Cambridge, MA: MIT Press.

Dalton, M. (1959). *Men who manage*. New York: Wiley.

Erickson, C.L., & Mitchell, D.J.B. (1996a, April). Information on strikes and union settlements: Patterns of coverage in a 'newspaper of record'. *Industrial and Labor Relations Review, 49*, 395-407.

_____. (1996b, August 7-9). *Labor standards and international trade: Background and analysis* (Working paper no. 96-2). UCLA Institute of Industrial Relations. Paper for a conference on "The Multilateral Trading System in a Globalizing World" sponsored by the East-West Center and the Korea Development Institute, Kehei, Maui.

Feldman, D. (1980, March-April). A socialization process that helps new recruits succeed. *Personnel, 57*, 11-23.

Freeman, R.B., & Medoff, J.L. (1984). *What do unions do?* New York: Basic Books.

Hansen, W.L. et al. (1996, August). Needed skills for human resource professionals: A pilot study. *Labor Law Journal, 47*, 524-534.

Hicks, J.R. (1932). *The theory of wages*. New York: P. Smith.

Hirschman, A.O. (1970). *Exit, voice and loyalty*. Cambridge, MA: Harvard University Press.

Hoxie, R. (1921). *Trade unionism in the United States*. New York: Appleton-Century-Crofts.

Ichniowski, C., & Lewin, D. (1987). Grievance procedures and firm performance. In M.M. Kleiner, M. Roomkin, R.N. Block, & Salzburg (Eds.), *Human resources and the performance of the firm* (pp. 159-194). Madison, WI: Industrial Relations Research Association.

Jacoby, S.M. (1995). Social dimensions of global economic integration. In S.M. Jacoby (Ed.), *The workers of nations* (pp. 3-29). New York: Oxford.

Kaufman, B.E. (1996a, August). Transformation of the corporate HR/IR function: Implication for university programs. *Labor Law Journal, 47*, 540-548.

Kaufman, B.E. (1996b). Why the Wagner Act?: Reestablishing contact with its original purpose. In D. Lewin, B.E. Kaufman, & D. Sockell (Eds.), *Advances in industrial and labor relations* (volume 7, pp. 15-67). Greenwich, CT: JAI Press.

Levine, D. (1995). *Reinventing the workplace.* Washington, DC: Brookings.

Lewin, D., & Boroff, K.E. (1996). The role of loyalty in exit and voice: A conceptual empirical analysis. In D. Lewin, B.E. Kaufman, & D. Sockell (Eds.), *Advances in industrial and labor relations* (volume 7, pp. 69-96). Greenwich, CT: JAI Press.

Lewin, D., & Mitchell, D.J.B. (1995). *Human resource management: An economic approach* (2nd ed.). Cincinnati, OH: South-Western.

Lewin, D., & Peterson, R.B. (1988). *The modern grievance procedure in the United States.* Westport, CT: Quorum Books.

Lewin, D., Feuille, P., Kochan, T.A., & Delaney, J.T. (1988). *Public sector labor relations: Analysis and readings.* Lexington, MA: Lexington.

Lewin, D., Kaufman, B.E., Fossum, J., & Verma, A. (1996, October). *Employer preferences for employee involvement/participation in the enterprise: A conceptual and empirical study.* Unpublished paper presented to the Conference on Collective Bargaining and Public Policy, University of Minnesota, Minneapolis.

Meyer, H.H., Kay, E., & French, J.R.P., Jr. (1965). Split roles in performance appraisal. *Harvard Business Review, 43* (1), 123-129.

Mitchell, D.J.B. (1993, May). Three suggestions for ensuring a future for the American labor movement. *Canada-U.S. Outlook, 3*, 5-40.

Mitchell, D.J.B.. Lewin, D., & Lawler, E.E., III. (1990). Alternative pay systems, firm performance, and productivity. In A. Blinder (Ed.), *Paying for productivity* (pp. 15-88). Washington, DC: Brookings.

Murphy, K. (1991, rev.). *Merck & Co., Inc. [A]. Boston, MA: Harvard Business School* [opN9-491-005).

O'Reilly, C.A. (1989, Fall). Corporations, culture, and commitment. *California Management Review, 31*, 9-25.

Perlman, S. (1922). *A history of trade unionism in the United States.* New York: Macmillan.

Roethlisberger, F., & Dickson, W.J. (1939). *Management and the worker: An account of a research program conducted by the Western Electric Company, Hawthorne Works, Chicago.* Cambridge, MA: Harvard University Press.

Roy, D. (1952, April). Quota restriction and goldbricking in a machine shop. *American Journal of Sociology, 57*, 427-442.

Schumpeter, J.A. (1947). *Capitalism, socialism and democracy.* New York: Harper.

Simon, H.A. (1957). *Administrative behavior* (2nd ed.). New York: Macmillan.

Sloan, A.P. (1964). *My years at General Motors.* New York: Doubleday.

Stephenson, K., & Lewin, D. (1996). Managing workforce diversity: Macro and micro level HR implications of network analysis. *International Journal of Manpower, 17* (4/5), 168-196.

Taylor, F.W. (1911). *The principles of scientific management.* New York: Harper.

Weber, M. (1947). *The theory of social and economic organization.* Glencoe, IL: Free Press.

U.S. General Accounting Office. (1987). *Employee stock ownership plans: Little evidence of effects on corporate performance.* Washington, DC: GAO/PEMD-88-1.

ABOUT THE CONTRIBUTORS

Orley Ashenfelter is Professor of Economics at Princeton University and editor of the *American Economic Review*. He has conducted many econometric studies on such topics as union growth and decline, employment discrimination, the returns to schooling and training, and public policy toward labor. His published work appears in the major economics and industrial relations journals, and he is also the author and co-author of several books. Ashenfelter formerly served as Director of the Office of Evaluation for the U.S. Department of Labor. He holds a B.A. (1964) from Claremont College and a Ph.D. (1970) from Princeton University.

Renae Broderick is an independent consultant in the field of human resource management, specializing in compensation and benefits. Her clients have included *Fortune* 500 firms (e.g., 3M, Lockheed, Hyatt Hotels, Sears, TRW), smaller businesses, and trade associations. Dr. Broderick has worked in corporate personnel at General Motors, labor relations and human resource planning at Philip Morris, and as a senior consultant for The Wyatt Company, an international consulting firm. She has taught at the John Anderson Graduate School of Management, UCLA, and Cornell University's School of Industrial and Labor Relations. Her research deals with workforce diversity, compensation strategy, and pay for performance, and she has published and spoken before professional groups in each of these areas. Dr. Broderick received her B.A. in psychology from Macalester College, her M.A. in industrial relations from the University of Minnesota, and her Ph.D. in industrial relations from Cornell University.

Janet Currie is a Professor in the Economics Department at UCLA. She has also taught at MIT. In addition to her work on gender differences in compensation packages, she has worked on the effects of legal structure on the resolution of bargaining disputes. Most recently, she is examining the effects of welfare programs on child care outcomes. Her work has been supported by a Sloan Foundation fellowship, the National Science Foundation, and the National Institutes of Health. She is currently serving on a National Academy of Sciences panel on the health of immigrant children.

Christopher L. Erickson is Associate Profesor in the Human Resources and Organizational Behavior Area of the Anderson Graduate School of Management at UCLA. He received his B.A. from Yale and his Ph.D. in economics from the Massachusetts Institute of Technology. He has been a member of the Anderson faculty since 1991, and was previously on the faculty of the New York State School of Industrial and Labor Relations at Cornell University. He has published widely in the areas of wage determination, collective bargaining, and international industrial relations/human resources.

John A. Fossum is Professor of Industrial Relations and Director of the Industrial Relations Center in the Carlson School of Management, University of Minnesota. His academic career includes positions at the University of Wyoming and the University of Michigan. He has held visiting faculty positions at UCLA, Cornell, the Warsaw School of Economics, the Universite Jean Moulin Lyon III (France), and the Olsztyn University of Agriculture and Technology (Poland). He is the author of *Labor Relations: Development, Structure, Process* and a co-author of *Personnel/Human Resource Management*. He is a member of the Academy of Management and the Industrial Relations Research Association and was formerly chair of the Personnel/Human Resources Division of the Academy. His research interests are centered around employee conpensation, human resource management and firm performance, and labor-management relations issues.

Barry Gerhart is Frances Hampton Curry Professor of Organization Studies at Vanderbilt University's Owen Graduate School of Management. Professor Gerhart has worked with a variety of organizations, including TRW, Corning, Bausch & Lomb, Blue Cross/Blue Shield of Maryland, and Petroleos De Venezuela. His research on compensation, rewards, and staffing has appeared in the *Academy of Management Journal, Industrial Relations, Industrial and Labor Relations Review, Journal of Applied Psychology, Personnel Psychology*, and *Handbook of Industrial and Organizational Psychology*. He was co-recipient of the 1991 "Scholarly Achievement Award," Human Resources Division, Academy of Management. Professor Gerhart received his B.S. in psychology from Bowling Green State University in 1979 and his Ph.D.

in human resource management and industrial relations from the University of Wisconsin-Madison in 1985.

Robert L. Heneman is director of Graduate Programs in Labor and Human Resources and is an Associate Professor of Management and Human Resources in the Max M. Fisher College of Business at the Ohio State University. Heneman has a Ph.D. in Labor and Industrial Relations from Michigan State University. Heneman's primary areas of research, teaching, and consulting are in performance management, compensation, and staffing. He has written two books, *Merit Pay: Linking Pay Increases to Performance Ratings* and *Staffing Organizations*. He has consulted with many organizations including IBM, Bank One, Time Warner, Whirlpool, the Limited, and the State of Ohio.

Larry J. Kimbell is Professor of Business Economics at the John E. Anderson Graduate School of Management, the University of California, Los Angeles (UCLA), where he teaches macroeconomics and business forecasting. He is also Director of the UCLA Business Forecasting Project, and he co-authors the quarterly UCLA National and California Forecast. He received his B.A. degree with honors from Yale University and his Ph.D. from the Univesity of Texas, Austin. His research has centered on the development, estimation, and policy application of large-scale economic models, including: microsimulation models of the U.S. and California health care systems; macroeconometric models of the U.S., California, and sub-state regional economies; and micro-analytic models of international trade in the Pacific Basin, water allocation in California, and air quality regulation in southern California.

Robert LaLonde received his Ph.D. in economics from Princeton University in 1985. He taught at the University of Chicago between 1985 and 1995 in the Graduate School of Business and the Harris School of Public Policy Studies. In addition he served as a senior staff economist at the Council of Economic Advisors during the 1987-1988 academic year. Currently, he is an Associate Professor of Economics at Michigan State University. His research has concentrated primarily on: program evaluation; education and training of the workforce; economic impacts of immigration to developed countries; the costs of worker displacement; and the impact of unions and collective bargaining in the United States.

Barbara A. Lee is Professor of Human Resource Management and Associate Dean of the School of Management and Labor Relations, Rutgers University. She received her B.A. from the University of Vermont, her M.A. and Ph.D. from the Ohio State University, and her J.D. from Georgetown University.

She has published extensively in the fields of employment law and higher education law, and chairs the editorial board of the *Journal of College and University Law.*

David Lewin is Professor, Vice-Dean, and Faculty Director of the MBA Program in the Anderson Graduate School of Management at UCLA. A specialist in human resource management and industrial relations, Professor Lewin has published 13 books and more than 125 articles in such journals as *Industrial and Labor Relations Review, British Journal of Industrial Relations, The Review of Economics and Statistics, Harvard Business Review, Organizational Dynamics,* and *California Management Review.* Among his recent books are *Research Frontiers in Industrial Relations and Human Resources* (1992), *International Perspectives and Challenges in Human Resource Management* (1994), and *Human Resource Management: An Economic Approach* (1995). In 1995 Lewin was elected a Fellow of the National Academy of Human Resources. He is senior editor of *Advances in Industrial and Labor Relations,* and a member of the editorial boards of *Industrial Relations* and *California Management Review.* In 1996 he co-chaired the first National Conference on Innovative Teaching in Human Resources and Industrial Relations. Lewin has consulted widely on human resource management issues and topics with business, government, and labor oganizations.

Brian McCall is an Associate Professor at the Industrial Relations Center, University of Minnesota. He received his Ph.D. in economics from Princeton University in 1988. His current research analyzes the incentive effects of social insurance programs, such as unemployment insurance and workers' compensation, and studies the economic consequences, of job displacement.

Daniel J.B. Mitchell is a professor in the Anderson Graduate School of Management and the School of Public Policy and Social Research, UCLA. In the latter school, he chairs the Department of Policy Studies. He was, for many years, the director of the UCLA Institute of Industrial Relations. Professor Mitchell has twice been associated with the Brookings Institution. During Phase II of the Nixon Administration wage-price controls, he was chief economist of the U.S. Pay Board. Professor Mitchell has been a consultant to the International Labour Organisation, the U.S. Bureau of Labor Statistics, the Federal Reserve Board, and other entities. He is the co-author with David Lewin of the textbook *Human Resource Management: An Economic Approach.* Mitchell is a regular participant in the UCLA Anderson Business Forecast and the Human Resource Outlook Panel.

Cheri Ostroff (Ph.D. Michigan State University, 1987) is an Associate Professor of Management at Arizona State University West. She previously served on the faculty in the Industrial Relations Center at the University of Minnesota. Her areas of expertise include: establishing links between human resource management practices and firm productivity and financial performance; staffing and selection; person-organizatin fit; employee training and development; socialization of employees; and job satisfaction. She received the American Psychological Associations Distinguished Scientific Award for Early Career Contribution in Applied Research in 1994, and was elected a fellow of APA in 1996. Dr. Ostroff is Associate Editor of the *International Journal of Selection and Assessment* and regularly reviews manuscripts for many other journals. She is an active member of the Academy of Management and the Society of Industrial/OrganizationalPsychology. Dr. Ostroff has provided human resource consulting to a variety of firms across the country.

Teresa J. Rothausen is an Assistant Professor of Management at Texas A&M University. She holds a B.A. in economics from St. Olaf College (1986) and a Ph.D. in industrial relations with specialties in staffing, training, and development, and organizational behavior/organization theory from the University of Minnesota (1994). Before getting her Ph.D., Dr. Rothausen worked for Arthur Andersen & Co., and taught for St. Olaf College. She currently teaches and conducts research in the areas of job satisfaction, person-organization fit, recruiting and selection, career-organization interfaces, work-family and work-life interface, and human resource management. She has published in the *Journal of Vocational Behavior* and the *Journal of Organizational and Occupational Psychology*. In addition, Dr. Rothausen has worked with Big Six accounting firms and *Fortune* 500 companies on employee staffing and training programs, work-family programs, and employee attitude assessment.

Donna Sockell is on leave as professor of Industrial and Labor Relations at the School of Labor Management Relations, Rutgers University. She was formerly th Associate Professor at the Graduate School of Business, Columbia University. She is the author of numerous articles and chapters on labor law and labor relations, and is a co-editor of the JAI Press series, *Advances in Industrial and Labor Relations*. She is currently completing a book on teaching effectiveness.

Calvin D. Siebert holds a B.A. (1958) and an M.A. (1960) in economics from the University of Kansas and a Ph.D. from the University of California at Berkeley (1966). He has taught at the University of Iowa since 1965 except for a year as Rockefeller Foundation Visiting Professor at the University of the Philippines. He was chairman of the Department of Economics at the University of Iowa for two terms and has published numerous articles in the areas of labor economics, investment behavior, health economics, and economic development in leading economic journals, including the *American Economic Review*, *Journal of Political Economy,* and the *Western Economic Journal.*

Courtney von Hippel is a Ph.D. candidate in Labor and Human Resources at the Max M. Fisher College of Business at The Ohio State University. She has served as a data analyst for the Consortium for Alternative Reward Strategies research project. Her research interests include perceptions of personal control, levels of commitment, and sources of satisfaction among temporary employees. She is also interested in staffing and compensation.

Mahmood A. Zaidi is a professor in the Industrial Relations Center, an adjunct associate in the Hubert H. Humphrey Institute of Public Affairs, and Director, International Programs for the Carlson School of Management, University of Minnesota. He received a B.A. with honors in economics and an M.A. in economic from the University of California, Los Angeles, and a Ph.D. degree in economics from the University of California, Berkeley. Dr. Zaidi's teaching and research interests are in the areas of international labor market analysis, international human resource management, and human capital and multinationals. Among his publications are *Labour Economics in Canada* (with Sylvia Ostry), and *The Economics of Human Resource Management* (with Daniel J.B. Mitchell). He has also served on editorial boards of various journals and at present is the co-editor of *The North American Journal of Economics and Finance*, a journal of theory and practice. Professor Zaidi has taught on the Los Angeles and Berkeley campuses of the University of California, the University of Western Australia, the University of New South Wales, Australia, the Université Jean Moulin Lyon—III, France, the Graduate School of Business, Zurich, Switzerland, and Wirtschaftsuniversität Wien, Austria. He is scheduled to teach at the Warsaw School of Economics in the spring of 1997.

INDEX

Current Topics in Management

Edited by **M. Afzalur Rahim,** *Western Kentucky University,* **Robert T. Golembiewski,** *University of Georgia,* and **Craig C. Lundberg,** *Cornell University*

Volume 1, 1996, 260 pp. $73.25
ISBN 0-7623-0150-3

CONTENTS: Preface, *Robert T. Golembiewski, Craig C. Lundberg and M. Afzalur Rahim.* Introduction, *M. Afzalur Rahim, Robert T. Golembiewski, and Craig C. Lundberg.* PART I. ORGANIZATIONAL SCIENCE. Organizational Science Inquiry: Toward the Appreciation of Equivoque, *Craig C. Lundberg.* Bases of Leader Power, Workgroup Commitment, and Conflict: A Structural Equations Model, *M. Afzalur Rahim and Clement Psenicka.* Burnout as Global and Strategic: Progress with the Phase Model, and Its Future, *Robert T. Golembiewski.* PART II. OTHER ISSUES IN ORGANIZATIONAL BEHAVIOR. The Psychology of Compliance: Revisiting the Notion of a Psychological Contract, *Adrian Carr.* Organizational Commitment and Instrumentality Perceptions: Differentiating the Concepts, *Nancy E. Day.* Examining Relationships Between Mangerial Self-Esteem and Selected Dispositional, Organizational, and Outcome Variables, *Bruce F. Mills.* PART III. SOCIAL ISSUES IN MANAGEMENT. Exploring Management in a Consumer Culture: An Introduction to Consuming Work, *Shayne W. Grice.* Public Policy: Toward New Philosophical Foundations, *Rogene A. Buchholz and Sandra B. Rosenthal.* Moral Development and Interpersonal Conflict: An Empirical Exploration of Stages and Styles, *Gabriel F. Buntzman, M. Afzalur Rahim, and Douglas E. White.* Comprehensive Organizational Wellness, *Craig S. Fisher, William S. Brown, and Angela W. Fleisher.* Assessing Shared Governance: An Example of Instrument Development in a Hospital Setting, *S. Patricia Minors, John B. White, and Tim Porter-O'Grady.* PART IV. INTERNATIONAL COMPARISON. Correlates of Leadership Effectiveness in the United States and Korea, *Dong-Ok Chah and Edwin A. Locke.* A Comparative Study of Personal Values in Yugoslavia, Russia and the United States: Implications for Management, Investment, and Political Risk, *Patricia L. Nemetz, John Mager, and Sonja Bjeletic.* Part V. Concluding Comments: Management Research in a Dynamic Environment, *Craig C. Lundberg, Robert T. Golembiewski, and M. Afzalur Rahim.*

J
A
I

P
R
E
S
S

J A I   P R E S S

Management Laureates
A Collection of Autobiographical Essays

Edited by **Arthur G. Bedeian**, *Department of Management, Louisiana State University*

Volume 4, 1996, 313 pp. $86.25
ISBN 1-55938-730-0

CONTENTS: Preface, *Arthur G. Bedeian.* Challenged on the Cutting Edge, *Kathryn M. Bartol.* Performing, Achieving, and Belonging, *Janice M. Beyer.* A Hopscotch Hike, *Geert Hofstede.* Roots, Wing, and Applying Management and Leadership Principles: A Personal Odyssey, *John M. Ivancevich.* A Common Man Travels "Back to the Future", *Fred Luthans.* Taking the Road Less Traveled: Serendipity and the Influence of Others in a Career, *Jeffrey Pfeffer.* A Taste for Innovation, *Derek S. Pugh.* Never Say Never!, *John W. Slocum, Jr.* Index.

Also Available:
Volumes 1-3 (1992-1993) $86.25 each

> **FACULTY/PROFESSIONAL** discounts are available in the U.S. and Canada at a rate of 40% off the list price when prepaid by personal check or credit card and ordered directly from the publisher.

JAI PRESS INC.
55 Old Post Road No. 2 - P.O. Box 1678
Greenwich, Connecticut 06836-1678
Tel: (203) 661- 7602   Fax: (203) 661-0792